Britain:
Leading, Not Leaving

Also by Gordon Brown

Maxton: A Biography
(Edinburgh, 1986), first edition

Scotland: The Real Divide
(ed. with Robin Cook) (Edinburgh, 1987)

*Where There Is Greed: Margaret Thatcher and
the Betrayal of Britain's Future* (Edinburgh, 1989)

Maxton: A Biography
(Edinburgh, 2002), revised edition

Speeches, 1997–2006
(London, 2006)

Courage: Eight Portraits
(London, 2007)

Wartime Courage
(London, 2009)

The Change We Choose: Speeches 2007–2009
(Edinburgh, 2010)

*Beyond the Crash: Overcoming the First Crisis
of Globalisation* (London, 2010)

My Scotland, Our Britain: A Future Worth Sharing
(London, 2014)

The Universal Declaration of Human Rights in the 21st Century
(Cambridge, 2016)

Britain: Leading, Not Leaving

The Patriotic Case for
Remaining in Europe

Gordon Brown

DEERPARK PRESS

First published in 2016 by
Deerpark Press
The Henhouse
Selkirk
TD7 5EY

ISBN: 978-0-9541979-6-4

British Library Cataloguing-in-Publication Data
A catalogue record for this book is available
from the British Library

Book designed by Mark Blackadder

Printed and bound by
Claro Print, Newton Mearns, Glasgow
claroprint.co.uk

Contents

Foreword

This book, *Britain: Leading, Not Leaving*, is a sequel to the book I wrote in 2014 during the Scottish referendum campaign, entitled *My Scotland, Our Britain*.

Then, as now, I wanted to understand the underlying issues at stake in a debate so critical to our future and to put a positive, principled and patriotic case for Britain. As I wrote *My Scotland, Our Britain*, I became convinced that it was not enough to defend the *status quo*: we had to set out our proposals for a new relationship between Scotland and Britain – a stronger Scottish Parliament within a reformed United Kingdom – and this played a part in creating the 'Vow' signed by all UK party leaders which, in turn, brought about the Smith Commission and the recent Scotland Act.

Similarly, as I have written my account of Britain's uneasy relationship with Europe, I have become convinced that we need a more forward-looking and comprehensive statement of how the European Union can best serve the interests of British people.

I suggest that the challenge is to get the right balance between the autonomy we desire and the co-operation we need and I set out five areas where Europe can do better by Britain and where Britain can lead Europe. We need to show where, through co-operation in Europe, we can create new jobs and do more to support communities that have come under pressure from wave after wave of global change. We need to show how, not least through using combined strength to combat tax avoidance, Europe can play a part in advancing a fairer society in a world people see as unequal and unsustainable. And in a world that people also see as insecure and unstable, we need to show how through co-operation we can deal not with just migration but with the challenge posed to Europe by what is happening on its eastern and southern borders – and thus how in a dangerous world we cope with the insecurity of the Middle East and Africa and the new aggression of Russia.

This book was only possible because of the expert help of Ross Christie, who has worked with me on detailed research on the history of the period, Andrew Hilland, Rachael Thomas and Ross Fulton. I have benefited greatly from the work that has been undertaken by Professor Iain Begg of the LSE, author of the first study showing the number of British jobs linked to Europe, and from conversations with Robin Niblett of Chatham House; Craig Calhoun, Director of the LSE; Nick Butler of the *Financial Times*; Jonathan Portes of NIESR; Michael Jacobs who is an expert on the environment; my friends Bob Shrum, Michael Wills, Jon Mendlesohn, Edward Morgan, Wilf Stevenson, Alison McGovern MP, Kirsty McNeill, David Muir, Alex Rowley and my brothers Andrew and John Brown.

I have worked closely with Nick Lowles and Cormac Hollingsworth of the organisation Hope Not Hate, who conducted an in-depth survey of British opinion from whose findings I have drawn, and I am grateful to Nick for undertaking interviews with people on their worries about the future of Britain. I have benefited also from conversations with Alan Johnson MP, Will Straw and David Sainsbury and from research conducted by Fabian Mushövel.

I am grateful to Bruce Waddell for advice throughout and to George Rosie and Reid Lidow for help with editing, to Mark Blackadder for his design of both the book itself and the cover, to Kate Blackadder, and to Alistair Moffat, who has been a patient and resourceful publisher as well as a trusted friend. As always our office staff – Susanna Pettigrew, Gil McNeil, James Cox, Jenny Mill and

Mary Bailey – and Fife and Met Police have provided great support in my travels.

This book could not have been written without the help of my wife Sarah. It has been penned with the future of our children, John and Fraser, uppermost in our minds. It is dedicated to the memory of my father and mother who, more than 50 years ago, taught me the importance of thinking beyond the confines of our shores.

Introduction

Andrew lives in Stoke-on-Trent, a city which has seen a sharp decline in many of its traditional industries over the past 30 years. In 2010 he was earning £30,000 a year working in a pottery. It was hard work but he felt valued. Since being made redundant, he has been in a series of short-term jobs with little security and even less self-worth.

Andrew, who has just turned 50, says: 'When the pot bank went bust I took whatever jobs were available but the reality is the only positions out there were in warehousing or in logistics and distribution.'

Today he works in a distribution centre on zero contract hours. 'At the beginning of the week I have no idea what hours – if any – I will be working,' he says. 'I work with dozens of Eastern Europeans, who do graft hard and I don't blame them for being there but there are so many of us chasing each hour of work that my boss only has to pay the minimum wage. He doesn't care. If we complain we get no more hours.'

Andrew hopes he has another 15 years left in work but is worried. He adds: 'What hope is there for the next generation?' He thinks Europe has done nothing for him and is only making his life harder. He is so pessimistic about his own future that, even although he is a lifelong Labour supporter and voter, he is thinking of voting to 'Leave'.

Danielle is from Dagenham. She is in her mid-20s, married and keen to start a family – when she can afford to. She works in retail, earning £16,500 a year. Danielle rents her home because she cannot afford to buy.

'On immigration,' she says, 'I agree we should help those who need it but at the same time I don't agree with them having a free ride, house, benefits and so on – not when working people like me are struggling to make a living.'

Danielle is proud of her working-class roots but does not think any of the main political parties really speak for her. 'I don't know a lot about the pros and cons of the EU, in all honesty. I just don't feel any political parties care about equality and it always sounds to me as if it's the rich looking after the rich.'

She is undecided as to how she might vote in the EU referendum but is swaying towards voting to 'Leave'. She says that she is starting to believe many of the things she reads in the press about exactly what's wrong with the EU.

Andrew and Danielle have their own unique stories and standpoints but their sceptical views are not unfamiliar. In recent months, as I have travelled across Britain, I have met men and women who describe their town's high street as 'run-down, dilapidated and a haven for vandals' and who think that it is not just their hometown that is decaying but 'the entire country'. They truly believe Britain is no longer the country they were born into. And, when pressed, they say it is now time to stand up for the Britain we have been losing. Unsurprisingly, they are thinking of voting to 'Leave'.

I have met many who have come to the conclusion that refugees are coming to Britain to take advantage of a free NHS and to gain access to our benefits and I have talked with others who are worried not only by the scale and the costs of migration but because, they say, 'the government has lost control of our borders'.

And even these heartfelt tales of anti-globalisation sentiment and resentment pale when set against the heightened concerns of families who – shaken by the recent onslaught of terrorism – blame our entanglement with the outside world, including our membership of the EU, for the risks we face.

We cannot disguise the fact that millions of our fellow British citizens have serious concerns about jobs, migration and the character of our country.

They want answers. They need answers.

The 2016 European referendum is not so much about the future of Europe as about the future of Britain – about the people of Britain and the kind of country we want to live in, now and in the future.

And the real crux of this is not what best serves the interests of the European Union. It comes down to what meets the needs and aspirations of the British people.

The question cannot be: how European are we? The question has to be: what best serves our interests as British patriots?

So, in assessing the case for Britain in the European Union, we build our case not from our similarities with Europe, crucial as they are, but from the uniqueness of Britain. And we start not from our strong sense of internationalism – important as that is to me – but from our even stronger sense of patriotism.

I will suggest that, when we look at the challenging demands of a global economy and an increasingly insecure and unstable world, the case for British engagement in Europe is even stronger than it was when we first joined the European Economic Community in the 1970s.

I will argue that since then we have entered a new world that is shaped by globalisation and defined by our interdependence. In this world, the real challenge for our nation – and indeed for every nation – is to balance the autonomy we desire with the co-operation we need.

The economic argument

Many pro-Europeans will base their argument simply on an updated version of the case we made in 1975, at the time of the only previous referendum on our membership of the EEC.

They will rightly emphasise Britain's exports of nearly £150 billion-worth of goods and over £85 billion of services to Europe as well as the estimated three million British jobs that depend on demand from Europe.[1] As I show in Chapter Seven, on the economy, thousands of the 240,000 jobs created by the car industry in manufacturing and its supply chain can be attributed to sales to Europe.[2] And from our whisky industry to pharmaceuticals, from aviation to financial services, the same picture can be painted: the majority of British sales are to the European Union, in a story of British jobs gained, British businesses created and British investment secured.[3]

There is still a belief among some that most of our exports go to the Commonwealth countries as they did for one hundred years of Empire, and an assumption among others that the world has changed so rapidly that our biggest export market is now fast-growing China. But the reality is that only a fraction of our goods exports go to these countries. The biggest share – 48 per cent last year – went to Germany, France and the European mainland and only a small minority went to China (4.5 per cent), India (1.5 per cent) and less still to Canada (1.4 per cent), Australia (1.4 per cent), South Africa (0.8 per cent) and New Zealand (0.2 per cent).[4]

We might hazard a guess that most outside investment in Britain's future – the money sent by investors from abroad that creates jobs everywhere from the car industry to high-tech medicine – comes from America or perhaps now from Japan, Korea or China. Yet that guess would be wide of the mark. Nearly half the foreign direct investment we secure – £450 billion in total – comes from mainland Europe.[5] Again, Europe matters more than we think.

And thousands of us are going to work today in the 200,000 individual British companies that are trading with mainland Europe or in the thousands of European-owned businesses which employ us, British workers, across our country.[6]

Britain has always been a trading nation. But in 2016, increasingly integrated into the global economy, we are even more dependent on trade than ever before – and far more dependent on trade with our European neighbours than when we first joined the European Economic Community more than 40 years ago.[7]

According to the Governor of the Bank of England, there is an even broader set of economic reasons for remaining part of the European Union. Membership has made Britain a more open economy and, in the Governor's words, 'reinforces the dynamism of the UK economy … and [increases] its ability to grow without generating risks … to monetary and financial stability … and to strong, sustainable and balanced growth.' Contradicting those who see European Union interference with our own financial sector as excessive and harmful, he argues that 'the need for national regulators and supervisors to have the flexibility in applying EU rules … has in the main been respected in the past' and concludes that 'the rest of the EU is more important to UK trade and investment than the converse.'[8] In his view, Britain needs the European Union more than the European Union needs Britain.

And so readers might ask: if the economic evidence is so powerful, and may even appear to be conclusive, then why do so many doubts about the European Union still exist? Why, according to the British Social Attitudes survey, do two-thirds of British voters consider themselves to be less than enthusiastic – and even sceptical – about the European Union?[9]

Why are so many ambivalent about the European Union when, according to another poll led by Professor John Curtice, nearly three quarters of the voting public – and thus millions who want to vote to Leave – think the economic alternatives to membership of the European Union would make us worse off?[10]

And why, according to a Hope Not Hate poll of English opinion, do millions of citizens by a 2 to 1 vote – 44 per cent to 23 per cent among those who have made up their minds – believe that 'Britain should be free to govern itself outside of the EU even if it means the country will be economically worse off?'[11]

The answer is that we are thinking not just of the jobs that have come from Europe but of the jobs that have been lost and our concerns about our future go far beyond the financial and the economic and extend to anxieties about our security – how safe we are – and our culture and identity – who we are and what we are becoming. Economic statistics about the benefits of membership are necessary but may not be sufficient to win over already sceptical citizens with concerns like these.

Some say that the referendum vote will now come down to a choice between two risks: whether the economic risks of leaving are seen to be greater than the risks to our borders – and the dilution of our sense of Britishness. Prominent commentators argue that in the battle between the head – economic reasons to remain – and the heart – our cultural concerns – the head will win. And this may turn out to be how the millions of people, who are culturally concerned but financially secure and who favour the economic *status quo*, will come to see their choice. But there are millions who are also concerned about what is happening to our way of life but who are financially insecure, who feel they have nothing left to lose, and who believe that even a reformed European Union will do little for them.[12] They too want answers.

The fact is that these apparently separate concerns – about what's happening to our livelihoods and about what's happening to our British way of life – arise from the same root cause, and are the product of the same underlying set of changes. We cannot easily respond to the economic and cultural anxieties millions express without explaining what has changed over the last three or four decades and how wave after wave of global change has created 'losers' as well as 'winners', and brought us insecurity as well as opportunity.

And so if we are to respond to the widespread worries about jobs, livelihoods and our British way of life – all of which affect our attitudes to Europe – we must start from where we are, a country hit by wave after wave of global change, and a people many of whom see globalisation as akin to a 'runaway train' that is out of control.

Perhaps in the 1975 referendum we could rest our case for Europe on the economic benefits of catching up with our competitors but, if we are to address the economic, cultural and security concerns that all of us now have about our future, we must start from the inescapable and seismic shift of recent years: the onset of globalisation. According to the Treasury our total trade – exports and imports combined – increased from 23% of our national income in 1965 to 64% in 2015. And while global change opens new doors for many of us, the very speed and scale of change all around us makes us fearful and uncertain. The very same globalisation that spreads opportunity across the world also spreads risks.

So we must also explain the new political reality – a more interconnected and integrated world which makes countries more dependent on each other. It creates not just a need to co-operate across borders, but also reawakens amongst individuals a need to belong and the heightened flow of money, goods and people across traditional borders has led to calls in a country like ours, always proud of our distinctive identity, to 'bring control back home'.

So we need to tell the story that lies behind the new economic realities, and explain why the same globalisation which produces economic opportunity and economic dislocation also brings in its wake a new set of fears about what's happening to our country, our borders and our future.

In this book, I will explain that from the 1980s onwards the context is globalisation. The theme is the interdependence of nations which is itself a direct consequence of the opening up of the global economy. The new political reality is the need to co-operate across borders, whether it be to secure economic growth and stability or address pollution, security or migration. The challenge for every nation is thus qualitatively different from anything that has come before: to get the balance right between the autonomy we desire and the co-operation we need. This will be important if we are to secure jobs and aid economic competitiveness, to address immigration and to counter terrorism, and to uphold and reflect our strong sense of Britishness.

Globalisation and an interdependent world

So, revisiting our relationship with Europe in 2016, we have to recognise the scale, scope and size of what has been a major and quite fundamental shift in the past 40 years – one that has transformed our relationships with the outside world and makes today's debates very different from those of 1975.

We are now living through a period in human history – sometimes called the era of globalisation – in which our national economies are increasingly integrated, our societies are more and more interconnected and our standards of living and quality of life are increasingly influenced by events beyond our borders.

When we joined the EEC in 1973 the majority of the goods we bought in our local high streets were made by British workers, manufacturing British-designed products in British factories. By contrast, we are all now part of a global economy in which most of the goods and many of the services we buy come from other parts of the world. Many of these are designed in one place and assembled in another, with their parts manufactured in not just one but several overseas factories, as part of a global supply chain and what is known as a 'trade in tasks'.

And while at the time we entered the EEC most of the investments made in Britain still came from capital raised in Britain, today our world is characterised by the free and uninterrupted flow of capital across borders.[13]

In the not-too-distant future the majority of the world's economic activity will consist of trade between countries rather than within countries financed by ever-increasing flows of capital across borders. And in the last two decades there has been one additional change in the way we connect with each other: each of us is also now part of a global cauldron where there is an instantaneous and continuous flow of information and communications that makes us more interconnected and integrated than ever before.

In 1962, President John F. Kennedy made a historic speech, which called on his fellow countrymen to complement their historic Declaration of Independence – which, he said, made sense for the last two centuries – with a new and equally historic Declaration of Interdependence that would make sense for the next two centuries. This Declaration of Interdependence would recognise that the freedoms and prosperity of each of us are inextricably linked to the freedoms and prosperity of all. It would envisage a world built not around the 'individual liberty of one but the indivisible liberty of all'. The task was to 'weave from all the tangled threads a fabric of law and progress'.[14]

Over 50 years on from Kennedy's speech, interdependence is not a choice. It is a fact. As Kennedy recognised, even the most powerful country in the world cannot act alone but has to co-operate in partnership with others. Indeed, our growing international interdependence is the most significant change since Britain voted Yes to Europe in 1975. Our future prosperity must now be sought in a new world from which there is a price to be paid for opting out and where, in pursuing our national interests, we can no longer afford to sit on the sidelines and leave British chairs empty in crucial international institutions and organisations.

I suggest in the chapters that follow that building a shared future is our insurance policy against a risk-laden world. These shared solutions are a protection against environmental pollution, financial crises and terrorist infiltration as well as, potentially, a stimulus to more jobs, higher growth and a better quality of life. And we argue that while divorce is always a messy and expensive business, international co-operation means that we can shape the future and not just be shaped by it. Membership of the European Union enables Britain to be a rule-maker and not just a rule-taker, able to define the agenda as opposed to simply following someone else's.

Identity matters

If the very openness of the world economy creates greater opportunities than ever before – to travel, to trade, to experience different cultures – it also brings greater insecurities. And millions of our fellow citizens have come to the view that the latest wave of seemingly unstoppable global change is threatening not just their own individual livelihoods, but the future of entire industries and the prosperity and security of whole countries.

The needs and aspirations of the British people are always best served by a policy that maximises opportunity and minimises insecurity. But because millions of people now feel that they live in a world of minimum opportunity and maximum insecurity, including the insecurity that comes from terrorist attacks, they are looking for someone or something to protect, insulate and shelter them from the (sometimes dire) effects of change.

As the biographical stories that I have cited at the outset of this introduction show, many citizens have come to the view that Britain is changing out of all recognition, is no longer the country they were born into and they feel they have been let down. The result is that mainstream political parties are losing support. While business fact sheets and trade statistics are important in persuading our fellow citizens of the case for remaining in Europe, right-wing political parties like UKIP are waging what is akin to a culture war – telling us our British identity is under threat. In particular, they link globalisation to mass migration and blame Europe for what they consider to be an open door for thousands of immigrants who have come to our country. In response we have to show that it is not only in our national interest to co-operate with our neighbours but also that we can do so without losing our sense of what it is to be British.

For many years, until recently, it was commonplace to argue that the political importance of national identity was waning in the face of the great global transformations of the last 50 years, not least the rapid dissolution of the British Empire which removed the institutions and symbols which had been so instrumental in defining Britishness. The ubiquity of air travel, the huge growth of television, the advent of the Internet – all drove huge cultural changes. Some would argue that a new global consciousness took root and with it came social changes that created a new 'politics of identity', laying emphasis on our individualism and individual characteristics such as gender and sexuality, turning our consciousness inwards to the individual and not outwards to the nation. But, for all these changes, the nation survives and remains a locus of our identity. In the midst of rapid and destabilising change, we tend to cling to the comfortable and to root ourselves in the familiar. It is not surprising that the dreadful shock of terrorist atrocities causes an upsurge in patriotic feeling as people understandably seek a mooring in an unexpected and savage storm.

And in many ways, a clear sense of national identity is more important than ever. The fact is that much of what roots us, politically, economically and culturally, flows from the nation state – from our systems of justice and education, to our public services like health and broadcasting.The ties that bind us, that root us in our own place and time – our shared language, culture, social and political institutions and norms – reflect our need to belong.

Globalisation has changed the way politics is practised. Roy Jenkins, one of the leaders of the 1975 'Remain' campaign, could say of British voters at that time that 'they took the advice of the people they are used to following'. No such deference exists now. In the past, politicians were judged on whether the alternative solutions they offered were credible. They could not secure an audience unless they had answers. Today in our debates there is far less emphasis on setting out alternatives than on articulating people's anger and on a political narrative that reduces complex arguments to over-simplified binary choices that suggest there are only ever two points on the spectrum. Are you in favour of self-government or Brussels government? Are you in favour of local control or central control? Are you in favour of independence or interdependence?

The real question, however, is how we can maximise our country's capacity to meet the needs and aspirations of its people. Throughout this book, I suggest that the real challenge in the modern world is to balance the autonomy we desire with the co-operation we need. I will make the case that the challenges ahead for Britain – from creating jobs and raising living standards to combatting pollution and ensuring our defence and security – can only be addressed by cross-border co-operation and co-ordination with our nearest neighbours. And as, chapter by chapter, I examine these challenges one by one – looking at the economy, energy, migration and terrorism – I suggest that in each of these areas of vital importance to our national quality of life we can best strike a balance between autonomy and co-operation by leading Europe, not leaving it.

Some will agree that we live in an interdependent world, but argue that Europe is not the best forum in which to leverage our influence. But as I show, Europe is where we are, where our economic interests lie, where our opportunity to leverage our influence is greatest and, indeed, where there is a ready-made opportunity for leadership which many of our neighbours want us to seize.

The anti-European argument has drawn support from the claim that the European Union plans to force upon us a federalist solution and compel a free country to accept a full economic and political union that will hold back our economy, jeopardise our prosperity and undermine traditional liberties. But increasingly the European Union of the second decade of the 21st century is defined less by old plans for a federalist state than by the pressure to be more flexible in the ways we structure our co-operation.

The very people who argue that Europe fails to deliver where it matters – on terror, on illegal migration, on climate change or on financial instability – believe that they are making an argument for leaving. But the reality is that *less* co-operation will not provide the answer to these challenges. We are going to share the future. The only question is: on what basis will we share? Will we share a future of tension, division and conflict by standing aloof from each other? Or can we jointly build a future of prosperity and security in which Britain is at the forefront? This book – *Britain: Leading, Not Leaving* – will, I hope, provide some of the answers.

The British way

All the time I was Chancellor of the Exchequer and then Prime Minister, I was acutely aware that there are two competing views of Britain and our standing in the world. Both views of Britain are held strongly by patriots, people who love and are proud of our country.

There is the popular image of Britain doing best when standing apart – a nation which can glory in its unique 'offshore island' status, a Britain that is wary of entanglements with outsiders, including Europe, and, in line with how they interpret the Dunkirk spirit, a country which thrives best when we emphasise our detachment and sturdy independence from outsiders.

But there is another patriotic view of Britain – one that interprets the Dunkirk spirit in a different way. It is of a Britain that has always done best when we have been outward-looking and engaged with events beyond our shores – a Britain whose history, values and general temperament impel us to lead when others fail to do so. It is this Britain that led the fight in Europe against fascism, totalitarianism, anti-Semitism and racism, and which has never allowed any one power – France, Spain, the Netherlands, Germany or Russia – to dominate our continent. It is this Britain that has a major role to play in Europe in the future.

These two views of Britain can take us in different directions. The pro-British Eurosceptics, who champion the idea of a Britain thriving on its own, complain that Britain is not what it used to be, that it is not the Britain they were born into. They argue that Britain should, as they put it, 'regain its independence.' The pro-British, pro-Europe supporters say that Britain has always been stronger for being open, tolerant, diverse and welcoming, and for being able to master change rather than resisting it. It is a view that sees Britain at its best when it looks outward, when it is engaged and leads.

If pressed, the 'Leave' supporters might tend to the opinion that what defines us as British is our ethnicity – that we are, in a sense, a race apart. Those who favour 'Remain' are more likely, if pressed, to tend to the opinion that Britain is defined best by what we stand for – a Britain proud of our enduring values, our historic commitment to liberty, fair play and an ethic of responsibility. One view stresses what separates us from the rest of Europe, while the other view sees what unites us with the rest of Europe.

Under pressure, extreme versions of Euroscepticism can descend into blaming foreigners, targeting immigrants and adopting a siege mentality. When pressed, Europe's supporters will argue that we do best when we are open to the world, and this has always been our greatest attribute. As a trading nation, it is argued, we will also lose if we are too protectionist and too isolationist in our outlook and approach.

Eurosceptics claim that Europe prevents us from doing what we need to do to advance British trade, British citizenship, and even British culture. Some will even argue that Britain under European law has no more constitutional status than a German or Canadian province or an American state. Supporters of European membership think the opposite: that if we abandoned this isolationist and protectionist thinking, our values and ideas are potentially so influential that they would enable us to lead the continent.

These are two patriotic views of what it is to be British. So the starting point is not whether 'Remain' voters are for Europe and 'Leave' voters are for Britain. It is not even whether pro-Europe 'Remain' voters identify less with Britain than do anti-Europe 'Leave' voters. The 'Remain-Leave' choice is not about whether one group identifies strongly with our country and another does not – or even about one group being more strongly patriotic than the other. No one should say pro-Europeans are anti-British. It is not about choosing Europe over Britain, or even about the intensity with which you express your Britishness. Pro-Europe 'In' voters believe they are just as proud and patriotic as Eurosceptic 'Out' voters are.

But of course history tells us that both these views can be held to a stronger or lesser degree by the same person. They are not mutually exclusive. What patriotism means to many of us is a combination of both: to be proud when we have to stand alone but also to be proud when we lead in the world. We can relish our uniqueness but also see the benefits of engagement. The question is: which view of what it means to be British will be uppermost in people's minds as they vote in June?

I agree with the words of the French President Charles de Gaulle who said that each country 'has its own genius, history and language, its own sorrows, glories and ambitions.'[15] The 'Remain' and 'Leave' positions come down to a different choice: not *whether* you identify with your country, or how strongly you do, but *how* you identify with your country. And as the need to co-operate grows, it is my view that we are more likely to think of ourselves in future as British people who are more outward-looking than inward-looking, more inclusive than exclusive, more progressive in the way we approach the world than parochial.

In this book, I will emphasise that we are the British people who did not stand aside but led on the mainland of Europe, sacrificing almost everything to overcome all forms of totalitarianism. And more recently we have led the way in taking a new approach to climate change, in championing great international causes from debt relief for the world's poor to banning land mines, and standing steadfast for human rights and the rule of law. And I argue that we, the British people, if we so choose, are now able to lead Europe against the forces of economic protectionism, xenophobic isolationism and anti-immigrant racism now rearing their ugly heads across this world.

I'll suggest that we have an opportunity to lead because Europe is now looking for a united front against a militarily resurgent but economically enfeebled Russia, a counterweight to over-powerful interests and a champion of a freer, democratic, accountable and competitive Europe.

And Britain – which is now likely to be Europe's biggest economy by 2050 and which can claim to be historically the most internationally minded of all European nations – is well placed to fashion what the continent needs most of all: an outward-looking, globally orientated Europe that can meet and master the challenges of a rising Africa and Asia and in doing so deliver for the British people a Britain that is better able to manage globalisation in the interests of working families.

PART ONE

Britain and Europe in the old world

CHAPTER ONE

Clinging to the past, 1945–57

Almost every adjective you can think of has been used to describe the complex relationship between Britain and Europe. *The Economist* recently described Britain, in the words of Janan Ganesh, as 'the reluctant European'.[1] We often say of ourselves that we are ambivalent Europeans. Sometimes we glory in being awkward Europeans. It seems to many people that we prefer being thought of as outsiders rather than insiders. Almost invariably the issue in our media is presented not as 'Britain and Europe' or 'Britain as part of Europe' but 'Britain versus Europe'.

Our neighbours often accuse us of being half-hearted and semi-detached – and sometimes of being wholly detached, unenthusiastic and uncommitted. Our attitude to Europe is often summed up as 'negative'. All too often we have favoured the empty chair rather than being centre stage; life on Europe's margins rather than in the mainstream; standing on the fringes and on the periphery even as we claim we are at Europe's heart. 'We are already something less than full members. We are in effect "Country Club" or "Associate members"', one former Chancellor of the Exchequer, Norman Lamont, has suggested. 'We are outside the Single Currency, the Schengen agreement and we have opted out from a large part of Home Affairs legislation … Perhaps, in time, the EU will leave us rather than we leaving them,' he argues.[2] Charles Moore of *The Daily Telegraph* has gone further by claiming that Europe is the only continent we have never led.[3]

Britain is not European, asserts one of our most pro-European politicians, Denis MacShane, who concludes from his time as Europe Minister that 'Britain has never had a European generation' which 'accepted Europe and our membership of the EU as a source of hope, ambition and desire.'[4] And some say that the best way of defining the referendum choice is not between 'in' and 'out' but between 'half-out' and 'fully out', a measure of how much most people think we are 'not fully in'.

Another well-known pro-European, Sir Stephen Wall, a Foreign Office adviser to Tony Blair, says our 'suspicion' towards Europe 'is rooted in our national psyche, the psyche of an island nation which has lived by resisting continental encroachment.'[5] The implication is that we are Europeans not by choice but by necessity. 'Europe was seen as a last resort, a final resting place for a country which had run out of options,' writes the historian Vernon Bogdanor.[6] Indeed, Jeremy Paxman argues that the very way we talk of Europe, with 'phrases like "joining Europe was a mistake", or "we should leave Europe", making it look as if the place can be hitched to the back of the car like a holiday caravan' says a great deal about our national attitude.[7]

But is this ambivalence recent, or was it always the case? Has Britain always been anti-European or at least invariably negative towards Europe? Indeed, if we ascribe significance to what George VI wrote to his mother after the French surrender to Germany in 1940, we might see glorying in isolation as a common feature of our history. He told her: 'Personally, I feel happier now that we have no allies to be polite to and pamper.'[8] Even at the moment when we were most deeply engaged in Europe, a monarchy with deep European roots felt little affinity for or attachment to our European neighbours.

'Europe produces … profound divisions … [it is] a toxic issue in British politics,' argued Bogdanor in a 2013 lecture series. 'It gives rise to the most fundamental issue of politics, the basic attitude toward national identity, about what it is to be British,' he said. Because of this, Bogdanor suggests: 'Europe has always been a problem for

Britain, in a way that it has not been for any other Member State ... perhaps our Euroscepticism was predetermined, that a European commitment did not follow from Britain's traditional understanding of her international position. It would have involved a radical discontinuity of approach, an imaginative leap, a leap of faith perhaps.'[9]

The argument of the 'Leave' camp is that Britain is just too different to be an integral part of the European Union – not just different in language but different because of its geography, history, politics, ideology, attitudes to government, culture and democracy. They emphasise this to sustain their claim that, set against the rest of Europe, Britain is so exceptional that we cannot be fully engaged within it without British values being undermined.

But David Cannadine writes that countries are 'rarely as homogenous, monolithic, or all-encompassing, or as naturally belligerent and as adversarially entrenched as their leaders and apologists, propagandists and historians like to claim.' Quoting W.S. Gilbert of Gilbert and Sullivan, Cannadine writes: 'When everybody is somebody then no-one's anybody.' He concludes that 'claims made for the homogeneity, the unanimity, and the innate bellicosity of such groupings inevitably break down under scrutiny, into myriad fragments, significant exceptions and many alternative competing identities.'[10]

I want to suggest that Britain's links with Europe have been much stronger than most Eurosceptics want to admit. Another historian, David Abulafia, writes: 'One way to describe this relationship would be to say that the United Kingdom has always been a partner of Europe without being a full participant in it ... 'Fog in Channel, Continent Isolated', the famous newspaper headline, does not represent the real nature of Britain's involvement in Europe, whether one thinks of the wool trade with Flanders that was such a source of wealth in the Middle Ages; or the English conquests that reached as far as Gascony; the 'longest alliance' between England and Portugal; or, indeed, in more recent times, the British presence in the Mediterranean that at various points brought not just Gibraltar but Minorca, Corsica, Malta, Corfu and Cyprus under the British flag. British and French guarantees to Poland were honoured in 1939, with the result that we found ourselves in a war to the death with Germany.'[11]

And when we look at geography, history, economics, commerce, culture and attitudes to law, democracy and governance, and similarities with our outlook and that of our European neighbours, I believe that we have been far too ready to accept there was a tension between being global and being European. As an island nation we have sought to trade with the whole of the world. But the balance of power in Europe has always mattered for our security. And even in times when our priorities were focused mainly on our Empire we could never afford to disengage from Europe for long or, despite the rhetoric, glory in 'splendid isolation' from Europe.

In fact, when we look at our history, we have consistently thought it right to engage with Europe to keep our sea routes open – either to maintain our world role or to ensure our own security at home. Ironically, some suggest, the time we should have engaged most was in the immediate aftermath of the Second World War, when Europe needed leadership and other countries were far too weak to lead.

Our current geography deceives us. True, we are an archipelago, but it is often forgotten that we were once a part of the European landmass. 'For most of prehistory, the lands which are now called the British Isles or the British and Irish Isles formed a broad promontory of the Continental landmass, an oceanside peninsula of the Peninsula,' writes Norman Davies in his book *The Isles*.[12] He continues: 'The transformation of the oceanside peninsula into a group of offshore islands took place in the course of the seventh or sixth millennium BC. In all probability it took place gradually, not as the result of a dramatic geological catastrophe or a sudden onrush of the sea. It was partly caused by the tilting of land surfaces rendered unstable by the retreating ice, and partly by the rising levels of warmer seas ... Sometime between 6000 and 5500 BC the land link disappeared entirely. "The Sleeve" was born, with its pinch point at the "Southern Straits".[13]

'The consequences,' says Davies, 'are often misrepresented or exaggerated.' He writes: 'It is often said that the new-formed islands were "isolated" from the Continent or "cut off". But this is hardly correct. Of course, in strictly geographical terms, the islands were isolated, since "to isolate" means "to turn into an island". Where once there was a strip of land, there now was a stretch of water.'[14] However, as Davies argues, we were far from secluded: 'There is every indication that communications actually improved. Even with the primitive boats then available, one could paddle or sail from one side of the Sleeve to the other more rapidly than one could previously have tramped across the isthmus or, in the intermediary phase, waded through the marshes. The birth of the Sleeve must have stimulated sailing techniques and marine transport of various kinds. In the period during the emergence of the Isles, the islanders became expert sailors. The islands were not cut off.'[15]

More controversially, Davies goes on to reference archaeologists who doubt how that most English of English icons, Stonehenge, represents anything that is distinctively English or British at all. It was built at a time, he says, when 'there was no country called "France" and nothing equivalent to it; there was no "England", and there was no "Britain', and no "Brittany". As yet, there were no ancient Gauls, no ancient Britons, and no ancient Bretons … Only two things can be said with absolute certainty about prehistoric life on "the Midnight Isles" [Britain]: it was *not* English; and it was *not* British.'[16]

If we take into account the 11,500 years of continuous human settlement, only 1,300 years can be described as English and 300 or so as British. And even then we were not cut off. So we have to put our island status into proper context. As Robert Tombs has written: Britain is a 'unique island': it is one of the three largest temperate archipelagos in the world, along with Honshu in Japan and the South Island of New Zealand, but unlike the other two nearly completely inhabitable. Britain is also closely moored to a continent. As Tombs argues: 'Most importantly, it [the British Isles] is in sight and easy reach of a continent. These seas – between 20 and 400 miles of often rough but predictable water – have been from earliest times a highway for traders, settlers and invaders in both directions.'[17]

The distance between Britain and the continent, writes Norman Davies, was 'not great enough to deter fair-weather voyages by hidebound coracles and kayaks, by dugouts, or even by rafts.'[18] He records: 'Even the "Great Crossing" between the Mainland and the Great Isle at the most convenient section of the Sleeve did not exceed 60 miles. It could be completed in a day, at most in a day and night … As a result, human settlement was increasingly concentrated in areas adjacent to the seaways and maritime trade routes.'[19] In this, we can see the beginnings of Britain as a nation of traders, explorers and merchant venturers, but also a nation closely linked to Europe.

Or, as a group of leading historians in *History Today*, tell us: 'Political, social, cultural, and economic life in Britain has always depended on, drawn upon, and given back to Europe. Since prehistory, migration into and out of these islands has defined their population and created generations of families with strong connections to Europe and elsewhere.'[20] Alternatively, as *The Economist* notes: 'After the Battle of Hastings in 1066 and the Norman conquest, England had a direct link to the western part of the continent for over 400 years, longer than it has been joined with Scotland.'[21]

Yet, for many, the 3,000 miles and more that separate us from North America seem a shorter distance than the 20 or so miles that separate us from the mainland of Europe. This is notwithstanding the fact that we were not only linked to the continent by our early history but for centuries have been more engaged in Europe than with the rest of the world. It was only after 1688 and during our long conflict with France that Britain's place in the world was transformed, as we inaugurated two centuries of global empire from the mid-18th to the mid-20th centuries.

To quote Shakespeare in Richard II, we are protected by a 'moat defensive,' but this has not prevented trade, communication or cultural contact. Despite our different histories, technological advances – from the telegram to the Internet – have brought us into close daily contact with mainland Europe as well as beyond.

No more can we say that our only route to mainland Europe is by sea and that we are invariably cut off by fog. There are now nearly 50 million outbound visits every year by UK citizens to Europe, which is 12 times as many trips to North America and five times as many as to the rest of the world.[22] What's more, Europeans are prepared to learn our language even when we refuse to learn theirs. When I first attended European ministerial meetings as a government minister in 1997, the French insisted on speaking in their own language. There was even a plan to make French the official language of the European Union. Now, in European secondary schools, over 90 per cent of pupils learn English.[23] English is the main business language and the working language of the European Union. It's spoken more in the European Parliament than even French or German. In short, our language is becoming Europe's language.

And while we will always be distinctive – situated between mainland Europe and North America – our desire to trade, explore and build up relationships with other countries has, over many centuries, been shared by many of our mainland neighbours who not only live by the sea – Europe borders on no fewer than four great seas: the Mediterranean, Black, Baltic and North as well as the Atlantic ocean – but also travelled widely, pioneered and made contacts across the waters. They were able to do this with ease because the European coastline, like ours, contains good natural harbours that make seafaring much easier. Of course, in past times, the Spaniards and the Portuguese were in the 'imperial game' long before us – with colonies in South and Central America, the Caribbean and Africa. At one time the French presided over more of North America and India than we did, while modern-day Sri Lanka, part of Brazil and the enormous archipelago of the 'Spice Islands' (now Indonesia) were run by the Dutch. By the 18th century the Russians had overrun all the tribes of Siberia and had leapt across the Bering Straits to settle in Alaska and as far down the American coast as San Francisco. The Norse had a settlement in North America centuries before Columbus set foot on Caribbean sand. Even a small country like Belgium had 'possessions' in the heart of Africa.

The overriding reason for Britain's first diplomatic and military engagements with Europe was obvious: to safeguard ourselves from invasion – at that time, mainly from the French – and to protect the sea routes essential to Britain's commercial success. But we soon saw that the best way of protecting our coastline *and* our trade routes was by preventing any one mainland European power becoming stronger than the others. So when we engaged to safeguard and advance our national interest, it was usually to balance the power of the strongest by building up the combined power of the rest. 'Splendid isolation' may have held its attractions but it was impossible in the circumstances as every British politician, general and admiral knew.

Of course it was also in the interests of others in Europe to prevent one power becoming too dominant. Whenever one power threatened to become a superpower – Spain in the 15th century, Venice in the 16th century, the Netherlands in the 17th century, France in the 18th and 19th centuries and then later Germany in the 20th century – Britain took action, and most of the time we did not need to act unilaterally but combined with others to head off continental dominance by one power.

And so one political fact of European history we should not ignore is that Britain could never *afford* to allow another power to dominate Europe for any length of time. Our interest in Europe included preventing one nation gaining the upper hand and being in a position to thwart our imperial reach. 'As an Empire builder and major trading power it was inevitable that Britain would come into conflict with rivals vying for the same territories and trade routes,' writes Sam Wilson.[24] It was always in our interests to prevent one country running Europe and to maintain a balance of power.

But we had our own – and different – needs and thus our own – and different – priorities due to our island status: 'Our trading pattern was quite different from that of the Continental powers', Vernon Bogdanor explains: 'As the first industrial nation, we had, from at least 1800, a much smaller agricultural sector than our Continental competitors. We were a maritime power that relied on cheap food from the Colonies, and our commercial system was based on free trade, unlike the high tariff countries of the Continent, with their large agricultural sectors.'[25] Our commitment to free trade was confirmed in 1846 with the Repeal of the Corn Laws.

Notwithstanding this, as James Ellison has argued: 'the British have always wanted to be at the [European] table … to this day Britain functions as a nation whose greatest interests are European.' The problem, as he sees it, is that 'the country is not at peace with this reality'.[26] All of this suggests that we are – and have been for centuries – necessarily a European power. The issue, Ellison contends, is not whether we are or are not European but why we apparently find it so difficult to admit it.

Great Britain, writes Robert Kagan, sat too close to the European continent to be invulnerable to attack, especially when the airplane and the long-range missile became major tools of warfare. But, unlike post-1945 America, which was able to maintain the peace because it was prepared to leave troops on European soil, 'Britain failed [in the pre-war years] because it had tried to play the role of balancer in Europe from "offshore" … [Britain's] main concern was always defence of their far-flung empire, and they preferred to stay out of Europe if possible. Their inability or unwillingness to station troops on the continent in sufficient number, or at least reliably to guarantee that sufficient force would arrive quickly in an emergency, led would-be aggressors to calculate that decisive British military force would either not arrive on time or not arrive at all.'[27]

Between 1914 and 1918 and 1939 to 1945, millions of British citizens had to fight or be stationed in mainland Europe. And our recent history of relations with Europe starts in 1945, with Britain – uninvaded and unconquered – the unmistakeable leading country of Europe and in pole position to shape the continent's future. There were four potential channels of influence for post-war Britain. We could leverage power through the Empire, which was now becoming the Commonwealth; through our Transatlantic Alliance with America; through Europe; or through newly created international institutions. The British choice was fateful: to base our foreign policy on relations with the Commonwealth and America, with the result that we suffered what one Foreign Secretary, Rab Butler, was later to call 'the bad start and the late start for Europe.'[28]

Churchill and the imperial legacy

Late in his life, Winston Churchill said he had devoted his entire career to what he described as 'the maintenance of the enduring greatness of Britain and her Empire'.[29] For him: 'Britain's standing in the world was indissolubly linked to its will to rule and to retain its Empire.'[30] Without India, as one of his biographers David Cannadine writes, Churchill had no doubt that British international prestige would be 'irretrievably damaged' and this would end Britain's status as one of the world's great powers.[31] When in the 1930s, Churchill had warned of the risks to the Empire, he claimed that: 'the continuation of our present confusion and disintegration will reduce us within a generation, and perhaps sooner, to the degree of states like Holland and Portugal, which nursed valiant races and held great possessions but was stripped of them in the crush and competition of the world.'[32]

For Churchill, as his official biographer Martin Gilbert has eloquently shown, the Second World War was not just about the defeat of Nazism and Japanese militarism, but also about securing India, reasserting Britain's leadership of the so-called Dominions and heading off US attempts to end both the Empire and imperial preference in trade. 'I have not become the King's First Minister in order to preside over the liquidation of the British Empire,' Churchill told the Lord Mayor's Banquet in November 1942, and as early as 1930 in the *Saturday Evening Post* in America he said: 'We are *with* Europe but not *of* it. We are linked but not compromised … we have our own dream and our own task.'[33] 'Each time we have to decide between Europe and the open sea, it is always the open sea that we shall choose,' Churchill told Charles de Gaulle.[34] When he met German Chancellor Konrad Adenauer in the early 1950s and told him Britain would always stand side-by-side with Europe, Adenauer replied: 'Prime Minister, you disappoint me somewhat. England is part of Europe.'[35]

But not everyone shared Churchill's enthusiasm for Britain's imperial role. Some believed that as the only major European power left standing after the war, Britain should take the lead in Europe. One civil servant of the time, Donald Maitland, who served in the Foreign Office after the Second World War before working at No 10 Downing Street under Edward Heath during Britain's successful application to join the EEC, recalls that he 'came back from the war absolutely persuaded that the imperial idea, the idea of us ruling other countries, was finished. We had to decolonise and if were we going to do that we had to have another kind of foreign policy.'[36]

The truth was that Britain had lost one quarter of its wealth because of the war. With war debts of nearly £5 billion, including £3.5 billion of deferred payments to Sterling Area countries, such as India and Egypt, the economist John Maynard Keynes argued that, unless overseas commitments were reined in, Britain's 'ability to pursue an independent financial policy in the early post-war years will be fatally impaired.'[37] Keynes argued that the British policy of defending the sea lanes, the Middle East and India showed that 'all our reflex actions are those of a rich man'.[38] But as Keynes predicted it would take many in Britain some time to see, in the words of one commentator of the time, that 'being on the winning side was not quite the same as winning'.

Under Churchill, British foreign policy was founded on 'three great circles among the free nations and democracies,' with Britain being at the centre of each: the Commonwealth, the English-speaking world and Western Europe. 'These three majestic circles are co-existent and if they are linked together,' Churchill argued, 'there is no force or combination which could overthrow them or even challenge them. Now if you think of the three interrelated circles, you will see that we are the only country which has a great part in every one of them.'[39] With Britain as the 'fulcrum' of the international system, his first circle was the Commonwealth. On the outside was a second circle, the English-speaking world, principally North America. A long way behind came the third, Europe. Our role in international institutions might have been added to his list but this was the frame of reference upon which politicians – both Conservative and Labour – formulated British foreign policy in the 1940s and 1950s.

The Labour government and the post-war world

Looking back from the perspective of today, what stands out in the Labour Government's list of achievements are the domestic advances: creating the National Health Service and Welfare State. Yet, when Attlee was asked late in life about his government's greatest challenges and successes none of those he listed were domestic. He had no doubt that his greatest accomplishment was Indian independence, achieved in 1947. His greatest problem, he said, was Russia with whom a Cold War had begun. His most pressing crisis was the Berlin airlift. And, in 1948, when Labour updated the Defence White Paper, it talked in traditional terms of the 'inescapable responsibilities of a great power'.[40] Nearly 10 per cent of the UK defence budget was devoted to India and almost 5 per cent to the defence of the Middle East.[41] Indeed the British Empire had five million soldiers based in 30 countries at the end of the Second World War.

It's easy to see why the economic realities of the time made many consider the new Commonwealth a better commercial prospect than a war-ravaged Europe. Aided by imperial preference in the 1930s and then by the breakdown of order on mainland Europe, Britain had become more dependent on its trade with the Commonwealth. Imports from the Commonwealth rose from just under 25 per cent in 1931 to nearly 37 per cent of total British imports in 1937, while exports rose from 32 per cent to nearly 40 per cent. By 1950, Commonwealth trade was up again to comprise 41 per cent of our imports and 48 per cent of exports, at a time when exports to what were to be the six original members of the Common Market had fallen from a pre-war level of 22 per cent to a post-war 17 per cent, with imports declining from nearly 18 per cent to 13 per cent over the same period.[42] As late as the mid-fifties, 61 per cent of our iron and steel exports, 52 per cent of engineering goods exports, 49 per cent of chemical product exports and 95 per cent of car exports went to the Commonwealth bloc, most of them to Australia, New Zealand and Canada. What's more, Britain's food supply depended on Australia, New Zealand and Canada, which between them provided 60 per cent of our imports of wheat. Australia and New Zealand, in turn, were responsible for 60 per cent of our meat imports.[43]

Britain's traditional links were cemented by the Bank of England and by the City of London's role as banker for the Commonwealth. Fifty per cent of all international payments were still made in sterling, a Foreign Office paper of July 1950 reported, most of them in trade with the old Empire.[44] 'The economics of the Commonwealth countries are complementary to that of Britain,' a 1950 Labour Party publication concluded, 'to a degree which those of western Europe could never equal.'[45]

Yet, as Lord Franks said in his 1954 Reith lecture, any policy to increase imperial preference was an attempt to call back a past that was already disappearing. The Australians, for example, were already signing deals that favoured America over Britain and they were later to pivot towards Asia. It was 'impossible and pointless,' Franks said, 'to argue the merits of this proposal for the simple reason it is out of date and has no chance.'[46]

Labour took the view that it was not supporting the old Empire but developing a new form of relationship with the colonies – what Attlee called 'a fourth Empire' – to convert an out-of-date imperialism into an ethical colonial policy. Africa, said the Foreign Secretary, Ernest Bevin, would become a 'surrogate' for the lost India.[47] 'If only we pushed on and developed Africa,' Bevin argued, 'we could have the US dependent on us and eating out of our hand in four or five years.'[48] It was this view of the world that gave rise to ambitious economic initiatives like the 'ground nuts' scheme that originated in Kenya to produce olive oil. (The tractors sent out to Africa were wrecked as they tried to cultivate untillable land, giving rise to the rewriting of a famous aphorism: 'give us the job and we'll finish the tools'.)

In his Reith lecture, Franks contended that, after Britain left India in 1947: 'The three circles of our life and power could have been realistically enhanced to considerable advantage as a means of a niche influence rather than global spanning power.'[49] In other words, Britain should have recognised that, while the ability to direct an Empire had gone, we could wield huge influence through the Commonwealth, with America and by actively participating in Europe. However, as Franks recognised, it was difficult for the leaders of the day to talk in this way. Such statements would be interpreted as 'defeatist'.

Attlee's government was clear that if Britain was to be influential – and maintain its position in the Middle East and Far East – it had to forge a modern relationship with the US in circumstances where our American friends were well aware just how financially weakened we were. 'The British are hanging on by the fingernails …,' the US Ambassador, John Winant, wrote in one of his cables to Washington, '… in the hope that somehow or other with our help they will be able to preserve the British Empire and their leadership of it.'[50] And having emerged from the war much strengthened, the American journalist, Walter Lippmann, hit the nail on the head when he said: 'War is hell but America had a hell of a war.'[51] The Americans were in no mood to defer to Britain. With America now making its own agreements directly with the Commonwealth countries, ending what one writer called 'the one indispensable precondition of the Dominion Idea', it was clear that 'a strategic revolution' was underway.[52]

The Labour Government stood apart from America on some issues – for example, the US and the UK disagreed on the recognition of Communist China – and at all times Attlee wanted to assure his party that he was not slavishly dependent on the USA. 'We are not pursuing an exclusive Anglo-American alliance,' Attlee's Parliamentary Private Secretary, Hector McNeil, scribbled in a note for backbenchers during a Commons debate in which Churchill had taunted Labour with a very pro-American speech. Foreign policy was based on collective security, Attlee assured them.[53]

However, Britain needed America more than they needed us. We needed their help to maintain the security of the sea and air routes to the Commonwealth and wanted US troops to stay in Europe. We may have been telling people that we had won the war but we needed the US to guarantee the peace. The need to secure new American financial support to maintain the Empire started with a plea for help in the Middle East. But America was reluctant to provide finance for two reasons that were put succinctly and directly by one American Congressman of the time: debt relief would be used to promote 'too much Damn socialism at home and too much Damned imperialism abroad.'[54] In particular America had no wish to finance the continuation of the British Empire.

In 1945, when Britain badly needed money not only to cover our imperial obligations but also to pay for both reconstruction and our imports of food, Keynes was sent to Washington to negotiate on the behalf of Britain along with the British Ambassador, Lord Halifax. Keynes' expectations proved unrealistic. He wanted a gift to cover Britain's post-war balance of payments or an interest-free loan. He got neither. The loan Britain was granted was at a fixed interest rate of 2 per cent – only finally paid off in 2006, my last year as Chancellor of the Exchequer.

The eventual outcome was, as Bevin put it, 'a pretty raw deal'.[55] James Callaghan, at the time a newly elected MP, called the terms of the economic agreement 'economic aggression' by the United States.[56] Robert Boothby, a prominent Tory backbencher, called it a 'monetary Munich'.[57] *The Economist* stated: 'The reward for losing one quarter of our wealth (in fighting the war) is to pay tribute for half a century to those enriched by war.'[58] The *New Statesman* said: 'the United States is nearly as hostile to the aspirations of Britain as it is to the Soviet Union.'[59] 'Why have the Americans acted like this,' asked Harold Wilson, soon to be President of the Board of Trade, only to answer his own question: 'There is nothing so irrelevant as a poor relative.'[60]

America had signed the 1943 Quebec agreement that committed it to sharing nuclear secrets with Britain and the use of nuclear weapons on the basis of mutual consent. But, in 1946, President Truman changed course, placing nuclear weapons under the US's own Atomic Energy Commission, and when the McMahon Act banned the sharing of nuclear information – which continued from 1946 to 1958 – Britain had to decide on its own deterrent, with what Bevin called 'a bloody Union Jack on it'.[61] 'We should make it clear to the US government that it was impossible for us to work with them,' Attlee said when US relations were discussed in the Cabinet, 'if they constantly took action affecting our interests without prior consultation with us.'[62]

But there was one overriding prize that justified tolerating these snubs in the minds of Attlee and Bevin: an American commitment of US troops, weapons and money to the defence of Europe under the umbrella of the new North Atlantic Treaty Organisation. Attlee's 'great achievement was to tie the United States into defending Western Europe in the event of any future attack', one of his recent biographers, Nicklaus Thomas-Symonds, has argued.[63] Of course the United Kingdom wanted to be the 'third force' alongside the US and the USSR but, recognising that it was too weak to defend Europe on its own, Britain needed America engaged on the continent.

The Attlee Government – aloof Europeans

Dean Acheson later said that the very phrase 'special relationship' was a dangerous intellectual obstacle to Britain's acceptance of a largely European role.[64] In retrospect, it is clear that Labour failed to distinguish between the temporary state of Europe – its debts, devastation and divisions – and its long-term prospects. One theme of Edmund Dell's account of the Treasury during these years is that Labour ministers just did not foresee the recovery of France and Germany. Neither did they see that such a recovery was not just in Europe's interests but in Britain's interests too.[65]

But we did not shun Europe. Initially, Bevin's 'great design' was a 'Western Union' underpinned by a demilitarised Ruhr outwith German control. He thought, as he told the Americans, that 'the whole of this region represents a single economic unit ... if the various countries were to pool their resources and eliminate the tariff barriers.'[66] One of his advisers wrote that 'if we became the recognised and vigorous leader of a group of Western Powers with large dependent territories we would gain ... weight.'[67] This view was made even more explicit in a memo to Bevin that stated: 'It may also restore us, if effective, and if we manage to become leaders of the union, as we should do if we do not bungle it, the former status of top dog which we have now lost to the USA and the USSR.'[68] Initially, then, Bevin saw advantages in building a British bloc to match those of the Americans and Russians. As late as January 1948, he talked of 'a Western European system ... backed by the resources of the Commonwealth and the Americans ... to develop our own power and influence to equal that of the United States of America and the USSR ... in a way which will show clearly that we are not subservient to the United States or the Soviet Union.'[69]

At the beginning of 1948, Bevin said that 'Britain cannot stand outside Europe and regard her problems as quite separate from those of her European neighbours', and, with the Commonwealth in mind, he argued that 'there is no conflict between the social and economic development of those overseas territories to the advantage of their peoples and their development as a source of supplies for Western Europe.'[70] In pursuit of this, Bevin sought co-operative arrangements with the Western Europeans, building on mutual defence pacts between Britain and other European states, namely a bilateral defence agreement with France (the Dunkirk Treaty of 1947), and a multi-lateral agreement with Belgium, the Netherlands and Luxembourg (the Brussels Pact of 1948).

However, Britain failed to capitalise on the potential strength it had as the undoubted leading power of post-war Western Europe. With the Cold War deepening and British economic difficulties more pressing, the idea of Britain as a 'third force' became harder and harder to sustain. Pivoting towards Europe became a more difficult proposition for Britain when fears started to grow that a European future might be a federalist one. And so, while initially enthusiastic about leading Europe, Bevin opted for an Atlanticist rather than a European future. At a meeting with his American and French counterparts – and in reply to Churchill's support for a Council of Europe – Bevin said: 'I must warn my colleagues that the United Kingdom – because of its overseas connections – could never become an entirely European country.'[71]

Yet there were good reasons to believe that Britain could have led a defeated and badly damaged Europe into a new era of co-operation, and some influential figures argued for this. As a Foreign Office paper of the time said: 'Unlike our two greater partners [America and the Soviet Union] we are not regarded in Western Europe either as gangsters or go-getters.'[72] But Britain did not seize the moment. One reason was that we still seemed to find it difficult to place our trust in the French. When Bevin was told in 1950 that if Britain opted for co-operation with France 'we shall perhaps be building on sand,' he retorted wryly that this was 'almost too optimistic'.[73] This was a reprise of Lloyd George's exchange with Clemenceau at the Versailles peace talks when Clemenceau said that post-war Britain could now get back to being the enemy of France. 'Hasn't that always been the policy of my country?', Lloyd George replied.[74]

Perhaps we did not understand, as Lord Franks later remarked, that the 'old Europe of independent, quarrelling, sovereign nations … [was] no longer fully alive'.[75] While it is true that up to the late fifties the German economy was virtually absent from world markets, Britain not only underestimated the scale of European recovery and the long-term importance of a growing trade with Europe but also feared that we might be landed with the financial burden of defending Europe and thus preferred the NATO arrangement which guaranteed European defence under an American umbrella.

More significant perhaps was Attlee's scepticism about European integration. He found the concept 'out of date' believing, as he later explained, that in an 'atomic age' concepts like spheres of influence and power blocs were superfluous.[76] Attlee believed that Britain needed to think of some form of world government. In this he was ahead of his time. During his period as Prime Minister the League of Nations was replaced by the United Nations and the 1940s saw the creation of the World Bank, the International Monetary Fund and the General Agreement on Tariffs and Trade as well as the adoption of the Universal Declaration of Human Rights. But while these institutions – in which Britain played a leading part – pointed to a multi-lateral system for managing crises, few yet saw them as an alternative or additional source of influence to the power we exercised through the Commonwealth, the transatlantic relationship or Europe. And while Attlee took a more internationalist view than some of his colleagues, he was not able to set out how British interests would be better advanced through our role in international institutions than through bilateral deals with countries like America. Right through until the 21st century few saw British leadership in multilateral institutions as a fourth avenue to international influence.

Attlee's reluctance to embrace Europe was not just because he felt multilateral institutions were the way of the future, it also reflected his ambivalence about European co-operation itself. Later, in his usual direct, curt way, Attlee explained: 'The so-called Common Market of six nations. Know them all well. Very recently this country spent a great deal of blood and treasure rescuing four of 'em from attacks by the other two.'[77] Far from making us Europeans, writes Vernon Bogdanor, the Second World War 'instilled into our consciousness the idea that our commitment to the Continent was bound to be limited, and could not be a total commitment.'[78] Attlee's views accorded with this.

Stafford Cripps, who became Chancellor in 1947, was pro-European and associated with a contemporary campaign to build a Christian Europe. Despite this, Cripps shared Attlee's scepticism about tying Britain too closely to Europe. If confronted with a direct choice, Cripps explained to Walter Lippmann, he would 'much rather go it alone and not be obligated to make agreements with the other European nations.'[79] 'They [the British] don't regard themselves as Europeans,' another famous American journalist, Sumner Wells, wrote in the *Washington Post*. 'They do not wish to stand in the same queue with the others and they have as a matter of policy manoeuvred themselves out of it,' he told his US audience.[80] Such reticence about European co-operation was confirmed in a confidential governmental paper of January 1949 in which the idea of a 'limited liability' for Europe was floated. It was argued: 'Our policy should be to assist Europe to recover as far as we can … [but] the concept must be one of limited liability. In no circumstances must we assist the Europeans beyond the point at which our own viability was impaired. Nor can we embark upon measures of co-operation which surrender our sovereignty and which lead us down paths along which there is no return.'[81]

So despite fighting – and leading – in a war to save Europe from the dominance of one power, building our relationships in Europe was not Britain's top priority in the post-war world. And so we gave a very guarded response to two big proposals for Europe's future: the Council of Europe and the European Coal and Steel Community.

A German diplomat explained later that when he tried to persuade Bevin of the benefits of the Council of Europe during a two-hour conversation, Bevin's argument against the Council was that the Labour Party could not support it because Churchill was its leading proponent.[82] But Bevin's reluctance to engage was also rooted in deeper worries. His priority was keeping the Americans in Europe. He welcomed the Marshall Plan. It meant American money that would be used to stimulate the European economies and world trade, helping to realise his aim of locking America into Europe. But his strategy did not include Britain joining European organisations other than in a titular or nominal way. At the time the Council of Europe was mooted, Bevin reluctantly agreed to endorse it but only so long as it had no power. Indeed, he dismissed it as of little relevance: 'We'll give them this talking shop in Strasbourg,' he said.[83] Yet, out of the Council of Europe came a common approach to human rights which, led by Britain, included the European Convention on Human Rights and the European Court of Human Rights. Nonetheless, Bevin wanted to kill off any attempts to give the Council itself any political authority.

Later, in 1950, the Labour Government had to consider a French proposal for a European Coal and Steel Community – the so-called Schuman Plan, named after France's Foreign Minister, Robert Schuman. The Coal and Steel Community, the forerunner of the European Economic Community, was founded to create a common, shared market in what had been vital materials of war – coal and steel – in order to ensure that the Germans could never monopolise the lion's share of them and never again rearm by stealth (as they had done in the 1930s). All six of the European Coal and Steel Community founding members – France, West Germany, the Netherlands, Italy, Belgium and Luxembourg – had been badly scarred by the Second World War.

First Britain agreed to engage – as we so often did when faced with a difficult choice. We did not want to appear to be wholly negative. By May 1950, however, Bevin was being advised by his Foreign Office mandarins that 'British participation is likely to involve us in Europe beyond the point of no return.'[84] They urged a 'consultative association' and nothing more. This was again a familiar British tactic of trying to limit the scope of a new European body. By June 1950, the Foreign Office was advising the government to reject membership entirely and for what were traditional reasons: 'We should not commit ourselves irrevocably to Europe either in the political or in the economic sphere … in view of our world position and interests.'[85]

What stands out in this statement is the reference to our 'world position and interests'. The Treasury took the view that 'no national Government [should] give up sovereignty over such essential elements in its economic structure without prejudice to its power of action in almost every other area.'[86] Britain's future, they implied, would always be elsewhere. The fear that justified reticence was, they claimed, the threat of European federalism: the real issue, though, was that Britain could not accept the principle of any pooling of its resources or its sovereignty. As the Head of the Foreign Office, William Strang, stated: 'To contemplate, even in principle, an agreement to pool the British coal and steel industries with those of other Western European countries, and make their decisions subject to the decisions of an independent European authority which are binding … would imply a readiness to accept a surrender of sovereignty on a matter of vital national interest … The decisions which the French are now summoning us to take is, in fact, the decision whether or not we are to bind ourselves irrevocably to the European Community.'[87] Herbert Morrison, by then the Foreign Secretary, was blunter: 'It's no good: we can't do it.'[88]

While the four potential channels for post-war British influence included working through a united Europe and through international institutions, Britain could not agree to put at risk the existing power blocs it thought more important: the Commonwealth and America. In November 1950, under pressure from America, Morrison signed a joint declaration with his French and American counterparts, the 'Washington declaration', supporting European co-operation as part of what was seen as a constantly developing Atlantic community. But when America asked Britain to participate in deeper European co-operation, Britain was reluctant to be seen as 'a one-man clearing house for ambiguous European plans dreamed up in Washington.'[89] America, we convinced ourselves, did not understand the details and complexities of Europe.

Thus, in the six years after 1945, Labour pursued a conventional policy of rejecting European entanglements in favour of working through the Commonwealth and the American alliance. We did so in preference to more extensive European engagement that would have involved, in the view of policy-makers, an unacceptable dilution of sovereign power and restrictions on our freedom and flexibility to act. In words that were to become familiar over the following decades, Hugh Dalton, Chancellor of the Exchequer from 1945 to 1948, explained that Britain should not put its sovereignty in peril by allowing vital decisions on great issues of national economic policy to be transferred from Westminster to a supranational European assembly. Or, as Attlee said, in rejecting the Coal and Steel Community, it was 'an irresponsible body appointed by no one and responsible to no one'.[90]

Churchill returns

As leader of the Conservative Opposition in the post-war years, Churchill led the way in advocating European unity, starting with his support for the new Council of Europe. Indeed, the speeches he made during this period in support of the idea make it possible for him to lay claim to be its father. When the Labour government rejected the European Coal and Steel Community, Churchill seemed to favour participating. Joining forces with the Liberal Party, he told the House of Commons in June 1950: 'The Conservative and Liberal Parties say, without hesitation, that we are prepared to consider, and if convinced, to accept, the abrogation of national sovereignty, provided we are satisfied with the conditions and the safeguards. The Conservative and Liberal Parties declare that national sovereignty is not inviolable and that it may be resolutely diminished for the sake of all the men, in all the lands, finding their way home together.'[91]

This was an extraordinary statement for a Conservative leader to make at that time. But it was never quite clear if this meant a united Europe including Britain, or a united Europe without Britain. Churchill said later: 'I never contemplated joining in this plan on the same terms as the Continental partners ... We help, we dedicate, we play a part, but we are not merged and do not forfeit our insular or Commonwealth-wide character.'[92] So when Churchill returned to power, his government did nothing to change the official British policy that rejected joining the Coal and Steel Community. When it came down to actual decisions in government the *status quo* was reinforced by the Conservatives.

In office, Churchill's grand strategy revolved around the same objectives that had guided Labour: maintaining Britain's world role through our leverage with both the Commonwealth and America. However, Churchill believed that he could do better than Attlee at persuading the Americans of the need to strengthen the Atlantic alliance to preserve Britain's global power. Furthermore, as when Labour was in power, under the new Conservative government there was little appreciation that the new international institutions that Britain had played a role in creating could be an important additional channel for British influence.

Churchill's main foreign policy attack on Labour's period in power from 1945 to 1951 was not that they were wrongheaded in their defence of Britain's world role but that they were half-hearted. 'The last six years has marked the greatest fall in the rank and status of Britain in the world which has occurred since the loss of the American colonies 200 years ago …,' Churchill asserted. 'Our Oriental Empire has been liquidated … and our influence among the nations is less than it has ever been in any period since I remember,' he claimed.[93]

And he had bolder objectives for Britain. He believed that the Commonwealth could, even in a fast changing post-war world, give Britain the weight and power to broker peace between America and Russia. 'We may regain our pinnacle of fame and power,' said Churchill, by keeping the colonies and pursuing a 'new policy' to effect the outcome of the Cold War.[94] Churchill was not alone among Conservatives in embracing such an idea. The view was also held by many on the moderate modernising wing of the Conservative Party. In May 1951, for example, the future Prime Minister, Harold Macmillan, said that the development of the Commonwealth into 'a unit as powerful as the US and Soviet Russia was the only possibility.'[95]

Churchill still believed that he could tell America what to do. But he underestimated the sheer scale of America's new power, the breadth of Washington's global ambitions and he still did not believe the Americans when they said that they wanted Britain to be integrated into Europe. In contrast, the Americans thought Churchill was out of touch with changing times. In his diary entry of December 1951, Dwight D. Eisenhower, then Supreme Allied Commander Europe, wrote that Churchill was 'living in the past'. He noted: 'Churchill refuses to think in terms of the present day. My regretful opinion is that he no longer absorbs new ideas.'[96] Eisenhower found Churchill's faith that 'all the answers to international problems were to be found merely in British-American partnership ... [to be] childlike.'[97] Churchill was to be disappointed at the degree of influence he could bring to bear on America. Not for nothing did Churchill call his memoir of the period *Triumph and Tragedy*. Famously, as David Cannadine remarks, he used the words *Finest Hour*, for the title of his war years' memoirs, suggesting that what was to come later was never to be as good as what had come before.

What Churchill sought – 'a revival of Britain's former influence and initiative among the allied powers' – and what the Americans were ready to offer was very different.[98] When he pressed for US support to maintain Britain's position in the Middle East, the US Secretary of State, Dean Acheson, said: 'Anglo-American solidarity on a policy of sitting tight offered no solution, but was like a couple locked in a warm embrace on a rowing boat about to go over the Niagara Falls. It was high time to break the embrace and take the oars.'[99] These were harsh and unsympathetic words, but it is clear that the Americans feared that supporting an old Empire in areas like the Middle East might undermine America's Cold War priorities, particularly its wish to win over to its side strategically important emerging nations. 'This role should not be sacrificed because of a very human feeling of decency and generosity towards an opinionated old gentleman who is still sufficiently sharp and selfish to grab every advantage with bland assurances of unwavering esteem,' wrote one Special Assistant to Eisenhower not long after his election as President in 1952.[100]

Throughout the 1950s, as power passed to Anthony Eden and later to Harold Macmillan, the Conservatives' position on the central aim of British foreign policy did not alter: Britain could not give up on a world role that should be maintained through our leverage in the Commonwealth and through the Transatlantic Alliance. Later Edward Heath claimed that Churchill would have supported integrating Britain into Europe as he realised that the Commonwealth could not be a real replacement for Empire and that the 'special relationship' with the United States was really one of a subordinate to a superior.[101] Others would argue that the clue to Churchill's position was that, although he favoured a united Europe, he did not favour an integrationist or federal Europe, but instead sought a Europe of intergovernmental co-operation. Whatever the truth, serious engagement with, and British involvement in, European plans for integration was not a UK priority. As one diplomat advised, if Britain were to do so, 'we shall have tipped the balance against the other two elements in our world situation, the Atlantic community and the Commonwealth.'[102] In other words, Britain would not risk its relationships with the Commonwealth and transatlantic partnership for a new relationship with Europe. Of course, we could understand that within mainland Europe there was a desire for co-operation as a welcome antidote to conflict, but we took the view that this was always bound to be felt more urgently in Germany, France, Italy and on the mainland itself than in Britain. As the father of post-war European co-operation, Jean Monnet, put it: 'Britain had not been conquered or invaded. She felt no need to exorcise history.'[103]

The Conservative governments – detached Europeans

If Dean Acheson said giving up our leadership of Europe was 'the greatest mistake of the post-war period,' others disagreed: for example, Vernon Bogdanor quotes the historian A.J.P. Taylor telling him that Churchill twice saved Britain – once by strenuous action in 1940; and once by inaction in 1951 when he refused to join the Coal and Steel Community.[104]

The truth is that the *status quo* was more attractive to the Conservative government. It wanted to hold on to the traditional relationship with the Commonwealth and the US to such a degree that it was prepared to forego playing a part in shaping the new Europe. The line adopted by the Conservative Government on the Coal and Steel Community was the same as that of the Foreign Office, which concluded that there was 'a danger in the longer term that a federalist union might constitute a neutral bloc in a world conflict,' with Germany emerging as 'the predominant economic partner' in Europe, and this would 'not be dangerous in the short term to the UK.'[105] The Foreign Office rejection of British involvement was unconditional: 'Owing to her position as a world power, the United Kingdom cannot join the integration movement … The aim of the United Kingdom should be so to guide the course of the integration movement that any continental union which emerges should take its place as a part of the wider Atlantic community.'[106]

In October 1950, what became known as the Pleven Plan (named after the French Prime Minister René Pleven) – a proposal for a European Defence Community – came forward in response to American pressure for Europe to do more for its own security. The Korean War was already seen by the Americans as a prelude to a Soviet offensive in Europe and they wanted European countries to spend more on their own collective defence. The idea of a European army had in fact first been suggested not by Pleven but by Churchill in one of his grandiloquent speeches to the Council of Europe in August 1950. 'We should make a gesture of practical and constructive guidance by declaring ourselves in favour of the immediate creation of a European army under a unified command, and in which we should all bear a worthy and honourable part,' Churchill pronounced.[107]

However, back in government, Churchill rejected a European

army and British participation in it. It was, he said, a 'sludgy amalgam', and that his proposal had been meant for continental Europe, not for Britain, despite his use of the word 'all'.[108] Once again, Churchill voiced the familiar refrain: Britain was too big to be in Europe and big enough to stand apart. 'I should resist any American pressure to treat Britain on the same footing as the European states,' he said, 'none of whom have the advantages of the Channel and who are consequently conquered.'[109]

Foreign Secretary Anthony Eden's rejection of the Pleven Plan, in a memo to Churchill, was even more definitive: 'It is in political trouble over fundamental questions of sovereignty. The plan does not permit national armies to exist in participating countries except for overseas garrisons … I have never thought it possible that we could join such an army.'[110] But again under US pressure, in May 1952, Eden recommended support for the plan even though Britain would not be a formal member. To avoid upsetting the Americans, Eden proposed an 'association agreement' – a treaty between the UK and the new defence community. 'This is the limit to which the UK can go in the way of association,' it was argued, and 'we shall be unable to respond to any future pleas that we must take … in order to save the whole project from failure.'[111]

Yet in 1953, after talks between Churchill, Eisenhower and the French, and in deference to American pressure, Britain softened its line by suggesting that a UK unit could join the European Defence Community. In April 1953, Eisenhower pressed Churchill for 'a more emphatic public endorsement from Great Britain [of the European Defence Community] … stating in your own inimitable and eloquent way the things that you have already announced that Britain is ready to do in support of these proposals.'[112] Later in July 1953, Eisenhower pressed once more, repeating even more forcibly his view that America believed 'earnestly that only closer union among the nations of western Europe, including Western Germany, can produce a political, economic and military climate in which the common security can be assured.'[113] In the end, the French National Assembly threw out the treaty. Churchill was furious but relieved: 'The French have behaved in an unspeakable way, execrable. No thought at all for others, ingratitude, conceit,' he said.[114]

But a third European initiative could not be so easily thwarted or dismissed. The proposals of the crucial 1955 Messina Conference (held in the Italian city of Messina in Sicily), involving the foreign ministers of the Member States of the European Coal and Steel Community, struck the British like a bolt from the blue. At its inaugural meeting an invitation was issued to Britain to participate in the negotiations that were to pave the way for the Treaty of Rome in 1957 and the creation of the European Economic Community in 1958. But Britain was dismissive of it from the outset. Rab Butler, the Chancellor of the Exchequer, spoke about Messina at an Organisation for European Economic Co-operation (OEEC) dinner. Not only did he anger people when he said: 'Britain was the normal chairman of Europe', but he ridiculed the Conference as 'some archaeological excavations at an old Sicilian town'.[115] We were, Butler said, a leader among 'sea-faring countries who should never want to exclude "the other world"'.[116] According to Butler, Eden, who had by now replaced Churchill as Prime Minister, was 'bored' by Messina – 'even more bored than I was,' Butler later remarked.[117] Macmillan, now Foreign Secretary, took a more nuanced view, arguing that Britain 'might be able to exercise a greater influence on the forthcoming discussions if we enter them on the same footing as other countries concerned and not in the capacity of an observer.'[118]

Subsequently the Foreign Office argued for the term 'delegate' while the Treasury talked only of sending an 'observer'. In the end it was decided that Britain should have a 'representative'. And so while other countries sent their foreign ministers to Messina, we decided to send a Board of Trade official, Russell Bretherton. As he later explained, Bretherton found himself 'confronted by something of a dilemma ... I thought personally that HMG would be most unlikely to give any clear undertaking to participate in a Common Market, but on the other hand we should not want to slam any doors.'[119]

The Messina Conference established the Spaak Committee, a steering committee chaired by the Belgian Foreign Minister, Paul-Henri Spaak, and composed of the heads of delegation from the Member States at Messina, including the hapless Bretherton. Spaak had been an early advocate of a European customs union, and had negotiated the Benelux agreement in 1944. It was in this year that he told Eden that the British 'have not yet realised how much all the countries of western Europe looked to them'.[120] The Spaak Committee was set up to draft recommendations for the formation of a customs union and the establishment of common European economic policies. Later in 1956 the United Kingdom withdrew and expressed a preference for negotiations towards a European free-trade area. The three reasons that Britain cited at a meeting of the Western European Council for standing apart were: British links with the Commonwealth; the fact that the Common Market could not be reconciled with a one-world system; and the risk that a European Common Market would impede the workings of the newly created organisation of advanced economies – the Organisation for European Economic Co-operation.

So, offered the chance to participate in the shaping of Europe, Britain opted for a restatement of its world role based on the primacy of relationships with the Commonwealth and America. Later, Butler said to the journalist, Michael Charlton: 'Why is it that a great maritime power, above all one that is accustomed to the uses of power through naval supremacy, does not make the political adjustment after the last war, when it's obvious among all facts that naval supremacy is no longer what is going to dictate the world balance?' He answered his own question by saying it was 'absolutely vital to the future understanding of British history, because we did not adjust ourselves from being a world power and an enormous maritime power depending on the resources of the sea.'[121]

Suez – the wrong type of European co-operation

Illusions about our global power were exposed in 1956 with the British and French decision to join with Israel to oppose Egypt's nationalisation of the Suez Canal Company and its control over the canal. The international consortium that had run it for nearly a century was summarily thrown out. Britain wanted to move quickly to protect its economic and wider interests, but right from the start the US was less than supportive, making it clear that it wanted the UK to wait for the 'broadest possible base' of support and 'the benefit of affirmative world opinion' prior to any action.[122]

When Eden decided to act, claiming Britain's world role was at stake, his Cabinet colleagues appeared – at least at first – to be even more bellicose than him. Harold Macmillan, who was now Chancellor of the Exchequer, told the Americans that 'if the final result was to be the destruction of Great Britain as a first-class power and its reduction to a status similar to that of Holland, the danger should be met now.'[123] It was statements like this that made the Americans consider the British to be out of touch with the new world. In his report to President Eisenhower, the US Ambassador in London wrote that Eden had 'not adjusted his thoughts to the altered status of Great Britain'.[124] Arguing against intervention, US Secretary of State Allen Dulles – whom Churchill said was the only case he knew of a bull carrying his china shop around with him – was characteristically blunt: Britain, he claimed, was unaware of the inadequacies of its military establishment to take on a 'real fighting job of this size'.[125]

But in the 1956 Suez crisis financial considerations came into play. And it was economics that would start to dominate in shaping Britain's changing views about membership of Europe. The dollar was now the undisputed international currency. Throughout 1956 Britain had maintained a current account surplus, but that was not enough: the value of sterling came under speculative pressure during the Suez crisis and the Bank of England was forced to deplete its US dollar reserves to defend the fixed value of the pound sterling against the dollar. The government viewed the exchange rate of $2.80 to the pound as appropriate for trade purposes. It feared the inflationary consequences of having to pay out in expensive dollars for oil imports while the canal was closed. And it regarded exchange rate stability as essential for preserving both the Sterling Area and sterling's role as a reserve currency. In short, the British needed American support to maintain the value of sterling.[126]

America understood this. Referring to Harold Macmillan's role as Chancellor, Eisenhower told Eden that 'Harold's financial problem is going to be a serious one and this itself I think would dictate a policy of the least possible provocation.'[127] Or, as it was put by one American official: 'You'll not get a dime out of the US Government until you are out of Suez'.[128] Eisenhower was adamant: Britain must withdraw from Suez. When the Treasury said that sterling needed urgent US support, his reply was simple: no ceasefire, no loan. The invasion was halted, British forces were pulled out and our French ally was abandoned. 'Europe will be your revenge,' Adenauer, the German Chancellor, said to Guy Mollet, the French premier.[129] Events were to show this to be true.

The historian Ronald Hyam concludes that Eden's decisions on Suez were founded on a misguided reading of Britain's past and an inability to comprehend the need for American support. He argues: 'Lacking historical knowledge, politicians can have an unhappy knack of seizing upon the wrong analogy. The classic case of this – the apotheosis of an embarrassing tendency – was Sir Anthony Eden's use of analogy during the Suez Crisis of 1956.' Eden concluded that Nasser was a 'Hitler on the Nile', viewing Suez through the prism of the 1930s. He forgot that much had changed in the intervening period. However, as Hyam concludes: 'Even so, analogies alone do not a disaster make. What was fatal was the devious way Eden, a sick man, bypassed the normal processes of government decision-making, refusing all advice except from one or two people who only encouraged him in his tragically mistaken and atavistic attempt to play power politics without American support.'[130] Hugo Young takes a broader perspective. By the time of Suez, he observes: 'the Empire was fraying at the edges and softening at the centre. The writing was on the wall for all those prepared to read it, and to study with detachment the financial data that underpinned its meaning ... [but] what took longer to follow was the quest for an alternative, a new matrix within which to fit Britain's strategic objectives.'[131]

When Suez was all over, Eden himself concluded that 'we must review our world position and our domestic capacity more searchingly in the light of the Suez experience which has not so much changed our fortunes as revealed realities.'[132] And he wrote that 'if we are to play an independent part in the world, even on a more modest scale than we have done here, we must ensure our financial and economic independence.'[133] Yet even if Suez highlighted the limitations on Britain's ability to act independently, the British political establishment were reluctant to change course.

What lessons Anthony Eden might have learned from the Suez debacle did not matter: a little over one month after the end of the Suez venture he was forced to resign as Prime Minister and left politics, never to return. The pillars of our post-war approach – seeing the Commonwealth and the transatlantic relationship as our channels of influence – were found to be wanting: would Britain now look to Europe?

CHAPTER TWO

Missed opportunities, 1957–70

Jean Monnet, who is regarded by many as the founding father of the European Union, once remarked: 'I never understood why the British did not join [the European Economic Community]. I came to the conclusion that it must have been because it was the price of victory – the illusion that you could maintain what you had, without change.'[1] With Suez, the illusion that Britain could hold what we always had was exposed. It was during the following decade that the UK realised it had to accept the need for change, but it could not agree on what form that change should take.

Harold Macmillan, Chancellor of the Exchequer at the time of Suez and then Prime Minister from 1957 to 1963, was to be the pivotal figure in steering British policy towards Europe. After Macmillan moved from the Foreign Office to the Treasury in 1955 – from what he termed the study of 'geography to arithmetic' – he became more aware of the rising financial and economic pressures on Britain.[2] As a result, when he replaced Eden as Prime Minister in January 1957, Macmillan ordered a wide-ranging reassessment of Britain's world role. The result was a report entitled 'The Position of the United Kingdom in World Affairs', which was blunt: it found that Britain could 'no longer operate from the position of overwhelming strength – military, political and economic – which we enjoyed in the heyday of our imperial power.'[3]

But while the report appeared to accept Britain's reduced status in world affairs, its conclusions held to traditional thinking, stating that we could still exercise a substantial influence in the world principally because of our relations with America and through being leader of the Commonwealth. However, Europe was seen in a new light, with Britain cast as a link between Europe, the Commonwealth and the United States. Even so, Europe remained on the outer circle of our foreign policy relationships: maximum Anglo-American cooperation was deemed essential and the connection with the Commonwealth was considered equally vital to the position of influence which Britain sought. The report, emphasising this, concluded: 'Commonwealth cohesion and Anglo-American solidarity are therefore major aims in themselves.'[4] Here the context was important: mindful that the pre-eminent struggle was the Cold War with the Soviet Union, it was argued that Britain should now bring what influence it could bring to bear not as a 'third force' but in support of the United States in the world struggle between the forces of freedom and those of tyranny.

The study argued that Britain needed to be faster on its feet in response to the decline of British power. In language that was prescient it stated: 'In the 19th century we had the power to impose our will. By contrast, we now have to work largely through alliances and coalitions.'[5] Ministers were warned, as Peter Hennessy shows in his summary of the report, that it would be impossible to maintain Britain's influence if it appeared to be 'clinging obstinately to the shadow of the old imperial power after its substance had gone'.[6] But while stating Britain had to come to terms with this changing world, the study rejected any retreat from the international arena, claiming that Britain could not put to 'best use the advantages of our special position, either as a link between Europe and the Commonwealth and the United States, or as the guardian and trustee of dependent peoples, if we took refuge in the neutrality and comparative isolation of the purely commercial powers such as Sweden or Switzerland.'[7] To play a continued world role, it was thought essential to foster the cohesion of the Commonwealth, promote UK trading interests, strengthen the pound and maintain the Sterling Area.

Where the report broke with the immediate post-war past was in bringing not just one but two pro-European arguments closer to the surface. The first was a reminder of Britain's old 'offshore balancing role', with the need to prevent one European power becoming too dominant. The second was an official recognition that, if the economy started to fall further behind other countries, joining with the rest of Europe might offer a solution.

Macmillan was the first senior British politician to argue that joining Europe would allow us to catch up economically with our competitors and his premiership was eventually to be dominated by European questions. But Macmillan's views on Britain's relations with Europe were complex and often conflicted. In 1958, Macmillan declared to de Gaulle, with great feeling, that 'the Common Market is the continental system all over again. Britain cannot accept it. I beg you to give it up. Otherwise we shall be embarking on a war which will doubtless be economic at first but which runs the risk of gradually spreading into other fields.'[8] Despite these comments, Macmillan had a more positive attitude towards Europe than his predecessors. As early as 1939, Macmillan had claimed that 'if the western civilisation is to survive, we must look forward to an organisation, economic, cultural, and perhaps even political, comprising all the countries of Western Europe.'[9] After the war, he had said: 'Britain's frontier is not on the channel; it is not even on the Rhine; it is at least on the Elbe.'[10] He was also worried that if Britain detached itself from Europe it would be unable to influence events. In 1951, Macmillan was privately warning people that it was through a European community that Germany would revive its power: 'It is really giving them on a plate what we fought two world wars to prevent,' he remarked.[11]

But while Europe featured prominently in Macmillan's new thinking he was not yet ready – or, because of his party, able – to be seen to downgrade the importance of the Commonwealth. America also continued to loom large in his thoughts. As he put it in his diary: 'Shall we be caught between a hostile (or at least less friendly) America and a boastful, powerful "Empire de Charlemagne" now under French, but later bound to come under German control? Is this the real reason for "joining" the Common Market (if we are acceptable) and for abandoning ... the Commonwealth: it's a grim choice.'[12]

How Britain viewed the world in 1960

Anxious to find a way forward, Macmillan set up – prior to the 1959 election – a group of officials to conduct a further review called the 'Foreign Policy Study, 1960–1970,' saying that it would be useful if, after the next General Election, the ministers of a new administration could have for their consideration an up-to-date and comprehensive forecast of the main economic, diplomatic and military developments in world affairs over the next decade.

Macmillan instructed his officials that this was not to be a standard exercise in assessing Foreign Office objectives without taking into account our economic position. He specifically instructed them to address how the UK should pay for its world role, informing them that Britain's ambitions should not run ahead of national resources and that to pay for future defence commitments, where decisions often took many years to deliver, broad strategic lines of policy should be established as far ahead as possible. Only in this way could they be aligned to the best use of available resources.

The resulting study was an important attempt to assess the best means of maintaining British power and influence in the world. The final Future Policy Study report stipulated that Britain's overseas policies depended upon three factors – world economic conditions; the adaptability and growth of the UK economy; and, finally, the willingness of the British people to devote a substantial proportion of their incomes towards such an objective.

The UK economy, it was accepted, would remain the most vulnerable of all the major economies in the 1960s, but still it was thought essential that sterling retain its status as an international reserve currency. However, a note of warning was issued: if, as in early 1960, London's gold reserves remained less than one-third of the sterling liabilities to other countries, Britain's worldwide defence effort would come under threat. 'It follows that the United Kingdom's first economic responsibility, and the necessary condition for maintaining our place in the world, is to keep sterling strong,' it was argued. The study concluded: 'This means keeping commitments within resources. If the future claims on the economy are allowed to accumulate so that the prospective increases in resources are already mortgaged in advance, there will be no margin available to meet unforeseen needs or to cope with the adverse changes in circumstances – which are bound to happen sometime in a ten-year period.'[13]

The logic was clear: defence and other spending had to be kept in check not just to balance the budget but also to safeguard sterling's international role. A weakening of sterling – and even more a depreciation – would have damaging results for the Sterling Area and Commonwealth. So sustaining the financial stability of the Sterling Area was set in concrete as a precondition of Britain's foreign policy objectives for the 1960s.

But there was a problem. As more countries in the Sterling Area acquired independence, Britain would become less able to control the extent to which these states drew on the gold and dollar reserves held in London. Concerned about this possibility, Treasury officials maintained that it would be necessary to further strengthen Britain's reserves to prevent a drain on them by sterling and non-sterling countries. Yet when the Bank of England's reserves came under pressure, the government had to react by defending the pound's value through deflation, which curbed growth. A vicious circle was set in motion: the consequent rise in interest rates, which helped limit speculation against sterling, would serve to undermine industrial investment.

During the 1960s, the study warned, Britain would have to constantly monitor the external financial position and the balance of payments, which were likely to forbid any ambitious expansion of overseas spending and limit internal spending too. It was clear, the report suggested, that Britain's best interests, as well as those of the West in general, lay in the government striking the right balance between doing too little and doing too much. Doing too little would be detrimental to the influence we could wield; doing too much would result in a series of sterling crises that would reduce British influence. The Treasury's view was clear: strengthening the reserves held in London necessitated a reining back of some of our international commitments, specifically those that were economically unproductive, including those located in the Far East. But upon this there was no consensus: it was not a view held by the rest of the political, diplomatic and military establishment.

The Future Policy Study was specific about how Britain should resolve the mismatch between commitments and resources. It was possible, the study said – at least in theory – for a country with Britain's standard of living and productivity to devote 8½ per cent of its GDP to support overseas policy objectives. However, finance for overseas expenditure was competing directly with other legitimate demands for resources, namely lower rates of taxation, greater social expenditure, expectations of higher living standards, increased consumption and more leisure time which would absorb valuable resources in the 1960s. On one point the Future Policy Study was clear: the public sector's share of resources was unlikely to decline. This meant that, if the government wanted to increase overseas expenditure, modifications in the level of investment in the domestic economy and/or the rate of taxation would become necessary.

Keeping the public sector's share of expenditure stable would mark a major shift in the general thrust of government policy. Between 1953 and 1958 the public sector shrank from 29½ per cent of GDP to 26½ per cent, and overall overseas expenditure fell from 11¾ per cent to 8¼ per cent. This decrease in the share taken by overseas spending had made room for expansion in other areas of the public sector, notably spending on roads and education, which had made a major contribution to the improved performance of the British economy in the late 1950s. The authors of the study reminded themselves of the economic consequences of financial imprudence: if the defence and aid programmes were carried out without a corresponding moderation in public and private spending, the impact would fall on the balance of payments and on sterling which would overload the economy with large and inflexible commitments. A resulting depreciation in the value of sterling would force drastic cutbacks in Britain's defence and aid programmes. If this were to occur, it was argued, the stability of Asia and Africa – where many of the currencies were backed by sterling – would be severely undermined.

But while it was blunt on these financial and economic realities, did the review's conclusions take them fully into account when determining UK foreign policy imperatives for the decade ahead? Britain's relative power would decline *vis-à-vis* the United States, the Soviet Union, and possibly the European Common Market bloc, said the study. Yet, because the Future Policy Study was of the view that Britain's contribution to the freedom and stability of the world was pivotal, it was deemed wholly inappropriate for the UK to restrict itself to a role limited to the European continent: 'We [Britain] are much too important a part of the free world to be able to retreat into a passive role like Sweden or Switzerland,' it was argued.[14] Any narrowing of Britain's international responsibilities and greater focus on a European or regional role was not an issue under serious consideration by the Future Policy Study, although sympathy for this idea was rapidly gaining ground in the Treasury. As we will see, in March 1960, not long after the completion of the exercise, Macmillan changed his mind on this and established the inter-departmental Economic Steering (Europe) Committee, chaired by Sir Frank Lee, the Permanent Secretary to the Treasury. This was the committee which was to eventually recommend Britain's first application for EEC membership.

Macmillan circulated the Future Policy Study to the Cabinet on 29 February 1960, instructing ministers that they ought to formulate future policy in line with this broad overview. A month later, Macmillan met with his senior colleagues in the Prime Minister's Room in the House of Commons to discuss the report. At the meeting, Macmillan said that he concurred with the main findings of the study, agreeing that Britain's relative power would decline. However, he also believed that the exercise of 'intangible' influence could compensate for this. In a statement on the importance of what was later to be called 'soft power', Macmillan told the assembled ministers: 'The best periods in our history had by no means been those, such as the 19th century, when we had a preponderance of wealth and power, and for the future we must be ready to consider how we could continue to exercise influence in the world other than through material means alone.'[15] So Macmillan saw that influence would supersede military and economic power, and that building alliances would be the alternative to going it alone. Britain would have to be ready to sublimate specific British interests, he argued, in favour of the interests of the West as a whole.

The responses to Macmillan were more in line with traditional thinking. Rab Butler, now the Home Secretary, considered the forecast of our international position unduly pessimistic, arguing that it 'did not sufficiently bring out the possibilities of development of the Commonwealth and Colonial system'. Butler seemed implacable in his opposition to accelerated decolonisation: 'Why,' he asked, 'should we assume that we had to follow an inevitable course in granting independence to our colonial territories and thus create trouble for ourselves in the United Nations? Did the Nigerians really want independence?'[16] The predicted economic growth rates of Germany and France, as well as of the European Economic Community generally, did concern Butler and he postulated whether Britain ought to take over the 'leadership' of Europe, although the language he used seems inappropriate: 'Should we not "invade" Europe and take the lead before it was too late, thus forestalling the possibility of France adopting isolationist policies with the consequent risk of [the] collapse of West European unity?' he asked.[17]

While accepting the general analysis that British power would decline, Lord Home, spoke as Commonwealth Secretary: the final document, in his view, failed to give due weight to the Commonwealth 'circle' in supporting Britain's world role. 'Without the USA we should be defenceless, without Western Europe we should be poorer, but without the Commonwealth our position in the world would rapidly decline,' he argued.[18] If the Future Policy Study was carried out to its logical conclusion, Home contended, Australia and New Zealand would become 'satellites' of the United States and India might be 'cut off' from the West altogether. Similarly, while the Defence Secretary, Harold Watkinson, accepted that 'the United Kingdom could not stand alone in the world in the 1960s', he did not think that this would preclude Britain from playing a significant role in international affairs and he suggested that 'the United Kingdom could take the lead behind the scenes,' directing the policies of other countries, namely the United States. By working through international alliances and the Commonwealth, Britain could, according to Watkinson, 'discreetly exert leadership in many fields where the Free World was in need of leadership'.[19]

Clearly, Derick Heathcoat-Amory, the Chancellor of the Exchequer, represented the department that was most favourable to reductions in the level of overseas expenditure, and he criticised the Future Policy Study for not adequately questioning the economic viability of Britain's world role. Heathcoat-Amory candidly asserted that he 'could not see how we could continue to carry out present commitments overseas, even with the help of our friends and allies'.[20] In particular, he doubted whether it was right to assume that Britain must continue indefinitely to carry part of the defence burden in Asia and the Far East. Embracing a subject other members of the committee had chosen to overlook, Heathcoat-Amory suggested that it could not lightly be assumed that Britain could continue to devote 8½ per cent of GDP to support overseas polices throughout the following decade. Rapidly expanding public spending programmes in social services and much-needed investment in industry would make it extremely difficult to maintain such high levels of overseas expenditure. In order to preserve the balance of payments and the strength of sterling, it would be necessary for Britain to curtail some of its existing overseas commitments. Yet, while the Chancellor's intervention secured general agreement that a stable balance of payments was important, the overall mood of the meeting was for maintaining the existing burden of taxation rather than reducing the proportion of national resources allotted to overseas expenditure.

The Macmillan Government – reluctant Europeans

The review and the findings of the Future Policy Study are at variance with some of the public statements that ministers made at the time. While there was, privately, pessimism about the ability to maintain Britain's traditional positions, Macmillan kept repeating what he had said in his first broadcast statement as Prime Minister: 'Every now and again since the war I have heard people say, "Isn't Britain only a second- or a third-class power now? Isn't Britain on her way out?" What nonsense. This is a great country and do not let us be ashamed to say.'[21] But Macmillan was prone to private bouts of pessimism about Britain's future influence, a preoccupation that was dominated by fears of relative economic decline and the emergence of Germany and a European bloc that excluded Britain: 'Britain – with all her experience – has neither the economic nor the military power to take the leading role,' he wrote in a private memorandum, entitled 'The Grand Design', in December 1960.[22]

The note continues: 'We are harassed with countless problems – the narrow knife-edge on which our economy is balanced; the difficult task of changing an Empire into a Commonwealth; the uncertainty about our relations [with] the new economic, and perhaps political, state which is being created by the six countries of continental Western Europe; and the uncertainty of American policies towards us – treated now as just another country.'[23] This reflection was typical of Macmillan. Shortly before he was Prime Minister, in December 1956, Cynthia Gladwyn, wife to the British Ambassador in Paris, Jebb Gladwyn, records in her diary Macmillan (then Chancellor of the Exchequer) being doubtful over the desirability of Britain sustaining its international commitments: 'Over port and brandy Harold held forth. The great thing for a country was to be rich as we were in the 19th century, he mused; and why should we not give up spending millions on atom bombs, why should we not give up Singapore ... and just sit back and be rich?'[24]

In May 1960, only a matter of weeks after the completion of the Future Policy Study, Macmillan privately ordered civil servants to address a set of questions specifically related to British entry into the European Economic Community. After three months' intensive work, officials produced a paper called the 'Sixes and Sevens' report (not because we were at 'sixes and sevens' in our approach to membership but because if we became a member the six would become seven). The official committee, under Sir Frank Lee, set out how Britain might maintain its power and influence in international matters, but all previous assumptions were now turned on their head, with the Lee report advocating the economic benefits of EEC membership.

In joining the Six, it was argued by Lee, Britain would be participating in a vigorous and rapidly expanding market, and there would
be good grounds for hoping that commerce and industry would
benefit. The UK could also gain from producing in bulk for larger
markets, and from the specialisation and higher efficiency that
resulted from trade competition and more rapid spread of technical
skills. 'All this we should miss – to the detriment of our industry – if
we remained outside,' Lee concluded. The inflow of new investment
into the United Kingdom would be greater if Britain joined, Lee
claimed, and the outflow of capital to the Six might be less than if
the UK remained outside.[25] In this respect, the report represented a
major shift: Britain would use membership of the European
Common Market to expand its economy and to catch up with our
more successful neighbours. From the early 1960s the pro-European
argument was to become an almost entirely economic one.

For the Lee Committee five big changes justified a new attitude
to European membership. First, the European Economic
Community was a reality: in the 1950s, at least from the British
perspective, it seemed very doubtful if the EEC would ever see the
light of day owing to the inability of a weak France to withstand
increased competition from her future partners, especially Germany.
Second, the idea of associate membership of a free trade area had not
worked. Britain had thought that, even if the Common Market did
come off, it should be able to write its own terms for association. The
Free Trade Area negotiations in the 1950s proved this wrong. Third,
France – and Western Europe generally – were no longer economically weak. The Common Market was becoming a powerful and
dynamic force, economically and politically. Fourth, in 1956, Britain
had (wrongly) thought that joining in European integration would
weaken its 'special relationship' with the United States. It was now
recognised that the United States attached increasing importance to
the views of the Community. Finally, in so far as Britain's previous
attitude was influenced by a desire to do nothing which might

prejudice the Commonwealth relationship, this consideration was now matched by a fear that the growing power and influence of the Six would seriously affect the UK's position in the world if it remained outside. 'If we stayed aloof from the Six, the relative decline in our status would reduce our influence in the Commonwealth and with the uncommitted countries we should run the risk of losing political influence and of ceasing to be able to exercise any claim to be a world power,' the Lee report concluded.[26]

Macmillan accepted the Lee Committee's recommendations on EEC membership, but that was only the first of many hurdles to be overcome: he had to persuade his Cabinet, his party and the country – and, perhaps even more difficult, the French President Charles de Gaulle. De Gaulle believed – as Macmillan explained in a memorandum sent to President Kennedy – that for 'so long as the "Anglo-Saxon domination" continues, he will not treat us [Britain] as European but American – as a junior partner of America'.[27] De Gaulle felt, Macmillan said, that 'while all this (NATO) machinery exists the vital decisions are made or not made between the American and British Governments in Washington'.[28] Accordingly, Macmillan argued, de Gaulle felt excluded from this club and partnership. He therefore asked Kennedy whether this might provide the basis for a deal. Britain wanted to join the EEC, while France wanted a greater role in NATO. Would de Gaulle be ready to withdraw the French veto, which alone prevented a successful UK application to the EEC, in return for a political and military arrangement which he would accept as recognition of France as a first-class world power? Macmillan asked Kennedy: 'Can we give him our techniques, or our bombs, or any share of our nuclear power on terms which are prudent … [and] the US will agree to?'[29]

It was over Christmas 1960 and the early days of 1961 that Macmillan decided on EEC membership. But it was not until 21 July 1961 that Macmillan took his proposal of membership to the Cabinet.[30] Confronted with opposition from within the Cabinet,

Macmillan was forced to find a compromise: Britain would negotiate possible terms of entry rather than apply for entry itself. The Tory Cabinet was one of 'reluctant Europeans'. The main barrier cited by Conservative ministers was the risk to the Commonwealth. The primacy of UK law was also an issue but what became the term that encapsulated it – loss of sovereignty – was yet to become the pre-eminent concern.

In his parliamentary statement of 31 July 1961, recommending negotiating for possible membership, Macmillan laid his greatest emphasis on the importance of UK access to a market approaching 300 million people. Macmillan told the House of Commons: 'This rapidly expanding economy could, in turn, lead to an increased demand for products from other parts of the world and so help to expand world trade.'[31] As we shall see, Harold Wilson would say almost exactly the same when he proposed to join the EEC in May 1967. As one prominent pro-European, the late Derek Scott has written, Macmillan's emphasis on the economic benefits of membership in his statement 'set the pattern for the way Europe was presented to the British people on many subsequent occasions by their leaders'.[32] However, with characteristic flair, Wilson was to add a reference to technology – 'an integrated strategy for technology on a truly continental scale' – to fit his theme that membership of Europe fitted in with the modernisation of Britain.[33]

All Macmillan's efforts were, in the end, to no avail. After a protracted series of talks, during which time Macmillan noted public opinion was moving against entry, de Gaulle turned him down. As Macmillan later wrote in his autobiography, he felt that de Gaulle's hatred of the close Anglo-American relationship was as great as ever. While Britain and France appeared to share the same view of Europe's future – united in opposing a federation – de Gaulle, in Macmillan's words, always went 'back to distrust and dislike like a dog to his vomit'.[34]

De Gaulle famously said that 'Britain will have to choose between

America and Europe: she cannot have both.'[35] However, in one conversation at Macmillan's country home, he admitted that the British were 'Europeans in their own special way'.[36] He personally wanted Britain in Europe but was concerned at how the British would shape Europe, telling Macmillan: 'The French did not want the British to change the character of their Europe, and therefore did not want [the British] to bring their great escorts in with them. India and the African countries had no part in Europe.'[37] This reflected what de Gaulle said in his rejection of UK membership in January 1963: 'England is an island, sea-going, bound up, by its trade, its markets, its food supplies, with the most varied and often the most distant countries', and it would be 'disruptive of a European Europe.'[38] Later in 1967, de Gaulle was to be crueller, telling Wilson that he considered that the British were 'a worn out people'.[39]

De Gaulle believed that all nuclear decisions were being made by the US with Europe left out. The young Henry Kissinger sensed this was a problem and wrote that France believed 'that the days of America predominating and European impotence were over … [and, on the one hand] there was legacy of (American) self-righteousness and impatience and on the other side (European) querulousness and insecurity.'[40] But Macmillan made no headway with America on sharing nuclear policy with the French, and France was caught by surprise when a nuclear arms deal with America was announced. In December 1962, during negotiations at Nassau on nuclear co-operation, Macmillan demanded submarine-launched Polaris missiles for Britain. President Kennedy was reluctant, believing bilateral arrangements would hinder British entry to the European Economic Community – yet, nevertheless, agreed to supply the missiles. Kennedy was right: de Gaulle's anger at Macmillan's failure to provide a clear signal of British willingness to engage in nuclear co-operation and inform him of the Polaris nuclear deal at Nassau gave him an additional reason to object to Britain's EEC membership. In contrast, Macmillan thought de Gaulle's desire for an independent

European nuclear force was no more than an excuse as he had told him that Polaris would be offered to the French under the same deal as Britain: part of NATO with independent control in a moment of supreme national interest.[41] In Macmillan's view, French hostility was more than about America's nuclear pre-eminence. It came down to something more basic: that de Gaulle wanted 'to be cock on a small dunghill instead of having two cocks on a larger one'.[42]

Macmillan's rebuff by de Gaulle came near the end of his premiership and may have contributed to its early end. It left him defeated. He even confided in his diary that 'all my policies are in ruins'.[43] When Macmillan failed to gain EEC membership, Dean Acheson appeared to write the epitaph on his efforts, controversially remarking: 'Great Britain has lost an Empire and has not yet found a role.'[44] What was perhaps more scathing and wounding at the time was his ridicule of British pretensions about the Commonwealth. The Commonwealth, Acheson said, had 'no political structure, or unity, or strength and enjoys a fragile and precarious economic relationship by means of the Sterling Area and preferences in the British market – this role is about played out.'[45] The very basis of British foreign policy was being challenged and Macmillan was outraged. Acheson, he claimed, had committed 'an error which had been made by quite a lot of people in the course of the last 400 years including Philip of Spain, Louis the XIV, Napoleon, the Kaiser and Hitler.'[46] However, confiding in his diary after the veto, Macmillan was forced to admit: 'The great question remains: "What is the alternative" to the European Community? If we are honest, we must say that there is none.'[47]

The Wilson Government – Europeans of necessity

On failing to secure entry to the EEC, Macmillan was savaged by his opposite number, the new Labour leader, Harold Wilson, who turned a phrase of Aneurin Bevan – 'don't send me naked into the conference chamber' – to his advantage, joking: 'Naked in the conference room is one thing: naked and shivering in the cold outside while others decide is an intolerable humiliation.'[48] Wilson could criticise and ridicule – but what would he do in government?

'We are a world power, and a world influence, or we are nothing,' Wilson asserted during his first major foreign policy speech as Prime Minister in November 1964.[49] One month later, he told the House of Commons, 'I want to make it clear that … we cannot afford to relinquish our world role. We have always been a world power; we should not be corralled in Europe.'[50] Britain's world role under Labour was built on two foundations that Wilson knew were under pressure. First, Britain's position East of Suez was still seen as pivotal. In December 1964, Wilson told the House of Commons: 'Whatever we may do in the field of cost effectiveness … we cannot afford to relinquish our world role – our role for shorthand purposes is sometimes called our East of Suez role.'[51] Second, Wilson saw maintaining the sterling-dollar parity at £1: $2.80 as fundamental to Britain's global standing and his biographer, Ben Pimlott, argues that this explains Wilson's decision to defend the parity of sterling for three years, even though this made it impossible for Labour to achieve its key domestic policy objectives.[52]

In his book on Britain's post-war relations with Europe, *This Blessed Plot*, Hugo Young captures Britain's predicament well when he suggests that politicians in the 1960s could look back on a moment when the UK had once been victorious in three intersecting world circles – with Europe, the Commonwealth and the transatlantic relationship – but were, instead, now in a no-win situation losing out in all areas. While many strong pro-Europeans in Labour's ranks, like Roy Jenkins, saw being part of Europe as a cause, the leadership from Clement Attlee to Hugh Gaitskell and then Harold Wilson thought otherwise. No one wanted to be accused of selling out the Commonwealth and they thought it essential to continue with Britain's traditional global role. In October 1962, a little under four months before his early death, Gaitskell told Labour's conference that joining the European Economic Community would mean 'the end of Britain as an independent European state … It means the end of a thousand years of history. You may say "Let it end" but, my goodness, it is a decision that needs a little care and thought. And it does mean the end of the Commonwealth. How can one really seriously suppose that if the mother country, the centre of the Commonwealth, is a province of Europe (which is what federation means) it could continue to exist as the mother country of a series of independent nations? It is sheer nonsense.'[53] Instead, Gaitskell wanted a bridge between the Commonwealth and Europe but, if Britain destroyed the Commonwealth by joining, there would be no bridge and we would be guilty, he said, of a historic error.

Gaitskell had no great passion for Europe. Roy Jenkins recalled that when he introduced Gaitskell to the Europhile Jean Monnet things did not go well. When talking of a European future, Monnet ended his comments by saying 'well, one must have faith,' to which Gaitskell replied, 'I don't believe in faith. I believe in reason and there is little reason in anything you have been saying tonight.' As Jenkins later recalled, 'I've never seen less of a meeting of minds.'[54] In 1962, when Jenkins wrote in *The Spectator* about the European question and addressed what would happen to the Commonwealth, he acknowledged that the best argument against EEC membership was that put by the future Defence Secretary and Chancellor, Denis Healey, who believed that Britain 'must keep clear of colonialising Europe in order to ensure leadership in the emerging third world' – a theme to which many later returned. Healey's argument was that if the UK threw in its lot with the other great European colonisers, Britain would find itself distanced from the Commonwealth. But Jenkins disagreed. The emerging nations, he said, did not want Britain to tell them what to do: they wanted independence from Britain and it was 'a pathetic illusion to imagine everyone wanted leadership from Britain'.[55]

On the face of it, Harold Wilson seemed as lukewarm on European membership as Gaitskell. When he spoke against membership in 1961, Wilson also used colourful language, saying of the Commonwealth: 'We are not entitled to sell our friends and kinsman down the river for a problematical and marginal advantage in selling washing machines in Düsseldorf.'[56] In Opposition, Wilson expressed his devotion to the Commonwealth and even pledged to reverse the cuts in Commonwealth trade that had taken place under the Conservatives. In office, however, the Commonwealth raised difficult questions, most notably Ian Smith's Unilateral Declaration of Independence of Rhodesia from Britain, leaving the British people confused and the Commonwealth divided: 'Sentiments of affection, which in 1964 were proposed as a central feature of Labour's world view and the viable basis for an alternative to Europe,' Hugo Young argues, 'began to vanish on both sides.'[57]

But it was the state of the British economy that was to colour every action of the Labour government. Just as in the mid-fifties post-Suez Britain had to come fully to terms with a diminished global military position, so in the mid-sixties Britain had to come fully to terms with a weakened economic position. The initial decisions Jim Callaghan had made as Chancellor had not stabilised the economy and, as a consequence of recurring balance of payments difficulties, Britain's economic prospects deteriorated markedly during the summer of 1966. Confronted with an unsustainable drain on London's reserves and speculation against the pound in the first half of July, the Labour government was forced into taking a number of stringent economic measures. On 12 July, Callaghan presented a paper to the Cabinet, warning that the economy was suffering from labour shortages, inflationary pressures, rising wages and excessive imports with public expenditure forecast to grow too rapidly. Callaghan saw no prospect of an improvement in the balance of payments during 1966 or 1967 when Britain had to pay off the loan it had acquired from the International Monetary Fund in September

1965 while it still owed £3,385 million to Swiss banks.

Sitting behind his desk in the Treasury, confronted with such a gloomy economic prognosis, Callaghan – hitherto a supporter of Britain's East of Suez role – became convinced of the need to withdraw. On 15 June 1966, when recording the deliberations of a meeting of the Parliamentary Labour Party, in which Wilson gave his 'usual Bevinite speech' denouncing the 'strange alliance' of pro-Europeans and left-wingers opposed to our presence East of Suez, Richard Crossman noted in his diary: 'His theme was that though he was prepared to withdraw and reduce the number of troops East of Suez he would never deny Britain the role of a world power … While he was talking, Jim [Callaghan] came in and sat beside me on the other side … Throughout the speech he whispered to me how totally he disagreed and told me that he thought Denis Healey holds much the same view … East of Suez is solely the PM's line … Undoubtedly, it's all a fantastic illusion. How can anyone build up Britain now as a great power East of Suez when we can't even maintain the Sterling Area.'[58]

In November 1967, when sterling came under massive speculative pressure from the markets, the game was up. Wilson and Callaghan agreed on 8 November that the appropriate date for devaluation should be 18 November, a Saturday and therefore a day when the markets would not be open.[59] On 16 November, at a meeting of the Cabinet, Callaghan formally recommended that sterling be devalued to a new fixed parity of £1: $2.40 from $2.80. Callaghan informed his colleagues that it had not been easy for him to make this recommendation, since in one sense it marked the end of the economic strategy hitherto pursued by the government.[60] Although Britain still had considerable reserves of foreign exchange and was not compelled to devalue because of insufficient liquid resources, speculation against the pound had reached such proportions that any other course would not work. If the policy of holding the pound's parity with the dollar remained unchanged, Britain could end up exhausting the reserves and should then be unable to defend even a reduced parity. In order for devaluation to succeed, Britain had to see a turnaround in the balance of payments by 1969.

Reductions in defence expenditure had been under discussion between Callaghan and Healey since the summer. Given the adverse economic circumstances, Cabinet ministers believed it right to substitute a more exacting target to match restrictive measures in areas of social provision, which included abandoning the decision to raise the school leaving age to 16. Social spending cuts would not be politically acceptable to Labour MPs without further economies in defence expenditure. On 21 November, as a result, the Cabinet considered the measures that would be necessary to make devaluation a success. Healey said that he was proposing to save a total of some £110 million of estimated defence expenditure for 1968–69.[61] Of this, some £60 million was accounted for by a wide range of small savings which had already been under discussion before the decision to devalue. The further £50 million of savings, Healey warned, would be concentrated upon cuts in Britain's defence capability, involving a substantial reduction in the UK's capability for operations outside Europe during the next five years.

On 4 January 1968, at a meeting of the Cabinet, Roy Jenkins, who had replaced Callaghan as Chancellor of the Exchequer, argued that more had to be done to restore foreign confidence in sterling. Jenkins argued that it would be necessary to increase taxation (both direct and indirect) and restrain public expenditure, involving large cuts in defence and overseas spending. He suggested that Britain withdraw from its political and defence responsibilities East of Suez by the end of the financial year 1970–71, instead of by the mid-1970s. These reductions in commitments, it was argued, should also be reflected in a corresponding reduction in expenditure on expensive defence equipment.

Having weighed up the arguments for and against an accelerated withdrawal, in some detail, the Cabinet decided in favour of

withdrawing from the Far East and Persian Gulf by the end of the
financial year 1970–71. It was a historic decision. It marked the end
of Britain's East of Suez role.

On 11 January 1968, George Brown, who was Foreign Secretary,
travelled to Washington to discuss the implications of devaluation.
He informed the US Secretary of State, Dean Rusk, that Britain had
'lost the battle [to defend sterling's parity with the dollar at £1: $2.80]
... because they had been trying to do too much at home and abroad
with too slender resources.'[62] Having been informed of the intended
post-devaluation measures, Rusk told Brown that he was 'profoundly
dismayed' by the proposed withdrawal from South-East Asia and the
Persian Gulf. Setting aside diplomatic protocol, Rusk asserted 'be
Britain', telling Brown that retrenchment would have 'profound and
detrimental implications' for both the US and UK. Rusk feared that
this decision would undermine the position of the West in the Cold
War, heralding as it did Britain's final retreat from major engagements in the world outside of Europe: 'This represented a major
withdrawal of the UK from world affairs, and it was a catastrophic
loss to human society ... We were facing a difficult period in world
affairs and Britain was saying it would not be there,' he complained.[63]
On the same day that Rusk held discussions with Brown, President
Johnson sent a telegram to Wilson, explaining the American position
in the bluntest terms: 'I cannot conceal from you my deep dismay
upon learning this profoundly discouraging news. If these steps are
taken, they will be tantamount to British withdrawal from world
affairs, with all that means for the future safety and health of the free
world.'[64]

All these events propelled a reconsideration of our position on
Europe. Roy Jenkins, the most eloquent supporter of European
membership, had always been in favour of joining. The Foreign
Secretary and Deputy Leader, George Brown, thought it was Britain's
mission to lead Europe. 'Willy, you must get us in so we can take the
lead,' Brown is said to have told West Germany's Chancellor, Willy

Brandt.[65] Barbara Castle records a July 1966 conversation with Brown: 'We've got to break with America, devalue and go into Europe,' Brown said. 'Devalue if you like, I said, but Europe no. I'll fight you on that,' replied the sceptical Castle. To which Brown retorted: 'I believe it passionately – we've got to go somewhere. We cannot manage alone.'[66] As Brown said in his autobiography: 'We have a role: our role is to lead Europe. We are, and have been for 11 centuries since the reign of King Alfred, one of the leaders of Europe. It may be that Britain is destined to become the leader of Europe, of western Europe in the first place, and of as much of Europe as will come together later on … I can't see where else leadership can come from other than from this country.'[67]

The decision to apply for EEC membership was taken during a Cabinet meeting at Chequers in October 1966. A paper written for the Cabinet away-day by Con O'Neill, a pro-European civil servant, put the reasons for applying within a wider context: 'For the last 20 years this country has been adrift. On the whole, it has been a period of decline in our international standing and power. This has helped to produce a national mood of frustration and uncertainty. We do not know where we are going and have begun to lose confidence in ourselves. Perhaps a point has now been reached when the acceptance of a new goal and a new commitment could give this country as a whole a focus around which to crystallise its hopes and energies. Entry into Europe might provide the stimulus and the target we require.'[68] But many Cabinet members present challenged this view. 'I regard Little England as the precondition for any successful socialist planning whether inside or outside the Common Market,' Richard Crossman said. He believed Britain 'shouldn't go into Europe in order to remain great'.[69] Tony Benn asked what was European about Britain and whether the Anglo-American relationship was not worth a great deal more than entry into Europe.[70] Crucially, though, Wilson was supported by his eventual successor, Jim Callaghan: 'My experience over the last two and a half years has led me to the conclusion … that nations are not free at the moment to take their own decisions,' Callaghan said, adding that 'the argument about sovereignty is rapidly becoming outdated.'[71]

This Chequers decision was followed by a tour of Europe in January-March 1967 led by Wilson and Brown. In March 1967 they reported back to Cabinet. Barbara Castle recorded this in her diaries: 'George [Brown] tried to urge that 1969 was a crucial year when policies in the Six would be reconsidered and that if only we could get in, even the CAP (Common Agricultural Policy) would be re-negotiable ... I thought Harold had maneuvered brilliantly. I remain convinced he is anxious to get in.'[72]

In May 1967, Wilson formally announced Britain's application to the House of Commons. Much like Macmillan before him, Wilson's 1967 statement emphasised the economic benefits of membership, saying that the decision was 'motivated by broader considerations of economic policy'. Wilson told MPs: 'All of us are aware of the long-term potential for Europe, and, therefore, for Britain, of the creation of a single market of approaching 300 million people, with all the scope and incentive which this will provide for British industry, and of the enormous possibilities which an integrated strategy for technology, on a truly Continental scale, can create.'[73]

Following his formal announcement of Britain's intention to join, Wilson pulled out all the stops. In Strasbourg, he delivered a speech that evoked British history in a way wholly different from Gaitskell's 1962 anti-European speech and his own at that time. Two thousand years ago, he argued, the British people were already created out of continental stock and, a thousand years ago, the very name England reflected the origins of European invaders and settlers.[74]

The negotiations were led by George Brown – 'little Brown' as de Gaulle said of him. 'I rather like him – in spite of the fact that he called me Charlie,' de Gaulle later said.[75] One of Brown's biographers, Peter Paterson, writes that 'Edward Heath can claim the credit for Britain's adherence to the Treaty of Rome, but George Brown was his

John the Baptist.'[76] Brown was a volatile figure and, as one of his aides put it, either the machine gun would open up or he would be totally charming. De Gaulle, however, was the problem yet again.

Having taken France out of the central counsels of NATO, his aim was to include defence issues in the next stage of European integration and make Europe a player in its own right in the Cold War. But there was not even a basis for a deal on this. There were other reasons, too. In May 1967, at a press conference, de Gaulle said that British entry to the EEC would cause 'destructive upheavals', a 'complete overthrow of its equilibrium', and that UK membership was incompatible with the weakness of sterling and its continued status as a reserve currency.[77] This was not a veto, but it looked ominous for Wilson. In June, Wilson visited de Gaulle in Paris, in an effort to convince him that the UK should join. Wilson left empty-handed. The *coup de grâce* was then delivered by de Gaulle on 27 November, one week after devaluation, when he said, again at a press conference: 'Non!' De Gaulle accused Britain of a 'deep-seated hostility' towards European integration. He said London showed a 'lack of interest' in the Common Market and that the UK would require a 'radical transformation' in attitude before joining the EEC. 'The present Common Market is incompatible with the economy, as it now stands, of Britain,' he declared. He then went on to list a number of aspects of Britain's economy, from British industrial practices to British agriculture, which he said made Britain incompatible with EEC membership.[78]

Wilson took the realistic view that 'if excluded we should not whine' and must instead be positive and robust.[79] In fact as Stephen Wall records: 'Harold Wilson and George Brown knew that de Gaulle did not want us to join, there was no question about that. The only question was whether he would feel inhibited or not by the attitude of his other partners, the Germans in particular; that was the doubt. So when the veto came, it was not a surprise; they were prepared for it. And in 1963, Harold Macmillan made a mistake really, because in the face of the French veto, he withdrew the British application whereas Wilson maintained the application in 1967 and that was very smart of him.'[80]

It would, after all, not be long until de Gaulle left office. Labour expected to win the 1970 election. If so, Wilson planned to appoint a more pro-European Foreign Secretary, Roy Jenkins, who would lead a new round of negotiations. In the end, the Conservatives won a surprise electoral victory, and, as we shall see in the next chapter, it fell to Edward Heath to finally secure British membership of the EEC.

CHAPTER THREE

Coming to terms with Europe, 1970–97

Edward Heath's commitment to European unity could not be doubted: it had been forged in response to the divided and strife-torn Europe he had witnessed at first hand in the 1930s. He had visited Nazi Germany, where he had been horrified at a Nuremberg rally and seen the evil that Nazi-fuelled German nationalism could unleash on the world. Then, as a supporter of the new Spanish Republic, he had visited Spain and come under fire while visiting the Spanish coast. Heath's maiden speech in the House of Commons in 1950 was in support of the Schuman Plan, championing the need to pool Franco-German coal and steel resources – a proposal for which neither his leadership nor the government of the day had much enthusiasm.

Ten years later, in July 1960, Heath was appointed Lord Privy Seal by Harold Macmillan, with responsibility for the negotiations surrounding Britain's first attempt to join the European Economic Community. While de Gaulle's veto of Britain's application was taken badly by Heath, he promised that Britain would not turn its back on the European project. 'We are part of Europe by geography, tradition, history, culture and civilisation,' Heath declared, following the veto. 'We shall continue to work with our friends in Europe for the true unity and strength of this continent,' he said.[1]

Heath addressed the US with 'un-sentimentality totally at variance with the special relationship,' Henry Kissinger claimed, '[unlike] other European leaders [who] strove to improve relations with us ... Heath went in the opposite direction.'[2] But Heath later quoted President Kennedy in support of European integration reminding people that he had said: 'The Atlantic alliance is bound to be based on two pillars, one on each side of the Atlantic. Of course, you can't have a very satisfactory basis if one pillar is much taller and rounder than the other pillar. You've got to have a balance.'[3] Moreover, by the early 1970s, the Commonwealth also looked very different from its original conception: India was now leading the non-aligned powers, Africa was asserting its independence and both Australia and New Zealand were starting to find their own way towards their Asian future.

But Heath faced a public sceptical about EEC membership. In April 1970, prior to his coming to power, an opinion poll had found 59 per cent of the British public disagreed with a positive pro-membership stance.[4] And so the Conservative Party's 1970 election manifesto could go no further than state a promise 'to negotiate, no more no less'.[5] Nevertheless, Heath entered office determined that Britain should join the EEC. As Heath told the Italian Prime Minister, Giulio Andreotti, he 'attached the highest importance to the formation of a European political policy.' 'Heath was a special sort of Englishman, very pro-European,' Édouard Balladur, President Pompidou's Secretary-General and later French Prime Minister, is quoted as saying. In fact, Balladur felt he had had more in common with Heath than he had with Willy Brandt, the West German Chancellor. Heath's biographer says that Pompidou concluded that Heath was an even better European than he was himself.[6]

Harold Wilson was to accuse Heath of wanting, in his enthusiasm for EEC membership, to sell out the Commonwealth and to surrender British control over its own defence. However, a binding commitment to nuclear weapons co-operation was the dog that did not bark in the 1971 negotiations on British entry to the EEC. The British had expected a nuclear alliance to be an issue: 'If only the

British could disengage from their entanglement with the Americans,' British intelligence reported of France's views, then there could be 'close co-operation between Britain and France on future delivery systems.'[7] Of course, Heath had to clear any such proposal with the Americans but he was prepared to consider the issue of an Anglo-French European deterrent. The surprise was that the French President, Georges Pompidou, did not raise it.

The central issues under discussion were, in fact, the future of the Sterling Area, Commonwealth trade (particularly Caribbean sugar and New Zealand butter) and the costs of paying into the Community budget, where a compromise was reached which would have long-standing implications for while initially Britain would pay only 3 per cent, the total UK contribution would rise to 21 per cent when fully phased in.

The negotiations were, in effect, sealed by May 1971, when Heath paid a state visit to Paris and met Pompidou. At dinner, Pompidou asserted: 'Through two men who are talking to each other, two peoples are trying to find each other again, to find each other to take part in a great joint endeavour – the construction of a European group of nations determined to reconcile the safeguarding of their national identities, with the constraints of acting as a community.'[8]

And at the press conference which followed, Pompidou said: 'Many people believed that Great Britain was not, and did not wish, to become European, and that Britain wanted to enter the Community only so as to destroy it or divert it from its objectives. Many people also thought that France was ready to use every pretext to place in the end a fresh veto on Britain's entry.' And then he turned to Heath and said, 'Well, Ladies and Gentlemen, you see before you tonight two men who are convinced of the contrary.'[9]

Pompidou then proceeded to say that he had put four questions to Heath. First, he asked Heath whether he accepted the very basis of the EEC's Common Agriculture Policy, and Heath replied that yes he did. He then asked whether Britain accepted the veto and rule by unanimity. Heath replied, yes. Pompidou then asked, 'Do you accept that sterling should end its role as a reserve currency and Britain should play her part in the development of monetary union?' Heath, again, answered yes. Pompidou then challenged Heath on what he thought of Europe – wanting to be sure that Britain was really determined to become European – and whether offshore Britain was indeed determined to tie herself to Europe. Pompidou asked whether Britain, an island, had decided to moor itself to the continent. Accordingly, the fourth question was: Would Britain really become European? Heath replied in the affirmative. Pompidou then told the press conference that he was able to say that the 'explanations and views expressed to me by Mr Heath are in keeping with France's concept of the future of Europe.'[10]

But, although Heath had a Conservative majority of 30 in the House of Commons, there was opposition within his parliamentary ranks to EEC membership. While he could rely on the support of five out of six Liberal MPs, Heath found himself dependent on the support of the Labour Party. Yet Labour MPs were under a three-line whip to vote *against* the terms of membership negotiated by Heath. In the end, 69 Labour MPs, led by Roy Jenkins, broke with the whip, with a further 20 abstaining. Heath secured a majority of 112: without the Labour rebels he would have been defeated.

Having won the decisive European vote on entry in the House of Commons, Heath went back to his Downing Street flat to play Bach on his clavichord. It was the right choice for that moment, he said, because 'Bach was an early master in the European musical heritage, in which the British share and to which they have contributed so much, and that particular piece of music, at once so serene, so ordered … brought us the peace of mind we needed before plunging into the busy round of celebration.'[11] This is but one illustration of the depth of Heath's European convictions. As he told an audience at the Royal Academy in 1971: 'The artists, the writers and the musicians have shown the economists and the politicians the way.

We have to bring to the creation of European and economic unity the same creative effort, the same interplay of ideas and aspirations, the same ability to share our achievements that enabled them to make a reality of European cultural unity.'[12]

So on the day Britain joined the Common Market, Heath's short speech to mark the occasion referred to a 'common European heritage' and he dropped from his text the idea that our leadership in the Commonwealth was complementary to European membership.[13] Indeed in his statement of foreign policy ambition, issued at the end of 1973, Heath went further by arguing that 'political co-operation anew needs to be fostered and the Community needs to develop a positive political personality in international affairs.' He wanted Europe to 'develop the habit of political co-operation and the corporate will to agree on further progress towards European union.' In Heath's view, it was the European Economic Community not the Commonwealth that now guaranteed our place in the world. As his adviser, Sir Con O'Neill, put it: outside the EEC we would be no more than 'a greater Sweden'.[14]

But what was Heath's long-term vision? What were his central objectives for British leadership in Europe now that we had joined? On that, Heath was strangely silent. Becoming an EEC member appeared to be the summit of his European ambition. 'I did not have the impression that he had at that time a coherent vision about what to do with it when we were in,' explained Robert Armstrong, Heath's Principal Private Secretary, 'and therefore how we would try and make it develop.'[15]

The Wilson and Callaghan Governments – hesitant Europeans

As Leader of the Opposition after 1970, Harold Wilson made an issue of the poor terms of entry negotiated by the Conservative government and promised to re-negotiate the UK terms of entry if Labour was re-elected. In a major speech to a special Labour Conference in 1971, Wilson claimed that Heath had not only sold the Commonwealth short but had, as a result of a poorly negotiated settlement, imposed on households an unnecessary tax on cheap, efficiently produced food for one purpose only: subsidising expensive, inefficiently produced food. Wilson declared: 'I cannot accept, and never have accepted, that the test of being a good European is one's willingness at great cost to subsidise inefficiency, nor that the very desirable objective of greater political unity in Europe, for which so many of us have worked, cannot be realised except at the cost of a burden of some £500 millions subsidy to French agriculture.'[16] Perhaps more significantly, Jim Callaghan in a speech in May 1971 took up the theme of British self-government and the threats to the Commonwealth. He lauded the distinctiveness of the English language and culture and famously said 'non merci beaucoup' to the proposition that we were about to exchange our allies in the Commonwealth and the United States for 'an aroma of continental claustrophobia', claiming that this would represent a 'complete rupture of our identity'.[17]

During this period, as Adrian Williamson argues, four schools of thought on Labour's approach to Europe existed, only one of which was strongly in favour of British membership of the EEC. First, the Left's view was that the EEC was a capitalist club which would prevent a Labour government carrying out its industrial policies. The leading light in this group was Tony Benn. Second, a group within Labour existed who believed that EEC membership meant the loss of self-government and the erosion of British democracy. The members of the Cabinet in this group were Peter Shore, Barbara Castle and Michael Foot. A third group, headed by Roy Jenkins, saw UK membership of the EEC as the central and defining issue in British politics: it was, ultimately, an issue on which they were prepared to divide the party. Finally, a fourth group of pragmatists in the party's leadership, namely Harold Wilson, Tony Crosland,

Denis Healey and Jim Callaghan (who softened his position when Labour was back in office) were supporters of but not enthusiasts for membership of the Common Market.[18]

In the manifestoes for the two elections that Wilson narrowly won in 1974 – in February and October – Labour promised to re-negotiate the UK's terms of entry and then hold a national referendum to determine whether the UK should remain in the EEC on the new terms. Most notably, during the two elections, Labour argued that the 1972 Accession Treaty was weak on protection for fishermen and not strong enough on protections for the Commonwealth, especially New Zealand butter (which had in fact gained concessions that cost the UK about £1 billion at today's prices over five years in its budget allocation), and both manifestoes said we needed a better deal on our Budget contributions.

Callaghan was appointed the lead negotiator in the talks. At the outset of his initial address to the Council of Ministers in April 1974, he made it clear that he wanted to ensure a fundamental re-negotiation of the terms laid down in the treaties of accession negotiated by the Conservatives. But Callaghan, a former trade union official and a skilled negotiator, also wanted to cut a deal. The government 'would not conduct the negotiations as a confrontation,' he told the House of Commons in March 1974, 'but in good faith, not to destroy or to wreck but to adapt and reshape.'[19] As Andrew Glencross, who has analysed the UK government's approach to the 1974–75 re-negotiation, writes: 'Negotiation by the Wilson Government hinged on the same two factors applicable today: the scale of the ambition and the ability to forge partnerships with foreign capitals. Foreign Secretary James Callaghan outmanoeuvred EEC-sceptics like Benn by settling for policy reform (notably regarding the budget and the Common Agricultural Policy) rather than treaty change. This move reassured other leaders, by showing that British unilateralism was nevertheless compatible with the existing rules of the game.'[20] In particular, Callaghan aimed to obtain an extension to the preferential terms on the transitional period, in order to allow the entry of Caribbean sugar and New Zealand butter into the United Kingdom. (Callaghan essentially wanted New Zealand farmers to get the same benefits as their European counterparts.) He also demanded a reduction in the contribution to the Community budget and the renewal of direct subsidies, what were called 'deficiency payments', to small farmers in poorer regions.

'Callaghan was very much in the driving seat,' writes Stephen Wall, who was later to serve as Ambassador and UK Permanent Representative to the European Union: 'He had been a former Chancellor of the Exchequer, and he saw very clearly that the biggest issue for the British national interest was the budget, while Harold Wilson did not really see that.' At that time, Wall suggests, Wilson was 'a tired man and he was focusing on issues such as New Zealand, and so on, and he did not really focus on the budget.' He argues that this was a mistake: 'It was evident from pretty early on in our EEC membership that this would be an issue,' Wall says, 'but initially it was thought that it could be solved by expenditure policies, hence Ted Heath's insistence on having a Regional Development Fund, but that did not work.'[21] The budget issue was to return with a vengeance ten years later.

At the Paris Summit of Heads of State in December 1974 and the Dublin European Council in spring 1975, the UK government claimed to have won a new regional policy, a budgetary correction mechanism (which favoured net contributors, with balance of payments problems, like the UK) and a re-negotiated agreement on market access for New Zealand dairy products. In a statement on 12 March 1975, Wilson said that the Labour government had 'now taken our discussions within the Community on re-negotiation as far as they could go.'[22] Callaghan, meanwhile, claimed that the majority of re-negotiation objectives from the February and October 1974 manifestoes had been achieved.

The Cabinet endorsed the results of the re-negotiation by sixteen to seven on 18 March 1975, with the House of Commons following suit on 9 April 1975: it was then agreed that a referendum should be set for two months later on 5 June.

When the Labour Cabinet discussed the issue Tony Benn said of the EEC: 'I can think of no body of men outside the Kremlin who has so much power without a shred of accountability for what they do.'[23] Similarly, Michael Foot argued: 'We are conniving at the dismemberment of Parliament, we are destroying the accountability of ministers to Parliament and if we elect a European Parliament by 1978 it will destroy our own parliament.'[24] In contrast, Jim Callaghan said the 'sovereignty of Parliament was not an issue, it wasn't even in the election manifesto'.[25] Harold Wilson tried to defuse the issue, comparing the divergent positions to 'the differences between the old and the new testaments,' while claiming that concerns about sovereignty could be met with the guarantee that 'the British Parliament has the power to come out at any time'.[26]

Wilson suspended the convention of collective responsibility for the period running up to the referendum allowing Cabinet members to publicly campaign against each other without being compelled to leave the government. In the House of Commons, Wilson stipulated that ministers speaking from the dispatch box must reflect government policy, which was continued membership of the EEC on renegotiated terms, but that they would otherwise be allowed to speak freely.

Wilson's compromise was messy but mass ministerial resignations were avoided – only the left-winger Eric Heffer resigned after speaking against EEC membership in the House of Commons – and, as Wilson later remarked, the offer of a referendum provided a lifeboat onto which the whole Labour Movement could clamber.

The campaign itself was conducted for the most part without the voice of Michael Foot, who was ill and in hospital for much of the time. There can be no doubt where he stood: Foot did not oppose EEC membership, like others on the Left, on the grounds that it was a capitalists' club. 'Foot's basic objection to Europe lay not in his being a socialist but in being a parliamentarian,' explains his biographer Kenneth O. Morgan. 'Throughout, his fundamental antagonism to Britain joining the Common Market lay in the fact that it undermined the sovereignty of parliament – the very foundation of Britain's constitution – and diverted control away to institutions overseas over which the British electors would have no control,' Morgan notes.[27] It was, Foot told the House of Commons, 'the most deliberate proposal for curtailing the powers of this House that had ever been put before Members of Parliament', and so when he spoke at the all-important pre-referendum Cabinet discussion of 1975 he warned of the danger of 'accepting an alien system'.[28]

In one memorable sentence, Foot said that Europe made the parliamentary system farcical and unworkable. With the superimposition of the EEC apparatus it was 'as if we had set fire to the place as Hitler had done to the Reichstag', and the Cabinet minutes record him stating that 'continued membership would lead to the dismembering of the United Kingdom, and of the authority of Parliament which had already lost much of its power in EEC affairs. If we remained in the Community, the seat of power would lie in future in permanent coalition in Brussels.'[29] Foot was well enough to address the special Labour Conference in April 1975, when he spoke out against British membership. 'I say to our great country, "Don't be afraid of those who tell us that we cannot run our own affairs, that we have not the ingenuity to mobilise our resources and overcome our economic problems",' he argued.[30]

On the other side, Roy Jenkins and Edward Heath – the two leading pro-Europe campaigners – agreed that they would fight the issue of UK membership on the biggest question of all: Britain's role in the world. As far back as 1962, Jenkins had argued that opponents of EEC membership 'all share a grossly exaggerated and completely outmoded view of Britain's importance in the world and her capacity for independent action', claiming that 'whether or not we join the

EEC is now subsumed in a bigger question: whether we live in an atmosphere of illusion or reality about our position in the world.'[31] And 13 years later in 1975, Jenkins said that, outside the Common Market, Britain would 'retire into an old people's home for fading nations.' 'I do not think it would be a comfortable old people's home,' Jenkins argued. 'I do not like the look of some of the prospective warders.' He asked people to 'free us from the continued debilitation of being hesitant and reluctant partners.'[32]

Instead of ignoring claims about the potential downgrading of the Commonwealth and Transatlantic Alliance, Jenkins and Heath were determined to take this argument head on. 'Neither did either of us attempt to downplay the importance of the issues,' Heath later recalled, 'or to suggest that all that was at stake was a narrow trade policy decision. It was political Europe in which we were interested. A Common Market, which existed and of which we were a part, was a vital step on the road but it was not the ultimate goal or the primary purpose.'[33]

Sovereignty was not something to 'be hoarded sterile and barren', Heath argued during the campaign, but something 'for us as custodians to use in the interests of our own country.' He contended: 'the question we have to decide, therefore, in carrying through this great political purpose ... for the peace and freedom of Europe and of our own country, is how we are entitled to use that measure of sovereignty which is required.'[34] Heath later claimed he was pleased to be told that the Keep Britain in Europe campaign – of which he was vice president – had not ducked the sovereignty issue. Indeed, one of their advertisements read: 'Forty million people die in two European wars this century. Better lose a little national sovereignty than a son or daughter.'[35] However, most pro-Europeans, as Heath's biographer argues, preferred to suggest that any possible sacrifice of power lay many years ahead and could easily be opposed when the time arose.[36] And reviewing the evidence of polls at the time, David Butler and Uwe Kitzinger said support for membership was 'wide but it did not run deep' and did not result 'in a girding of the loins for a great new European adventure'. 'The vote had been for the *status quo*, rather than for a fundamentally new and integrated future,' they concluded.[37]

So in practice most of the arguments that were made in favour of membership during the 1975 referendum were economic. Europe's faster economic growth was the main theme of an official 16-page pamphlet issued by the government to every voter setting out its views. The pamphlet's title was *Britain's New Deal in Europe*. On page five it set out the aims of the Common Market:

- To bring together the peoples of Europe.
- To raise living standards and improve working conditions.
- To promote growth and boost world trade.
- To help the poorer regions of Europe and the rest of the world.
- To help maintain peace and freedom.[38]

Hugo Young's assessment was that the economic argument came to the forefront in the campaign out of fear and anxiety, arguing that 'the national psyche had been battered by ... dire economic straits that hung like an albatross round the national mind.'[39] This is undoubtedly true. Moreover, going back to read their speeches and writings, it seems clear that Wilson's case, like that of Macmillan and most campaigners, was based on economic benefits. In particular, Macmillan regularly pointed out that the Treaty of Rome did 'not deal' with defence or foreign policy. As we shall see, Mrs Thatcher backed a narrower economic role for the European Union – as the champion of the Single Market – and preferred a strategic alliance with the US. It was only Edward Heath who dared to suggest that the UK's leading role in the Common Market was the platform upon which to 'contribute to the universal nature of Europe's responsibilities', and to argue, as he did, even when the UK's first application for entry was rejected in 1963, that we were part of Europe by geography, tradition, history, culture and civilisation.[40]

Perhaps unsurprisingly neither 'Fanfare for Europe,' the publically funded festival organised after UK entry into the EEC in 1973, nor the 1975 referendum, elicited much enthusiasm from the British public (turnout in the referendum was 65 per cent at a time when General Elections regularly secured 70–80 per cent turnouts). And in the years that followed Britain would be less than enthusiastic about the benefits of Europe. During the late 1970s, there were two major issues on which Britain took a fundamentally different stand from the rest of Europe. First, in 1978, Callaghan rejected the French and German plans for monetary union on the grounds that he could not favour being locked into too high an exchange rate at a time of rising unemployment. (Later Mrs Thatcher worried about being locked into too low an exchange rate to tackle inflation.) And in the same year, Callaghan reignited the controversy over the British contribution to the EEC budget, which he believed to still be too high. These two issues were to become defining subjects under his successor as Prime Minister, Mrs Thatcher.

The Thatcher Government – stealth Europeans

In September 1988, almost a decade after becoming Prime Minister, Mrs Thatcher warned an audience at the College of Europe, in the Belgian city of Bruges, against creating an 'identikit European personality'.[41] The Bruges speech is now seen as a watershed moment in her career, deepening a rift with Cabinet colleagues, notably Geoffrey Howe and Nigel Lawson, and considered central to the division over policy that led to her fall from power. Yet, in her Bruges speech, it is important to remember that Thatcher was at pains to demand a reappraisal of Britain's relationship with Europe, not a severance. She argued: 'Britain does not dream of some cozy, isolated existence on the fringes of the European Community. Our destiny is in Europe, as part of the Community.'[42]

And we must remember that reluctant as Mrs Thatcher was in Bruges to embrace Jacques Delors' plans for a more integrated Europe, she accepted the basis of the post-1973 settlement. In her speech, she acknowledged Britain was linked not just by geography but also by history and shared values to Europe; that the UK's place was to be at the centre of Europe; and that there was much to gain from engagement in the future. 'Our destiny is in Europe as part of the Community,' Mrs Thatcher said at Bruges.[43] At this time at least the issue was not 'in' or 'out' but reducing the speed and scale of European integration. Lord Powell, Thatcher's Principal Private Secretary, has said that she was surprised at the reaction to her speech, especially the way some saw it as a Eurosceptic attack on Europe. 'She thought she was setting a different agenda for Europe,' he has argued. 'In office she remained a European,' Powell says.[44] Mrs Thatcher, he suggests, wanted to see Europe more united and with a greater sense of purpose, believing that Europe was stronger when it worked more closely, whether it be in trade, defence or in relations with the rest of the world.

But from Mrs Thatcher's Bruges speech onwards the shape of Britain's political discourse about Europe changed. From then on, every new extension of integration was seen as the first steps onto a slippery slope. From then too Britain's partners as a consequence would always expect the UK to be the first to object to any extension of European Union competences. The Bruges speech even spawned a think-tank, the Bruges Group, which became a rallying point for Conservative anti-European rebels in the 1990s. It is still celebrated by Eurosceptics today.

But Mrs Thatcher's speech came at a time when, as I will show later, globalisation and a sense that we were losing control of our destiny were becoming issues that made many people more sceptical of international entanglements. Mrs Thatcher's position was however a more traditional one: during her tenure in Downing Street, she was at pains to build up the 'special relationship' with America, putting this at the top of her international priorities. For her, Britain was America's Cold War partner, part of a conflict in which she considered it vital that the UK play a leading role. One of her biographers, John Campbell, has written: 'The unshakable cornerstone of Mrs Thatcher's foreign policy was the United States. She had no time for subtle formulations which saw Britain as the meeting point of overlapping circles of influence, maintaining a careful equidistance between America on the one hand and Europe on the other, with the Commonwealth somewhere in the background.' This was further solidified by her close relationship with an ideological soulmate, Ronald Reagan. 'She had no doubt,' Campbell writes, 'that Britain's primary role in the world was as Washington's number one ally.'[45] Consequently, as Sir Percy Cradock, a foreign policy adviser during the second half of Thatcher's period as Prime Minister, has said: 'Solidarity with the US as a cardinal principle of foreign policy acquired a special sanctity under Margaret Thatcher.'[46]

The single biggest European question faced by Thatcher was Britain's membership of the Exchange Rate Mechanism, the ERM, about which she had doubts over joining while Nigel Lawson, the Chancellor of the Exchequer, and Geoffrey Howe, the Foreign Secretary, were both very much in favour. After much pressure from the two, she finally agreed to the 'Madrid conditions', a promise of eventual ERM membership. But when her economic adviser, Alan Walters, claimed that the ERM was 'half baked', Lawson saw it as a resigning matter.[47] Lawson's replacement as Chancellor, John Major, took a different view: he thought he could shift responsibility for unpopular policy decisions from the UK to the European Union by joining the ERM.

But when Jacques Delors called for democratic power in Europe to rest with the European Parliament, Mrs Thatcher denounced his proposals: 'The President of the Commission, Mr Delors, said at a press conference the other day that he wanted the European Parliament to be the democratic body of the Community, he wanted the

Commission to be the Executive and he wanted the Council of Ministers to be the Senate.' 'No. No. No,' she declared.[48] Two days later, Geoffrey Howe resigned, making clear that this anti-European tone was unacceptable to him. His resignation set in motion a challenge to her leadership and an inconclusive ballot that led to the end of Margaret Thatcher's time as Prime Minister.

However, prior to this, there were notable achievements in negotiation, including Britain's rear-guard campaign at the famous 1984 summit in Fontainebleau, when Mrs Thatcher threatened to stop paying into the European Community budget if she did not achieve a rebate. In the many years of negotiation running up to the summit, Britain argued that we were unable to benefit much from farm subsidies (which still made up 70 per cent of Europe's expenditure) and that, without being the richest country in Europe, Britain was now about to become the biggest net contributor to the Community budget. First we achieved a temporary rebate over three years. Then, in 1984, at the last minute following Britain's threat to block agricultural payments and after juggling with complex formulas, a simpler rebate was agreed – one that has stood the test of time. Mrs Thatcher then immediately moved to the next fight: reform of the Single Market.

The European Commissioner who led the programme to complete the internal market, Lord Cockfield, was a Thatcher appointee who shared many of her views on market principles. The agreements of the mid-eighties included the replacement of national vetoes by qualified majority voting and the commitment to further economic union. As we show later, the Single Market has helped create the conditions for higher growth and more job creation as Europe has broken down cross-border barriers to trade. It has become part of the Thatcher fiction that she never fully understood all that she had signed up for in the Single European Act of 1986, and did not foresee the regulatory measures that would be placed on an unsuspecting Britain. Her own explanation is more straightforward: 'I took the view that I could not quarrel with everything, and the document had no legal force,' she explained in her autobiography, when discussing the 'Declaration on European Union', which committed signatories to ever closer co-operation: 'So I went along with it.'[49]

She not only encouraged the Single Market but was also in the vanguard of another major shift in the way the European Union has evolved – supporting the strategy of 'widening', what she counterposed to 'deepening' and which was driven by the approach Thatcher took to confronting the Soviet Union and helping to end the Cold War.[50]

So even when Mrs Thatcher rejected European 'dreams' of a federal superstate she did not reject engagement with Europe. When asked afterwards if she had any doubts about surrendering power to the European Commission to oversee the Single Market, Thatcher was unequivocal. She had wanted the Single Market to work – that was her main objective – and was prepared to support extra powers for the Commission and the end of vetoes to achieve it. But her general hostility to Europe – and, in particular, her poor relationship with a fellow Conservative, Helmut Kohl – blinded her to subtle shifts in both American and European positions. Kohl, along with President François Mitterrand of France, sensed that America would become more Pacific-orientated in its outlook and believed that America and Europe would work better together if Europe offered more. In 1984, as Stephen Wall recalls, Kohl asked to see Mrs Thatcher for an in-depth 'where do we go from here' discussion on long-term issues. He told Mrs Thatcher that talk of a bridge across the Atlantic was an inadequate concept: a bridge, he said, needed a pillar at both ends and the European pillar was not strong enough. This was a repetition of the view expressed by President Kennedy just over 20 years earlier. Mrs Thatcher responded by arguing that in strengthening the European pillar we should be careful not to undermine the arch over the Atlantic.[51] Thus, while global change was making the world a more interconnected and integrated place and nations were becoming ever more dependent on each other, Mrs Thatcher still held to a traditional view of where Britain's interests best lay: she did not see the growing importance of international institutions or a European global role and was ultimately not willing to countenance building a stronger Europe to work with an already strong America.

The Major Government – divided Europeans

'It is because we care for lasting principles that I want to place Britain at the heart of Europe,' John Major said six months after being appointed Prime Minister. He promised to 'fight' for change 'from the inside, where we will win'.[52] Major has subsequently written of terrible misjudgements made on Europe by his predecessors – the same kind of misjudgement to which Rab Butler himself confessed being guilty of in the 1950s, when he talked about 'the bad start and the late start for Europe'. In an interview with Hugo Young, Major said that our previous stance on European engagement had been 'unfortunate' and 'a historic error of very grave proportions'.[53] But if John Major genuinely wanted to be at the heart of Europe, it was Europe that was at the heart of all his government's troubles. Major was derailed by the Maastricht Treaty which divided his party, then suffered an ignominious exit from the European Exchange Rate Mechanism which destroyed the Conservatives' reputation for economic competence. And Major's later years were dominated by months in which he stood aside from European engagement, pursuing a policy of the empty chair in protest at decisions in Brussels which he said harmed Britain.

Major had been elected with Eurosceptic support in preference to Douglas Hurd and Michael Heseltine, who were more avowedly pro-European. He himself fell between the two camps. Major told Hugo Young late in his premiership: 'Unlike any other European nation, we are genuinely split as to where our interests lie, pretty evenly split. So I ask myself why do we have to choose one way or the other? Why should we make an artificial choice where our interests are almost equally divided between two great blocs – the Americas and Europe?"[54] Major's answer was that Britain should not make such a choice. Britain, he said, would always be different from its neighbours because the UK was 'traditionally used to doing things in its own way'.[55]

The bitterness of the Maastricht negotiations – including a walk-out by the then Chancellor, Norman Lamont, over an attempt to name a date for the beginning of the single currency – is recorded by Major in his memoirs. At Maastricht where he claimed to have won 'game, set and match', Major exempted Britain from the new single currency, but, as we show in a later chapter, found it more difficult to persuade fellow Europeans to keep Britain out of Europe's growing social dimension, the Social Chapter. His greatest difficulty, however, was about to come: securing the passage of the legislation for Maastricht through the House of Commons. At one point, he lost a vote after an opportunistic Labour amendment that tied the implementation of Maastricht to Britain's adopting the Social Chapter. This marked the beginning of a period of six years until 1997 in which the Major government was split on the European issue. His efforts at party management, which included expelling MPs from the Conservative Whip, calling fellow Cabinet members 'bastards' and standing for re-election as Conservative leader did nothing to end the divisions. In his memoirs, Major claimed that opposition came from the 'dispossessed' (ex-ministers) and the 'never possessed' (the permanent backbenchers).[56] However, opposition also came from senior members from within and from Mrs Thatcher who said in her first speech in the House of Lords that she 'could never have signed that Treaty'. As Major records: 'It was a unique occurrence – a former PM openly encouraging backbenchers in her own party to overturn the policy of her successor.' This made winning 'an almost impossible task'.[57]

Nevertheless, as Major recognises, the 'genesis of the divisions' within the Conservative Party went much further back: the legislation to enact the Maastricht Treaty was the 'trigger', not the cause, of internal splits. Some in the party had never been at ease with Europe.[58] The imperial tradition within the Conservatives was keen, he said, to establish clear blue water between Britain and our neighbours. The allegiance of this group always lay across the Atlantic or with the Commonwealth. However, as Major records, it was when 'the Single European Act whetted the continental appetite for communal decision-making and fed the ambitions of the Commission that bitterness set in.'[59]

But much worse European news was to come for John Major when Britain's membership of the ERM plunged the economy into crisis. Like his negotiation at Maastricht, the ERM at first seemed to be a success, but within two years the whole policy lay in ruins. UK membership of the ERM lasted from October 1990 to September 1992. Under the conditions of ERM membership, sterling was pegged at a central rate of £1 to DM2.95, with the flexibility to fluctuate within a 6 per cent margin on either side of this benchmark. ERM membership was supported by Major as the best weapon available to the government in its battle against inflation. By being forced to adjust interest rates in line with the policies of the Bundesbank, it was hoped that the government's credibility in getting inflation down to German levels would be increased.

Throughout the period leading up to the Conservatives' re-election in April 1992, Norman Lamont repeatedly made statements that the economy was heading towards recovery. In October 1991, for example, Lamont claimed: 'What we are seeing is the return of that vital ingredient – confidence. The green shoots of economic spring are appearing once again.'[60] In fact, Lamont was presiding over a severe recession. By the end of 1991, unemployment had increased by 700,000 on 1990 levels, business failures ran at nearly 1,000 a week, and house repossessions were rising. The second quarter of 1992 saw

UK GDP decline 3.6 per cent from its 1990 level, industrial production fall ever faster, public borrowing and mortgage debt rising. With
the US economy volatile and the long-term inflationary consequences of German reunifi-cation unclear – and as Germany's tightening of its monetary policy led to difficulties for the UK economy –
Britain took the decision to defend the pound's position within the
ERM when it came under heavy speculative attack on 16 September
1992, and raised interest rates by 2 per cent, then another 3 per cent
without success – and so Britain left the ERM. It has been estimated
that the ERM experiment led to Britain losing £67.2 billion – £3
billion on 'Black Wednesday' itself. While the Major government
continued until 1997, it was in the words of Norman Lamont 'in office
but not in power.'

But the Conservatives' difficulties on Europe did not just arise
from a failure to manage crises; theirs was a failure to understand the
changing world. Ironically, the very ministers who had championed
the opening up of global markets were slow to recognise that we had
moved from an era defined by Great Powers – and indeed for a time
defined by America's pre-eminence alone – to a world defined by our
interdependence. It was this seismic change that had begun to shape
the economics, culture and politics of a new generation. In the three
chapters that follow, which comprise the next section of this book, I
deal with this new world. I start with how the 1997–2010 Labour
Government saw our international role and where Europe fitted in;
explain how wave after wave of global change has changed public
attitudes to Europe and the world; and suggest that in an interdependent world the real challenge is to balance the autonomy we seek
with the co-operation we need.

PART TWO

The impact of globalisation

CHAPTER FOUR

The dawn of an interdependent world, 1997–2010

Ten months after becoming Prime Minister and at the invitation of Senator Edward Kennedy and the John F. Kennedy Presidential Library, I delivered a public lecture in Boston about the new world I saw around me.[1] My starting point was that the world had changed and that each country's independence was now limited by every country's interdependence, a fact of life that was true even for the most powerful and richest superpower in the world, America.

The new reality of our interdependence was a theme I returned to again and again as Prime Minister: that globalisation marked a break with the past and that we were now in the global era – not the imperial era, nor even the American era. I argued that we were living through the first period in human history that was defined by interdependence – and our growing integration as economies and interconnectedness as societies meant us relying on each other as never before. The conclusion was obvious: we were going to have to share the future and the real question was on which basis we would share.

Interdependence

In my speech in Boston, I explained that the economy of 50 years ago was built around national flows of capital and the domestic production of the very goods and services that we bought in our high streets and shopping centres. Now, in contrast, global flows of capital had superseded national flows. The global sourcing of goods and services meant that the clothes and electronic goods we bought could come from anywhere and less and less were made in our own factories and workshops.

When President Kennedy was alive, I argued, countries communicated with each other primarily through private conversations among an elite of ambassadors sent abroad for that very purpose. Now, in 2008, we were able to communicate with each other across borders instantaneously and continuously. I often used the example of how in the 1990s, in totalitarian regimes, sentries would stand over fax machines to stop information from the outside world coming into their country. In this new world, regimes might try to suppress information from getting through – but not for long.

The lecture was followed by a private lunch with Ted Kennedy and several dozen prominent Americans. Then, in a short speech, I elaborated on the significance of the Declaration of Interdependence that John F. Kennedy had called for in 1962. I reminded them that Kennedy believed co-operation between Europe and America could 'ultimately ... help to achieve a world of law and free choice, banishing the world of war and coercion'.[2]

Of course there was another great shift underway. The world of the future would no longer be Western-dominated. Around us we were seeing the growth of emerging economies and what the Goldman Sachs economist, who is now Britain's Minister for Infrastructure, Jim O'Neill, has called the power of the BRICS: Brazil, Russia, India, China and South Africa. Indeed, one LSE economist, Danny Quah, has charted the changing centre of economic gravity: it is no longer situated midway between America and Europe but is now on the edge of Europe; soon it will be located between Europe and Asia; and then it will move close to the heart of Asia.[3] While military power rested with America, we were witnessing, as Jonathan

Glennie of the Save the Children has written, 'mega-shifts' in what he calls 'the geography of power'.[4]

But if the rise of the emerging market economies had changed the balance of economic power, no one country, whether a rising or established power, was untouched by the growing interdependence of nations. The rise of Asia did not negate the overriding significance of interdependence: indeed, the rising economic powers had already accepted that they were in an interdependent world by working within the existing 'architecture' of the world's economy – the United Nations, the International Monetary Fund, the World Bank and the World Trade Organisation. Nor did they propose to fundamentally challenge this as was to be confirmed when, in late 2008, we created the new leaders' G20 which all agreed to join. I found that the emerging market powers also wanted us to act on our interdependence by addressing not just financial contagion but other shared problems such as climate change; the spread of epidemics and antibiotic resistance; terrorism and conflict; and the general stability and prosperity of the global economy. They too recognised that there were problems which were not just common and shared but global in nature and these could not be solved by bilateral or regional actions alone. As I kept saying during the financial crisis, 'there are global problems that need global solutions'.

Of course the needs and aspirations of the British people had not fundamentally changed. They looked to a government to deliver peace, stability and prosperity. What had changed was the world around us: our needs and aspirations had to be met in a world that was so different from the one in existence after the Second World War that our relations with different countries and continents were now bound to change. As an island economy, we needed a world economy that opened the way for trade, investment and thus jobs across the whole globe. We now had to deal with new threats to our security and prosperity. Right across the world we wanted to win friends for our values and to be a vehicle for progress – a force for good. However, we had to operate in a world in which even the smallest country could now pollute, destabilise and disrupt the richest and most powerful countries. If, in the old world, a neighbour or a competitor became a weak or a failing state this was their problem and their weakness might even be seen to be in our interests. Their loss, after all, could be viewed as our gain. In the new world the fallout from a failed state – that could bring instability, pollution, mass migration or the growth of terrorism – could hurt us all. Their loss could be our loss too. Given that we depended more on each other than ever before – given that our independence was limited by our interdependence – it was in our interests not only to have the best possible relations with small and large states but also to help them avoid breakdown or collapse. It made less sense than ever to divide the world into 'enemies' and 'friends': while we should never diverge from our outspoken commitment to human rights and democracy, we should, I argued, think of a world of 'friends' and 'potential friends'. Of course there would be exceptions – for example, countries such as North Korea – but elsewhere co-operation was normally in our interests, would usually make us stronger, and Britain would benefit from building strong connections and good relations with every part of the world.

Power

It was not just the nature of economics that were changing; so too was the nature of power.

As Labour came to power we were under no illusion that Britain's position had undergone dramatic change over the course of the 20th century. In the year 1900, Britain was home to 2.2 per cent of the world population, but was responsible for 10 per cent of world economic activity, 20 per cent of the world's manufacturing and oversaw an Empire covering 500 million people. By comparison, in

1900, the United States had a population of 75 million and Russia had 119 million inhabitants. In the First World War, we were able to summon up four million troops from our imperial Dominions and in the Second World War we enlisted 4.5 million Commonwealth troops, half of whom came from India and half from Australia, New Zealand, Canada and South Africa. We were, as we have seen, in a position to require the Dominions – who were much less prosperous than us – to lend us £3.5 billion to help pay for the war.

While we must never underestimate the importance of investing in our defence forces, our ability to meet people's needs and aspirations now depended less on the power that we wielded directly but more and more on the influence that we could exercise. If power is defined by the ability to prevent or direct a course of future action through muscle, values, the ability to persuade and through the rewards you can offer, as Moisés Naim's argues, we needed to bring not just military power but economic aid and diplomatic resources – soft and smart power as well as hard power – to bear.[5]

All this, as I sought to show in Chapter Two, had been a subject of discussion in official circles since the 1957 review on Britain's position in the world commissioned by Harold Macmillan, which found that while a century before 'we had the power to impose our will, by contrast we now have to work largely through alliances and coalitions'.[6] And the conclusion that the 1957 study drew was that we had 'to adapt our tactics to changing situations' was even more relevant now when what was at issue was an effective capacity to deliver for the British people.[7] The countries that would be most successful in the future would be the ones that found ways of complementing their military strength with influence in all other arenas: in Britain's case, within international institutions, in the Commonwealth, through the transatlantic relationship and as a member of the European Union.

What is more, our influence no longer depended just on state power. A new set of actors were appearing on the stage, from multinational corporations to non-governmental organisations that had a global reach. And it was their expanding presence across the social media that, in time, was going to demonstrate, in the words of Professor Joseph Nye, that 'states are no longer the only important actors in global affairs, security is not the only major outcome that they seek, and force is not the only or always the best instrument available to achieve those outcomes'.[8]

Governments such as ours had to operate in a world where, in the words of Nye, the distribution of power increasingly resembled a complex, three-dimensional chess game. On the top chessboard, military power is still largely unipolar and the US is likely to remain the only military superpower for some time. On the middle chessboard, economic power was already becoming multipolar. But we were now seeing the evolution of a bottom chessboard – of cross-border transactions that occur outside of government control and range from the undesirable – terrorists, hackers and 'bankers electronically transferring sums larger than most national budgets' – global problems which require a co-ordinated global response – to the desirable – grass roots and community leadership in an emerging global civil society.[9] Because, as Nye argues, 'there are more and more things outside the control of even the most powerful state', it is the case that the future is more about the 'the ability to affect others to obtain the outcomes one wants through attraction rather than coercion or payment.'[10]

So there was a new dimension to our international relations. We not only had to leverage the important channels of influence we had in our transatlantic, European and Commonwealth partnerships, and acknowledge the influence we could bring to bear through international institutions, but we had to build our relationships and in turn our influence through a wider platform – with other non-state players and other countries, particularly in the emerging markets. As we could no longer downplay the importance of sustaining our links with the emerging markets, I made a point of working with

Manmohan Singh of India, Luiz Inácio Lula of Brazil and Michelle Bachelet of Chile, with Thabo Mbeki and Jacob Zuma of South Africa, as well as with Kevin Rudd of Australia and Helen Clarke of New Zealand. Nor could we ignore the fact that if we wanted to secure success on climate change, economic reform through trade liberalisation, development aid or the rebuilding of international institutions, we had to build a coalition that included NGOs, concerned citizens' foundations and the private sector.

Where did that take us to in relationships with our European neighbours? In the pages that follow, I show how in the first few years of the Labour Government our growing influence in Europe was not at the expense of global influence – indeed each reinforced the other – until, that is, the crisis of Iraq which became a major source of contention between leaderships in Europe and America. In the years after 2007, when we faced a global financial collapse, co-operation in Europe was the springboard from which we tackled the global financial crisis. We showed that by building a strong cohesive European position, Britain and Europe could have a significant influence on global decisions. If, in the immediate post-1997 years, influence in Europe was not at the expense of global influence, in the latter period of Labour government influence in Europe was the means by which we exercised global influence: in other words, our global influence was at its most effective when we worked through Europe.

The Blair Government – pragmatic Europeans

More so than anyone before him and more so even than his fellow pro-European predecessor Edward Heath, Tony Blair, who took over as Prime Minister in 1997, had a vision of a Britain that played a positive and constructive role in Europe. And while Tony used the same words as John Major about being at the 'heart of Europe', he meant this not in the way Major did – as a signal to his party that he

wanted its attitudes on Europe to change – but instead as a signal to
the country that he wanted Britain as a whole to change and become
more comfortable with Europe. Both Tony and I rejected any idea
that Britain under Labour would be sitting on the sidelines or tolerating an empty chair. He would show Britain that by being engaged
we could change Europe to Britain's benefit.

Reflecting his commitment to Europe, Tony was awarded in 1999
the Charlemagne Prize for his 'outstanding contribution to European
unification'. In a speech in that year, charting the mistakes in post-
war British policy towards Europe, Tony said: 'The failure of vision
was partly economic. The British establishment at the time failed to
see that the tectonic plates of our international trade were moving
in favour of Europe.'[11] But Tony was more direct about wider
mistakes: 'It was also a failure to seize a political opportunity. And we
had to pay a high eventual entry price – the Common Agricultural
Policy had been shaped in our absence, for example. We did not
shape the institutions that make up "Europe" – the Commission, the
Parliament, the Council. We thought we didn't need to: we had won
the war after all. So it was not surprising to find Europe an uncomfortable fit when we finally joined. That was not a conspiracy. That
was not the foreigners trying to undermine Britain. It was simply the
price paid for our original miscalculation.'[12]

But while Tony had a vision for Europe, he was also pragmatic,
arguing that 'any British Government, governing for the true national
interest, always comes back to the same place. It is not weakness, or
the beguiling embrace of European allies; it is stark reality, good old-
fashioned British pragmatism that brings us there.'[13]

Tony also wanted Britain to be the 'bridge' between Europe and
America. His use of the 'bridge' metaphor could be seen as a modern
version of Churchill's idea that we were a unique player in a set of
interlocking circles, which enabled us to influence America and
Europe and to lead them both. As with Churchill its ambiguity
softened Eurosceptic opposition. Talk of being the 'bridge' or the 'go-

between' allowed us to be pro-European while still standing aside from mainland Europe. Tony used the term regularly and for some time too my speeches – those at the turn of the century – talked of the UK as a bridgehead for American investments in Europe. But the idea of Britain as the go-between would look less convincing when up against what became 'unbridgeable' differences between Germany and France on the one side and America and the UK on the other over Iraq. In these circumstances it became difficult to think of co-operation between Europe and America as the linchpin of the new international order.

But from day one in May 1997, Tony and Robin Cook, our Foreign Secretary, brought fresh energy to our European relations as they took over from John Major in the negotiations to agree a new European Union Treaty, which was concluded in Amsterdam just over a month after we came to power. We immediately signed up to the Social Chapter and, as we had promised in Labour's manifesto, reversed our opt-out from Social Europe. We were, however, cautious about other measures of integration, did not enter the Schengen agreement that opened up European Member States' borders, and in line with public opinion we adopted what has been called a 'pick and mix' approach that enabled Labour to be positive about Europe as a whole while choosing where and when we co-operated in full. Later at the Nice Inter-Governmental Conference in December 2000, Tony agreed 17 new measures where qualified majority voting replaced traditional vetoes, reminding people that Mrs Thatcher had been prepared to do the same to secure the Single Market extensions. But we refused to compromise on tax and social security, on how we made European Union decisions on its Budget, and on border controls. Indeed, in the ten years from Amsterdam onwards the number of UK opt-outs on Justice and Home Affairs measures was as big as the number of opt-ins.[14]

But quietly, behind the scenes and without much publicity, as I show in the discussion of defence and security, Tony made headway on enhanced defence co-operation with France that included a new treaty between the two countries. Britain also tried to lead discussion across Europe on a common agenda of economic and social reform as countries across the continent attempted to marry measures for economic competitiveness, such as opening up the Single Market in finance, energy and IT, with commitments to social protection, like on working hours and holiday pay, challenging the illusion that economic progress had to be bought at the cost of social cohesion. For a time, the Third Way movement that embraced both Bill Clinton's America and Gerhard Schröder's Germany, along with Tony Blair's Britain, was to play a pivotal role.

But in the end, Tony's time as Prime Minister was to become dominated not by social and economic reform and common European or Western approaches to it, but by foreign interventions, first in Kosovo and Sierra Leone, later in Afghanistan and then, most controversially of all, in Iraq. The final judgement on Iraq, what caused it and what it achieved will have to be made at another time, when all the facts are known. It is not the purpose of this chapter to analyse that.

The American decision to go to war in Iraq tested to its limits the very idea that Britain could act as a 'bridge' between America and Europe. Tony had been explicit in his first major foreign policy speech at the Mansion House in November 1997 that 'we are the bridge between the US and Europe. Let us use it.'[15] And when in the immediate aftermath of 9/11, the UK led the world in standing 'shoulder to shoulder' with the US, European countries joined us as part of the US-led action in Afghanistan. However, as opinion polarised in Europe over an intervention in Iraq that was opposed principally by the French and Germans but supported primarily by Spain, Portugal and the UK, and as the American right divided Europe into 'Old' and 'New', Britain's European relations became more fraught. At times Tony seemed to argue that opposition across Europe to American policy on Iraq amounted to an attempt to set up Europe in opposition to the US. 'What we have witnessed is indeed the consequence of Europe and the United States dividing,' he said, opening the 2003 debate in Parliament on the Iraq war. 'The heart of it has been the concept of a world in which there are rival poles of power – the US and its allies in one corner, France, Germany, and Russia and its allies in the other.'[16]

Yet Tony did not give up on fostering a European-American rapport. His argument was that in return for his support on Iraq the American administration would not only commit to a two-state solution for Israel and Palestine but also deliver it: a policy around which Europe and America could again unite. Yet, by 2003, the very idea that Britain was a 'bridge' between Europe and America had become less easy to sustain. After she left government, Clare Short spoke of 'our total incapacity to act as a bridge'; Robin Cook, who also left government over Iraq, was even more scathing, saying that 'the concept of a bridge is perfectly tailored for New Labour, as a bridge cannot make choices, but by definition is in the middle.'[17] Christopher Meyer, our ambassador in Washington at the time of Iraq, recorded in January 2003: 'Transatlantic relations were in a trough. Blair's famous bridge between Europe and America was sinking beneath the waves.'[18] In one speech in 2004, Tony was reduced to saying of the transatlantic relationship: 'Call it a bridge, a two-lane motorway, a pivot or call it a damn high-wire, which is often how it feels; our job is to keep our sights firmly on both sides of the Atlantic, use the good old British characteristics of common sense and make the argument.'[19]

And so, in the aftermath of the Iraq invasion, Tony tried to rebuild US-European relations. As I show in a later chapter, he acknowledged French and German worries about American predominance in NATO and tried to find ways that would bring America and Europe closer together on defence co-operation – something that might illustrate that the 'bridge' still worked – even though the damage to European unity that arose over Iraq was not easily repaired.

Some have argued that Tony – and I – placed too much stress on the similarity of values we shared with America and spoke of nothing more than the similarity of interests we shared with our neighbours in Europe. I do not believe that this was the case. There was, ultimately, no substitute for a strong American-European partnership founded on our shared values as the best way of managing globalisation.

But in these early years of the new century there were at one and the same time two processes at work: the European Union was dividing on Iraq and thus on foreign policy and security issues, and a core European group was uniting around a more integrationist constitution. By then the Labour Government had already made its single biggest decision on our future in Europe by rejecting membership of the Euro, the details of which I discuss in a later chapter. My argument throughout was that there was no contradiction between being outside the Euro and being at the heart of Europe. But we faced another difficult choice in 2004 and 2005: how to approach the European Constitution proposed by the former French President, Valéry Giscard d'Estaing. Having first refused to contemplate a referendum on the new proposals, Tony was persuaded that if he did nothing it would be an election issue on which he would be on the defensive – and so he changed tack. He announced in April 2004 that the new European Constitution would be put to a referendum. The 2005 Labour Party election manifesto pledged to 'campaign wholeheartedly for a "Yes" vote to keep Britain a leading nation in Europe'. The new Constitution was commended as 'a good treaty for Britain and for the new Europe'.[20] Inside Europe, Britain would, it stated, 'help spread democracy and freedom around the world' and the government would be 'leaders in a reformed Europe'. Accordingly, in the run-up to the 2005 election, legislation was introduced to prepare for a referendum and for the ratification of the Constitution. But all this changed when there were 'No' votes in referendums in France and the Netherlands in May and June 2005. We decided to postpone

the Second Reading of the European Union Bill 'until the consequences of France and the Netherlands being unable to ratify the
treaty are clarified'.[21]

Even after offering a referendum, we remained on the back foot
on this European issue, as Stephen Wall's comments about the
possible referendum reveal. Wall was part of an umbrella group
brought together from inside and outside government that was
charged with preparing for the referendum. He noted that extensive
polling of British attitudes suggested that the government might just
have been able to persuade people to ratify the Constitution if all
nations supported the Treaty. Only then might the British public be
persuaded out of a concern that Britain would be isolated as the odd
one out. However, as Wall writes, the 'odds were against' winning a
referendum even in these circumstances. In his view, Britain was
always on the defensive on Europe because Britain joined too late
and the 'degree of our commitment to the European project came
into question'.[22] One of Tony's close advisers, Jonathan Powell, argues
that a referendum could have been won – but only on the general
question of membership of the European Union not on a specific
policy measure.[23] In contrast, Peter Riddell, a well-known commentator, believed that insufficient groundwork had been done to make
the case and that with Europe '[i]t was always a case of tomorrow.
There has been an occasional speech and then nothing.'[24] I myself
felt strongly that we could win a European referendum. But the
hostility of the media to Europe was a factor – something Tony
complained about before he left office when he made a ferocious
attack on the anti-European bias of the press: 'I have long since given
up trying to conduct a serious debate about Europe in certain
quarters,' he said. 'The fevered frenzy of parts of the British media
don't exactly help.'[25]

One writer, Oliver Daddow, who has studied both Tony's speeches
and his European policy, identifies three 'schools of thought' on why
implementing his European vision became difficult: distinguishing

between what he calls the 'blown off course' interpretation, the 'no strategy' interpretation and the 'electoral considerations' interpretation.[26] The events of 9/11 and Iraq, it is suggested, did blow the government off course. However, Stephen Wall's more fundamental observation is that America loomed too large in British calculations. In so far as Britain was a 'bridge' between America and Europe, says Wall, it was 'carrying traffic from west to east across the Atlantic and not in the other direction.'[27] Wall records: 'Under Blair, the idea that the British government might seek to take the lead in achieving the common EU view before talking to the United States was to my knowledge never entertained.'[28] Tony's instincts, he argues, were too similar to most of his predecessors: given a choice between the United States and Europe, America would always come first. I disagree. Until the run-up to the war in Iraq, our government had measurable success in influencing Europe on matters of trade, development, defence co-operation and in bringing America and Europe closer together in the interests of both. Throughout we pursued a pro-European policy of engaging with the rest of Europe and championing reform that would promote economic flexibility and competitiveness alongside social cohesion and we played an important part in shaping the EU's direction. 'From the self-congratulatory official wisdom of the "blown off course" to the highly critical "no strategy" school,' concludes Daddow, 'we arrived at the "electoral considerations" school in the middle.'[29] Winning elections, he suggests, mattered more than winning Britain to a pro-European position. But this is wrong: we were a government of committed Europeans even when public opinion was less than enthusiastic. And even as he left office in 2007, after four years of the occupation of Iraq and with questions growing about the failure of reconstruction there, Tony was still trying to rebuild our relationships with our European neighbours.

Europe and the world, 2007–10

In my first months in office, I made an effort to build a stronger alliance between Europe and America. Within a few days of becoming Prime Minister, I had met the American President, the German Chancellor, the French President, the heads of the European Union and other European leaders. We were now working with a new German Chancellor, Angela Merkel, who had defeated Gerhard Schröder; with Nicolas Sarkozy who had replaced Jacques Chirac in France; and with Romano Prodi, who became Prime Minister of Italy for a second time, as well as his successor as President of the European Commission, José Manuel Barroso. We also had the benefit of allies from the left-of-centre – José Luis Rodríguez Zapatero and José Socrates in Spain and Portugal respectively – and I made a point of working with the socialist group in Europe, a group that Tony had held at a distance. From the right-of-centre, we worked well with Jan Peter Balkenende in the Netherlands, as well as Angela Merkel and Nicolas Sarkozy.

I felt that in an interdependent world Europe and America had to work more closely together. For much of the last century, we had thought there was a choice between global influence and influence in Europe – that, if we focused on Europe and not the Commonwealth or America, we would be marked down as less of a global player. As we saw in Chapter Two, this was after all Sir Alec Douglas Home's argument for resisting the push to Europe in the Macmillan Cabinet. In the first years of Tony Blair's premiership, I believe British people had started to believe that the way to maximise our global influence and go global was to act with and through Europe. I wanted to go one step further: to bring Europe and America closer together and show in practice that there was no contradiction between being pro-European and being a global leader. I also wanted to show that Britain could be a bigger force for influence in the world through Europe and not at the expense of our relationship with America but in a way that enhanced it. Within a few months all our attention would be on the global financial crisis and economic recession, but in my first year as Prime Minister I tried a different approach from that of Tony – not talking of Britain as the 'bridge', but instead pressing for Europe and America to work more closely together. The problem as I had found with talking of a 'bridge' is that each pillar on both sides of the Atlantic had to be as strong as the other and the link between the two had to be seen as credible from both sides. But, divided over Iraq, Europe looked weak to many in Washington. And, out of step with most of Europe on Iraq, Britain could not easily be the link. I saw how relations might improve if Europe could be a more cohesive, stronger partner of America and if we accepted that not just Britain but, on occasion, Germany, France or even America itself, as well as Britain, acted as the 'go-between'. In other words, my view was that the outcome – America and Europe working more closely together – was more important than who claimed credit for delivering it.

Reshaping the global architecture

Part of my strategy was that Britain should exercise a more important influence in the decision-making of international institutions. The UK would benefit, as I argued in my Boston speech, from the strengthening of international institutions and making them more credible channels for change. By 2007, Britain had a role in 80 international institutions, making us one of the most networked countries in the world. Moreover, we had important positions: one of the eight in the G8, one of the five permanent members of the UN Security Council, along with permanent seats on the boards of the World Bank and the IMF, and, of course, a place as the acknowledged leader of the Commonwealth. And we had ideas for reform – for example, a new Marshall Plan for Africa, a restructuring of the international financial architecture that would have given the IMF a role as a surveillance institution and making the World Bank a stronger institution to deal with the challenges of development.

Whether it be climate change, multilateral disarmament, international aid or the banning of arms sales, my preferred strategy was to call for change through internationally co-ordinated action that would often start by building a European consensus – and, if possible, with transatlantic support – for such a change. Then, I believed, 'punching above our weight', we could work through colleagues such as Manmohan Singh, Kevin Rudd, Luiz Inácio Lula, Thabo Mbeki and Jacob Zuma to secure international agreement and support. This was, as I record in a later chapter, the approach through which we tried to win global agreement for a new climate change treaty. It was also how we approached winning support for further global action against nuclear proliferation.

But the practical test for our faith that international co-operation and action through stronger international institutions could make a difference came in an unwelcome form: a global financial crisis. From the moment I became aware of the scale of the global banking collapse, I made it my mission to create an international response that was equal to the scale of the crisis. Clear in my own mind that no country on its own, not even America, could be the engine of recovery and that established fora like the G8 were too narrowly based to undertake the task, I quickly won support for co-ordinated action in September 2008 from Presidents Sarkozy, Barroso and Lula, and Prime Ministers Rudd, Zapatero and Sócrates for the creation of a leaders' G20 which Britain would chair. This happened after we commandeered a remote room within the United Nations building for a very private get-together. Having secured agreement for a new G20 from colleagues in Europe and beyond – and an undertaking from President Lula that he would pass the G20 chair early to the United Kingdom – I left the UN General Assembly in New York to fly to Washington in order to persuade President Bush of the need for action.

When the G20 met in London in April 2009 and underpinned the world economy with a $1.1 trillion guarantee, we saw international co-operation at its best. The creation of the G20 – and our chairmanship of it – was a vindication of my view that strong and effective international institutions in the 21st century could be a vehicle for enhanced British influence. Britain had also played a part in creating the Financial Stability Forum and as Prime Minister I wanted it to become a tougher monitor of the global financial system, as well as a catalyst for higher global financial standards, so I fought to see it expanded into a Global Stability Board with responsibility for providing early warnings of global financial problems.

Just as Britain had promoted reforms in response to perceived gaps in the global architecture after the Asian crisis in 1997, we sought to learn lessons from the global financial crisis about how to co-operate to even better effect in the future. Accordingly, I persuaded Manmohan Singh, the Prime Minister of India, to lead a review into possible reforms we could make to our international institutions. But when the peak of the crisis had passed, the willingness to work globally was more difficult to cultivate and after we left office in 2010 the G20 – and, with it, international economic co-operation – assumed less importance.

There was a practical limit to how much influence international institutions could exercise. With no direct democratic mandate of their own, international institutions were only as effective as national governments allowed them to be. To create a stable post-1945 world order, America had understood that unilateral action – or even action in conjunction with the other Great Powers – would be seen as unacceptable, akin to a new form of imperialism, and they recognised that the world needed broad-based institutions capable of building consensus. But with the power of veto at the UN held by five big states – Britain, France, China, America and Russia – and with the IMF and the World Bank having an inbuilt Europe-America dominance, the international institutions were starting to look like the creations and hand-me-downs of another era. So, while I and others tried hard to make international institutions work more effectively – and there were many examples of where, under the hard-working and committed UN Secretary-General, Ban Ki-Moon, and other leaders they did – we knew that what still mattered more for British influence in the world – and getting things done – was how we set our relationships with the Commonwealth, America and Europe.

Influence through working with the Commonwealth

From 2007 to 2010, we tried hard to bring the Commonwealth into play as an important leader on the world stage in its own right. Of course there was no question of us ever telling the Commonwealth countries what to do. The Commonwealth consists of independent nations each of which is proud of the freedoms they have won from Britain. But I did believe that, if we were able to work more closely together, the Commonwealth could be a more important and dynamic force in the 21st century world. It made sense because, in our interdependent world, smaller states now had more influence and the confidence amongst the peoples of Africa and on the Indian sub-continent was on the rise.

When I spoke to the 2009 Commonwealth Heads of Government meeting in Uganda, I said we had moved on from when, at the time the modern Commonwealth was born, the defining feature of international relations was the end of Empire and the start of a post-colonial age; and when countries were, for the first time, embracing independence and the world appeared to be an ever larger collection of individual nation states. This meant the theme of the times was independence, but now the defining issue was our interdependence. 'The old colonial ties and colonial rivalries have been replaced by globalisation,' I stated, 'and some rightly now ask how the Commonwealth fits in with this new era.'[30] I argued that the enormous issues

we faced – on climate change, international terrorism, nuclear proliferation, poverty and securing economic prosperity – meant states
were powerless to act alone and here the Commonwealth could take
a lead. It represented some 800 million Hindus, 500 million Muslims
and 400 million Christians. Among its 53 Member States were, I said,
some of the world's richest and some of the world's poorest, some of
the most powerful and some of the most vulnerable. The strength
and clarity of our shared values across such a diverse group of
countries, I argued, gave the Commonwealth a unique legitimacy
and ability to tackle the tough global challenges that confronted us
all. Despite our differences, each and every one of us was committed
to freedom and democracy; to the eradication of poverty and
inequality; to peace and the rule of law; and, of course, to opportunity
for all. These values, I contended, should underpin the Commonwealth's future work.

However, when the Commonwealth comes together – as it does
every two years in a conference of heads of state and in ministerial
round-tables – you also find it is weighed down by its own internal
problems. In my time as Prime Minister, the issues that necessarily
had to absorb our time included the exclusion of Pakistan and the
suitability of Sri Lanka to be our host in 2011. It is also weighed down
by past grievances yet to be resolved – one issue I had to deal with
was Uganda's claim against the British for atrocities in the 1920s –
and, unsurprisingly, the shadow of Zimbabwe has hung over our
deliberations for 50 years.

Moreover, in recent times, the Commonwealth has been undermined by differences in world views among its leading participants:
from India's neutrality and its role as a leader of the non-aligned
countries during the Cold War to different interpretations of human
rights and of repeated changes in constitutions to allow elected
leaders to stay in office The emergence of the BRICS and thus South
Africa and India's strong links with China, Russia and Brazil has also
changed the way the Commonwealth is seen as does the work of the

Group of 77, the loose coalition of developing nations that includes many members of the Commonwealth and which is designed to enhance their joint negotiating capacity in the United Nations. And of course there were differences on climate change – as well as long standing differences over Iraq. The Commonwealth did not escape from the most divisive issues of world politics in the early years of the 21st century: what divided Europe also divided the Commonwealth.

And trading relationships are also no longer the glue that once held the Commonwealth together. The 'south-south' trading relationships between China and Africa, and within Asia, are becoming far more important than British trade with these continents. Individually, little more than one per cent of our exports goes to Australia, Canada and South Africa respectively and less than 1 per cent go to New Zealand. As Australia and New Zealand pivot to Asia, and as Africa builds its own position as a world player through the African Union, the Commonwealth's role is changing and, despite its great potential to be a bloc of powers that influences the course of events, the Commonwealth's 53 nations have found it difficult to unite to influence the rest of the world around common positions. I wanted the Commonwealth to become more important than it had been in influencing global events. But in the real world of alliances, interests and calculations we found that potential to be a force for good on the global stage has yet to be fully realised.

American relations

When I became Prime Minister, our relationship with America was as controversial as it had been at any time in the post-war period. Iraq and the presidency of George Bush had divided British opinion and while there had been a party consensus between Conservatives and Labour on going to war, a strong reaction to the war and to its aftermath – the continuing civil war in Iraq – existed amongst a large section of the general public.

I came into No 10 with my own timetable – that we would exit Iraq within 18 months. However, at the time I became Prime Minister, a new President was in the process of being elected in the United States. America, I found, was also undergoing a process of reappraisal and change: Washington was starting to view Asia as the continent to which they wished to 'pivot'.

Every year for nearly four decades after the Second World War, one-quarter of a million American troops were billeted in West Germany. However, with the end of the Cold War, US troop numbers dropped to just over 100,000 by 1993. By 2000, just 69,000 American military personnel remained. And, with the rise of China, the balance between Europe and Asia was shifting. Today, as a result, a minority of US overseas troops (65,000) are stationed in Europe and a bigger number (78,000) are to be found in East Asia and the Pacific area. The pivot to Asia was not just expressed in changing American defence priorities: in preference to pursing a world trade agreement, America now sought to complement the proposed new EU-US trade treaty with an even more ambitious Trans-Pacific trade deal which included the rest of Asia but not China.

'I feel I can do something to bring Europe and America closer together for the future,' I said on my first visit to Washington as Prime Minister.[31] But I avoided focusing on the 'bridge' metaphor. Instead, I wanted to focus less on what Britain thought of itself in terms of the 'special relationship' – and more on what we could achieve if Europe and America moved closer together. In the 18 months I worked with George Bush, I urged him to reach out to more European leaders. With the Iraq War virtually over, I said that 'now is an opportunity for an historic effort in co-operation' between America and Europe.[32] However, if a new dawn in collaborative action between Europe and the US was to happen, both America and Europe would have to change. As part of that, I supported President

Bush over NATO membership of Ukraine and Georgia, while wanting to offer an olive branch to Russia so that they too could think of their future as part of a wider Europe. But the key would be America and Europe working collaboratively on matters where we could strike a consensus, particularly climate change, global economic reform, international development and in the fight against terrorism.

'The 20th century showed that when Europe and America are distant from one another, instability is greater; when partners for progress the world is stronger,' I said in my first annual foreign policy speech at the Lord Mayor's Banquet in November 2007. 'And in the years ahead – notwithstanding the shifts in economic influence underway – I believe that Europe and America have the best chance for many decades to achieve historic progress – working ever more closely together on the project of building a global society.'[33] I took the view that the country that does not matter inside Europe will never be taken seriously in the US: indeed I cannot think of any American president who has not urged closer integration between Britain and mainland Europe. I also had never understood why some have seen our strong ties with the US as a reason for withdrawing from Europe. Some say that under my leadership from 2007 the Labour government was too ready to follow the US uncritically. I do not accept this: in the period from 2007 to 2010, Britain led on climate change and on global economic policy, both in the creation of the G20 and in trying to secure (successfully) a stronger Global Financial Stability Board and (unsuccessfully) a world trade treaty, in each case urging America to join us while being solid in our support for action to hold back the Taliban in Afghanistan and in the fight against terrorism.

I was happy that France wanted to build a stronger relationship with America and I was encouraged by President Sarkozy's decision to bring France closer to America, back into the core of NATO. During this period, some said that Chancellor Merkel was taking over from the British Prime Minister as the favourite 'go-to person' in Europe for Washington. But this was not the problem as I saw it. I was not unhappy that President Obama saw Angela Merkel as a leader he could deal with directly. He may have surmised – rightly, of course, as it turned out – that she would outlast myself and Sarkozy in office. Most of the time it was Britain, but I was happy if, on occasion, it was France or Germany who provided the link between Europe and America. What I wanted was the two continents to work together. I was not interested in cutting other countries out nor in being a 'bridge' just for the status it gave us – I was interested only in what we could achieve. The reason was that I was confident about the ideas we, Britain, were putting forward and were contributing to the agenda for international action. I had no fears about our ability as a country to be listened to if we championed the right initiatives – as happened with our response to the economic crisis – and I wanted to see stronger bonds between Europe and America as a way of resolving major global issues.

There were useful annual meetings between the European Commission led by my friend José Manuel Barroso and the US administration. I was also happy that – as often happened – the Italians and the Spanish as well as President Barroso were central to any joint initiative between ourselves and the United States. And despite being outside the Euro I had regular talks with the European Central Bank President Jean Claude Trichet. We achieved most, however, when French, German and British leaders worked together with the US. In the old world, we could back Germany against France or France against Germany, in order to secure an equilibrium in the European balance of power, thus preventing one power from becoming too dominant and securing our world position. By contrast, in the new world, working with France to contain Germany or vice versa will impact on what happens within Europe but may have little effect on the rest of the world. Indeed, if European powers end up at odds with each other this may be counterproductive to the interests of all of us. Each European power had more chance of carrying global influence if we were part of a united front. Instead of thinking of a world where one European power is set against the other and of a return to spheres of influence, it makes more sense in our interdependent world to think of collaboration between all the European powers in the pursuit of our collective interests and security.

I found in the years between 2007 and 2010 that there is a fifth channel for influence for Britain – in addition to the channels for influence that we build through our European, American and Commonwealth partnerships, and through stepping up our role in international institutions: we needed to cultivate our collaboration with non-state actors and friendships with other countries. I think that I was one of the first to see the importance of working with global NGOs – as we did to achieve 100 per cent debt relief for Africa at the 2005 Gleneagles summit – although I was perhaps slower to appreciate the need to work with social media. The friendships we developed with leaders in India, China, Brazil, South Africa and Australia helped us form the G20 initiative and was central to the British push for a climate change deal. Nevertheless, in the end, a common approach from America and Britain was vital to success.

Co-operation between Europe and America should have grown because of a common anxiety about Russian aggression. It is said the last time Britain and Russia had good relations was in 1696 when Peter the Great visited Britain and worked in our shipyards. But if the British-Russian relationship has always been difficult – even when we were allies in the last years of the Second World War – the context has changed substantially in recent years from the old Cold War stand off as a result of the European Union's advance into the East and more recently the requests by Ukraine, Georgia and others to join NATO. My immediate problems with Vladimir Putin arose from the assassination of Alexander Litvinenko on the streets of London. We were clear that the assassination had been ordered from the top – as was concluded in January 2016 by a public enquiry led by Sir Robert Owen – and what was also clear was that further assassinations on British soil were possible; indeed, we believed one new assassination was being planned. This led to the diplomatic stand off that has characterised our relations with Russia ever since. During the time I was Prime Minister, Putin was not President but Prime Minister of Russia, so I dealt mainly with President Medvedev, whom I met regularly. But Putin left us in no doubt that he was in charge. I particularly remember the G8 meeting in 2008. After we thought we had secured a common G8 position on Zimbabwe, Russian President Medvedev's acquiescence was immediately overruled by Prime Minister Putin.

Russian aggression has come just at the moment when the end of the Cold War means, in Robert Kagan's words, 'for the first time in Russia's long history it does not face a strategic threat on its western flank.'[34] But that is not how Russia sees it. The European Union's Eastern Partnership, the Western embrace of Ukraine and the discussions of NATO membership for Eastern European countries is viewed in Moscow as an attempt to undermine Russia. It was Catherine the Great who said: 'I have no way to defend my borders but to extend them.' And relationships between the whole of Europe and Russia deteriorated badly in 2008 with Russia's military action in Georgia. This led to the suspension of formal meetings of the NATO-Russia Council until spring 2009 as we urged Russia to step back from its recognition of the Georgian regions of Abkhazia and South Ossetia as independent states. The renewed Russian assertiveness made my point: Europe and America needed to co-operate more effectively. General Ismay, the first Secretary General of NATO, described the military alliance's policy as to keep America in, Germany down and Russia out. Things have changed: I certainly wanted to keep America in but I also wanted Germany, France and Britain in it together. Sadly, and for the very reasons that we now have a referendum on Europe, the new Coalition government sought to distance themselves from European co-operation for domestic reasons – in order to appease the Conservative Party's Eurosceptics and keep them in line.

Europe

It has been a constant criticism that my relationship with Europe was an ambiguous one because I did not recommend we join the Euro but that is not how I saw it. Tony Blair had started in government as a wholehearted European – with a broad vision of what a united Europe could achieve and his speeches were unequivocal about the centrality of Europe to Britain's future. However, Iraq made it difficult for him to be seen as a leader that could bring greater European unity and, despite my trying hard on his behalf, I could not persuade my fellow European leaders to accept him for the position as first President of the European Council. More because of the divisions within his party than out of choice, Tony's immediate predecessor, John Major, was forced to view Europe from the narrower perspective of British party politics and having won the leadership with the support of Eurosceptics he was – at all times in his premiership – forced to take on board a strong Eurosceptic opinion within his party.

I was more interested in how we could change and reform Europe and make it more competitive, more outward-looking and more engaged with the rest of the world. I wanted Britain to change its mind about Europe and I wanted Europe itself to change because of a Britain that championed what I felt Europe could become – a Global Europe. And this is still my view: a globally oriented, internationally engaged European Union that stops looking inward and builds its links with Asia, Africa and the Middle East as well as remaining a strong and vibrant part of the West. But all this was derailed by the global recession which led Europe to look inwards, become self-absorbed and more focused on the minutiae of

European reform rather than on the potential for growth through building a stronger trading and strategic relationship with the three regions around it: Asia, Africa and the Middle East.

Global Europe – a proposal I outlined to my European colleagues – had allies in the Netherlands, France, Spain and Portugal – all important European Union countries with former overseas Empires and with a commitment to an open trading system and a shared interest in a global role. Nevertheless, in my view, no one was better fitted to persuade Europe of the need for a global role than Britain with its links to each continent. And there was a prize: we could lead a Global Europe without any need for a trial of strength with other European powers for the same role. While attitudes were slowly changing, Germany was still generally reluctant to have an 'out-of-area' presence. France faced its own internal problems, struggling to reform out-of-date institutions and more focused on its relationship with Germany than on anything else. In 2007, no other European power was as strong globally as Britain and by working through Europe and deploying our relationships with NATO and the US, my view was that we could play a unique role. A Global Europe was a good route from which a Global Britain could strengthen its engagement with the world.

Of course, Europe had to reform and I set out an economic reform programme focusing on competitiveness, openness and stronger trading links with the rest of the world. In January 2008, in a speech on Europe, I argued: 'What is clear is that at this time of global economic uncertainty, we should not be throwing into question – as some would – the stability of our relationship with Europe and even our future membership of the European Union – risking trade, business and jobs. Indeed, I strongly believe that rather than retreating to the side lines we must remain fully engaged in Europe so we can push forward the reforms that are essential for Europe's, and Britain's, economic future.'[35] I said that Europe should take the lead, as we did, in global negotiations over climate change and after the financial crisis broke in reforming the global financial system and in the creation of the G20. Even when others had written a world trade deal off, I argued for Europe to play a leading role in seeking a new trade agreement, while, at the same time, I was an early proponent of European-China investment and trade treaties.

I urged that we champion reforms to modernise international institutions – principally the IMF and World Bank – even if this was at the cost of diluting some of Europe's previous voting strength. While I resisted merging all Europe's votes into one bloc, I did so because it would weaken Europe not strengthen it. I agreed, instead, that the European members should attempt to formulate common positions. Moreover, while agreeing in principle that the post of Managing Director of the IMF should go to the best candidate no matter which part of the world they came from, I continued to support European candidates for the IMF leadership whenever the position became vacant. I did so because I wanted Europe to play a leading role. During my time as Chancellor and Prime Minister, I championed the appointment of three European leaders of the IMF: one from Germany, one from Spain and one from France.

In 2007, when I was appointed Prime Minister, British support for the European Union was running at not more than half the European Union average with openly critical attitudes over twice as high in Britain compared with the EU as a whole.[36] Like Tony Blair, I started from a desire to convince our country of the patriotic benefits of Britain being in Europe. But as Oliver Daddow has put it, Tony Blair and I encouraged the public to see see the 'Britain and Europe story' not as a history of our 'eternal separateness from the continent but always as an always-European one'. However, as he suggests, it was always going to be difficult for the Labour government to alter attitudes on an emotive question in such a short space of time.[37]

Conclusion

Because the European Union has the potential to affect the full spectrum of British foreign policy goals, from delivering prosperity to improving our security, Jonathan McClory told an important House of Lords Committee into Britain's Power and Influence, it should be 'seen as the UK's most important multilateral membership – despite the tone of current domestic political debates'.[38] In evidence to the same committee, Professor Joseph Nye detected similar benefits: 'From Britain's strategic position, I would think [EU membership] gives you a second arrow in your quiver.'[39] What he meant was that if we do 'punch above our weight' we do so best when we use our connections to Europe to the full. 'The biggest risk to Britain's soft power in the near-term is if it detaches itself completely from its closest and deepest institutional network: the EU,' Robin Niblett has counselled. 'This would risk the UK becoming … a consumer of global public goods, standards and norms, rather than a shaper of the international environment.'[40]

But something changed between 2010 and 2015 as the new government became more Eurosceptic and to make its point intensified its search for alternative alliances. In these last few years, ministers have compared our role in the world to a 'hub', a 'pivot' or, as the then Foreign Secretary, William Hague, put it, 'a centre with many spokes coming from it'.[41] And thus the idea of Britain as 'a connecting node in a networked world' gained currency. It allowed ministers to justify distancing themselves from Europe. Indeed, it sometimes seemed that our allies were to be found anywhere but in Europe.[42] But does it add up to a strategy that makes sense for Britain's future needs?

As the world defined by the 'Great Powers' became, in the wake of the changes wrought by globalisation, a world defined by our interdependence, Britain, like other countries, had to rethink and to re-engineer our strategic relationships. One answer is that offered by Robin Niblett who argues that '[f]or Britain to be economically successful, secure and influential internationally in the future, its leaders need to think of the EU as constituting Britain's first or "inner circle" – from which it can leverage its strengths to maximum effect,' America as the next circle and the UK's other key bilateral and multi-lateral relationships – from the UN Security Council, G7, G8, G20, and the Commonwealth to its relations with major emerging economies such as China – making up an outer circle of influence arrayed around these two.'[43]

His delineation of separate 'circles' is not meant to imply a set of exclusive relationships. But Niblett's argument is that the more influence we have in Europe, the more influence we have across the world – with America, with the Commonwealth and with other states. We can show that after 1997, influence in Europe was not achieved at the expense of global influence. Of course, as we found with divisions over Iraq, we will not always persuade Europe of a common course and, even when Europe has a united position – as on climate change at the 2009 Copenhagen summit – we will not always be able to persuade the rest of the world. But when, as we found in addressing the global financial crisis, the conditions are right – with well-thought-through initiatives, a united front and a strategy for heading off vested interests – Britain can play its part in leading Europe and Europe can lead the world. The stronger Britain is in Europe, the stronger we are in the world.

Our growing international interdependence underpinned the Labour Government's foreign policy. And the growing interdepend-ence came as a result of seismic shifts in the way the global economy was working. But, of course, the very same forces that make us more connected to each other and challenge us to co-operate with our neighbours also create economic dislocation and insecurity and a desire to 'bring control back home'. Understanding how we address these pressures – and respond to them – is the theme of the next chapter.

CHAPTER FIVE

Globalisation:
'a runaway train'?

Jim had been a car plant worker for years. When that job went he took redundancy and set himself up as self-employed, driving his own taxi. But first his trade was threatened when Eastern Europeans migrating to Britain undercut him. They had entered the business as unregistered drivers. Now both Jim and his competitors have been hit by the newest threat: global giant Uber has come to his town and zero hours contract drivers are beating them on price and speed of response – and doing them out of business.

Uber is the face of globalisation that Jim sees and he does not like it: he feels he can do nothing against its power and strength and it seems to be sweeping all before it. Jim now sees Uber and companies like it as alien interlopers impinging on his livelihood, turning globalisation from an opportunity – that for years he has been told it was – into a threat to his work, his income and his security. After losing a once-secure job and now losing his taxi business to outsiders he is asking: what has Europe or the rest of the world ever done but harm him? Jim's story has been recounted to me by a colleague in the last Parliament and it is people just like Jim who are thinking of voting to leave the European Union.

Jim is one of millions of British citizens who feel they have lost out in successive waves of global change. Some, as I have suggested, compare globalisation to an out-of-control, runaway train. Others think of themselves akin to travellers marooned at sea, with no lifeboat or lifejackets and no anchor, map or compass to chart a way forward.

In this chapter I explain how globalisation – its scale and scope and the international interdependence it creates – has brought about the most profound shift in our lives that has occurred since Britain entered the European Economic Community. I will argue that while many want to 'bring control back home', globalisation is here to stay and the issue that matters is whether we either manage it well or badly; that solutions are not to be found in walking away from co-operative action but in making it work better; that the only legitimate corrective to new forms of transnational power exercised by others over us is new forms of transnational democracy exercised by us; and that the EU is not the cause of the insecurities people are experiencing but is part of the solution. In fact, the case for British co-operation in Europe is stronger today than it ever has been.

Globalisation and economic dislocation

Some people think of globalisation as a new cultural phenomenon: we buy the same global brands, listen to the same global music, trawl the same global Internet, favour the same global lifestyles and are part of a long revolution creating a common cosmopolitan culture we increasingly share. Others see globalisation as no more than the latest phase of a neo-liberal free market capitalism and write of it in purely economic terms.

I see globalisation, however, as a phenomenon that starts from deep-rooted economic change but is qualitatively different from what has come before it in the social and culture changes it brings about. Global flows of finance, goods and services rose from $2 trillion in 1980 to $29 trillion in 2007. They then subsequently declined as a result of the global financial crisis and recession, before rising again and reaching $28 trillion in 2014. According to McKinsey this figure could triple – to $84 trillion – by 2025.[1] And this is what global change is about: the replacement of predominantly national flows of capital – which used to dictate what was invested, where it was invested and how – by global flows and of the national sourcing of goods and services by global sourcing. While in the past the goods that we bought on our high streets – TVs, washing machines and clothes – were, in the main, designed, manufactured, assembled and serviced at home; today most of the goods and even many of the services we buy are designed, manufactured, assembled and serviced elsewhere in the world.

In 1860, nearly 20 per cent of the world's manufacturing output came from Britain, the world's first industrial nation.[2] However, once the pre-eminent manufacturing power, Britain accounts for just 3 per cent of the world's manufacturing output today.[3]

It is instructive to take an overview of the scale of the change. In 1900 the UK represented 2.5 per cent of the world population – just 41 million out of 1.56 billion. By 1950 our share had fallen to less than 2 per cent of the global population – 50 million out of 2.5 billion. Today, we are less than 1 per cent – 60 million out of 7 billion. However, in 1900, the UK produced just under 30 per cent of all the world's manufactured goods, three times as much as the USA and 50 per cent more than Germany. By 1950 we still produced 20 per cent of global manufacturing output and, while we had been surpassed by the USA, we still produced more than the war-ravaged economies of France and Germany combined.[4]

But the change in the last half of the century and particularly from the 1980s has been dramatic. By the year 2000, Britain's share of world manufacturing fell from 20 per cent down to 4 per cent. By 2000, Germany produced twice as much as we did and the USA five times as much. Now the three great manufacturing pioneers – France, Germany and the UK – are responsible for producing less than one-third of the world's manufactured goods between them.[5]

So Britain is not alone in experiencing the downside of globalisation. However, in Britain's case, 90 per cent of our clothes and many of the all textile goods that we buy are manufactured abroad.[6] Nor is it just low-tech goods that we buy from overseas. Many of our electronic goods are manufactured in other countries, mainly in Asia. For example, 70 per cent of the world's mobile phones are made in China.[7]

Fifty years ago, the vast majority of the world's entire economic activity was conducted as commercial transactions within nation states between national buyers and national sellers. At some point in the coming decades more than half of the world's economic activity will come from the cross-border trading of goods and services.

Take the Apple iPad, designed in America and China, assembled in Taiwan, Korea and Vietnam and sold around the world. Alternatively, take the British company, Dyson, which sells vacuum cleaners, fans and hand dryers in 60 countries. By any measure Dyson is a great British success story. It employs 5,000 people worldwide and has over 3,000 patents or patent applications for 500 different inventions. Everything Dyson produces is designed and tested at its home base in Malmesbury, Wiltshire, where the firm employs around 1,000 engineers. But production of the bag-less vacuum cleaners, fans and hand-dryers is done in Malaysia while the digital motors for these products are built in Singapore.[8]

This reflects a new truth: we now have a more sophisticated division of labour in which a single product is designed in one country, assembled in another, invented in another and repaired in yet another. What is often called 'flexible specialisation', 'vertical production' or 'the trade in tasks' means that companies can move the production of goods and services around the world to where it is most cost effective, but can also break the production cycle for each good and service down into a series of discrete tasks that can be off-shored or outsourced to just about anywhere.

As global flows of capital, goods and services have taken over from purely national flows in the last 30 years, over one billion people have entered the global industrial workforce to create a labour force now dominated by lower-paid Asian manufacturing and service workers.[9] There are more manufacturing jobs today – around 300 million – than ever before as consumer spending power rises, but Britain's share of the global workforce has fallen from 6 per cent to 1 per cent.[10] Fifty years ago the UK had nine million men and women employed in manufacturing. Today the number employed in manufacturing is one third of what it was – below three million. Employment in our manufacturing and mining industries is down from nearly 40 per cent of our workforce 50 years ago to just 8 per cent today.[11]

TABLE 5.1

Manufacturing jobs as a percentage of total jobs

	Manufacturing as per cent of total jobs
1964	36
1973	26
1982	22
1990	15
2000	13
2010	10
2015	8

Source: Stephen Broadberry and Tim Leunig, *The Impact of Government Policies on UK Manufacturing since 1945* (London, Foresight, Government Office for Science, 2013) and Chris Rhodes, *Manufacturing: Statistics and Policy* (London, House of Commons Library, 2015)

It is when technological change and global economic competition come together that the impact on the working lives of millions of people is dramatic. The collapse of established occupations started with the hollowing out of the boilermakers, typesetters, riveters, bookkeepers and clerks who were at the heart of the first industrial revolution. More recently, the skills of workers from machinists and cashiers to secretaries and typists – occupations that were at the heart of the second industrial revolution – have been digitalised, computerised or off-shored to cheaper locations, with jobs like those of radiologists, accountants and even lawyers the next to be transformed. In just fifteen years, since 2001, it is estimated that we have lost the jobs of 204,000 secretaries, 108,000 typists, 83,000 bank and office clerks, 72,000 retail cashiers and check-out operators, 64,000 postal workers, mail sorters, messengers and couriers, 60,000 assemblers of electrical and electronic products, 51,000 metal machine setters and setter operators and 47,000 sewing machinists.[12]

So while globalisation may mean lower prices for clothes and electronics and a wider range and higher quality of goods – it is estimated that because costs have come down, Americans now buy twice as many items of clothing a year as they did 20 years ago – the gains individuals experience as consumers are more than counteracted by their loss of job security as producers.[13] There were nearly five million skilled workers in the UK in 1990. There are little more than three million now. White-collar jobs have been hit too. Administrative jobs fell by 0.7 million between 1990 and 2010, declining from 4.4 million to 3.7 million. This trend is forecast to continue to 2020.[14] According to a study by researchers at Oxford University and Deloitte, more than ten million of today's 30 million jobs – 35 per cent – are at high risk of computerisation over the coming 20 years.[15]

Insecurity at work has been accompanied by a decline in the value of earnings. Real household disposable incomes – a yardstick of living standards that takes account of incomes, benefits, taxes and inflation – fell 0.6 per cent lower in the five years from 2009 to 2014.[16] And the tax and benefit changes implemented by the Coalition government lowered average household incomes by just over £1,000 a year.[17]

It is important to put all these changes into their global context. When companies moved production from high cost parts of the world to low costs parts, they brought about, in the words of Branko

Milanović, the 'biggest reshuffling of income since the Industrial Revolution'.[18] At the top, a global elite of around 60 million people – half in the USA – have raced far ahead of the rest. At the bottom the relative position of more than one billion people living on less than $2 a day is little improved. In between, as China lifted more than 500 million poor people out of absolute poverty, the global middle class has rocketed upwards from half a billion people around 1980 to two billion people. But while the new middle class in China and the emerging markets have seen their real incomes doubled even after inflation (with many on incomes just above $10 per day meaning their incomes still place them as high as only the top six and seven deciles of the world) the old Western middle income groups (who are in the top 90 per cent), including British skilled and clerical workers, have seen their incomes squeezed.[19] 'Initially, the winners easily outnumbered the losers, although the losses suffered by the losers were bigger than the gains for the winners,' explained Larry Elliot in *The Guardian*, 'but the last period of globalisation was a lot more fragile than it looked … The recession and its aftermath have meant an increase in the number of people who think that the economic system may be working for the owners of multinational companies and the global super rich, but is not working for them. The sense of unhappiness has been fanned … [as] the recovery has been skewed in favour of the have nots … [and] the traditional parties of the centre appear to have nothing [new] to offer … [adding to] their sense of being ignored or left behind.'[20]

Milanović believes the hard-pressed Western middle classes are the victims of what he calls the second Kuznets curve: the first – in the industrial revolution years – is the story of a sharp rise in inequality as incomes diverged at the outset of industrialisation. But then we saw inequality decrease as Western societies developed welfare states financed by higher rates of taxation on income and capital. By the late 1970s, as a result, inequality in Britain had been substantially reduced.

But a second wave of inequality began in the 1980s with the adoption of policies to deregulate, privatise and liberalise. This led to what Milanović calls the second Kuznets curve – the story of how incomes at the very top started to diverge from the rest as wages at the top rose fast and as the same people used their capital to earn high rates of return. Inequalities, he suggests, will widen as a privileged minority of 'millennials' inherit substantial sums of wealth while the rest who have little parental financial support find it difficult to buy their first home.[21]

This will change the patterns of inequality and how we view them across the whole world. Until recently, Western countries were so far ahead of the developing world in wealth and income per head that 70 per cent of the world's inequality could be explained by your location – by whether you were fortunate enough to be born in a rich county or a poor country. Over the next few decades living standards in China will converge with the West and the focus will move from the wide disparities in wealth and income between countries to the disparities within the same country. Soon your class position will come to explain around 50 per cent of the world's inequalities.[22] Indeed, inequalities could worsen if the returns to capital remain higher than returns from employment and if more middle-class skilled jobs are computerised or offshored. 'How long will the current upswing in the Kuznets wave continue in the rich world and when and how will it stop?' Milanović asks. 'I am sceptical that it will be overturned soon,' he says.[23]

Milanović helps us explain why there is anger and bitterness among skilled workers and middle-income earners who were, once, beneficiaries of industrial change. It is unrealistic, he concludes, to expect that the type of jobs that people will be employed to do in the future are going to be protected from foreign competition and be anything other than precarious. 'It's a perfect storm,' he says. 'It's been forgotten by the Establishment in the rich countries that you have to pay attention to the losers … [or face] a political backlash.'[24]

The patterns described by Milanović have meant that in the UK, the top 1 per cent have doubled their share of the national income: between 1990 and 2013–14 their share of income has risen from 5.7 per cent to 8.3 per cent.[25] For the first time since the Second World War, middle- and lower-income parents with little to pass on in inheritance to their children are worried that their children will not fare as well as them. The economist and now ITN political editor, Robert Peston, detects a European-wide phenomenon – 'year after year of low growth and high unemployment which has prompted millions of Europeans to fear that globalisation and the EU is enriching the privileged few at their expense.'[26]

While most British cities have done well – as urban and regional centres for such fast-growing sectors as retail, finance, entertainment and universities and colleges – towns have been unable to replace their traditional manufacturing industries and indeed have simultaneously lost jobs in retail, finance and entertainment to the cities. So, while Manchester has become Europe's biggest education centre, with more than 80,000 students, nearby towns such as Bury, Burnley and Oldham have lost out badly as their citizens lose jobs in traditional iron, steel and textile industries and at the same time gravitate to nearby cities for shopping, entertainment and sport.[27]

And economic upheaval has undoubtedly led – at least in the short term – to a more protectionist view of what is seen, in Anthony Giddens' words, as an out-of-control 'runaway world'.[28] And while a former President of the EU Commission, Jacques Delors, wanted us to see Europe as 'a shelter in a world turned upside down from globalisation,' many people blame Europe for the downside of globalisation and look to national leaders to shelter, insulate, protect, or, at least, cushion them in the face of these bewildering and seemingly alien forces.[29] Matthew Goodwin and Caitlin Milazzo have spoken of 'social groups that are distinctly unlikely to perceive the EU as bringing any benefits – the financially insecure, who have few or no qualifications and little flexibility, who are (or feel) more exposed to competition as a result of the Single Market and the free movement of labour, and who feel under threat from rapid economic change. The Eurosceptic vote, some argue, is driven mainly by (this) group, and in response to these economic considerations.'[30] Polling evidence supports this thesis. Both the UK Social Attitudes Survey and the UK General Election Survey show that support for continued membership is highest among young graduates in white collar occupations but is lowest amongst those without any educational qualifications and especially among older people in this position. Those people who feel most threatened by global change are most likely to blame the European Union for their fate or at least be more sympathetic to the idea of leaving.

'Bringing control back home'

Even many who have benefited with material gain feel there has been a cultural loss. 'The fearful and fearsome reaction against growing inequality, social dislocation and loss of identity in the midst of vast wealth creation, unprecedented mobility and ubiquitous connectivity,' writes Nathan Gardels, editor of the *World Post*, 'is a mutiny, really, against globalisation so audacious and technological change so rapid that it can barely be absorbed.'[31] Statements such as 'Britain is not the country I was born into' or 'Britain is barely recognisable from the country I used to know' express a strong sense that things are 'slipping out of control'. This gives rise, according to Goodwin and Milazzo, to 'concerns over cultural issues like immigration and perceived threats to identity, culture and values. The argument is that anxieties over European integration are less about trade, regulation and economics than about a pooling of national sovereignty and communities. The EU and its enlargement drives public concerns because it fuels not only the expansion of economic markets, but also the integration of different peoples and national cultures.'[32] A survey analysed by Goodwin found that when voters were prompted with concerns about what is happening to our British identity, Labour 'Leave' vote rose from 27 per cent to 34 per cent and the 'Remain' vote fell from 53 per cent to 50 per cent. The Conservative 'Leave' vote rose from 49 per cent to 53 per cent. Overall, when cultural concerns were raised with the public, the total 'Remain' vote fell to 39 per cent, while the 'Leave' vote rose to 41 per cent.[33]

British responses to changes happening around us are not dissimilar from views expressed across mainland Europe. When people all across Europe were asked to respond to the statement – 'there are too many foreigners in my country, sometimes I feel like a stranger in my own country' – 50 per cent agreed. In France, Germany and Italy the figures were 47 per cent, 53 per cent and 70 per cent respectively. An equally provocative statement was made about the effects of migration on the welfare state. In Britain 59 per cent agreed that foreigners were a burden on the welfare system and only 41 per cent disagreed. But in Germany, France and Italy, the figure was as high – 58 per cent to 42 per cent in Germany and 59 per cent to 41 per cent in France and Italy. In Poland, which has relatively few immigrants, 71 per cent of interviewees believed that foreigners were a burden.[34]

Thus what begins as a set of economic grievances about the impact of global change can easily descend into something akin to a set of cultural concerns that lead citizens to believe that their country is changing out of all recognition and is a spur for anti-globalisation movements – and a wide-range of protectionist, nationalist and anti-immigrant parties across Europe. And, while their appeal and emphasis vary depending on the specific traditions of the country, the common theme is the desire 'to bring control home' – out of the hands of what are often seen as anonymous and impersonal decision-makers in faraway places who currently seem to determine our fate.

Political parties used to be judged by whether they offered a viable alternative; now people will vote for a candidate that expresses their anger, even if they fail to provide any answers, and this can give encouragement to political forces whose main weapons include blaming foreigners, targeting immigrants and engendering a siege mentality across Europe. 'I really believe that our generation of politicians can for the first time make a difference and get back what belongs to us, which is national sovereignty,' stated the Netherlands far-right leader, Geert Wilders.[35] In France, the anti-EU politician, Marine Le Pen, argues that 'the basic problem is that the state no longer protects you.'[36] These 'populist movements' represent 'a refusal to live in the world as it is and a desire to go back to the way it used to be,' writes Tim Bale, arguing: 'It's symbolic of a wider worry of the way the world is changing.'[37] Or, as Paul Ames puts it, all across Europe, despite the risks, the economic appeal of nationalism continues to grow and this is 'fast reshaping the continent's political landscape, blurring traditional left-right divides and throwing up surprising – and disturbing – new alignments.'[38]

Twentieth-century political debate focused on how to change systems of production and distribution in modern industrial societies, and made social class the predominant and determining factor in people's affiliations. Twenty-first century alignments revolve around identity. In response to insecurities people experience in a rapidly changing and unfamiliar world an increasingly resonant claim is not that 'we the working class have lost out and are being left behind' but that 'we the British people have lost out and are being left behind'. And for many this is expressed in an anger about the way immigration encouraged by European Union membership puts pressure on established local communities. 'Those who feel most negatively towards immigration – who simultaneously feel that migration is having negative effects on Britain's economy, culture and welfare state – have nearly a 50 per cent likelihood of being an "outer",' conclude Goodwin and Milazzo. 'In contrast, those who hold more positive attitudes toward immigration – who simultaneously feel that migration is good for Britain's economy and culture and is not a burden on the welfare state – have only an 11 per cent likelihood of voting to leave the EU.'[39]

While a new report from the European Policy Centre, *Europe's Troublemakers – The populist challenge to foreign policy,* has no doubt that populism will remain part of the political landscape, it suggests there is something to be done about it, calling politicians to address the root of the problems that create populism in the first place.[40] For as attractive a solution as it may appear on the surface, we cannot simply 'bring control back home'. The problems that have caused protectionism and nationalism cannot be solved by protectionism and nationalism. And many left-of-centre parties struggle too to find answers: they now know that they cannot just pull the old national levers of state control 'to bring power back home' – through nationalisation, import controls, capital controls and other types of protectionist policies – with impunity. Nation state-only policies offer no solution to climate change and pollution which do not recognise geographical borders. Nor is there any solution to financial instability without recognising the interconnected nature of the world's financial system and acting in concert to manage it. Nor is there any solution to inequality without clamping down on the widespread use of tax havens and that requires international agreement for exchange of information and if necessary sanctions on tax evaders. But in Paul Mason's words social democratic parties do not ask and cannot answer the question 'what would a non-neoliberal centrist socialism look like?'[41]

But there is one starting point for those seeking answers: to show that we will have more control of their lives – and our national interests will be best served – not by retreating into our national silos but by embracing more effective forms of co-operation. As I seek to argue in the next chapter, we have to balance the autonomy we desire with the co-operation we need. And doing so will involve us working closely with our European partners to manage globalisation in the interests of the British people. This is the modern case for being part of the European Union.

CHAPTER SIX

All the autonomy we can secure, all the co-operation we need

At the turn of the century, just after the launch of the Euro, I found that tax harmonisation had moved to the centre of the European Union agenda. Corporate tax harmonisation – a standard corporation tax rate charged across the whole of Europe – was not just a distant prospect but a very real threat. VAT rate bands and exemptions were already harmonised – as we found when we tried to abolish the rate of VAT on domestic and electricity bills and instead had to settle for a 5 per cent minimum. The immediate threat, however, was the imposition of a European-wide tax on savings. The plan was to set a rate of tax on dividends on all forms of savings across Europe – a single tax which, while collected by national governments, would be the same for the whole of the European Union.

While the demand for tax harmonisation was a European Commission initiative, the proposal was given added urgency by tax avoidance by German savers who were setting up bank accounts in Luxembourg. Ordinary German citizens would travel across the border once a year to collect their dividends from Luxembourg banks, well away from the clutches of the German taxman. And attempts to persuade these individuals to declare their savings income had proved fruitless: Luxembourg's bank secrecy laws made sure of that.

The answer the Germans came up with was to centralise tax decisions and to adopt one single savings tax rate throughout Europe.

This accorded with broader European Commission ambitions across the European Union, and many countries saw the harmonisation of taxes as the next stage of European integration after the currency union. When attending my first meeting of the European Group of Finance Ministers in 1997, I was surprised that the discussion was dominated by a debate not about job creation or economic competitiveness – Europe's real challenges – but about the inevitability of uniform taxes across income and corporation taxes as well as savings taxes.

The movement for tax harmonisation reached its high watermark with the Commission's savings tax proposal. I was instinctively against it and I argued that even a federal state like the United States did not need to harmonise taxes to make its single currency work. Across the United States, sales, corporate and income tax rates varied from state to state without rendering economic management impossible. But the savings tax was a hard case for Britain to oppose: many finance ministers suspected that our reservations were nothing more than a reflection of the vested interests of the City of London where large sums of savings were deposited. And London's desire to defend the *status quo* came up against the strong ethical imperative that something needed to be done to deal with tax avoidance and retrieve billions of lost revenues that were depriving our (and other countries') public services of resources – and was, anyway, unfair to millions of law-abiding citizens.

When the debate began, Britain was in a minority of one in opposing a EU-wide savings tax. We all agreed of course that savings should not be moved from one country to another within the European Union simply to avoid tax. But I had to persuade the other Member States that there were ways other than harmonisation, centralisation and blanket uniformity for dealing with the problem. I quickly saw that those supporting the harmonised tax had one fundamental difficulty with their proposal: if we legislated to impose a savings tax in Europe, thousands of savers would simply move their money outside Europe to Liechtenstein, Switzerland, Hong Kong or another part of the world – quite possibly with the expert assistance of lawyers in Panama. European-wide tax harmonisation would prove powerless to prevent people using countries outside of the EU to deposit savings without paying tax. And this was the crux of the argument I put. To impose a European tax that accelerated the flow of savings out of Europe would deprive all European countries of revenue and be counterproductive and worse than useless – it would be simply cutting off our noses to spite our faces.

My answer was to reject harmonisation of tax rates in favour of an exchange of tax information between national tax authorities – a proposal that each country who had foreign savers should report details on their dividends to the home country of the saver. Of course it was also an answer that could only work if it applied to all tax jurisdictions that could be persuaded to adopt it, rather than only to European Union jurisdictions. While we could not impose a European savings tax on Liechtenstein, we did however have a chance of persuading them to exchange information on their foreign savers. So I proposed that we negotiate exchange of information agreements with Switzerland, the United States, Hong Kong and in time other countries. In short, we had to recognise that we were living in an integrated global economy, and that the success of our policies depended on co-operation with countries both inside as well as outside of the European Union. No one European country has the muscle to bring Switzerland or Hong Kong into line. Of course in the absence of a collective European position nothing would have happened: without the clout of the EU there would have been little chance of persuading other states to help us tackle this tax avoidance. Europe had to act together as one. Without doing so we could not persuade others to join us.

It took many months of negotiation to persuade fellow members of the European Union to support the UK position, but eventually the majority of fourteen to one against us became a unanimous

decision in favour of a new policy based on the exchange of information. And over time we persuaded Switzerland and other tax
authorities outside the EU to adopt our proposals.

The savings tax controversy is important to tax reform because
exchange of information will become an essential tool in addressing
the loss of around €1 trillion of public revenues across Europe
because of the use of tax havens and tax avoidance, and $7 trillion
across the world.

While it has taken time to get Luxembourg and Austria on board,
Europe's system of automatic exchange of information led directly
to the initiative that President Sarkozy and I championed at the G20
in 2009 to blacklist 'unco-operative' tax havens; to the Multilateral
Competent Authority Agreement on common reporting standards
for exchanging information on tax, which 80 countries have now
signed; and to a unilateral US initiative under their Foreign Account
Tax Compliance Act which required tax havens to report the offshore
accounts of US citizens. In April 2016, a joint French-British-Spanish-
German-Italian initiative proposed to go further by agreeing to
exchange information on the beneficial ownership of trusts, although
not all trusts were included. Clearly Britain cannot root out tax
evasion and end tax avoidance on our own. We will have to persuade
America and others of the need both for the automatic exchange of
information and for public registers of beneficial ownerships and,
more than ever, we will need the clout of a united Europe – and then
the strength of the G20 and the Organisation of Economic Cooperation and Development – to bring tax havens into line.

But the savings tax debate raises an even more important set of
lessons for decision-making across a wide range of areas in the
European Union. Our European neighbours came to reject a
proposal for tax harmonisation, which involved centralisation of
decision-making and a blanket uniformity in approach, in favour of
a more flexible policy, namely the exchange of information. Coming
just after the turn of the century, it represented the beginnings of

more general shift in outlook. First, we saw decision-making firmly grounded in intergovernmental negotiation and compromise – a top-down European Commission dictat was rejected. Second, with each country still free to set its own tax rates, we saw the blanket uniformity that uprooted existing national systems of taxation rejected in favour of a flexibility of approach which respected indigenous traditions and ways of doing things. Third, we saw that the importance of European unity was not that we did exactly the same things but that we used our collective strength to negotiate the best deal with the rest of the world and so, as individual nations, we achieved far more by working together than we could have achieved in isolation on our own. In short, the savings tax decision demonstrated a United Europe of States at work rather than a United States of Europe. And the controversy showed that, with its ideas and insights, Britain could lead Europe. Outside the European Union we would have had no influence on the savings tax debate. Inside we were not only part of the discussion but shaped it.

In the previous chapters, I made the case that in an increasingly interdependent world, we have no choice but to embrace international co-operation and co-ordination and that, for Britain, co-operation in the European Union was the best way forward. But I also argued that every nation in Europe has traditions, customs and a strong sense of identity – and a desire, where possible, to make their own decisions – which has to be respected. In this chapter, I will show that Britain can best achieve a balance between the autonomy it desires and the co-operation it needs by being part of the European Union and working to reform it. I begin by taking on the assertion that Europe will impose a federal solution upon Britain. I argue that the modern European Union is, instead, coming to be defined more by its greater flexibility than by an older fixation with federalist uniformity: allowing varying degrees of integration across different spheres of policy and in different ways for different Member States. I then examine other ways of balancing autonomy and co-operation and look at models that have been canvassed as alternatives to membership of the European Union – in particular the Norwegian option and the Swiss option. I argue that none of these would enable Britain to strike a better balance between autonomy and co-operation than membership of the European Union. Finally, I address the argument – advanced by prominent proponents of Brexit – that international co-operation through the European Union has to be rejected because it undermines Britain's national sovereignty.

The high tide of European federalism

Some 'Leave' campaigners argue that it is impossible for the United Kingdom to strike the right balance between autonomy and co-operation within the European Union. They argue that the European Union is moving inexorably towards becoming a federal superstate. On this view, Britain will be forced to accept greater economic and political integration against its will, and this will restrict our autonomy and limit our ability to control our own affairs. This view assumes that, far from receding, the high tide of the movement towards a federal Europe has not yet been reached.

In the 1980s, I met the President of the European Commission, Jacques Delors, many times – often with my friend and fellow Scot, John Smith, who died so tragically in 1994. I remember vividly the time when sitting in his Presidential office at the Commission headquarters in Brussels, Delors explained to John and me – half joking, half serious – that Mrs Thatcher hated him for eight reasons, and then went on to list them. She hated him, he said, because he was a socialist, a trade unionist, a collectivist, a bureaucrat and because he was French, pro-European, an internationalist and a federalist.

This was in the late 1980s when Delors was at the peak of his powers – and when he made a fateful intervention. In July 1988 Delors added unscripted words to a speech proclaiming his view that 80 per cent of all legislation on tax as well as on economic and social policy would be initiated and executed at a European-level in the not-too-distant future. His loyal assistant Pascal Lamy immediately recognised that Delors had struck a disastrous note, later writing: 'I buried my head in my hands as I heard Delors make this claim.'[1] Delors was seeking what he called 'an embryo European Government'.[2] But he had overreached himself, and in doing so allowed his detractors to find a way back.

In 1990, Delors made a similar mistake, when he said that he wanted the European Parliament to be the democratic body of the European Community, the Commission to be the executive and the Council of Ministers to be the Senate. It was this speech that led Mrs Thatcher to famously exclaim to each of his three proposals: 'No. No. No!' And it is this spectre of a federalist superstate that still drives Eurosceptic opinion today.

For decades, of course, leaders across Europe have made the case for wholesale integration. As far back as 1930, when France was concerned to contain a rising Germany, the French Prime Minister Aristide Briand proposed a 'federal bond for Europe' that was to be more than an 'economic association'.[3] Post-war Germans too spoke of a federal Europe, often as part of their desire to secure support for bringing East and West Germany into a single German state – something they knew could not be agreed unless a united Germany was contained within a united Europe.

Yet as my explanation of the retreat from tax harmonisation shows, the high tide of European integrationist ambitions was reached at the beginning of the century and has since been receding. Some see the turning point as 2005 when the French people rejected President Jacques Chirac's proposal for a new European Constitution. 'Ever since then, we've been on a slippery slope,' Fredrik Erixon, the director of the European Centre for International Political Economy in Brussels has suggested. 'Every elected national leader knows there is no political mileage to try to lead on European issues or push for more integration.

The European idea is now a rapidly declining trend,' he argues.[4]

Even some of the governments of Europe's founding members have put a brake on further European integration. While Germany has supported – at least in theory – a political union, it has come close to hollowing out some of the key integrationist projects including fiscal and banking union. There can be no doubt that pressures will grow for more integration within the Eurozone – from which Britain, has of course an opt-out – but the same kinds of strains and tensions – and differing priorities – exist within the Eurozone as within the European Union. As we shall see later, Berlin's resistance to the idea of debt mutualisation has been an important brake on economic and political integration and the German Finance Minister has opposed any fiscal union that could in any way be seen in the way fiscal unions normally are – as a transfer union. He does not wish to see German taxpayers transfer more resources to Greece's pensioners or their unemployed.

It is clear then that, even without British reservations, divisions would run deep between EU Member States on the extent of economic integration. Just as European unanimity could not be found on fiscal union, despite many attempts to achieve it, so too agreement cannot be reached on the taxation of goods – such as cigarettes and alcohol – where politicians have placed national traditions, cultures and preferences well above any desire for harmonisation. Member States resist plans for European-wide income taxes and demand, as we shall see, special exemptions to suit their own national agendas. When President Juncker stated in his 2015 State of the Union speech that there is 'not enough Europe in this Union' and 'not enough Union in this Europe', he did so not as a call to action but out of frustration that he could not achieve more.[5]

While the European Union has the authority to override national governments on issues relating to trade and the Single Market, it lacks what in earlier times were the two fundamental building blocks of any successful state: the power to declare war and peace (including the possession of an army) and the power to raise taxes. Without armed forces, the European Union cannot discharge what is for many the first and most fundamental duty of any government, namely offering security. Without the power to tax at its discretion, the European Union cannot pay for defence or make easily redeemable promises about living standards and the welfare state.

And I believe that it would be one of history's most dramatic turnarounds if, in only one generation, what was a divided, fragmented and quarrelling continent, composed of nations proud of their own identities, quickly became a centralised federal state. The truth is that for all the global forces at work pushing greater homogeneity, there are as many forces that are marking Europe out as much for its centrifugal tendencies as for its centripetal ones. And this is not going to change anytime soon. 'In the 21st century, Europe will undoubtedly continue to consist of nation states, each with its own language and history,' the former German Chancellor, Helmut Schmidt, said in a valedictory address to the German Social Democratic Party in 2011. 'For that reason, Europe will definitely not become a federal state,' he concluded.[6]

A flexible Europe?

As we will see, while the old division of competences into three pillars – European Communities, Common Foreign and Security Policy and Police and Judicial Co-operation in Criminal Matters – has been formally abandoned, the European Union's new scheme of exclusive, shared and supporting competences does not reflect the true picture. And I want to suggest that the modern European Union is becoming an association that is defined less by its uniformity than by a tendency towards greater flexibility, one in which there are varying degrees of integration across different spheres of policy and between different countries.

The Schengen Area, for example, guarantees free movement between Member States without border controls, but a number of Member States, namely the United Kingdom and Ireland, do not participate fully in Schengen co-operation. At the same time Norway, Iceland, Liechtenstein and Switzerland are part of Schengen, despite not being members of the EU.

Flexibility is advanced by the highly visible abstentions of Member States across the Area of Freedom, Security and Justice and from the Eurozone; 'emergency brakes' in the Common Foreign and Security Policy and in the Area of Freedom, Security and Justice on judicial co-operation in criminal matters; Spain and Italy's opt-out from the unified EU patent; Sweden's opt-out from *Snus* (loose tobacco); and of course the transitional arrangements in the Accession Treaties accompanying the last three waves of enlargement in 2004, 2007 and 2013.

This set of opt-outs and exemptions has led one group of academics to rationalise the development of the EU as a 'system of differentiated integration'. In their article, *The European Union as a System of Differentiated Integration: Interdependence, Politicization and Differentiation*, Frank Schimmelfennig, Dirk Leuffen and Berthold Rittberger state: 'Rather than restricting differentiation to a temporary, accidental, or non-systematic feature of European integration, we argue that differentiation is an essential and, most likely, enduring characteristic of the EU.' And this, they suggest, will grow as the European Union widens its membership. 'Differentiation has been a concomitant of deepening and widening, gaining in importance as the EU's tasks, competencies, and membership have grown.'[7]

The authors proceed to distinguish between two types of differentiation that they term 'vertical differentiation' and 'horizontal differentiation'. By 'vertical differentiation' they mean that policy areas have been integrated at different speeds and reached different levels of centralisation over time. By 'horizontal differentiation' they refer

to the territorial dimension, specifically that many forms of integration are neither uniformly nor exclusively valid in the European
Union's Member States. The authors draw a further distinction
between internal horizontal differentiation – where many Member
States do not participate in all EU policies, and external horizontal
differentiation – where some non-members participate in selected
EU policies. A policy area is characterised by *internal differentiation*
if at least one Member State does not participate in integration – the
Euro is the most prominent case in point – and by *external differentiation* if at least one non-Member State participates: this is true for
the internal market, which extends into the European Economic Area
(with Iceland, Liechtenstein and Norway). Internal and external
differentiation can go together, as in the Schengen Area, which
combines the membership of EU non-members and the non-
membership of EU members.

Differentiated integration is an academic term to characterise
what we now have – flexibility in ways of co-operating – and this
development has been variously described as 'a multi-speed Europe'
(states heading in the same direction but at different speeds), as a
'multi-tier', '*à la carte*' or 'variable geometry Europe', or as a 'Europe
of three pillars' – with different states pursuing different forms and
levels of integration. While the boundaries between different
categories are often unclear and there is often substantial overlap
between one characterisation and another, what is clear is that greater
flexibility in the ways we co-operate is becoming the new normal.
And it is a multi-tier rather than a multi-speed vision of Europe's
future that is becoming more commonplace: less is now heard about
all Member States heading towards the same destination but at
different speeds – a multi-speed Europe – and we now hear more
about Member States enjoying different kinds and degrees of participation – a multi-tier Europe.

And it is easy to see why it is that not just Britain but many other
countries favour that greater flexibility in their relationship with the

European Union. Anyone assessing the development of the EU since the 1970s would discover that Europe's desire for political unity and conformity has often had to take second place to the need to break deadlock by compromise. This has led to opt-outs, exemptions and transitional arrangements which can become permanent. Even if countries' reasons for supporting differentiation are varied, the practice is now endorsed not only by Eurosceptics – as a way out of decisions they oppose – but also by pragmatic pro-Europeans, who consider it necessary to hold a larger and more diverse Union of 28 states together.

An important consequence of the EU's development as a system of differentiated integration is that intergovernmentalism is emerging as the dominant structure of decision-making. All the major decisions on the bailouts and future structure of the Eurozone and on migration have been made in the European Council by Europe's leaders. There has been a decisive shift in the balance of power from the European Commission to the European Council. Ten years ago the Commission did not just have a formal right to initiate new policy but was the driving force for change. Decisions are not just formally made by the Council of Ministers but they are initiated and the fine print is negotiated there between governments. And because decisions are now made by 28 national governments that have to resolve differences between one another, we are likely to see more opt-outs, enhanced flexibility and a greater proclivity towards mutual recognition of each others' practices. 'The references to ever closer union among the peoples,' said the European Council itself at its meeting in June 2014, 'are compatible with different paths of integration being available for different Member States and do not compel all Member States to aim for a common destination.'[8] This statement was echoed in the agreement reached during Britain's recent re-negotiation, which now promises a treaty change to clarify that 'the UK … is not committed to further political integration into the EU … The references to ever closer union do not apply to the UK.'[9] But perhaps it is more significant that the statement categorically affirmed a broader agreement about the future of the European Union: that the concept of ever closer union cannot be used to extend the powers of the European Union, or be used as a basis for its decisions by the European Court of Justice, or employed as an argument to prevent powers being handed back to Member States. The 2011 Sovereignty Act contains a further safeguard for Britain: requiring a referendum if and when any aspect of sovereignty becomes the competence of the European Union.

In a system of differentiated integration, EU policies are likely to continue to vary in both their level of centralisation and their territorial reach. In short, Member States are and will be able to influence the balance that is struck between their autonomy and their level of co-operation within the EU.

Far from being caricatured as some great adventure in federalism embarked on by our leaders in our name, could the European Union come over time to be seen more as a practical and workmanlike attempt to allow a collection of small and medium-sized states to do together things they could never achieve separately – in other words, a United Europe of States, as opposed to a United States of Europe?

The alternatives to the EU

Many Eurosceptics argue that Britain can achieve a better balance between autonomy and co-operation outside the European Union – either as part of the European Free Trade Association (EFTA) or as part of the European Economic Association (EEA). That way, it is argued, we can still enjoy the trading benefits of the European Union without the huge costs of membership and without the political baggage of accepting a European regulatory framework.

The Norway option

Opponents of the European Union say that the EEA shows it is possible to be part of the European market but not part of the European Union. One road to the EEA is to join EFTA first. Brexit campaigners say Norway is able to benefit from membership of the Single Market without being subject, as Britain is, to EU regulation and bureaucracy. They argue that we would negotiate an even better deal than Norway because we are a larger country and a greater trading partner, buying more from Europe than we sell to it. Thus it is claimed that there would be no difficulty in a non-EU Britain securing a preferential free trade agreement with the EU. But are they right?

It certainly wouldn't be simple. Securing the Norway option means that we would first need to apply to join EFTA, which would have to agree to our membership unanimously. When the agreement was adopted between the European Union and EFTA, the EFTA nations were treated favourably because they were seen as future European Union members. The final terms of entry, if Britain were to apply to join EFTA, would involve our neighbours balancing off our importance as a large market with resentment against us for walking out of the European Union.

While there is no formal membership fee for being part of the EEA, the UK would still be required to contribute financially to the operation of the European Union, through a separate EEA grant. Norway is the tenth largest contributor to the EU per capita: it paid per capita contributions of £106 in 2011, compared to the UK's net contribution of £128 (i.e. after rebates).[10] If the UK left the EU and instead contributed to the EU budget on the same basis as Norway, its contributions would fall only by around 17 per cent (including rebates, but before taking into account the other financial benefits of EU membership such as agricultural subsidies).

Moreover, the UK would be required to retain a range of legislation: over 11,500 EU legal acts have been incorporated into the EEA Agreement as of 2015.[11] This is determined by whether an EU act has EEA relevance. Although incorporation can be delayed in the most controversial cases, it normally goes ahead. Rather than freeing Britain from the EU's laws and regulations, any EEA agreement Britain might sign would comprise EU law backed up by procedures designed to ensure that the rules are applied in the same way in the EEA-EFTA states as they are in the European Union.

However, the UK would lose all formal voting rights and ability to formally influence that legislation. Rules affecting trade within the Single Market are set at the EU-level. Norway, Iceland and Liechtenstein have no seat around the negotiating table and no voting power – although they may be able to exert some 'soft influence' through membership of committees. The UK would therefore not be adequately represented in decision-making and legislative processes that would have direct consequences for the country.

Further, the EEA and EFTA states have no MEPs or votes in the European Parliament, no veto in the European Council, no votes in the Council of Ministers, no European Commission staff and no judges or staff at the European Court of Justice – notwithstanding that those states are affected by the decisions of all of these institutions.

In February 2001, this led the then Norwegian Prime Minister, Jens Stoltenberg, to call Norway's relationship with the European Union a 'fax democracy' – in that Norwegian officials sat by government fax machines waiting for the latest rules to arrive from Brussels.[12] More recently, Nikolai Alstrup, the spokesperson on European Affairs for the Norwegian Conservative Party, cautioned: 'If you want to run the EU, stay in the EU. If you want to be run by the EU, feel free to join us in the EEA.'[13]

But while EFTA states like Norway are not subject to monitoring by EU institutions, they are supervised by the EFTA Surveillance Authority (like the European Commission) and the EFTA Court.

EFTA's procedures for dealing with infringements are similar to the mechanisms for monitoring compliance in EU Member States. And although the EFTA Court does not have the same authority as the European Court of Justice to issue binding decisions – it can only issue recommendations and advisory opinions – it is not correct to say that outside the EU and inside EFTA Britain would be free from supervision and the possibility of reproach.

Under the Norway option, the UK would no longer be covered by trade agreements entered into by the EU, but could join existing EFTA trade agreements. Currently, EFTA has 25 free trade agreements covering 36 countries, compared to more than 50 countries that are covered by the EU's trade agreements. One of the arguments advanced by 'Leave' campaigners is that the UK could potentially strike quicker and deeper trade agreements, including with countries such as China, with whom the EU is stalling on a deal. Yet the EFTA states have no agreement with the United States and, depending on the outcome of the Transatlantic Trade and Investment Partnership (TTIP) and Trans-Pacific Partnership (TPP) negotiations, EFTA countries – who are excluded from these big treaties which give preferential access to their signatories – could face new market access restrictions, discrimination and trade distortion, even in situations where they already have free trade agreements.

What would be the overall impact of leaving the European Union to join the EEA? When Open Europe conducted a survey of what they called 'the 100 costliest EU-derived rules in force in the UK' – which collectively impose a cost of £33.3 billion on the UK economy – they discovered that 93 of them would apply anyway if the UK joined the EEA.[14] All of the five single costliest pieces of EU-derived legislation in force in the UK would continue to apply in the EEA, including the Renewable Energy Strategy, the Working Time Directive and the Temporary Agency Workers Directive.

In short, it is not surprising that the Norwegian leaders advise against the Norway option: it would not be in Britain's interests either.

The Switzerland option

Switzerland is in a different position from Norway. It is not a member of the EEA, but only a member of EFTA. A Swiss referendum held in December 1992 rejected EEA membership; and, in 1994, Switzerland and the EU started negotiations about a special relationship outside of the EEA.

Why did Switzerland need an agreement with the European Union? For the same reasons as Norway – to reduce the risk of discrimination against the country and its companies. Switzerland participates in specific parts of the Single Market on the basis of bilateral agreements concluded with the EU in 1999 and 2004. All in all, there are 20 principal bilateral agreements and around a hundred supplementary accords. The important point to note is that Switzerland enjoys access to certain aspects of the Single Market, although only in areas where it can successfully negotiate bilateral agreements. As a condition of access, it is required to comply with the relevant EU law and regulations.

Switzerland does not have an agreement with the EU in respect of financial services. Major Swiss banks are able to get around this block on cross-border market access by establishing subsidiaries in a EU Member State, often in the UK. However, this approach results in higher costs because it requires additional personnel and separate capitalisation. Claude-Alain Margelisch, CEO of the Swiss Bankers' Association, warned in 2013 that the impact of new EU regulations 'is a further deterioration in the *status quo*' for Swiss banks and wealth managers. He concluded that 'in the end we may even have to negotiate a services agreement for medium- and long-term access to the EU market.'[15] Any agreement with the EU which excludes financial services would be unsatisfactory for Britain.

Moreover, in order to gain access to the Single Market and thus the free movement of goods, services and capital, Switzerland had to accept the EU principle of freedom of movement of workers, something it is now objecting to with possible repercussions from the European Union. In fact, like Norway – also a Schengen member – Switzerland currently has far more EU migrants per head than the United Kingdom. Proportionate to their populations, net EU immigration was in 2013 four times higher in Switzerland than in the UK. Today 15.6 per cent of the Swiss population were born in another EU country, while only 4.2 per cent of the UK population were born in another EU country.[16] The Swiss experience highlights the improbability of a state outside the EU being granted access to the free movement of goods, services and capital without accepting some requirements on the free movement of workers.

But how much autonomy does Switzerland have to shape its own decisions when in return for Single Market access it has to implement Union law it plays no part in formulating? In this respect, Switzerland is in a worse position than Norway, for unlike Norway, the Swiss have few consultative structures in place to exert 'soft influence' in the EU decision-making process. In fact, because they came to the view that they had too little say on European Union legislation, Switzerland recently sought to gain a right to extensive consultation and early engagement in the drafting and deliberation of new European laws.

Adopting the Swiss model would not only leave us implementing laws we did not shape but also paying financial contributions. While the Swiss contribution is substantially lower than the Norwegian contribution, this is partly because – as a neutral country – Switzerland is not part of the Common Foreign and Security Policy and does not contribute to its costs.

Brexit supporters portray a world where, freed from the European Union, we are also freed from constraints on our ability to act independently but this objective could not be achieved through the Norway option or the Switzerland option. Like Norway and Switzerland, we would find ourselves a member of the EEA or EFTA tied into arrangements that bind us to the standards and regulations of the EU Single Market but without any say in their formulation. Like

Norway and Switzerland, we would have to agree to translate all relevant EU laws into our domestic laws without any greater ability to shape them or veto them. Like Norway and Switzerland, who also contribute to the European budget, we would pay out money to the European Union but without a say in its direction.

The WTO option

There is another option: what is sometimes called the WTO option – to rely on the World Trade Organisation rules for trading access to mainland European markets. This would leave Britain in the same position as third countries which do not have free trade agreements with the EU. Specifically, UK businesses would then be subject to the EU Common External Tariff and this would reduce their competitiveness compared to competitors from the EU or from countries with free trade agreements (which may soon include the EU-US agreement). Tariffs could be imposed on around 90 per cent of the UK's goods exported to the EU. These tariffs could range from 10 per cent for cars, to 11 per cent for clothing to around 15 per cent for food. WTO terms are more limited for many services and, specifically, the UK would not enjoy its current level of preferential access to the Single Market for financial services. It is difficult to see what we would gain: UK businesses wanting to sell their products into mainland Europe would still have to abide by and adhere to EU-set product standards and regulations. The difference is that we would not have any influence in their formulation. It is difficult to see how this offers a better balance between the autonomy we desire and the co-operation we need and it is impossible to deny that we would lose influence within Europe.

What are our chances of negotiating a better deal than Norway or Switzerland if we leave? Eurosceptics argue Europe could ill-afford to retaliate, because we buy more imports from mainland Europe than we sell in exports and thus the rest of the European Union gains more from trade with us than we gain from trade with them. In 2013, we exported £155 billion of goods to the bloc and imported £221 billion of goods to the UK – leaving a deficit on current account of £66 billion. This, they say, supports five million jobs on the continent. However, not only would we be at a disadvantage, negotiating from a position where we have walked away, but as the CBI highlights: 'The UK is more dependent on the EU for its trade than the EU is on the UK. Around half of the UK's total trade is with the EU, while just 8 per cent of EU trade is with the UK.'[17] Our deficit in exports with the rest of the EU has to be weighed against the benefits we gain from access to the European market. Nothing should be said that prejudges a negotiation in the national interest but it is true to say that no one believes that we would be handed a UK-EU free trade agreement that would bring all of the current benefits and incur none of the current costs. Again, 'in' or 'out' of the European Union, Europe remains a crucial market for us – and all the evidence suggests that the best way to secure the best deal for Britain is by leading Europe, not leaving it.

Sovereignty

Achieving the best balance between autonomy and co-operation – and retaining our influence in Europe – is the best way we can meet the needs and aspirations of the British people and achieve the employment creation, financial stability, environmental sustainability and social cohesion we seek. Doing so is the answer to those who say that Britain has lost its ability to influence events and given up on its sovereignty by being part of the European Union. Setting out his 'Leave' argument it is Michael Gove's thesis that 'our membership of the EU stops us being able to choose who makes critical decisions which affect all our lives.' The problem, according to his article, is that 'laws which govern citizens in this country are decided by politicians from other nations who we never elected and can't throw out'.[18] Like Michael Gove, Boris Johnson states that European Union membership is incompatible with parliamentary sovereignty. And so many proponents of Brexit claim that, even if leaving the EU has a price, it is worth paying that price to regain control.

There are, of course, a number of strands to the sovereignty argument. The first is the concept of parliamentary sovereignty. As a matter of fundamental UK constitutional law, Parliament is sovereign. The constitutional mechanism through which the EU treaties have effect in UK law – and EU institutions are able to pass legislation that directly affects the UK – is the European Communities Act 1972, a British parliamentary statute. If the UK wishes to withdraw from the EU, Parliament can simply repeal the European Communities Act. The very fact we are having a referendum – passed into law by Parliament – is testament to the fact that we have not lost our ability to make that decision.

It was Lady Thatcher who recognised that European law is necessary for the EU to function properly when she pressed for the full implementation of the European Single Market. To make all that happen Lady Thatcher was also prepared, as I have shown in the discussion of her government's policy on Europe, to argue for qualified majority voting on key decisions and, in these areas, renounce the veto we held. She recognised that the Single Market needed EU law to enable all companies and consumers – including those based in the UK – to sell and buy products and services across the EU on an equal footing. In this way the sale of chemicals or pesticides, for example, produced in the UK in accordance with the relevant EU legislation, cannot be prohibited by other EU countries. And UK citizens and businesses can enforce their EU legal rights in the courts. In practice, the UK has had more influence over the development of Single Market legislation than most other Member States – and particularly in relation to telecoms, energy and financial services where EU legislation is largely based on the UK model. When

it comes to pharmaceutical regulation and competition law, UK legislation is closely modelled on EU law. Even if the UK were outside the
EU, European competition law would continue to affect us. Access
to the European market would require us to abide by European rules
– but we would cease to have any influence over the future development of that law.

More fundamentally, those who employ the concept of sovereignty against Britain's membership of the European Union assume
an abstract and absolutist notion of sovereignty which ends up
suggesting that power only matters when it is exercised alone.
Johnson and Gove talk of being sovereign as if it were like being
pregnant: one either is or is not. The truth is more complex. Britain
has always pooled sovereignty and in doing so has not lost control
of events. We have signed some 700 international treaties that
impinge on the kind of sovereignty espoused by 'Leave' campaigners.
We have to ask if signing the Convention against Torture or joining
the United Nations or NATO really undermines our ability to control
our own destiny or, instead, are these simply means by which we can
achieve better outcomes than if we acted on our own? Only if we
think that sovereignty does not involve relationships with other
countries and we glory in isolation or solitude, can we cling to the
view that it is absolute. A country can claim complete and absolute
sovereignty yet have no influence on events. 'The castaway alone on
a desert island may be sovereign over all she or he surveys,' wrote
Philip Stephens of *The Financial Times*, but is also 'impotent.'[19] In a
similar vein, David Cameron has warned potential 'Leave' voters
against pursuing what he called the 'illusion of sovereignty'.[20]

When we led an Empire and then created the Commonwealth,
we took on legally binding obligations to act in certain ways and
assumed responsibilities for others that limited our freedom to do as
we wanted. So it is with the European Union. In the real world we
pool sovereignty not to diminish our control over events or our
ability to deliver for the British people but to increase our control

and enhance our ability to deliver. 'Those opposed to Britain's role in Europe argue about sovereignty: that the gains we have made are outweighed by the fact that in many areas national sovereignty is no longer absolute,' Tony Blair said in a speech in 2001. 'My answer is this: I see sovereignty not merely as the ability of a single country to say no, but as the power to maximise our national strength and capacity in business, trade, foreign policy, defence and the fight against crime.' Sovereignty, as he concluded, has 'to be deployed for national advantage. When we isolated ourselves in the past, we squandered our sovereignty – leaving us sole masters of a shrinking sphere of influence.'[21]

And today's world is, indeed, very different from the 17th and 18th centuries, when the notion of sovereignty first took root. National independence is constrained by our international independence, something that is true, as I have suggested, for America which has shared its sovereignty by accepting obligations under NATO (to support other countries under attack), within the World Trade Organisation (to accept others may penalsie them for protectionist policies) and within its own free trade area in North America, NAFTA. Its influence is enhanced by the strength of its international partnerships. 'A country that refuses outright to pool authority,' writes *The Economist*, 'is one that has no control over the pollution drifting over its borders, the standards of financial regulation affecting its economy, the consumer and trade norms to which its exporters and importers are bound, the cleanliness of its seas and the security and economic crises propelling shock waves – migration, terrorism, market volatility – deep into domestic life. To live with globalisation is to acknowledge that many laws (both those devised by governments and those which bubble up at no one's behest) are international beasts whether we like it or not.'[22] So hoarding a sovereignty we cannot deploy is not the answer to the threats posed by climate change, financial crises or cross-border crime and terrorism.

Being pure but impotent – theoretically powerful but practically powerless – is no answer to the environmental, economic and security challenges we face in the world of today. A 21st century conception of sovereignty would focus on maximising a country's capacity to meet the needs and aspirations of its people and seeing the real challenge as securing the right balance between the autonomy we desire, the co-operation we need and the influence we can gain.

Britain has an opt-out from the Euro and from the Schengen agreement on open borders. We are protected – as are other non-Eurozone countries – from discrimination by Eurozone members that might harm our ability to benefit from the Single Market. We are not required – and nor are other non-Eurozone members – to fund Eurozone bailouts. A protocol of the Lisbon Treaty insulates Britain from the effects of the Charter of Fundamental Rights.

And it is important to remind ourselves in conclusion that, as before, the UK government retains complete control over almost every area of our public spending; interest rates; and taxation as well as public services like healthcare, education and public transport.

Delivering the best results for the British people in other areas, however, can only be achieved by balancing this autonomy that we value with the co-operation we need. And in the chapters that follow, I show in detail how Britain can best strike that balance across a range of policy areas – from the economy and social policy, to security and migration – to meet the needs and aspirations of the British people in the 21st century.

PART THREE

Balancing autonomy and co-operation

CHAPTER SEVEN

Can Europe help us create jobs?

During the 32 years I was a Member of Parliament, including the 13 years I was a government minister, first as Chancellor of the Exchequer and then as Prime Minister, the story of industrial Britain can be told through the dramatic change in the fortunes of the mining, textiles, shipbuilding, and iron and steel industries. Indeed, a new chapter in the decline of steel is being written now. But as one group of heavy industries faltered, one sector that has bucked the trend has been the car industry. Today, from a time in the 1980s when the UK produced 900,000 passenger cars, our vehicle manufacturing work-force now produces over 1.5 million cars. The car industry's survival is not because of an absence of crises but because it has weathered its crises. In my time in government, we saw Ford pull out from car assembly, Rover go bankrupt twice, the near collapse of Jaguar and Land Rover during the global financial recession and the battle to keep Vauxhall at Ellesmere Port. The car industry thrives today not because of the domestic market but because nearly 80 per cent of its output is exported, most of it to Europe, with Britain acting as the bridgehead for South Korean, Japanese, Indian and American car producers to sell into mainland Europe. They invest in Britain as their platform for investment in Europe.

Take Nissan, which last year manufactured 500,000 cars at its plant in Sunderland. In total, 120 cars came off the Nissan production line every hour, a tenfold increase on the mid-1980s shortly after the plant opened when just 12 an hour were produced. But fewer than 100,000 of those cars – less than 20 per cent of what they produced – were sold domestically in the UK.[1] The 7,000-plus workforce – and the 40,000 jobs linked to Nissan's supply chain – exist on exporting primarily to mainland Europe.[2] In 2015, 250,000 cars were exported to European Union countries, plus another 100,000 to the rest of Europe if we include non-EU European countries and Russia. Only 50,000 Nissan cars, around 10 per cent of production, were exported to the rest of the world. Nissan's future, like that of the British car industry, is inextricably linked to Europe.

The Sunderland plant is Nissan's main producer in Europe, responsible for production of 70 per cent of all Nissan cars on the continent.[3] It is through Sunderland that Nissan enters the European marketplace. Moreover, Nissan's European Design Centre is located in Paddington, London, which employs around 50 people. Nissan's European Technical Centre is based in Cranfield, Bedfordshire and employs around 500 people. And Nissan's Sunderland plant has the only Nissan Global Training Centre outside Japan.

As 7,000 workers are employed by Nissan, with nearly 40,000 workers benefiting from the company's work, it is reasonable to say that, as half its cars go to the European Union, 3,500 of Nissan's jobs and 20,000 of the supply jobs are dependent on demand from countries in the European Union. Of course, no one is saying these jobs would disappear overnight if the UK left the EU, but the fact is that Nissan in Sunderland is producing not just to sell into Britain, or even to the rest of the world, but to sell into mainland Europe.

Outside the European Union there would be far less incentive for Nissan to make its European investments within the UK. Britain acts as a 'bridgehead' to European markets for the firm. As Trevor Mann, the chief performance officer at Nissan, has argued, Nissan and other multinational companies invest in Britain to export to Europe not just to sell in Britain.[4]

And the Nissan story is not unique: the same story could be told for Honda, Toyota and Vauxhall and for the thousands of firms in the supply chain who are British companies relying on trade with Europe. The automotive industry in Britain as a whole currently provides employment for more than 770,000 people – 161,000 of whom are employed directly in manufacturing.[5] The UK motor vehicle manufacture industry contributed 8 per cent of manufacturing output in 2014.[6] It is a big exporter accounting for 10 per cent of the UK's trade in goods.[7] The UK produced 1.6 million cars and commercial vehicles and almost 2.6 million engines in 2013.[8] As a result, Britain is now the fourth largest vehicle manufacturer in the EU and when it comes to top-of-the-range luxury cars we are second only to Germany.[9] According to Eurostat data, the UK now has the most productive automotive sector in the EU, with an industry-wide turnover of £64 billion and £12 billion in added value.[10] There are now more than 2,350 companies in the UK operating in the automotive sector.[11]

The industry is one of our major exporters. While Nissan sells 80 per cent of its cars abroad the industry as a whole comes close to matching this figure: 78 per cent of all vehicles produced in the UK were sold overseas in 2014.[12] And vehicle production is forecast to increase from 1.6 million vehicles in 2013 to 2 million in 2017, a near record level of output.[13] This projected increase is not to meet a big rise in domestic demand. It is to meet a rising demand from abroad, particularly from the European Union.

It is to our credit that UK automotive exports to China, for example, increased more than six-fold between 2008 and 2013. Indeed some of our sales to China go through Europe. But it is the European market itself that we will rely on for the years into the future. European Union vehicle registrations outside the UK are expected to increase by an astonishing 30 per cent from approximately 10.7 million in 2013 to almost 13.5 million by 2018.[14] It is this demand that the expansion plans of British car manufacturers are seeking to meet. As a consequence, we are investing for the future and it is why investment in automotive Research and Development (R&D) doubled from 5.3 per cent of total UK R&D in 2006 to over 10 per cent in 2012.[15]

'The EU market will remain key for UK automotive manufacturing,' claim the Association of Motor Manufacturers. There are, they say, 'some arguments that the UK government should focus on the emerging economies rather than the EU for future trading links', but they conclude that 'the EU automotive market is expected to remain the largest automotive market for the UK.'[16]

Access to the EU market means that 49 per cent of UK-produced vehicles are sold across the largest Single Market in the world, unhindered by any tariffs or costly regulatory barriers. This is more than saying 49 per cent of our exports go to Europe: it is 49 per cent of all sales even after home sales are included. While for most manufacturers, domestic trade will be the biggest share of their sales, this is not so for UK vehicles. Furthermore, if we take motor trades as a whole, including wholesale and retail, we find that there are 240,000 auto-industry jobs associated with demand from the EU.[17]

One other feature of the car market should give us food for thought. Our automotive exports are not just in the form of completed cars but also of engines. The UK produces almost one million more engines than we do completed cars.[18] These engines are then assembled into cars in the rest of Europe. Being specialists in engines, we use our skills to prepare the most important part of the machinery for assembly in other EU countries. If we lose membership of the European Union, the case for this fragmentation of production or trade in tasks – what is sometimes also called 'vertical specialisation' – becomes less powerful.

The British car industry benefits from the tariff-free Single Market and from Europe's strength as a bloc in trade negotiations that set standards for the worldwide car industry. This is to Europe and Britain's benefit. While bad regulation hampers everyone, common regulation and standards are vital for manufacturers to compete across the Single Market. Standardisation of regulations at an EU-level removes the complexity and cost to conform with varying national standards. Innovation is more cost-effective if the gains from it are not just to one country but to the other 27 countries in the European Union. And winning recognition for EU standards globally helps our trade with the rest of the world.

Eurosceptics argue that the UK could have more influence in standards bodies if it were not represented by the European Union. Outside the EU, it is suggested, the UK would be working directly – not indirectly through Europe – with these organisations, building alliances with like-minded nations and playing a far bigger part in deciding the rules. Yet, it is not clear how much one country's representation would be worth given the size and working methods of the Word Trade Organisation – it is a one member, one vote organisation of more than 162 members – set against Europe's clout as the world's largest trading bloc. By making its case in and through the EU, and often leading it, Britain is able secure its interests more effectively than it would as an individual member.

European standards should form an essential element in preventing abuses such as those exposed in the Volkswagen emissions scandal. The US Environmental Protection Agency checks cars to establish whether they are meeting the standards agreed. It was through their rigorous checks that Volkswagen's cheating software was revealed. Europe now needs to have similar standards.

But the upside is that new EU-wide emission standards have led to investment in areas such as new fuel efficiency technologies. As a result, Britain has benefited from Nissan's decision to site the European production of its LEAF electric car in the UK. This was accompanied by a brand new battery plant built next to the car assembly plant in Sunderland. As of January 2014, 100,000 Nissan LEAF cars had been sold worldwide, making it the best-selling electric car globally.[19] As EU standards have become global standards this has been to the benefit of producers in European countries.

Balancing sovereignty and co-operation

I have started this chapter with an audit of the car industry's gains from membership of the European Union and the jobs that flow from it. The argument of this chapter is that, in a world in which each country's independence is limited by every country's interdependence, the real economic challenge for Britain is to achieve the right balance between autonomy and co-operation when it comes to jobs.

Britain is one of the most open economies in the world. Whereas just over 10 per cent of American economic output is exported, exports represent 30 per cent of Britain's GDP.[20] Historically, we have been one of the economies most exposed to the world, and our biggest trading partner is the European Union.

So how do we get the balance right? The more we co-operate, share and integrate, the more we are exposed to shocks that are not of our own making but come from forces external to Britain. In the financial sphere, contagion is an ever present threat, as we've all learned to our cost. Of course, even outside the European Union, we would be affected by contagion. The question is whether we gain overall from the strength that can come from being part of a wider union and the connections this allows for companies that are networked and global.

So, in this chapter, I seek to show how Britain benefits economically from EU membership and how we can in future maximise the benefits of co-operation in the best way possible.

A recent Bank of England report, referred to in the Introduction, found 'To the extent it increases economic and financial openness, EU membership reinforces the dynamism of the UK economy. A more dynamic economy is more resilient to shocks, can grow more rapidly without generating inflationary pressure or creating risks to financial stability, and can also be associated with more effective competition.'[21]

The downside is that 'increased economic and financial openness means the UK economy is more exposed to economic and financial shocks from overseas and that as a result of closer integration within the EU and, more recently, with the Euro-area crisis, this may have increased the challenges to UK economic and financial stability.'[22] Even so, as the Bank of England points out, these problems can be overcome by policies that manage such shocks as they arise.

The conclusions of the Bank of England study are not just about benefits in theory; they testify to benefits in practice. As the Governor of the Bank of England, Mark Carney, argues: 'For the majority of the period since the UK joined the EU, the first factor – greater openness and deeper integration afforded by EU membership – very likely increased the UK's dynamism. To be clear, by dynamism I mean the ability of an economy to grow and progress. Dynamism is reflected in the rate of productivity growth, the degree of labour engagement, the pace of new business creation and the rate of new innovation.'[23]

So, in the Single Market, UK industry and jobs benefit – as the car industry example shows – from the absence of tariff and non-tariff barriers that override any risk that comes from the exposure to potential shocks from the weaknesses in other countries' economies; we benefit too from being part of a larger marketplace; and it is clear that many companies, and maybe even most, invest in Britain not just to benefit from the British market but as the platform from which to sell to the European market as a whole.

In 1975 we were prevented from tariff-free trade with the Commonwealth. There are now, in contrast, few EU tariffs that prevent trade between the Commonwealth and the UK.

There is one further benefit: Europe's clout as a bloc undertaking trade negotiations mean that we are an influential part of global standard setting and possess a key role as a rule-making player.

We can, if we choose, help shape the EU rules for the future. Outside, by contrast, we risk being a rule-taker. By engaging directly, we can tap into the very large markets that are opening up in services and digital trade, and, without us, the European Union's struggle for competitiveness would arguably falter.

And, finally, by pooling and sharing investment in research and innovation, Britain gains. There are benefits in co-operation for research and development where by pooling and sharing resources we can achieve more working together than we could achieve by acting on our own. If the UK were to change the balance between autonomy and co-operation in its relations with the EU by leaving, or even by forming a relationship similar to that of Norway or Switzerland, we would not fare so well.

Benefits to Britain

Scotch whisky exemplifies the benefits we gain – and the UK food and drink industry gains – from European membership. Whisky is one of Britain's biggest exports, a £5 billion industry that employs directly 10,000 people and 30,000 indirectly.[24] It is bigger in size than the whole of British shipbuilding, British textiles, or UK iron and steel – it is even larger than our computer industry. In Scotland, whisky is the third biggest industry, only behind oil and financial services, and whisky represents two-thirds of the entire Scottish food and drink sector. The industry is nearly three times the size of Scotland's digital or life science industries.[25]

There are 113 distilleries, with 30 more in train and a planned investment of £1 billion in the years to 2020. Of 1.2 billion whisky bottles sold each year only 100 million or so are purchased within the UK and only 20 million in Scotland. Myths may die hard but less than one bottle in every 50 that is produced in Scotland is consumed in Scotland and less than one bottle in every ten is consumed in Britain.

Today the Scotch whisky industry relies on exports outside the UK. Before the Second World War exports accounted for 50 per cent of what we produced. Now they are around 90 per cent of what is produced. It is by exporting that we make money and create jobs from whisky.

There is another long-held and convenient myth that most of our whisky sales are to America, China or Japan. While we certainly want to build up sales in these countries, the fact is that of the 1.2 billion bottles sold every year less than one bottle in ten – 118 million – goes to the USA. China is only the 26th largest market by value, even if we include China trade through Hong Kong. In Japan, whisky drinkers consume less than 20 million bottles a year.

Where then is whisky's biggest export trade to be found? The biggest market is the European Union and the biggest consumer of whisky in Europe is France. France consumes 183 million bottles a year. More Scotch whisky sells in one month in France than cognac sells in a whole year. With just 66 million people, France consumes one and a half times more than the USA's 318 million people. Exports to France are worth nearly half a billion pounds a year. If France leads with 183 million bottles sold, Spain is the second biggest export market consuming just under 60 million bottles, and Germany is not far behind with imports of 50 million. Even Poland and Latvia purchase just under 20 million bottles each. And the Netherlands, too, purchases around 20 million bottles. Latvia, Poland and the Netherlands all consume more than Japan.

In 2014, European Union countries took 444 million bottles of whisky and Europe as a whole 470 million, dwarfing sales across the Atlantic and to other regions of the world. In total, Europe consumes 36 per cent of UK whisky exports; North America, including Canada, 15 per cent; Asia as a whole comes in at 20 per cent; Africa, 7 per cent; and the Middle East, 4 per cent.

Whisky is one example of where European sales thrive because there are no tariff and few non-tariff barriers to access to the world's largest trading bloc of 500 million people and its 21 million potential business partners that between them generate £11 trillion in economic activity.

There's a popular myth that our exports go mainly to the Commonwealth or China. However, as I reported in the introduction of this book, only a fraction in fact do. As table 7.1 below shows, the biggest bulk of the £300 billion or so of UK goods exports – 48 per cent last year or just under £150 billion – went to Germany, France and the European mainland, with China taking only £12.7 billion (4.5 per cent) and India £4.2 billion (1.5 per cent). We export £47 billion of goods to the USA – one third of the exports that go to the EU. Our old Commonwealth partners used to take over 40 per cent of our exports in the years after the Second World War, but today each of the major Commonwealth nations take an export share of around 1 per cent each, and the Commonwealth as a whole is no more than 10 per cent: Australia takes £4 billion (1.4 per cent) of UK exports, Canada £4 billion (1.4 per cent), South Africa £2.3 billion (0.8 per cent) and New Zealand less than £600 million (0.2 per cent). Even the rising economies linked to the Commonwealth take little compared with Europe. In 2015, exports to Singapore were £4 billion (1.4 per cent); Nigeria took £1.2 billion (0.4 per cent); and Malaysia received £1.5 billion (0.5 per cent). Exports to the small country of Belgium, which has a population 11.2 million, are three times as high as to India's population of 1.5 billion. The UK exports more to Ireland (£17 billion) than it does to China (£13 billion). We export more to our fellow EU member Sweden, which receives £4.4 billion of UK exports in goods and services, than to either India, Canada or Australia.

Membership of the Single Market is key to the future of jobs in Britain. An independent study by the Centre for Economics and Business Research (CEBR) has found our membership of Europe could add £58 billion a year to the UK economy by 2030 due to further economic reforms, equivalent to a 2.8 per cent boost in UK GDP, or £2,800 per household. This boost to GDP, provided that the assumptions used by the authors prove to be realistic, could deliver 300,000 new jobs by 2020, rising to 790,000 in 2030. The CEBR study

TABLE 7.1

Top 50 UK international export destinations, 2015

	Country	Value (£ million)	per cent of total UK exports	Cumulative percentage
1	United States	47 501	16.6	16.6
2	Germany	30 590	10.7	27.3
3	France	17 984	6.3	33.6
4	Netherlands	17 349	6.1	39.7
5	Irish Republic	16 810	5.9	45.6
6	China	12 748	4.5	50.1
7	Belgium and Luxembourg	11 778	4.1	54.2
8	Spain	8 953	3.1	57.3
9	Italy	8 580	3.0	60.3
10	Switzerland	7 336	2.6	62.9
11	United Arab Emirates	6 238	2.2	65.1
12	Hong Kong	5 730	2.0	67.1
13	South Korea	4 975	1.7	68.8
14	Saudi Arabia	4 709	1.6	70.4
15	Japan	4 571	1.6	72.0
16	Sweden	4 436	1.6	73.6
17	India	4 276	1.5	75.1
18	Canada	4 034	1.4	76.5
19	Australia	3 995	1.4	77.9
20	Singapore	3 941	1.4	79.3
21	Poland	3 643	1.3	80.6
22	Turkey	3 597	1.3	81.9
23	Norway	3 294	1.2	83.1
24	Russia	2 832	1.0	84.1
25	South Africa	2 329	0.8	84.9

TABLE 7.1 (*continued*)

	Country	Value (£ million)	per cent of total UK exports	Cumulative percentage
26	Denmark	2 322	0.8	85.7
27	Brazil	2 249	0.8	86.5
28	Qatar	2 132	0.7	87.2
29	Czech Republic	1 964	0.7	87.9
30	Austria	1 574	0.6	88.5
31	Malaysia	1 411	0.5	89.0
32	Mexico	1 353	0.5	89.5
33	Finland	1 315	0.5	90.0
34	Thailand	1 293	0.5	90.5
35	Hungary	1 293	0.5	91.0
36	Portugal	1 278	0.4	91.4
37	Nigeria	1 268	0.4	91.8
38	Taiwan	1 224	0.4	92.2
39	Israel	1 155	0.4	92.6
40	Egypt	1 077	0.4	93.0
41	Romania	980	0.3	93.3
42	Greece	908	0.3	93.6
43	Azerbaijan	701	0.2	93.8
44	Kuwait	607	0.2	94.0
45	New Zealand	598	0.2	94.2
46	FYR Macedonia	557	0.2	94.4
47	Pakistan	538	0.2	94.6
48	Morocco	520	0.2	94.8
49	Indonesia	503	0.2	95.0
50	Gibraltar	494	0.2	95.2

Source: Office for National Statistics

says even without further reforms, exports to the EU are worth £187 billion a year to the UK economy and that could rise to £277 billion a year by 2030. These figures are all predicated on the UK retaining its current status within the EU.[26]

Academic economists Brian Ardy, Iain Begg and Dermot Hodson found that, in 1997, almost 3.5 million jobs in the United Kingdom were associated with demand from the European Union, which included 2,500,000 jobs directly supported and 900,000 indirectly created from demand created by those jobs.[27] An updated analysis performed by CEBR in 2015 shows that, in 2011, 4.2 million jobs, or 13.3 per cent of the UK workforce, were associated with demand from exports to the EU. Within this 4.2 million, an estimated 3.1 million jobs were directly supported by exports to the European Union and 1.1 million jobs were indirectly supported – i.e. through spending income earned from exporting.[28]

Table 7.2 shows that London had the highest number of jobs reliant on EU exports, with the South-East coming second and North-West third. However, as a share of each region's total work-force, the highest reliance on EU exports was found in the East Midlands, followed by the West Midlands.

Total income associated with demand from EU exports was £211 billion or £3,500 per head of the population in 2011. As Table 7.3 shows, the number of jobs connected with EU demand in profes-sional, technical, scientific services and in the area of business and administration support services rose particularly rapidly between 1997 and 2011, with the numbers of jobs in both of those industrial sectors almost doubling. The part of UK manufacturing industry that exports to the EU has also done well by the standards of that sector, and, in total, around half of UK jobs linked to the EU are to be found in manufacturing.

Let us take yet another industry: the pharmaceutical industry. The chemicals and pharmaceuticals sector represents 15 per cent of total UK manufacturing output. With exports of £53 billion, 56 per cent

TABLE 7.2

EU-associated jobs by region, 1997 and 2011

	1997	2011
North-East	153,949	156,156
North-West	441,233	477,005
Yorkshire	338,513	363,464
East Midlands	307,713	337,131
West Midlands	408,796	384,976
East of England	319,631	373,615
London	426,345	541,707
South-East	458,698	538,988
South-West	309,914	362,861
Wales	169,795	191,332
Scotland	315,203	336,326
Northern Ireland	94,280	111,480
United Kingdom	3,744,069	4,175,042

Source: Centre for Economics and Business Research

of which go to EU countries, this sector is one of the UK's largest exporters, accounting for 18 per cent of the UK's goods exports.[29] Pharmaceuticals are an export-oriented industry which produces far more for our foreign markets than for the domestic market and far more for the rest of the European Union than all other markets combined. Pharmaceuticals, which employs around 73,000 people directly in the UK – 23,000 of these are highly skilled research and development roles – has many jobs dependent on demand in the European Union.[30] And, of course, pharmaceuticals have a long supply chain which also generates thousands of jobs in related industries.

TABLE 7.3

EU-associated jobs by sector, 1997 and 2011

	1997	2011
Public Administration	105,450	137,704
Health	92,483	122,432
Education	63,856	64,340
Business Admin and Support	206,082	410,085
Professional, Scientific and Technical	143,530	281,058
Property	10,553	16,510
Finance and Insurance	177,826	261,738
Information and Communication	67,185	124,360
Accommodation and Food Services	237,881	235,227
Transport and Storage	163,957	213,508
Motor Trades; wholesale; retail	179,976	241,426
Construction	68,573	82,083
Manufacturing	2,011,475	1,706,294
Mining, Quarrying and Utilities	61,808	90,127
Agriculture, Forestry and Fishing	63,538	76,184
Other	89,897	111,964
Total	3,744,069	4,175,042

Source: Centre for Economics and Business Research

The prospect of Britain's departure from the EU has been a matter of concern for the pharmaceutical industry. For example, John Lechleiter, chief executive of the US pharmaceutical company, Eli Lilly, which employs 2,800 people in the UK, has said it would be a 'shame and a mistake' if the UK left the EU.[31] Sir Andrew Witty, CEO of GlaxoSmithKline, has said: 'Europe has gone from 27 fragmented, independent, not-talking-to-each-other regulatory authorities in the healthcare space to one. That's a big deal.'[32] To take one example, Baxter Healthcare, a US-based manufacturer of medical devices and pharmaceuticals, saw the attractiveness of the UK as a place to invest significantly increased by the development of the Single Market. Their plant at Thetford in Norfolk manufactures healthcare products, employing over 400 people, and has recently completed a £20 million investment programme. The Single Market enables Baxter to supply products from its Norfolk site across the whole EU based on harmonised regulatory procedures.[33] Lord Darzi, a former Health Minister, has said: 'EU membership is one of the reasons why major pharmaceutical and med tech companies have significant operations in the UK, including every single one of the world's top 20 pharmaceutical firms. The Life Science industry and its supply chains employs approximately 180,000 people with thousands of highly skilled workers based within life science companies owned by EU-based parent companies. The burden of unpicking the synergies and efficiencies that exist within this huge, single trading market for science and its related outputs are numerous.'[34]

What then are the practical day-to-day benefits of Britain's membership of the EU to the pharmaceuticals industry? Firstly, the harmonisation of laws that aid the approval of medicines is in the industry's interest, and the creation of the European Medicines Agency has greatly simplified the procedures for approving new medicines across the EU. The decision to locate the European Medicines Agency in London also has undoubtedly boosted the UK's attractiveness to foreign investors.[35] As Darzi states: 'Leaving the EU would lead to significant disruption, financial expense and significant regulatory upheaval by necessitating new authorisation systems for medical devices and pharmaceuticals. Being able to combine and share data like this across geographical and national boundaries provides the scale and population size needed to drive healthcare innovation in today's connected world of big data.'[36]

No industry is more dependent on innovation than pharmaceuticals. Protecting and honouring patents is an important part of the innovation process and again the European Union plays a key role in harmonising intellectual property processes and thus encouraging innovation. A co-ordinated approach to research and innovation across Europe helps Britain too. Research funding through programmes such as the Innovative Medicines Initiative has contributed to the UK's competitiveness in the pharmaceutical sector. All of the 40 projects funded through this € 2 billion programme has involved companies and universities in the UK working as part of pan-European initiatives to develop new medicines and healthcare solutions. This makes it possible for the pharmaceutical industry to carry out more research than any other industry sector in the UK, bringing major health benefits to patients in Britain and all over the world.

Exiting the European Union would, as many industry experts point out, leave UK companies bound by the same EU legislation, meaning they would have to meet its standards and terms to sell in the European Union marketplace, but with far less input on the future development of these rules. Today, Britain balances its autonomy with co-operation in a way that gives it a major say over the direction of the regulatory framework in which UK and UK-based pharmaceutical companies operate. Outside the European Union and inside EFTA or the EEA, the UK would only have the right to comment on new rules after EU members had already had the discussion and made the decision.

'In Norway, pharmacists will soon have to go about the task of electronically authenticating medicines (like every country in the EU), as a consequence of the Falsified Medicines Directive,' points out former Secretary General of the Pharmaceutical Group of the European Union, John Chave. 'Whatever the merits and demerits of that, Norway had no say in the legislation,' he observes.[37] Similarly, Richard Bergström, Director General of the European Federation of

Pharmaceutical Industries and Associations, has argued: 'It is very difficult to see other EU Member States allowing the UK to cherry pick what they like and do not, while they stomach all of it.'[38]

Financial services

Financial services, account for 8 per cent of UK output and around 3½ per cent of our employment. The sector employs 1.1 million people in the UK, while almost another one million work in associated professional services, such as legal accountancy. Of these two million or so employees, more than half work outside London and the South-East: cities like Edinburgh, Manchester, Glasgow and Leeds have financial districts of their own. The financial sector in total accounted for around 65 per cent of the UK's recorded trade surplus of £89 billion in 2014. Most would call our financial services industry global and not just European. The UK is the leading country alongside the USA for cross-border bank lending, several forms of derivative trading activity and insurance services. Indeed, the UK accounts for nearly half – 49 per cent – of the global market in over-the-counter interest rate derivatives and 41 per cent of turnover in foreign exchange.[39] Some say that that leaving the EU will make no difference to UK financial services because the industry is so important to the global economy and our non-EU markets are growing so much faster. However, I will show how important the European connection is to the success of financial services and how leaving would hurt.

There's no doubt that the City of London is the heart of Britain's financial industry, contributing £66 billion to HMRC's coffers in 2014–15.[40] And while it is often thought that the City's trade is mainly with the rest of the world, rather than with European countries, this is a mistake. The City benefits more from trade with the EU than it does with our friends in the USA. We certainly have good trading relationships with the USA: it's where 26 per cent of UK financial services are exported. But 41 per cent of our financial services exports go to the European Union.[41] The industry exports to the world: but its main business is with Europe, which generates for us a trade surplus of £18.5 billion.

And it is our leadership in Europe that has changed the City out of all recognition. It is often forgotten that, in the 1960s, the City of London was still predominantly an international clearing centre for sterling-based transactions and even then there was a focus on the Commonwealth. Indeed, leadership of financial services in Europe was disputed between us and France: if we compared the two countries in Europe fifty years ago, the more international and market-oriented London had no greater banking assets than France.

There are many reasons offered for London's revival back in the 1970s and 1980s. One is that US and continental investment banks moved their operations to London after American governments enforced taxes which made it costly for international companies and foreign governments to raise loans and issue bonds on Wall Street. As a consequence, raising loans and credits in foreign currencies became a task performed in London. After this, London also benefited from both the liberalisation of financial markets – the Big Bang – which loosened regulations to make financial dealing less difficult, thereby enabling the City of London to become a yet more international financial centre.

The City, furthermore, benefited from the dismantling of controls on the flows of cross-border capital, which happened in London far earlier than in the rest of Europe. London also gained from the evolution of the Common Market into a Single Market and was able to present itself as a bridgehead for foreign, and especially US, financial institutions' operations in the EU. 'The City's extraordinary transformation will deceive UK citizens into thinking that the growth is endogenous, based on genuine internal strengths, and to overlook its external dimension, above all in a European context,' says Karel Lannoo, chief executive of the Centre for European Policy Studies.[42]

In particular, under the Single Market's single banking licence and common prudential and regulatory minimum standards, a bank located in one Member State is able to set up branches in others while supervised at home to prevent a race to the bottom. The presence in the City of US-domiciled financial institutions, banks, institutional investors, fund managers and ratings agents is linked to the Single Market's passporting rules that allow for the free provision of services all over the EU, a facility that has been further enhanced in recent years. As a result, London has mirrored New York as a genuinely global financial centre, a market-maker in multiple currencies and in providing services from bank lending, asset management, insurance, derivatives, trade and maritime finance right across to securities and currency trading. Around half of the world's largest financial firms have their European headquarters in the UK because London is a centre for European trade.[43]

Currently around 250 foreign banks operate in London which is far more than do in Paris, Frankfurt or New York and over 200 foreign legal firms have offices in London and elsewhere in the UK. If these firms were to reconsider their location in the event of a Brexit, or relocate some of their staff or business, the potential impact on the UK economy might be considerable. It could reduce domestic employment and tax receipts enough to make our economy falter.

London trades heavily with the rest of Europe and can genuinely be said to be the leader in Europe. The UK financial sector accounts for almost a quarter of all EU financial services income and as much as 40 per cent of EU financial services exports.[44] European trade accounts for over a third of the financial services trade surplus that Britain enjoys.[45] Indeed, London does more Euro-denominated foreign exchange trading than the whole Eurozone, and accounts for 85 per cent of EU hedge fund assets under management, over 70 per cent of over-the-counter derivatives traded and 51 per cent of marine insurance premiums.[46]

What London says it fears is inappropriate EU-wide regulation, an EU-wide tax on financial transactions, EU curbs on bankers' pay and more red tape arising from the proposed EU banking union. Indeed, countries like France feared that Britain was using the EU referendum negotiations to secure a backdoor veto on European financial regulation.

Yet even outside the European Union the City of London would still be bound by European Union rules. The EU insists that so-called 'third countries' – those outside the club – must have regulation and supervision of their financial sectors that are equivalent to that of the EU in exchange for access to EU markets. Thus, if we were inside the wider European Economic Area, Britain would have to pay the costs when rules are imposed without having the freedom to shape them. If we were like Switzerland, there would be no passporting and the London market would decline because non-EU firms would no longer be able to site their European operations in the UK and trade freely throughout the Single Market.

In theory, if outside the EU, Britain could become the sovereign regulatory body for hedge and private equity. But because hedge and private equity funds operating in European Union countries are required to comply with capital requirements, pay guidelines and other rules if they are based outside the EU's borders, London-based funds that wanted to continue to market their services within the EU would have to comply with these rules.

One of Britain's biggest bank, HSBC, which has recently decided to remain headquartered in London after a £40 million study of the pros and cons of leaving for Hong Kong, estimates that it may have to move 1,000 jobs from the UK to Paris if Britain left the EU.[47] Goldman Sachs, which, along with the New York's J.P. Morgan, is supporting the 'Remain' campaign, says up to a third of the 6,000 or so staff at its London HQ will have to shift to Frankfurt if Britain leaves the EU.[48] As a Brexit campaigner, Alex Brummer of the *Daily Mail*, says: 'This is understandable … being based in an EU country provides financial institutions with a so-called "passport" which allows them to trade currencies, bonds and shares across European borders more easily.'[49]

To sum up, EU membership is vital to jobs in the financial services industry, many of which are based outside London. It has, for example, been estimated by Iain Begg that some 261,738 UK finance and insurance jobs are dependent on demand from the European Union.[50]

Reform

Eighty per cent of Britain's exporters trade with mainland Europe and, if we thought of UK exports to Europe in terms of average sales per person, they are worth an average of £3,500 per person per year.[51] Britain can claim to have led in the creation of the European Single Market, which is designed to make it easier to trade. It can be viewed as the distinctive British contribution to a European Union that started off as a Custom Union, then became a Common Market and is now a Single Market, which does not only promote free trade, but – more so than any other trade area – makes possible not just the free movement of goods and services but also capital and labour, both of which are crucial to the very notion of a Single Market, and which stands in contrast to North America where NAFTA is only a trade agreement. And while it is not easy to estimate the impact of liberalisation, greater competition, lower transaction and distribution costs and the economies of scale that come with the Single Market, and difficult too to assess the counterfactual – what would happen if Britain was not part of it? – one study suggests that a more open and reformed Single Market – more open to trade in services, capital markets, digital and energy (which is the subject of a future chapter) – could add 2.5 per cent to our national income with the possibility of 790,000 extra jobs by 2030.[52] Britain gains from access to the Single Market. While Tim Congdon's study for UKIP says that the costs of remaining in the European Union was 11.5 per cent of GDP, even he concedes: 'When the UK joined the then Common Market, access to the large industrial free market on its doorstep was worth having, and did lead to worthwhile gains in economic efficiency and resource allocation.'[53]

When a team led by Paolo Cecchini, a widely respected economist, looked at the gains from opening up markets in the 1980s, they found that the benefit could be an increase of around 5 per cent – between 4.25 per cent and 6.5 per cent – of the European Union's GDP, a 6 per cent decline in prices and an extra 2 million new jobs rising overtime to five million jobs.[54] Nearly 30 years on, an updated study by Britain's own Department for Business, Innovation and Skills suggested income had risen by 6 per cent per head as a result of increased trade (and GDP could fall by between 1.22 per cent and 1.74 per cent if Britain left the EU).[55] And while the European Commission has calculated that the Single Market generated an extra 2.8 million jobs and an additional 2 per cent of GDP between 1992 and 2008, it is clear that only around half the expected gains have been achieved – highlighting that more has to be done in services, finance, energy and in the new areas of e-commerce and IT where non-tariff barriers frustrate cross-border trade.[56] It is possible to argue that implementing the EU Services Directive in full would do more for British jobs and exports than any other trade agreement under consideration. If the directive on services were fully implemented and we applied the 'country of origin' principle this would allow a trader in one country to trade in all countries of the European Union. The removal of trade barriers to the services sector alone could boost EU-wide output by over 2 per cent, adding an estimated £300 billion to the European Union's economic output, with Britain, the leading service provider, the biggest beneficiary.[57]

With 80 per cent of Britain's output now in services we could, as the Chancellor of the Exchequer, George Osborne, has said, create millions of jobs by economic reform in services.[58] However, in order to achieve an integrated market for services, Britain will be required to persuade a Germany that has been reluctant to proceed with service liberalisation to make reform of the Single Market a priority.

A Capital Markets Union has the potential to break down one of Europe's biggest barriers to growth and jobs: delivering more loan and equity finance on better terms, especially to Europe's small and medium-sized businesses. Unlike American small business, Europe's companies are over-dependent on banks. A Capital Markets Union creates an opportunity not only to broaden the base of business financing but to expand Internet banking. Over the past decade or so, Britain has become one of the world's most important centres for so-called FinTech, the digital financial revolution for the next generation. Internet banks, offering highly personalised services on the web, and companies such as Worldpay which arranges secure Internet payment systems and was recently floated as a £6 billion company on the London stock market, show what we can achieve in this field.

There has already been progress within the EU through an agreement on roaming that will cut the cost of mobile phone bills for businesses and tourists across Europe. However, as the Chancellor has pointed out, if we can purchase CDs from a German shop with a UK credit card when in Berlin, but cannot log-in to a German website with a British account to download music, then we are missing out badly. As a share of our economy, Europe's information and communication technology capital stock was on a par with the USA 25 years ago. However, during the digital revolution of recent years, Europe has fallen back to about two-thirds that of the US today. During this period, IT productivity growth was higher in American companies and they contributed more to US growth than in Europe.[59] Yet banking, shopping, wholesale supply, logistics and scientific research, as John Springford has highlighted, can be part of the Internet revolution and bring Europe's fragmented services markets up-to-date.[60] The challenge is to use fast-developing technologies, such as machine learning, robotics, sensors, and synthetic biology so that Europe like America improves its digital productivity across a range of industries from cars and energy to telecommunications and healthcare.[61] Securing mutual recognition or harmonisation of online standards and thus reducing transaction costs could, if the assumptions made in one study by the CEBR hold, add £3 billion to UK national income by 2020.[62]

In addition, reform must also include a further opening up of the continent's agricultural sector. The share of agriculture, forestry and fishing in European Union economic activity is now down to 1.4 per cent. It is 0.6 per cent in the UK and 1.6 per cent in France but is as high as a 10 per cent and 15 per cent in the more remote rural areas of Hungary, Romania and Bulgaria. And with the share of agriculture now down to 1.6 per cent of GDP in a France which has held out for decades against reducing the agriculture budget (which is still under the EU's seven-year budget agreement, projected to still cost €300 billion over the seven years from 2012 to 2019) there is an argument today that France might endorse switching support to rural communities and to biodiversity, enabling the costs of the Common Agriculture Policy to be reduced.

It is often argued that reform cannot succeed because of European red tape and bureaucracy. Indeed, Open Europe estimate that the cost to the UK economy of the 100 most burdensome EU regulations is £33.3 billion a year and claim that the benefits of these regulations, estimated in government impact assessments at £58.6 billion a year, have been vastly overstated.[63] But no-one can be sure and it is difficult to devise a counterfactual about what deregulating too much would do. Nevertheless, Europe has struggled for years with the way the Single Market is implemented – caught between what seem overbearing prohibitions and pressures for harmonisation, with derogations usually justified only because of national concerns about safety, health, environmental security or consumer protection. The problem, as one writer puts it, is blanket prohibitions 'erase the capacity of Members States to regulate if only for correcting or overcoming market failure'.[64]

The idea of 'mutual recognition' – that Member States must allow a product lawfully produced and marketed in another Member State into their own market without having to meet a second set of requirements in the country to which they are exporting – dates back to a European Court of Justice decision in the 1970s. More recently, in 2010, Mario Monti produced a further plan for a more efficient system of mutual recognition in 2010 and Michel Barnier, as Commissioner for Internal Market and Services, enacted several new initiatives in 2012. The idea behind mutual recognition is that even 'deep' market integration can respect 'diversity' and show that the Single Market is not about eliminating differences in culture, identity or traditions, allowing regulatory discretion for nation states. It has been suggested that mutual recognition could only be rejected in favour of harmonisation when public health, consumer safety or the environment are at risk. Of course the majority of goods traded within the EU, from toys and machinery, to medical devices and pharmaceuticals, are already covered by harmonised rules, but mutual recognition applies to goods including foodstuffs, furniture, bicycles and precious metals, which no longer need to harmonise their detailed technical specifications (or their testing, approvals, inspection or certification) and for services where the focus is on essential regulation only: safety rules, environmental rules and minimum qualifications such as strict rules for working hours. In professional services, for example, the rules are national. In some cases – vocational qualifications or in areas like accountancy – mutual recognition is proving complex and difficult, but the principle has been established that we consider innovative ways of avoiding over-centralisation of regulations and thus balancing autonomy and co-operation.

At its best, mutual recognition of each other's standards and rules entails both respect for Member State's national regulations and acknowledgement of the subsidiarity principle under which decisions are taken as close as possible to citizens. At one and the same time, we can remove barriers to the free movement of goods and avoid time-consuming legislative procedures for harmonisation of each and every national requirement or procedure at the European-level. And this is the best way to balance the autonomy we desire with the co-operation we need. The evidence is that mutual recognition can generate greater economic benefits than we can gain by a simple act of deregulation or by full harmonisation and this enables us to avoid the heavy costs of centralisation and a uniformity imposed from the centre. Europe should do more to enshrine a principle of mutual recognition that elevates local control: we should favour harmonisation only when essential.

In this chapter we have shown how a British agenda on economic reform of the Single Market could yield considerable benefits in jobs. So too can the European Union's €315 billion infrastructure initiative – from which Britain should gain its 15 per cent or so share of projects – and Europe's role in opening up world trade. However, as our discussion on globalisation has shown, we have to minimise the insecurities of those who lose out from globalisation as well as maximise the opportunities of those who gain from it. Today, Europe produces only 10 per cent of the world's steel while China is responsible for half the world's output. Both China and Europe now face large redundancies as the overcapacity of the steel industry is reduced. But it is clear that not enough has been done to prevent the dumping of goods at artificially low prices and not enough is being done to help those in danger of losing their livelihoods. Low European tariffs on steel imports are controversial but this is at least in part because the UK government blocked attempts to toughen up anti-dumping measures. But all this has to be balanced against the risk that outside the European Union we might have to pay tariffs on our exports, nearly 50 per cent of which go to mainland Europe. Side-by-side with an economic reform programme to create new jobs,

Europe must do more to assist the reconstruction of traditional industrial areas. I turn to Europe's Social Market in Chapter Eight but first I answer those who say that outside the Euro we cannot be at the heart of Europe.

CHAPTER EIGHT

Outside the Euro but still at the heart of Europe?

I was present at the very first meeting of the Eurozone heads of government held in Paris on 12 October 2008. I was lucky to be there. The meeting was meant to be exclusive, to be attended only by the then fifteen Eurozone heads of government and Britain was not a member.[1] I know that some Eurozone leaders opposed an outsider, a non-member, being present, even though none of them said this either at the meeting or directly to me in private.

Just as Britain was outside the Euro Committee of Finance Ministers – the Euro Group – so too Britain was to be on the outside at the first ever meeting of the Euro Group held at a presidential and prime ministerial level. But thanks to President Sarkozy an invitation was issued to me and I was asked to join in the discussion on the fallout from the financial crisis. As a result, Britain can justifiably say that it was present at the creation of this new group. In particular, the Eurozone leaders wanted to know why Britain had broken with US policy, had decided to recapitalise and take partial ownership of the top British banks and why our analysis was so different from the common view in America and Europe at the time.

At the Paris meeting, I was the first to be called by the chairman to speak. I argued the problems which the banks faced were caused not just by a lack of liquidity but by a lack of capital. To my astonishment, most European leaders thought they were dealing only with the indirect consequences, the fallout from an Anglo-Saxon financial crisis. And, of course, they believed that Britain had been unwise because instead of backing a European future it was their view that the UK had allowed itself to be locked into an American financial boom for which it was now paying a heavy price.

They did not know that half the American sub-prime assets that had been bought were by reckless banks in mainland Europe. At that time, they understood even less about the scale of their own banks' exposure to falling property markets. They did not fully appreciate the depth of the entanglements between European banks, like the German Landesbanks, and those of the US and other global financial institutions. I remember the disbelieving glances across the table when I explained that European banks were now even more vulnerable than American banks because they were far more highly leveraged.[2]

But my presence at the meeting emphasised one important point: that not all European economic matters can be subdivided, cordoned off and labelled 'Euro' matters and 'non-Euro' matters. In my view, then as now, it makes little sense to think, as many currently do, that the best way forward is to erect a 'Berlin Wall' between the Euro and non-Euro members. Non-Euro members, I believe, require safe-guards when Euro Area members take decisions about their economies. The Single Market project, which embraces 28 countries, cannot be directed by 19 Eurozone countries deciding European economic policy as a whole. So I favour provisions that make it clear that the European Union is a multi-currency union and that Euro countries must take the interests of non-Euro countries into account, referring important matters and decisions to all 28 members. This builds on the guarantees that I sought and obtained in 1998 when the Euro was being formed.

The emphasis on a Berlin Wall between the Euro and non-Euro countries, as some Eurosceptics advocate, rests on a misconception: an erroneous assumption that the real danger Britain faces is that Eurozone decisions will spill over and pollute the British economy, landing us with additional costs we should not have to pay. As big a danger is that were we on the outside of European decision-making on all the big economic issues of the day – growth, trade, exchange rates, financial stability, Europe's economic position in the world – Britain would be denied the chance to engage in and shape decisions. Without a dialogue and the chance to secure a meeting of minds on matters of common interest, we would lose out entirely on the benefits of a shared approach. In other words, a Berlin Wall does not fully protect Britain against decisions affecting us made in Europe.

But the debates of October 2008 at the height of the crisis raise even more important questions relevant to the issues of the coming British referendum. Just for me to be at that meeting in Paris as Prime Minister was controversial because the Euro itself is controversial in Britain. If they had a say in the matter, some British MPs would have argued that I should not have agreed to be even present. But those MPs would fail to recognise that getting the right balance between co-operation and autonomy means that Britain should not exclude itself from the Single Market and omit itself from general economic debates and decisions. It is wrong to suggest that because we are outside the Euro we cannot lead: the 2007–08 financial crisis proved Britain can be a leader on economic matters irrespective of whether it is in the Euro or not. At the summit in Paris, despite Britain not being a member of the single currency, we successfully urged EU leaders to copy the British model for tackling global financial turmoil. And, with Britain leading, the Eurozone countries adopted the rescue plan launched by the UK as the template for an increasingly global approach to the financial crisis.

As Chancellor and Prime Minister, I tried to prove that we could be at the heart of Europe while still being outside the Euro. And I want to suggest that it is in our interests to be at the heart of European decision-making wherever possible. Of course, when it comes to assessing the right balance between the autonomy we desire and the co-operation we need, the Euro is the most difficult of issues. At one extreme, many Euro-enthusiasts say that in order to be at the heart of Europe we have to be inside the Euro. Eurosceptics, at the other extreme, say that it is not only right to be outside the Euro but that we should either leave the EU or erect a Berlin Wall between the Euro and non-Euro countries.

My argument is different: Britain can co-operate in the Single Market without being in the Euro and still also lead. What Britain must do is strike the right balance between autonomy and co-operation. The right balance for Britain is being in the EU, playing a central role in economic decision-making and stopping the emergence of a permanent divide or stand off between Euro and non-Euro groups, while rejecting departure from the EU and rejecting membership of the Euro because we have not found it in our interests to join.

The importance of the Euro

'We can't join the Euro? Is that what you said?' Tony Blair said to me in 2003. 'We can't join the Euro,' I said. 'We can't join the Euro? Is that what you said?' Tony repeated. 'Yes, I said we can't join the Euro,' I told him. 'You can't say that,' he replied. 'But the evidence is clear,' I argued, 'it just won't work for us.' No European issue has perhaps been so important to the politics of Britain in recent years as whether or not to join the Euro. On this matter I drew a different conclusion from Tony Blair. For Tony, membership of the Euro was important if we were to be at the heart of Europe. For myself, we had to make a decision on the merits – and this meant an assessment of the benefits gained from balancing autonomy and sharing. If the economic test was not met and it was not in Britain's interests, I was clear that we should not join. While many wanted to make support for the Euro a test of our pro-European credentials, I was of the view that we did not need to be in the Euro to be at the heart of Europe. Getting the balance right between autonomy and co-operation, I believe, should not require us to join in for the sake of joining. It was not Europe right or wrong: it was supporting co-operation when it was in our interests to do so and rejecting it when it was not.

Not surprisingly, the Euro has divided British opinion probably more so than any other European issue with the exception of immigration. As a cause of controversy inside Europe it is even more divisive than the Common Agricultural Policy.

Some will continue to argue that being pro-European and pro-Euro are interchangeable: in other words, you cannot be one without being the other. However, it is important to understand why the Euro – and not, for example, a common defence and security policy as floated in the 1950s – became an acid test of whether leaders in Europe were serious about European unity. While economic and monetary union was set out as one formal objective of the European Union as early as the 1970s, it was German unification and reactions to that possibility which brought the Euro into existence. The then President of France, François Mitterrand, decided that he would agree to German unification only if Germany was hemmed in under a European umbrella. This he thought would ensure that Germany could not become too dominant. So Germany had to accept that its room for manoeuvre was circumscribed and that a united Germany was only possible within a united Europe. A defence union was one possibility. However, as one prominent German supporter of greater integration, Wolfgang Schäuble, has said: Europe had shown from the 1950s that because of British objections and French suspicions of Germany it could not unite around a common defence policy. If it had been mooted in the 1990s, a shared defence policy would have alienated America, marginalised Germany at the expense of France and the UK would have vetoed it. Another possibility was an industrial union, with industrial policy subject to greater integration. But with the Left in power in France and the Right in power in Germany there was a basic disagreement over the limits of state intervention.

The prospects for a shared currency seemed much brighter. There was an economic motive too: French concern about an over-powerful Germany. The more Germany grew in economic and political stature in the 1960s, 1970s and 1980s, the more Western European leaders came to regard European integration as their best safeguard against the prospects of an over-powerful Germany. This was recognised by Helmut Schmidt, Chancellor of West Germany from 1974 to 1982, who as the powerful managing editor of the *Die Zeit* newspaper warned his fellow countrymen that 'the present generations should not forget that it was suspicion of Germany and its future development that paved the way for the start of European integration.'[3]

So, determined to ensure that a united Germany could only happen under strict European supervision, leaders in Europe sought to contain German power. And because of its past history, Germany itself felt it necessary to say it supported the objective of European unification in order to achieve its real aim: German unification. And when France insisted on monetary union as the next step towards an integrated Europe, the very real doubts that the Bundesbank had about the prospects of a common currency were swept aside.

As Chancellor of the Exchequer, I knew the decision on Euro membership was one of the biggest economic decisions that Britain would have to make in decades and that the consequences would live with us for decades to come. Approaching the issue with all the seriousness it deserved, we – and principally Ed Balls, the Chief Economic Adviser to the Treasury at the time – produced our own studies on the implications of membership. Having set five tests – about the impact on investment, jobs, financial services, the housing market and the possibilities of convergence for the UK economy as a whole with the Eurozone – we commissioned 18 separate studies which explored the differences between the British economy and the Euro Area, namely our distinctive housing market, our disproportionately large financial services sector and our post-war proclivity towards inflation.

These studies, which were all published, provided solid evidence the like of which no other country, other than Sweden, had produced. I then talked to Cabinet ministers who tended to support joining. I faced a seriously hostile press, too, who were determined to show that any objections I had to the Euro were not based on solid evidence but on personal ambition, and I was reluctant because I wanted to draw a line between Tony Blair and myself. In fact, before entering government, Tony had penned an article for *The Sun* about the importance of the pound.

But, in the end, my reason in 2003 for recommending not joining the Euro was simple: I was a strongly pro-European Chancellor but the evidence before me showed that the economics of the Euro did not work for Britain. I saw detailed – what I believed irrefutable – evidence which confirmed our economy was out of sync with that of the rest of Europe and was likely to stay out of sync for some time.

At the same time, I came to the view that the Euro, as planned, could not avoid regular crises and under its current guidelines would push Europe towards becoming a low-growth, high-unemployment economy. As events transpired, the next crisis started in America where waves of speculation in the sub-prime market triggered a banking collapse, but, although the crisis came first to America, Europe was harder hit than even the United States, suffering six years on the edge of recession or in it. While no one country escaped losses in output or jobs, Greece saw a fall in output of over 25 per cent, while unemployment reached 50 per cent among young people and over 20 per cent for the adult population in both Spain and Greece.

Jean Monnet, the Frenchman who was one of the founding fathers of European integration, used to say that Europe 'would be forged in crises, and would be the sum of the solutions to these crises.'[4] But for the first ten years of its existence, from 1999 to 2008, the Euro looked like an unqualified success. There was growth, low interest rates, currency stability and living standards in the poorer countries of the Eurozone seemed to be rising closer to the levels of the richer ones. Yet beneath the surface, national economies had begun to diverge rather than converge. The Euro had brought not only a drop in interest rates which fuelled excessive demand, but opened up new credit, forcing up prices and wages.

What is more, Germany was undergoing painful economic reforms, which made it much more competitive than other countries in continental Europe. Indeed, while Northern Europe saved and focused on higher productivity, Southern Europe was consuming, caught in a speculative bubble and becoming more and more uncompetitive when it should have been making much-needed structural reforms. As a consequence, Northern Europe was accumulating external surpluses while Southern Europe went deeper into debt. And the more that demand grew in the South, the more inflation in the South exceeded that of the North.

And when the bubble burst, with all its costs in lost revenues and higher social security payments, public debt for the Eurozone as a whole rose from 69 per cent of GDP in 2008 to 92 per cent in 2014.[5] But debt grew far faster in Greece, Spain, Portugal and Ireland, with debt spiralling upwards to near or well above 100 per cent.[6] And European decision-makers realised for the first time that despite a complex machinery for setting monetary policy there was nothing in place to resolve crises, not even a mechanism in place to come to the aid of countries cut off from access to the bond market – with the result that the price paid for adjustment on the periphery of the Eurozone was high indeed. Between 2007 and 2014, not only did the Greek economy contract by a quarter but Italy lost nearly 10 per cent of its national income and Portugal and Spain lost 7 per cent and 6 per cent respectively.[7]

Post-crisis measures

Europe's leaders have been forced to set up a permanent fund (the European Stability Mechanism) to support members that require bailouts, to agree supervision of the systemically important banks by the European Central Bank, to constitute a new mechanism for rescuing or disposing of failing banks without immediately turning to taxpayers, to strengthen financial regulation and to impose tougher budgetary disciplines. Some of what is now being considered was foreshadowed more than 20 years ago in a paper co-authored by Wolfgang Schäuble, Germany's veteran finance minister. Schäuble's paper, 'Reflections on European policy', called for 'cores of co-operation within the EU that enable smaller, willing groups of Member States to forge ahead with integration'. Schäuble and his co-author, Karl Lamers, a leading member of Germany's Christian Democratic Union, argued that the EU should focus mainly on the following areas: a fair and open internal market; trade; currency and financial markets; foreign and security policy; and the climate, environment and energy. In these areas, Schäuble and Lamers claimed, lasting success could be achieved only if Member States acted at the European-level. Once responsibility for these tasks was situated where they could be tackled most effectively, they argued, each tier of government – regional, national or supranational – should be given the appropriate legislative powers and authority to enforce the rules.[8]

More recently, writing in August 2014, Schäuble and Lamers suggested that there should be an EU Budget Commissioner with powers to reject national budgets if they do not correspond to rules. They also favour a 'Eurozone Parliament' comprising MEPs from Eurozone countries to strengthen the democratic legitimacy of decisions affecting the single currency bloc.[9] The heads of the Bundesbank and Banque de France, Jens Weidmann and François Villeroy de Galhau, have also called for a Eurozone Treasury, to reinforce control over national budgets.[10] Similarly, Italy's finance minister, Pier Carlo Padoan, has stressed that the Eurozone crisis provides an opportunity to deepen European integration, like many other times before in the history of the EU. 'A crisis is always a good opportunity if you are alive after the crisis,' Padoan argues, echoing Jean Monnet. 'Let me recall an obvious similarity with the debate at the end of the 1990s,' Padoan said. 'The topic was why do we want a single currency? The answer is because we want monetary stability. To have monetary stability we need a supranational monetary authority. Today we are in a similar situation.'[11]

So, as in the early 1990s, proposals for much closer economic union are now being floated. But the most likely outcome is far more modest, with a likely roadmap set out in the proposals of the June 2015 report of the Five Presidents – named after European Commission President Jean-Claude Juncker, together with the Presidents of the European Council of Ministers, the Euro Group, the European Central Bank and the European Parliament.[12] These proposals build on, but also water down, the 2012 four presidents' report (the President of the European Parliament was later added as the fifth member) and call for for changes to be implemented not before 2025.

The Five Presidents' report has been attacked as federalist. 'At a time when Brussels should be devolving power, it is hauling more and more towards the centre, and there is no way that Britain can be unaffected,' wrote the Mayor of London, Boris Johnson, about the Five Presidents' report: 'The fundamental problem remains: that they have an ideal that we do not share.'[13] But when we look at the practical proposals in the four areas itemised by the Five Presidents – closer integration of budgetary policies, better co-ordination of economic policies apart from fiscal policy, banking union and a strengthening of democratic legitimacy and accountability – we can see that they struggle to resolve a divide between the risk-sharing that France supports as the best way forward and the risk-control that is the essence of the German approach.

Germany favours a tougher centralised regime for disciplining fiscally imprudent countries, believing that hard-working German taxpayers will not be prepared to pay for the pensions of Greek civil servants, and so it wishes controls over the budgetary process. In contrast, the integration that some others, most notably France, want involves fiscal transfers. So there is a division between those who support greater economic integration to achieve fiscal discipline and those who support greater integration to achieve fiscal transfers. One side wants to impose new rules, the other side to have explicit mechanisms for sharing the burden of adjustment. The divisions reveal how fragile is the consensus on what to do next.

There are other issues that lead to a watering down of previous integrationist proposals. In the early days of the Euro, Eurozone politicians – French ministers in particular – wanted all European Union countries' individual seats at the IMF and World Bank to be replaced by one bloc representing Europe as a whole. A proposal was also mooted at the time to replace the individual G7 country representation of Germany, France, Italy and the UK with one European representative. As Chancellor, I spent a huge amount of time arguing for the continuation of a distinctive British representation and I was able to find other European allies who resisted this centralisation.

But this is not the proposal that is now coming forward. It is clear that Euro Area countries like Belgium which, for historic reasons, have a special status in the IMF, do not want to see their role diminished, nor does Germany want a fundamental change for it has no wish to explain to its public that the head of the Bundesbank, who is the German representative at the IMF, has been replaced by a European politician. If it is no longer proposed that the European Union take on all the separate country seats at the IMF and World Bank, then there is little threat to the position of the United Kingdom from Europe in this regard.

The Five Presidents' final set of proposals for completing banking union is more controversial. There are three elements of banking union, the first two of which are now in place. The first is the creation of a single supervisory mechanism (SSM), in which the 130 large and systemically important banks are now directly supervised by the European Central Bank, while other banks are supervised by their respective national authorities, though with oversight from the ECB. Britain chose not to participate in the SSM, but other 'Euro-outs' such as the Danes and Poles are considering joining. The second is a common approach to resolving failing banks: the single resolution mechanism, backed by a single resolution fund which will be built-up from levies on banks. This will take at least ten years to reach its target size of €55 billion, prompting the Five Presidents to propose a bridging facility to underpin the fund in the interim. Again, the UK has chosen not to participate, even though, as with the SSM, non-Euro countries have the option to do so.

The third proposal to establish common deposit insurance has been diluted in response to opposition from creditor countries like Germany who prefer to focus first on reducing the risk of bank failures before they countenance sharing the potential costs of dealing with insuring depositors against bank failures. The timetable for reinsurance is a long one: on 24 November 2015, a plan was published requiring national reinsurance to be backed-up by a common European reinsurance; later there will be co-insurance, that is a hybrid with insurance liabilities shared between Member States and the European Union scheme. Full common insurance will only come in ten years, when the Germans hope the moral hazards of today will be substantially reduced because of tougher controls to risk.

Britain has encouraged the Euro area to do what is necessary to ensure the long-term sustainability of the Euro, but has sought guidelines to manage relations between itself and a more integrated Eurozone. The UK worries that the Eurozone may caucus and push through rules that damage the Single Market in financial services or the City of London. However, in evidence to a House of Lords inquiry, Thomas Wieser, the very influential President of the EU's Economic and Financial Committee, pours cold water on this idea, noting: 'I have participated in every Euro Group meeting that ever was, and I can assure you that the diversity of views is enormous. There is maybe some ganging up against the people who produce the coffee there – and rightly so – but there is never any monolithic bloc deciding on what should be decided.'[14] The UK also has guarantees of non-discrimination and an emergency brake – the right to ask the European Council to intervene if the Single Market as a whole is being undermined by the Euro.[15]

And the new procedures to ensure greater transparency in the discussions of the Euro Group are similar to the agreement our government reached in 1998.[16] At the start of the Euro, I had an argument with others who wanted to downgrade the European Economic and Financial Affairs Council, Ecofin, and hand everything over to the new Eurozone committee. I insisted that when decisions were being discussed, as far as was possible, Britain should be involved. In contrast, the French Prime Minister, Lionel Jospin, and his finance minister, Dominique Strauss-Kahn, wanted a form of Eurozone economic government. They wanted a Euro Group that was an effective political counterpart to the ECB. When we demanded representation at the Euro Group – we said: 'We want to be at the table not an ear at the door' – the reply from France was that the UK 'could not be both in and out.' Lionel Jospin said: 'The UK which invented clubs should agree it was not unfair not to be included.' Strauss-Kahn likened our demand to that of a voyeur insisting on the right to gain access to a married couple's bedroom.

But after a series of meetings, it was agreed in November 1998 that Ecofin should not be superseded. In the end a compromise was struck: the then four non-Euro members were guaranteed full information from meetings of the Euro Group; given the agenda of Euro Group meetings in advance, with the right to raise objections if there was a matter which was of common interest; and it was agreed that an official would be in attendance at the meeting to prepare a report back. The settlement of February 2016 agreed between the UK and EU Member States reinforces the constitutional position that Ecofin remains the main economic decision-making body for Europe.

I recount this history because in my view it does not serve our interests well to glory in exclusion. Instead of the Berlin Wall approach, we should maximise the role Britain plays in discussing major economic issues: from macro-governance where co-operation between the UK and Euro Area will be of increasing importance to both trade and financial stability.

Nevertheless, Britain has to be careful not to claim it speaks for all countries outside the Euro. Some of the non-Euro countries in Central and Eastern Europe want to join the Euro (only Denmark is under no obligation like the UK to join). Indeed, all the other non-Euro states are now signatories to the separate intergovernmental treaty establishing the 'fiscal compact' – the arrangement under which fiscal policy is more closely co-ordinated among countries.

Post-crisis measures in the European Union reveal the extent and the limits of European integration. The EU not only remains a multi-currency union but as it debates competing visions of risk-sharing and risk-control the Euro Area itself has stopped short of an early push towards a fiscal and banking union.

How do we get EU growth?

One other argument of the Eurosceptics has to be addressed: the claim that Europe's low growth and high unemployment arise from a flawed Eurozone, and because of this Britain must extricate itself from any connection with such a doomed project. One economic historian, Brendan Simms, says Europe faces a series of interlocking challenges that are individually and cumulatively bringing the continent to its knees: 'The Eurozone ship is like the Titanic, it will sink sooner rather than later … It is better to be sitting in a lifeboat than to be dragged down,' he has argued.[17] The US investor, Jim Mellon, has predicted the end of the common currency itself.[18]

Europe's economic challenges should be seen in proper perspective. A growth rate that is slower than that of America is not unexpected because of lower population growth in Europe. And of course some economies – like the German and Dutch – are very competitive. Nor should we blame low Euro Area growth on the Euro alone and ignore a series of macroeconomic mistakes – namely, excessive pre-crisis borrowing used to fund consumption not productivity and investment, as well as the failure to deal quickly with the banking crisis and the austerity which depressed growth. As a study edited by Baldwin and Giavazzi demonstrates, the crisis has many roots and was not just about shortcomings in one area of policy.[19]

'Failure to restore growth, bring inflation back on track and address major labour market imbalances and inequality in the distribution of income is making a joke of traditional parties' pretence to economic competence,' writes Jean Pisani-Ferry.[20] And while many commentators believe that European leaders could not deal with the Euro crisis in the absence of a fiscal union, one writer, Martin Sandbu, claims that the Euro Area can return to growth and avoid future crises without a fiscal union or political union if it pursues the right macroeconomic policies.[21] He suggests that centralised control is not needed and envisages coalitions of countries being able to issue Eurobonds with the weaker economies employing fiscal tools for adjustment.

What he calls Europe's 'deeply disappointing' low growth has led the former Chairman of the US Federal Reserve, Ben Bernanke, to claim the obvious answer is 'no' to the question: 'Is the Eurozone's leadership delivering the broad-based economic recovery that is needed?'[22] He attributes the Eurozone's high unemployment levels primarily to an inadequate monetary and fiscal stimulus. While unemployment rates in the United States and Europe were both about 10 per cent in late 2009 and 2010, unemployment has fallen to 5.3 per cent in the US and risen to more than 11 per cent in Europe in 2015. Europe's overall jobless rate would be above 13 percent, Bernanke suggests, if it was not for Germany's unemployment rate of less than 5 per cent. Tight fiscal policies, he implies, have dampened consumer demand in Germany, providing a boost to exports and a lasting trade surplus with other countries at the expense of jobs being created in the rest of the Eurozone. The problem for Germany's trading partners is that they cannot devalue their currency to boost their own exports. In turn, this puts them at an economic disadvantage that has kept unemployment high.

The Euro Area as a whole produces an excess of savings over investment: at 3.7 percent of GDP, or nearly € 400 billion, its current account surplus represents the biggest imbalance in the world.[23] This money is exported rather than consumed or invested in Europe and thus undermines growth. To mirror its rules that prevent high budget fiscal deficit, the Eurozone should, as Bernanke suggests, adopt rules that prevent sustained trade imbalances – thus meaning Germany and other countries with large trade surpluses would have to boost domestic demand through more appropriate fiscal policies. One recent budget shift – meeting the costs that arise from Middle East migration – will provide a stimulus of up to 1 per cent of GDP for a number of European economies by 2020.[24] More importantly, though, if the European Union could speed up its € 315 billion programme of infrastructure investment, this could lead to a push for growth over the entire continent.

In this chapter, I have tried to show Britain benefits from our economic engagement with Europe and that with the right policies Europe can grow faster. In the next chapter, I make the case that Britain benefits not only from the Single Market but from what has been called a 'Social Market'.

CHAPTER NINE

Does Europe's social dimension help or hinder us?

Of all the issues that has divided Britain on party lines over Europe perhaps the bitterest and most controversial has been whether the European Union should have a social dimension. Debates over the rightness and wrongness of a 'Social Europe' spanned all the time I was an MP from 1983 onwards – as a Labour economic spokesman in the 1980s and 1990s as we made the case for Britain joining the European Social Chapter and for Britain's inclusion of it in the Maastricht Treaty; in the decade after 1997 when Britain finally signed the Social Chapter and supported a stronger social policy for Europe; and in the debates that led to the Lisbon Treaty that I signed on behalf of Britain in which for the first time a social dimension was enshrined at the very heart of European legislation with the agreement of all Member States.

In other countries support for a social dimension to the European Union has been bipartisan, coming from parties of the Right as well as the Left. But when we look at how vehemently the Conservative governments of 1979 to 1997 opposed a European social dimension – and the lengths to which they were prepared to go to prevent this – we can see how opposition to a Social Europe has been central to the Eurosceptic case.

'Social and employment policy is one of the most controversial areas of EU competence and the debate about whether or not the balance is right between the EU and Member States goes to the heart of what the EU is about,' the UK government's own 'Balance of

Competences' review explains.[1] Some of the arguments are philosophical – whether there is or is not such a thing as a shared European social ideal – while others are about whether working hours and holidays should be a matter for European Union laws and thus whether or not social policy is in itself an intrinsic element of a Single Market. I have always thought that for Eurosceptics it always came back to their original argument: that Europe should be a free trade area and nothing more.

Not until the Maastricht and Amsterdam Treaties in the 1990s was there was any real legal basis for European social or employment policies. When it started, the Common Market was about economics – with no social dimension at all. However, when European governments from the 1980s onwards argued that social and employment rights were at the heart of a modern European Community they justified social interventions not on social but on economic grounds by citing abuses of health and safety regulations that damaged the Single Market.

This did not satisfy the then Conservative government, who used their power of veto in the Council of Ministers to block social and employment policy directives, including proposals to give enhanced rights to part-time workers in 1981, to temporary workers in 1982, for parental leave in 1983, and to outlaw sex discrimination in 1986. Even in areas where all other right-of-centre European leaders agreed upon the need for a social action programme at the Hanover European Council in 1988, Mrs Thatcher's government held back – refusing to accept the European Commission's preliminary draft of the Social Charter, despite the Social Affairs Commissioner, Vasso Papandreou, giving an assurance it would only constitute 'a political commitment, not a legal obligation'.[2] She went on to reject the Social Charter at the Madrid Summit in 1989 and blocked proposals that flowed from the European Community's Social Action Programme. While the President of the European Commission, Jacques Delors, told the British TUC, 'it is impossible to build Europe on deregulation', Mrs

Thatcher 'considered it quite inappropriate for rules and regulation about working practices to be set at Community level'.[3]

The Maastricht Treaty negotiations are now famous for the decision to create the Euro currency with an opt-out for Britain. But as Sarah Hogg and Jonathan Hill, two of the most important advisers to John Major at the time of Maastricht, have written, 'the biggest problem' for British negotiators was not the Euro but the Social Chapter. As Hogg and Hill note, Major 'wanted to keep the Social Chapter out of the treaty' and adopted a 'high-risk strategy' to oppose the entrenchment of employee rights as agreed by both France and Germany.[4]

So worried was Britain about the French version of the Social Chapter that officials in the Department of Employment drafted a British alternative to be held back in reserve by negotiators. But Michael Howard, the Secretary of State for Employment, opposed any compromise: as a result, Britain did not submit what a Foreign Office civil servant of the day, Stephen Wall, called a 'less problematic' set of proposals. Indeed, Howard was so determined to stop the Social Chapter that he is said to have made many telephone calls to John Major during the negotiations and, according to Wall, made it 'subtly, but plainly, clear that this was a resigning matter'.[5] Recalling Maastricht, Wall has subsequently said: 'What occupied my time at Maastricht itself was the whole question of the Social Chapter opt-out, where Major was being put in a corner by Michael Howard … Michael Howard was ensuring that John Major had no room for manoeuvre. It would have been perfectly possible to devise [a compromise] at an early stage, before Maastricht – the Department of Employment had worked on a version of the Social Chapter which may have been negotiable. But Michael Howard made that impossible.[6] 'Either the Chapter had to be drastically amended,' recalled Douglas Hurd, the then Foreign Secretary, 'or we had somehow to negotiate an opt-out,' while accepting that 'increasingly our isolation appears but that can't be helped'.[7]

The danger was that the Maastricht negotiations would break-down on the issue of the Social Chapter even after agreement had been reached on Britain's Euro opt-out. But Major himself was opposed to the Social Chapter because of concerns about the impact on business and he thought it would be impossible to get Maastricht ratified by the House of Commons with it in the treaty. As Hogg and Hill recall, on being 'door-stepped' at the start of the first day of the Maastricht negotiations, Major said the Social Chapter would impose huge costs on British business: 'It is very strongly opposed by British industry and commerce and it would cost jobs, it would cost competiveness,' he said.[8] As Major writes in his own autobiography: 'I disliked the Social Chapter intensely, and knew well enough the necessity of rejecting it if I wished to obtain approval in Parliament of the treaty as a whole ... I preferred no chapter at all.'[9]

The French view was that there could be no Maastricht Treaty unless there was a Social Chapter, but for Major there would be no Maastricht Treaty if there was a Social Chapter. President Mitterrand said: 'Europe must commit itself to it or France would vote against the treaty.' He threatened to 'oppose a sham charter'.[10] The Spanish Prime Minister, Felipe González, argued that 'there can be no political union without the social title'.[11] At the negotiations, Major recalls saying: 'Some [European] colleagues won't sign without the Social Chapter; I won't sign with it.'[12] He insisted that he was not prepared to replace, overrule or undermine the legislation that the Conservative government had passed in the employment field over the previous decade: 'I saw no purpose in adding Community programmes to our domestic effort,' he later said.[13] As Hogg and Hill recount, officials then worked on alternative drafts trying to see if it was possible to reduce the Social Chapter to a 'meaningless shell', but it was 'dangerous territory and the Prime Minister did not like it'.[14]

As they tried to stand firm in a minority of one, the Conservative government's position was undermined, when at a meeting of employers and trade unions, the British CBI agreed to participate in a European Commission consultation on the Social Partners' Agreement, which proposed to entrench in Community legislative processes a constitutionally recognised role for employers' organisations and trade unions. This, as Hogg and Hill argue, 'undermined the British position' and was taken as 'a signal that Britain was ready to give in'.[15] While the CBI then withdrew its support for the Social Partners' Agreement, following ministerial pressure, the announcement weakened Major's hand and the UK appeared even more isolated. John Kerr, the leading civil servant in the negotiations, believed that all the government could do was to go on 'seeing if they were bluffing, keeping the issue going to the end'.[16]

When at the last minute of the Maastricht negotiations, the host of the discussions, Dutch Premier Ruud Lubbers, offered the UK a watered down Social Chapter that was technically outside the Treaty and left most powers with nation states, Major still refused, replying: 'It's no good asking me – I can't do it and I won't do it.'[17] As Major says in his memoirs, Lubbers 'dangled some tentative offers of watering down the social proposals, but there were none I could accept. He suggested amendments … I considered them and said no.'[18] Meanwhile, as Major writes: 'John Kerr was walking round with an upside down Social Chapter we had drafted in which everything was agreed by unanimity except when specific to the contrary.'[19] Major toiled over the ground with Lubbers, says Hurd, '[but] our partners could not accept our diluted alternative text … never was ingenuity more necessary among weary men.'[20]

Lubbers, he recalls, 'met the moment' with a device by which 'our partners could agree the Social Chapter among themselves without Britain being involved at all.'[21] Pascal Lamy, then *Chef de Cabinet* to the President of the European Commission, is thought to have drafted the solution under which there was to be no protocol that Britain alone had to sign. Instead there was a protocol that all the rest of Europe had to agree: Member States would secure a separate Social Chapter outside the Treaty, thus satisfying the UK's demand that a text should not be inserted inside it. Lubbers later said: 'If I had known that John Major needed in all circumstances an opt-out I would have played it differently.'[22]

But matters did not end there as I recall from my time in the Labour Shadow Cabinet. The Social Chapter had been key to persuading British trade unionists to support European membership and to reverse their opposition that had been apparent in the 1975 referendum. Labour's anger at the exclusion of the Social Chapter went so deep that it was prepared to put the Maastricht Treaty at risk. So, in April 1993, Labour championed a tactical amendment to the Maastricht Bill that tied ratification of the treaty to acceptance by Britain of the Social Chapter. What emerged was described by John Major as 'a mad hatter coalition' between those who wanted to stop Maastricht altogether and those who wanted Maastricht with Britain signing the Social Chapter too.[23] The amendment required that there be another vote on the Social Chapter before the treaty could be officially ratified and come into effect. The Labour amendment resulted in a tied vote, 317–317, with the Speaker voting that night to maintain the *status quo* (as is required by parliamentary procedure). The vote, in any event, was amended the next day to 317–318 after a recount. But the government's main motion that night was lost by eight votes and had the effect of stopping ratification of the treaty, despite the fact that Parliament had already approved the legislation. It almost brought the government down: John Major was now pencilling in a General Election date for early September 1993, only a year after regaining power in 1992, and it was only when he submitted to and then won a Motion of Confidence by 38 votes that his government survived.

Why was the Social Chapter – and a social dimension to the European Union – so divisive in Britain when it was a unifying and almost consensual piece of legislation in Europe? After all, Britain is already signed up to the United Nations, the Council of Europe and the International Labour Organisation, all of which have agreements on social rights to which the UK are committed. One reason for the controversy, as we have implied, is that social legislation was a late-comer to European legislation: that from the early years of the Common Market employment law was seen as a national responsi-bility and that British citizens looked to their own governments for social protection. Eurosceptics also found it difficult to accept what they considered to be empire-building by the European Union.

But no one can deny that the Social Chapter has strengthened the individual and collective workplace rights of UK employees. Annual leave, agency worker rights, part-time worker rights, fixed-term worker rights, collective redundancy, paternity, maternity and parental leave, protection of employment upon the transfer of a business and anti-discrimination legislation flow from it, are generally popular and might all be re-opened if we left the European Union. During the 1960s, Harold Wilson's Labour government legislated to protect workers from discrimination on the basis of gender and ethnicity, a protection subsequently extended to those with a disability. It was only later, however, that the European Union's Treatment Directives extended protection from discrimination on the grounds of age, sexual orientation, religion and belief. And there is no doubt that, more generally, European social policy has delivered support for some of the most disadvantaged in Britain. At the last count, 87,000 disabled British people were helped towards work by European-funded training schemes.[24] Moreover, under discussion is a European-wide general Accessibility Act that could further help the mobility of millions of people.[25] All of this makes 'Social Europe' more than just a phrase devised by a Brussels-based bureaucrat.

But even after the 1997 General Election, when Labour signed the Social Chapter, European social policy remained a divisive issue. When in his draft Constitutional Treaty, President Giscard d'Estaing advocated an increase in the social policy element contained in the Treaties, putting this at the heart of the new Constitution, the battle over social policy was re-joined. When that fell and a milder version

– the Lisbon Treaty – was signed, enshrining a commitment to 'combat social exclusion and discrimination' and to 'promote social justice and protection and solidarity between the generations', the Conservatives in Britain again complained about the scope of Europe's social dimension. They opposed the clauses committing the European Union to facilitate dialogue between their social partners, employers and trades unions, and the social clauses of the Charter of Fundamental Rights which guarantee safe working conditions, reasonable working hours, protection against unfair dismissal and freedom to seek employment in any Member State.

Balancing autonomy and sharing

So what is the right balance between the autonomy that Britain enjoys and the co-operation we agree on a social dimension to the Single Market? Why should basic rights be guaranteed and, in some cases, applied at the EU-level and not just by national states on their own? The reason is that the emphasis in the European Union's social provision is on minimum rights without which we risk a 'race to the bottom' in which the losers would be hard-working people and their families. The case for intervention, accepted by politicians of the Right as well as Left across Europe, is driven forward by a simple argument: that a market must have a social dimension and that the Single Market should also be a Social Market. The Social Chapter has reflected a basic idea that a market needs a set of minimum social rights if it is to work successfully and if we are to prevent the good employer – or country – being undercut by the bad and the bad by the worst.

One of the first and most important areas in which Europe has influenced British practice at work is in the area of women's equality. Although the UK had enacted legislation in this area – notably the Equal Pay Act of 1970, introduced by a Labour government – a European Court of Justice (ECJ) judgement in 1982 strengthened the law. The European Union has also played a significant role in protecting working parents and supporting improvements in maternity leave and pay. The 1992 Pregnant Workers' Directive further extended these rights, establishing a minimum entitlement to paid maternity leave and protection from unfair dismissal.

Perhaps the best known change the European Union has brought about in employment rights has been in the area of working time and holidays. The Working Time Directive was adopted in 1993. The Directive laid out a framework for working time – based on protecting health and safety – and set a limit to unacceptably long working hours. In 1998, the Working Time Regulations, which guarantee four weeks' paid holiday a year, was implemented in Britain. Until then, UK workers did not have any statutory rights in respect of weekly working hours or paid holidays. Initially set at 20 days a year, paid holiday entitlement was subsequently extended by our government to 28 days a year with the inclusion of bank holidays. The Directive also brought in a maximum working week of 48 hours, averaged over 17 weeks. There has been a decline in long hours working since 1998 – it is possible that this is, at least in part, due to the Working Time Directive and introduction of the 48-hour week.

In a third area, European Union directives have been fundamental in strengthening rights for the collective voice of workers in both the UK and Europe. Workers in large multinational companies that operate within Europe now have the right to request a European Works Council be set up to discuss any transnational issues with managers when there is a request from at least 100 employees in two or more countries. This right derives from the European Works Council Directive, which was agreed in 1994 and extended to the UK in 1997 when the Labour government signed up to the Social Chapter. The Information and Consultation Directive that was agreed in 2002, and transposed into UK law in 2005, gives employees – in the event of any corporate restructuring – a further statutory right to be informed and consulted on a range of issues that affect their employment.

A fourth area in which the EU has improved workplace rights is in the protection for employees facing redundancy when an employer's business is in the process of undergoing sale. The Transfer of Undertakings Regulations (TUPE) were introduced in the UK to implement the Acquired Rights Directive of 1977 and offers protection to employees whose work is being transferred to another employer. These employees have to be consulted about the transfer, and some basic protection of their employment and terms and conditions is written in. The TUC, rightly, described this as an example of where the EU 'has been a real pathfinder for national policy'.[26] A follow-up Collective Redundancies Directive requires employers to consult with recognised trade unions on collective redundancies.

There is a fifth area – general protection for health and safety – where European law has helped British workers tackle diseases like asbestosis and protected whistle-blowers who highlight breaches. There is some evidence that workplace accidents have fallen as a result.

In the UK government's 2014 review of European Union social and employment policy, concern was expressed about the 'judicial activism' of the ECJ in social affairs and how a 'one size fits all' approach to 28 different Member States – with diverse traditions and social practices – contrasts with Britain's traditional emphasis on the rights of the individual.[27] But, in reality there is a limit to how far European rules and regulations alone can protect workers' rights and in practice there is a balance to be struck between autonomy and integration. As the government's own review acknowledged, it is difficult to quantify costs associated with European social policy. Indeed, those who complain most about empire-building by the European Commission also admit Britain has some of the lightest-touch employment laws in the developed world. And, as the government's own review concedes, the flow of new legislation has 'tailed off and we have instead seen a greater emphasis on the EU's role of co-ordinating policy across Member States.'[28]

The Treaty of Lisbon, which we signed, strengthened the social dimension of the European Union and allowed for qualified majority voting in regulations outlawing discrimination and protecting health and safety. But it also made clear that the development and implementation of social policies should remain principally the responsibility of Member States. 'European unification on the basis of a union of sovereign states under the Treaties may, however, not be realised in such a way that the Member States do not retain sufficient room for the political formation of the economic, cultural and social circumstances of life,' the German Constitutional Court ruled when it issued its interpretation of the Lisbon Treaty in 2009. 'This applies in particular to areas which shape the citizens' circumstances of life, in particular the private space of their own responsibility and of political and social security ... and to political decisions that particularly depend on previous understanding as regards culture, history and language and which unfold in discourses.'[29] For good measure the Court added: 'To the extent that in these areas, which are of particular importance for democracy, a transfer of sovereign powers is permitted at all, a narrow interpretation is required. This concerns in particular ... the shaping of the circumstances of life by social policy.'[30]

So it is not surprising that today the European Union has no power to regulate in areas as important as pay and salaries, collective bargaining, social security, dismissals and workplace discipline which are recognised to be the sole competencies of Member States. And while there is some support for a common approach to minimum wages, there is no European law that could force states to follow instructions from the European Commission. In 1993, the European Commission asked Member States to 'take appropriate measures to ensure that the right to an equitable wage is protected', and a report from the European Parliament encouraged them 'to establish a minimum wage which amounts to a certain proportion of the national average wage'.[31] But the idea was more or less abandoned by the second half of the 1990s. In 2007, the European Parliament revisited the issue, expressing its regret that 'the minimum wage is set very low or at below subsistence level' in many European countries and in 2008 it called on the Council 'to agree an EU target for minimum wages … to provide for remuneration of at least 60 per cent of the relevant average wage'. The Parliament later asked the European Commission to study the impact that the introduction of an EU-wide minimum income would have in each country, but nothing has come of this.[32]

As I showed in a previous chapter, membership of the European Union leads to more UK exports, more UK investment and more UK jobs. But it is my conviction that the case for remaining in Europe must extend far beyond this. The Social Market is the linchpin of the European Union. Markets, I suggest, should be free. But markets should not be value-free. As I said during the global economic crisis, markets need morals. And so, in this chapter, I argue that again a balance has to be achieved between the autonomy we desire and the co-operation we need and from which we can benefit. While Britain has – and will retain – the freedom to design our social security system and thus decide the levels of benefits (from child benefit to pensions); set its own minimum wage and the ways it is enforced; and retains the power to set our own tax rates, there are substantial benefits to be gained from EU co-operation. I have said that we benefit from the setting of minimum standards under European-wide arrangements like the Social Chapter which raise standards in competitor countries and helps minimise what is called 'social dumping'.[33] But we also do so because we learn from each other and, in significant areas like scientific research, we pool and share resources for a common cause that supports the public good.

Social Europe

Unsurprisingly, mention of the phrase 'Social Europe' raises more hackles than it does plaudits and it certainly defies a comfortable consensus. And, while many argue that the continent's Social Market expresses what it means to be European, defining what we mean by the 'European social model' has proved elusive.

Europe cannot afford to forget that the inequalities between Member States – particularly between the richest and poorest regions of the Union – are far bigger, far more deep-rooted and far more intractable than the major inequalities that exist within the USA, and that this is a source of discontent. As Iain Begg, Fabian Mushövel and Robin Niblett argue, differences partly reflect national traditions and preferences, but also result from countries' differing economic conditions and the varying proportion of revenue raised for social purposes. For example, while Denmark generates only 20 per cent of its social protection receipts through charges on employers and workers, in Estonia it is nearly 80 per cent of all social protection revenues.[34] Variations in the share contributed by employees as opposed to their employers are also striking: Slovenia and Germany are among those countries asking workers to take on more of the burden.[35]

This reflects the fact that there is not one but at least three different social policy models in continental Europe – one giving priority to social insurance and earnings-based benefits as in Austria, Germany and Luxembourg; another emphasising universal entitlements available to all citizens, as in Finland, Norway, Sweden and Denmark; and a 'Southern European' model where social insurance policies are less to do with universal coverage and are linked to employment.[36] This has led writers such as Anthony Giddens and Patrick Diamond to say that there is no such thing as one European social model and that it is more accurate to speak of Europe's 'social models'.[37] However, what's clear, is that Europe's social policy provision is much higher than that of America, whose model of limited welfare leaves higher numbers in poverty even in good times.

Some have argued that Europe could instead ally social reform to economic modernisation. The debate arises from a concern that high welfare spending undermines European competitiveness. As Tony Blair put it back in 2005: 'There is not some division between the Europe necessary to succeed economically and social Europe. Political Europe and economic Europe do not live in separate rooms. The purpose of social Europe and economic Europe should be to sustain each other.' Controversially he challenged Europe to change by asking: 'What type of social model is it that has 20 million unemployed in Europe, productivity rates falling behind those of the USA; that is allowing more science graduates to be produced by India than by Europe; and that, on any relative index of a modern economy – skills, R&D, patents, IT, is going down not up.'[38]

Globalisation does not require Europe, it is argued by Roger Liddle, to dilute its commitment to social justice but to emphasise social investment to improve the quality of public spending and enhance the incentives for reform.[39] One recent attempt to find common ground across Europe to foster adaptability, flexibility, security and employability is what has been called the 'social investment' model. Based on active labour market policies that are linked to social protection – pioneered in the Nordic countries and the Netherlands in the 1990s – the focus in this model is more on prevention than on cure, seeing welfare as a springboard for work, not as a 'sofa' for remaining unemployed.

Focusing on social investment – and making social provision an instrument of greater economic competitiveness – can also help counter the myth that Europe's social provision fosters welfare dependency. Some right-wing ideologies have taken the results from a UN dataset – contained in an article 'Golden Growth: Restoring the Lustre of the European Economic Model' – and made a series of extraordinary claims which have been taken up by Chancellor Angela Merkel and the British Conservative Party.[40] It is alleged that the 28 nations that make up the EU, who account for around 7.2 per cent of the world's population and make up 25.8 per cent of world GDP, account for 50 per cent of 'welfare' spending. But the figure is wrong:

the claim that Europe spends 50 per cent of all world welfare spending is based on computing data from only half the world's countries (and excluding countries like Canada and Mexico). But more important, the 'wasteful public spending' that forms part of the calculation includes contributory pensions, health and help for children and thus laudable attempts to distribute money and invest in people across the life cycle to ensure children at the start of their life and pensioners approaching the end of their lives are not impoverished.

Globalisation, as we have found, has altered the structure of unemployment and industry, creating an ever-widening gap in wealth, income and opportunity between the well-paid elite and the great majority. This is often described as social and economic 'polarisation'. So while Europe continues to generate a large and encouragingly healthy number of high-skilled jobs, lower-skilled jobs – particularly in retail, hospitality and the care services – have replaced middle income jobs as a result of both global competition and technological advance. Low pay among workers is thus a structural problem that can be addressed by upgrading skills and through active labour-market policies.

While it is recognised that welfare systems across Europe are all in need of modernisation, we must be clear: no one is proposing a uniform European welfare state – neither Britain with its own distinctive Welfare State, nor Germany which prides itself in its own policy of co-determination, nor France with its own unique social insurance system.

While cohesion policy is an important element of the Single Market, it also has a pivotal role to play in promoting the idea of 'Social Europe'. But the measure of success should not just be the money we have received or the contracts British firms have won: it should also be the jobs that have been created.[41] There is a strong case for targeting regional policy more effectively to eliminate the disparities between and within countries – disparities which, if dealt with, may reduce the pressure for the migration of workers from poor countries to richer countries like our own. It cannot be stressed too often that the inequalities between and within Member States are far greater – often 5:1 – than in America where the differences between per capita incomes of individual states are much smaller. The difficulties of catching up – usually the rationale for Eastern European states joining the EU – are apparent when we find that, despite annual transfers of around 4 per cent of national income from Western Germany to Eastern Germany, the gap in per capita incomes remains such that incomes are still 25–30 per cent lower per capita in the East compared to the West. More worryingly, every single region of Bulgaria, Greece, Croatia and Slovenia have incomes per head that are below the EU-28 average. In 19 regions in Eastern Europe, income per head is less than half the EU-28 average. The three Bulgarian regions of Severozapaden, Severen tsentralen and Yuzhen have incomes per head that are less than one third of the EU-28 average.[42] Regional inequalities can arise from geographic remoteness, sparseness of population and from the failings of the old Communist economic systems but they manifest themselves in social deprivation, poor-quality healthcare, sub-standard education, high levels of unemployment and grossly inadequate infrastructure.

According to Dawid Sawicki the majority of Eurozone countries have seen income inequality increase substantially since 1990.[43] He argues that this is partly because there are few policy levers available to the Eurozone to compensate for economic shocks, with the result that one in six Europeans are currently living below the poverty threshold.[44] Over 17 million Europeans currently live on less than five euros per day. This poses, as Sawicki argues, 'a challenge for policy-makers as the need to satisfy both ends of the polarised income distribution impedes the design of meaningful reforms.'[45] Perhaps the best way of reducing poverty within Europe and of slowing the exodus of people from East to West is creating prosperity in the East. More than one third of the EU's budget is devoted to cohesion policy which focuses on helping restructure declining industrial areas, assisting rural areas to diversify and supporting the economic development of the low income 'convergence' regions. According to the government's own review of cohesion policy, there is 'increasing convergence between Member States', with the least developed, on average, growing faster than the most developed since 2000.[46] And while they state, 'the evidence is inconclusive as to whether the [cohesion] funds have been effective in achieving their objectives', they can at least conclude that 'where significant positive impacts have been identified they tend to have been in the poorer regions of Member States'.[47] The emphasis now should be on improving the effectiveness of European funds, strengthening the emphasis on competiveness and targeting them on the poorest areas who face the greatest difficulties in catching up.

Pooling and sharing for the public good

There is one area where Europe pools and shares resources to great effect – in research, development and innovation. One prominent writer, Wolfgang Münchau, has stated that 'the main economic argument in favour of the EU, looking forward, is not trade, but policy on research, science and innovation.'[48] Lord Darzi, the leading surgeon, has said: 'As a surgeon and researcher working in the NHS, I know that leaving the European Union would have a catastrophic impact on our status as the world leader in medical science and innovation … The European Union has helped Britain to sustain our world leading position.'[49]

But even this is not uncontroversial. When the Conservative government were negotiating the last paragraphs of the Maastricht Treaty in 1992, the last outstanding issue was decisions on a common research and development budget. As Sarah Hogg recalls, many Member States requested that decisions on the research and development budget should be reached by qualified majority voting, rather than by unanimity. Here again John Major dug in and said he favoured no changes. There was, she recalls 'a terrible pause'. Then Helmut Kohl flung up his hands and slapped the table, rolling with laughter. Unanimity is agreed, Ruud Lubbers quickly and quietly said, closing the meeting before anyone else had a chance to speak.[50]

The promotion of scientific and technological advancement in its own right has become a specific objective of the European Union. By coupling research and innovation, the goal is European leadership in world science, the removal of barriers to innovation and the creation of strong public and private partnerships. Previously, the EU aimed to promote research activities when they were deemed necessary to support the competitiveness of industry. However, at the time of the Lisbon Treaty, we reached agreement on the idea of the European Research Area which encourages the free movement and exchange between countries of researchers, scientific knowledge and technology. The Lisbon Treaty also defined the distribution of research technology and space policy competences between the EU and the Member States.

The most recent EU research framework programme, Horizon 2020, will make almost €80 billion available over seven years (2014 to 2020), in addition to the private investment that this money will attract. The UK receives more EU research funding than its economic or demographic size would entitle it to receive. As the Royal Society has made clear, the UK is one of the largest recipients of research funding in the EU and, although national contributions to the EU budget are not itemised, independent analyses suggest that the UK receives a greater amount of EU research funding than our *pro rata* contribution. In fact, in the six years to 2013, the UK received €8.8 billion in direct EU funding for research, development and innovation activities.[51] And in receiving €1.9 billion of structural funds for research and innovation activities Britain was the second largest recipient after Germany.[52] Adjusting these figures for the relative sizes of economies, the UK outperforms Germany and is second only to the Netherlands.

Examining Framework Programme 7 funding more closely, namely funding from the European Research Council and Marie Skłodowska-Curie Actions, we find that the UK was the top performer among participating countries. Researchers based in the UK received 16 per cent of EU R&D funding, and 20 per cent of its grants for scientific research in the last budget period, while our contributions were 11 per cent of the EU's total budget.[53] As José Manuel Barroso, President of the European Commission between 2004 and 2014, says, the UK is a very important player in European research and education 'as a result of the excellence of research in many of the British universities'.[54]

Of course, if Britain left the EU, more research funding would have to be made available from the Treasury to make up this shortfall in funding. However, there could be risks: the UK would lose out unless it is able to negotiate terms, similar to Norway, to continue to be part of collaborative European Union projects in areas such as aerospace, medicine, transport and energy. This would be to the huge detriment of our nation's competitive performance. In contrast, if the UK's performance in attracting EU framework funding is maintained, UK universities, research centres and businesses could expect to receive €2 billion in the first two years of Horizon 2020. This is about 20 per cent of all British government spend on science. In circumstances when UK funding for Research Councils is decreasing in real terms, as a result of the Conservative government's cuts, the European Research Council has given British science a funding increase of 60 per cent.

Professor Sir Paul Nurse, the Nobel Prize winner, has said that UK research would suffer if the country were to leave the EU. A British exit would make it harder to get funding for science and sell 'future generations short', he argues. Nurse, who is director of the Francis Crick Institute and the former President of the Royal Society, believes those who campaign for a Brexit are jeopardising 'the long-term future of the UK for short-term political advantage'. He contends: 'We need a vision for our future that is ambitious and not to run away and bury our heads in the sand, and we can best do this by staying in the EU. We should not be side-tracked by short-term political opportunism.'[55]

Lord Darzi has pinpointed the €800 million for health research received from European Union research budgets between 2007 and 2013 and the fact that Britain led 20 per cent of all health-related projects, striking up partnerships with other scientific institutions across Europe. He also points to the success of the Oxford Parkinson's Disease Centre as an example of a project given European Union support. Darzi says leaving Europe would be an exercise in self-harm that would risk our economy, degrade our scientific research and undermine our NHS.[56]

Similarly, Professor Steve Cowley, who runs the UK's national laboratory for fusion research – a technology that could be an answer to supplying the world's electricity by the end of the century – has said that long-term projects such those funded by Horizon 2020 would not be possible outside the EU: 'At this point, we have the greatest capability for fusion in the world … [and] that capability is supported largely by European money. Where the science gets closer to market, then access becomes harder and harder for people outside the EU,' he maintains.[57] Professor Dame Janet Thornton, Director Emeritus of the European Bioinformatics Institute, says that in her field of analysing genetic and genomic information to tackle diseases such as cancer, projects were only possible thanks to EU scientific structures and co-operation: 'We cannot do it on our own, because it needs data for millions of people … If we are going to try to collaborate with 27 European Member States [outside the EU] and negotiate how we do it with every one individually to share biomedical data, that is going to take a long, long time to achieve.' Asked what would happen if the UK were to leave the EU she replied: 'We would lose so much.'[58]

CHAPTER TEN

Is there a case for an energy and environmental union?

In 2008, we agreed to create 'The North Sea Offshore Grid' as part of the European Energy Super Grid. Germany, France, Denmark, Sweden, Belgium, Ireland, Luxembourg and the Netherlands, as well as the UK, signed up. And in 2010 the European Commission document, 'Blueprint for a North Sea Grid', set out the detailed case for high-voltage cables transmitting, selling and exchanging energy over thousands of miles.

The benefits of co-operation were clear. The intermittent and variable supplies of renewable energy – wind, wave and solar power – could be harnessed more cheaply and efficiently as part of the widest possible pool of customers. The wind does not blow all the time and the sun does not always shine. However, with Norway's hydroelectric power plants acting as a 'giant battery' – storing the power and releasing it at peak times or when the wind strength is low – a cable between Norway and the United Kingdom, with interconnections to Germany, could contribute greatly to delivering a low carbon future and potentially help decarbonise Europe's energy sector to help reach the European Union's target to reduce CO_2 emissions by 80–95 per cent below 1990 levels by 2050. Over the next five years, the UK government is planning 'to double our ability to import electricity with similar new connections to France, Belgium and Norway. And there are potential new projects with Denmark, Iceland and Ireland further down the track. These new connections alone could save British households nearly £12bn over the next two decades by driving down the price of electricity.'

There are enormous gains from using the variable power that comes from wind farms in the North Sea and Germany, combining it with solar energy from Spain and Southern Europe, and adding this to the power supply generated from base-load nuclear generators in France and hydroelectric stations in Scandinavia. This would, first and foremost, ensure we have a reliable source of clean, low-carbon energy. The existence of such a network, moreover, would not preclude imports of gas through pipelines from Russia or Algeria, or through liquid natural gas facilities from the Middle East and Central Asia, but a European grid would limit our dependence on energy supplies from unstable regions and avoid the risks that come with that. It would also reduce the risks that changes in the weather or loss of supply from any particular facility might cause in individual countries. And using renewables to best effect and reducing the need for back-up facilities – often gas or coal-fired power stations – would cut costs for energy consumers. This is not a science fiction fantasy; it is a practical possibility which is now within reach. Wind farms are already being planned on the Dogger Bank, an area of submerged land in the middle of the North Sea.

In its first stage, the wind power from the North Sea will be supplied into the UK. Hydropower can also be accessed from Norway and further lines could be built from Holland and Germany. Other links might also be added: for example, power could come from wind farms in Scotland that would link to the established European Grid. Using the most advanced available grid technology would reduce transmission losses by up to a factor of ten. Such a hub, once in place, would also encourage further investment in wind.

Of course these new links do not depend upon our European Union membership, but almost certainly they could not easily be built without it. The technology for distributing electricity right across Europe is developing fast. Of course, all transmission systems lose energy between the generation point and the end consumer as the electricity encounters resistance in the wires along the way. Usually, the greater the distance between systems and consumers, the more energy that is lost. In China the main sources of power are often thousands of kilometres from where the electricity is most needed. As a result, the Chinese have installed seven ultra-high-voltage lines which carry power at around 800,000 volts or more (compared to the maximum 450,000 volts in Britain) and are producing from this one source the equivalent of half the energy Britain uses each year.[1] At the United Nations last September, the Chinese President, Xi Jinping, proposed a Global Energy Network with 'an intercontinental backbone grid' to enable the world to obtain 80 per cent of its energy from renewables. In addition, China suggested 'discussion on establishing a global energy network to facilitate efforts to meet the global power demand with clean and green alternatives'.[2] As Jeremy Plester highlights: 'Transmission lines already connect the UK with France, the Netherlands and Ireland and there's a proposal for a 600-mile power line to connect Iceland to the UK and export Iceland's abundant hydroelectric power from rivers and geothermal power from underground hot rocks.'[3] But the use of high voltage currents will make even longer transmission lines viable. One day, given further scientific advances in areas of research such as solar thermal technology, we may also be able to make use of the abundant sunshine of the Sahara Desert to produce energy for Europe. But for the moment there is more than enough of a challenge within the EU itself.

In 2010, in a major lecture at the Council of Europe in Bruges, the German Chancellor, Angela Merkel, highlighted her support for this new form of European co-operation. There was, she said, a need not just for 'smart grids' throughout Europe but for what she called 'energy reservoirs' – capturing energy that is then stored for later use when needed. 'It must be clear that without new energy networks, there will no competition gains,' Chancellor Merkel said, and 'without new energy infrastructure, no expansion of renewable energies.'[4] In other words, a fully connected European-wide network across Europe will reduce costs, cut emissions and enhance energy security by limiting the need for imports.

According to energy economist, Dieter Helm, 'integration of these networks has multiple pay-offs to the European economy. Integrating networks increases Europe's security of supply,' he states, 'and reduces the pressure of those countries exposed to Russia's aggressive threats to gas supplies; reduces the costs of meeting the capacity requirements in each member-state; and brings competition to the heart of the dominant national incumbents and hence helps to harmonise prices.'[5] According to a European Parliament study, 'an economically and physically more integrated energy market in Europe could deliver at least €50 billion in efficiency gains per year' across the continent.

The scientific advances that are making the case for an energy union represent an important dimension of the new global climate change policy that was agreed in Paris during December 2015. There is wide-ranging support for action to reduce emissions and to limit the risks of global warming and the disruption of weather patterns. It is equally clear that such action can be best achieved faster and more cheaply if Europe works together. That is one reason why Europe needs an effective common energy policy and why the UK should be taking the lead in designing it.

'The EU energy union is a concept whose time has come,' Helm states, while pointing out that there is 'little consensus as to what it should contain.'[6] As things stand, Europe's energy policy is in an embryonic form and its scope and shape are still to be defined in detail. The key policy issues – the mix of fuels, the nature of regulation, questions of ownership, pricing and taxation – are still predominantly matters for individual Member States.

Energy policy, as it developed through the 20th century, was set at the national level. In many countries, including the UK, gas and electricity supplies were publicly owned monopolies. Cross-border co-operation was limited and energy supply was seen as an issue of national security in narrow terms. Different countries adopted different policies, usually dictated by the resources available within their own territory. Britain and Holland found extensive resources of oil and gas in North Sea waters. France, under de Gaulle and his successors, sought to avoid over-dependence on supplies of oil from North Africa and the Middle East by developing civil nuclear power. The coal industry, once the dominant source of supply in both France and the UK, declined dramatically but remains a significant force and an important source of power in Germany and in parts of Eastern Europe.

In the UK during the 1980s, the Thatcher Government transferred most of the energy sector into private hands. In contrast, in France and many other parts of the EU, energy supply remains a sector dominated by state-owned enterprises. The division of Europe after the Second World War led to the creation of a distinct energy economy in the East, dominated by the Soviet Council for Mutual Economic Assistance (commonly known as Comecon) under the leadership of Russia. And, today, many Eastern Europe states still depend on their infrastructure links with Russia. As a result, 25 years after the Cold War ended, the physical connections between Western and Eastern Europe are limited and inadequate, and confirm the fragmented nature of the European energy market.

But by building on new technologies and gaining a better understanding of how we can harness energy in an environmentally friendly way, a more co-operative approach in Europe should yield beneficial results. There are clear gains to the United Kingdom in ensuring that we get the balance right in future between autonomy and co-operation. As a producer of both oil and gas, and as one of Europe's biggest sources of wind and wave power, we would benefit from leading a European-wide debate on new energy policies and helping to secure the continent's energy supply.

Energy security is usually defined as keeping the lights on. Governments that fail to do that, as Edward Heath discovered in the

1970s, don't last long. We need to ensure that adequate supplies of energy are always available to keep normal, daily life running smoothly. Electricity is needed for factories, shops, schools, hospitals, airports, traffic lights and a myriad of other uses. It is critical that it is never (or hardly ever) interrupted. And environmental security is about ensuring that we can meet all of our energy needs without doing irreparable damage to the natural environment on which we all depend. The challenge is global and Europe can lead on this. However, unless we can help other countries, including some of the poorest in the world, whatever we do will have only a limited impact on global outcomes.

We cannot afford either to ignore the impact which energy prices have on our economic security, on jobs and on livelihoods. Pricing ourselves out of world markets by forcing up energy prices will only result in industrial activity and jobs being exported to areas where costs are lower. And that will do nothing to reduce total global emissions.

So we need a carefully balanced mixture of policies to meet our objectives and it is clear that the best way of avoiding harsh trade-offs is for the countries of Europe to work together rather than at a distance from each other. Co-operation can enhance security by spreading risks and can also make a material – and, perhaps, decisive – contribution to the achievement of wider international objectives on the reduction of emissions and the development of a thriving low-carbon economy.

Energy co-ordination

The recent history of energy policy in Europe demonstrates what has been achieved and also what remains to be done. The European Coal and Steel Community, which was one of the forerunners of the EU structure, was all about the need for the free and open movement of coal supplies. But in 2007, as concern about climate change grew, Europe for the first time adopted a set of common, medium-term objectives to ensure that renewables provided 20 per cent of Europe's total energy mix by the year 2020.[7]

Individual countries, including the UK under the last Labour government, have since set higher, longer-term targets. And after 2013, in response to the crisis in Ukraine and concerns about Russian dominance of supplies of gas, the European Union began to develop a set of policies designed to limit dependence on any single supplier and to improve infrastructure links between Western and Eastern Europe.

In the past two years, in advance of the Paris agreement on global climate change targets, European policy-makers brought the twin objectives of reducing dependence on one supplier and targeting reduced carbon emissions together into one policy. In February 2015, the European Commission tabled a plan, which the Council of Ministers adopted, setting out the basis of the EU's Energy Union proposal.

Each of the advances made over recent years has been important but none of the initiatives have yet come to full fruition. In the spring of 2014 the Commission presented studies promoting dozens of major new infrastructure projects which would enhance energy security, including lines linking the Baltic states to the main suppliers of energy in Central and North Europe, with links through Italy to Central Europe and through Spain into France. There is a strong case for each of these projects – many of which would help businesses and communities in some of Europe's poorest areas. The reality, however, is that no projects have yet been started. The infrastructure links necessary to maximise the use and minimise the cost of renewables, such as wind and solar across the European Union, remain undeveloped.

Europe's energy imports have therefore grown as oil and gas production from mature areas, such as the British and Dutch sections of the North Sea, have declined. Without the infrastructure links necessary to ensure sources of supply, Europe's dependence on imports from particular suppliers – for example, Russia and Algeria – can only increase.

The way forward

Energy policy across Europe has become a divisive issue because of claim and counter claim about costs to the consumer. The Energy Secretary, Amber Rudd, claimed that total household bills could rise by as much as £1.5 million a day outside the European Union's internal energy market. Citing research by Vivid Economics in support of her contention that the UK faces an 'electric shock' of £500 million a year to UK energy investment costs, Ms Rudd also claimed that Brexit would make the UK more at risk of Russian 'hijacking'. The 'Leave' campaign responded the UK did not depend on the EU or Russia for supplies; that EU membership actually pushed costs up; and that, like Norway, we could negotiate to remain part of the internal energy market if we thought it of use. However, as Ms Rudd questioned, 'does anybody really think all of that investment would continue if we left the EU and with no extra costs?' She proceeded to refer to National Grid research which suggests that, although uncertain, the impact of leaving the EU on the UK's energy capability is 'very likely to be negative'.[8]

In the confused and hostile debate within the UK ideas can all too easily be twisted out of shape. Co-operation for common purposes does not mean the imposition of uniformity. There is no need – and little value – in forcing a single solution on every different Member State of the European Union. For historic and cultural reasons different countries have taken and will continue to take different views on the energy mix. A policy which attempted to force Germany to keep its nuclear power stations which are being phased out would simply not succeed. Nor would a policy which attempted to make the French embrace fracking and the production of gas and oil from shale rock.

Nor is it realistic at this stage to base a common approach to energy in Europe on an objective of self-sufficiency in the same way that a primary American strategic objective is 'energy independence'. UK gas imports are predicted to rise from providing 45 per cent of our needs today, to 75 per cent by 2030. A European goal of energy security is better achieved by diversity, the aim being to reduce the risks that can come from having one dominant supplier by buying from a wide range of suppliers. European policies that have led to the unbundling of energy markets and greater pricing transparency transparency facilitate this objective. In short, we need a policy which respects the reality of differing resource bases, differing local needs, differing public pressures across Europe and that gets the balance right between the desire for autonomy and the need for, and benefits of, co-operation.

To assume that co-operation in an energy union means the imposition of an absolute uniformity or that it requires us to isolate ourselves from world markets in the interests of self-sufficiency is both inaccurate and unfair. As we have shown with the energy grid, what can be achieved by co-operation could not be achieved if we worked in isolation from each other. The whole is clearly greater than the sum of its parts. This insight should influence the next stage of policy development in Europe: recognising the need for creative co-operation based on the reality that Europe can do together what no nation state can do alone.

Security remains an important consideration. But that means a diversity of sources and supply so that no one is completely and permanently dependent on a single supplier. Russia in turn has to compete on normal commercial terms while unable to use their gas supply as a political lever. Other countries would benefit enormously from being able to access the European gas market through new infrastructure links. Additional links could also connect Europe to a wider range of supplies including those available from the countries of Central Asia and the Eastern Mediterranean. Trade routes through the Balkans and South-East Europe could bring resources and revenue to some of the poorest countries in the region. In this way, energy policy need not be concerned only with protecting our own security but could be developed in ways which enhance the stability and prosperity of our neighbours through open markets and fair competition.

Europe is ahead of most parts of the world in its energy efficiency and in the reduction in emissions. Indeed, measured by energy per unit of output, our carbon emissions per capita are half those of the US.[9] The challenge now is to reduce the cost of renewables not least to avoid the risk that carbon emissions are simply exported elsewhere as industry moves to areas with lower standards and lower costs.

I have focused on one major step forward – infrastructure which could link supply and demand across the widest possible area, from Scotland to Greece, to reduce the cost of intermittent wind and solar. The Brussels-based think-tank, Bruegel, has suggested that 'much more electricity could be generated from the same capacity of deployed solar panels if they were installed in the sunniest locations, rather than in the Member States that provide the highest subsidies.'[10]

That remains unproven but what we do know is that Europe has world-class science, technology and engineering alongside pioneering companies in and around the energy sector capable of commercialising technical advances and marketing them across the globe. And, as we have shown, co-operation on research, scientific and technical work need not be fragmented and resources duplicated.

Across Europe there is a multiplicity of alternatives being researched – from use of advanced materials such as graphene to a range of technologies which can help transform the market by allowing energy (including electricity) to be stored rather then used instantly. Individual companies are developing more efficient vehicles, heating and lighting technology, and advances which can transform waste to energy. Technology can increase the effective supply and value of renewables and allow us all to manage the ways in which we use energy in order to maximise efficiency. In this area Europe can lead the world and the UK can help to lead Europe. A fragmented approach will not achieve the potential which could be unleashed through co-operation.

To quote Bruegel again: 'Individual Member States cannot meaningfully support a sufficiently large portfolio of technologies necessary to ensure resilient decarbonisation. For transport decarbonisation, for example, there is still no certainty whether the future will be fuel-cell hydrogen, battery electric, modal shift, biofuels or something else. So European coordination should ensure that we do not put "all eggs in one basket" by only going big on one single technology, but coordination should also ensure that fragmentation cannot prevent efficient support to the most promising technologies.'[11]

So a union for energy is preferable to a 'ragbag' of national policies. Of course, though, the Germans will continue to argue for their compulsory national renewables targets; the Poles will do the same for coal; the Spanish for investing in an interconnector to France to export their surplus solar; and we British will continue to press for competitiveness and lower electricity prices.

All countries have their own worries about the issues involved but the conclusion is clear: an energy policy in one country is now almost an impossibility. Energy is a global business, with prices set by events far away. The role for countries in Europe is to make sure they are as resilient as possible to cope with events beyond their control and as productive as possible in developing and deploying new solutions. The conclusion is that co-operation across Europe makes eminent common sense.

Climate change

We should take pride in the fact that the UK was the first country in the world to adopt a comprehensive approach to reducing carbon emissions – a lead which others are now following. Indeed, Britain was the first to put emissions reductions into law in the Climate Change Act, which committed us to reduce greenhouse gas emissions by 26 per cent by 2020 and by 80 per cent by 2050 compared to 1990 levels. Under our government there was also a target to eliminate fuel poverty by 2016.[12]

And if Britain led on legislation, the European Union led as the first continent in the world – the first in any region – to adopt an emissions trading scheme. It was also the first to push for a legally binding set of climate and energy targets (a 20 per cent cut in greenhouse gas emissions (from 1990 levels), 20 per cent of EU energy from renewables and a 20 per cent improvement in energy efficiency, all by 2020). Because it understood that reducing emissions in Europe would not itself be the solution to global climate change, it was the European Union that led the push for a Climate Change Treaty at Copenhagen in 2009. And it was the Europeans who after Copenhagen kept pressing for ambitious targets and again helped bring people together in 2015 to secure a further climate change deal. While the deal between America and China paved the way for Paris, it was Europe's work with developing nations that clinched the deal.

Of course, Europe did not succeed in getting all its own way in the negotiations. But even if the agreement does not specify the size of each country's carbon reductions, Paris has given us the first legally binding universal agreement to tackle climate change. And, with the commitment to net zero emissions in the second half of the century, it is the first global statement on how radical emissions reduction has to be and signals to business 'that it has to shift investment in the direction of low-carbon technologies – solar power, electric cars or nuclear energy'.[13]

It might be argued that Europe has accepted obligations on itself that no other continent is willing to assume. The 28 Member States of the European Union have agreed to be bound by targets to cut emissions by at least 40 per cent by 2030, for renewables to account for 27 per cent of energy and for energy efficiency to increase by 27 per cent.[14] It, and the joint action across Europe to improve our seas, landmass and our natural environment, shows how a Union that was established as an economic union has also evolved into an environment union. The effects of pollution do not stop at any national border and if European Union environment laws did not exist to help us tackle common challenges to our air, soils and rivers we would have had to invent them. As Lord Deben, Chair of the UK Climate Change Committee has said: 'Europe is about gaining sovereignty as it allows us to face environmental issues, such as air pollution, which we share with our neighbours.'[15]

Britain was instrumental in the design and passage of the Habitats Directive which protect valuable sites that are home to many of Europe's most threatened species. It is said that we have lost 60 per cent of our plant and animal species over the previous 50 years.[16] Before the Directives we were losing 15 per cent of protected sites every year. That is now down to 1 per cent. And European Union collaboration in research and development allows us to expand the 'green' economy which already stands at £112 billion with a £5 billion trade surplus in green goods and services.[17]

As a group consisting of former heads of environment agencies has said: 'The environmental rules of engagement with the EU after Brexit are very uncertain and would be subject to lengthy and protracted negotiation due to our new status as an outsider.' Most importantly, we would not be able 'to shape EU policy and our influence on the environmental performance of other Member States would decline very sharply once we were no longer at the negotiating table. We therefore conclude that Brexit would be damaging for Britain's environment … the case is clear: We will better able to protect the quality of Britain's environment if we stay in Europe.'[18]

CHAPTER ELEVEN

Migration

In a 2011 study, 60 per cent of our fellow British citizens said that immigration was bad for the country; in a similar poll asking the same question in 2016 the figure was 50 per cent.[1] The main complaint in 2016 is about the impact of immigration. In a poll carried out by Hope not Hate, 78 per cent agree that migrants add to the already severe pressures on overstretched public services and only 7 per cent disagree.[2] When asked to choose their greatest concerns, one quarter of unskilled workers are concerned about immigrants taking their jobs, but overall the impact of immigration on wages and jobs is less of a priority than the perceived pressure on public services, such as hospitals and schools, which was raised by nearly 50 per cent of those surveyed.[3]

Exactly 50 per cent agree 'immigrants often do jobs that need doing but British people don't want to do' and 37 per cent of British people accept that 'immigrants are often prepared to work harder for lower pay than British workers'.[4] And when asked if many organisations, including in the public sector, couldn't cope without immigrants, 40 per cent agree and 29 per cent disagree.[5] Surprisingly perhaps, even a majority of those who oppose further immigration appear to accept it is a two-way street: that there are benefits as well as costs. These findings accord with the evidence from a separate study, analysed by Professor John Curtice, that found 60 per cent of people accepted that migrants should get the same benefits as British residents after two years in the country and 44 per cent agreed this should happen after one year.[6] These results are important because they point to British citizens' main concern about immigration: incomers using already under-pressure public services and the fear they are giving nothing in return.

The 'Leave' campaign feel they will make headway by making immigration their major issue, conjuring up pictures of the overcrowded Calais camps, lorries smuggling in illegal immigrants and the overcrowding of hard-hit communities. All of this is blamed on membership of the European Union. And when the Hope Not Hate poll put the more general statement – 'Leaving the EU would allow us to take back full control of Britain's borders' – 57 per cent agreed with only 15 per cent opposed.[7] Few are prepared to entertain the truth that, while our benefits system may be open to European Union workers, Middle Eastern and North African migrants have no claims on it that are derived from European laws.

Little too is said by the 'Leave' campaign about the 1.2 million British citizens who live in mainland Europe.[8] This fact reminds us that people, generally, are far more mobile than ever before; that the global movement of people is part of a process of global change that includes the global movement of goods, services and money; and that, whether we are 'in' or 'out' of the European Union, more and more people are on the move – in particular millions who are seeking to move from poorer countries to richer countries such as the UK. What are called 'push factors' – conflict and natural disasters – and 'pull factors' – a growing recognition that you will be better off poor in a rich country than rich in a poor one – have little to do with the generosity of welfare provision in the United Kingdom and suggest that, while the general public of today may consider the entry of EU workers into Britain to be our greatest migration problem, the biggest long-term challenge is illegal immigration. And in future years in every rich country, including our own, we will be under pressure to strike the right balance in our national interest between the autonomy we desire, including our ability to impose border controls, and the co-operation that we will need, including co-operation across Europe to root out illegality and abuse.

Without co-operation through the European Union, we will be unable to track the flow of illegal immigrants or slow it before people try to enter our country. Without co-operation we will be unable to address the root causes of migration and to help tackle the poverty in migrants' home countries that propel them to leave. And without co-operation we will also be unable to address the violence and conflict in the Middle East and Africa that forces people to flee their homes and become a new wave of refugees and asylum seekers. Each nation is in a far better position to cope if there is co-ordinated cross-continental action – using continent-wide surveillance and the sharing of intelligence, the European Arrest Warrant, negotiated agreements with countries of origin to return illegal entrants, and EU missions to improve conditions in the neighbouring regions.

Of course much of what needs to be done has to be done within the UK. And I will show that where there is abuse of the system we can act more boldly within the UK, in particular where law, order and criminality are affected, where our public services are under greatest pressure and where ruthless employers are using immigrants to undercut British workers' wages. It is within the power of our own parliament and government to secure better enforcement of the minimum wage, more protection from exploitative employers and – an issue I deal with later – the reallocation of public spending to ease pressure on services in the hardest hit communities. But, again, national measures will be far more successful when matched by the co-operation of our European neighbours. In the chapter ahead, I want to analyse the problem in more depth. I start by placing our British concerns into their global perspective and conclude by suggesting how we can do better in our responses.

Global migration

It is too easy to think that immigration is a phenomenon confined to Britain or Europe: it is, instead, a global problem and there are good reasons why it is on the rise. Recent migration into Europe is driven by the same economic, social and political forces that are affecting migration patterns in the Americas and Asia. Already 230 million of the world's population live and work in countries that are not the countries of their birth. That represents 3 per cent of the world's population.[9] The numbers of people displaced by conflict or natural disasters have risen to an all-time post-war high of 60 million people, with the world's displaced almost equivalent in number to the population of the United Kingdom.[10] Because the number of unstable countries and 'failed states', which fell after the end of the Cold War, has started to rise again – there are currently more than 30 separate conflict zones – and because of the incidences of natural disasters, most recently the earthquake in Nepal, movements of people driven by war, conflict and natural disaster are likely to increase. And while most displaced people stay close to where they once lived – 86 per cent do so – there are now 20 million officially recognised refugees worldwide living away from their home countries.[11] This pattern is revealed in its starkest form by what is happening in Syria where there are now between 12 and 13 million displaced persons, around eight million of whom are internally displaced within Syria and four million of whom are in the neighbouring countries – including Turkey, Jordan and Lebanon – with around one million – only one in 12 of the displaced – headed for Europe or another continent.[12]

But people are also on the move for financial and economic reasons and increasingly leave poorer countries for richer countries – with this number rising fivefold over the last 50 years from an estimated 20 million to 100 million out of the world's 230 million migrants. A skilled or semi-skilled worker doing the same job – for example in the construction industry – can earn 15 times as much if he or she moves from, say, Yemen to the United States.[13] To take another example: moving from the rural areas to the city in Nigeria doubles your wages but moving from Lagos to London can raise your wages six-fold on what you were paid in Lagos and 12-fold overall.

The 2012 World Gallup Survey contained an astonishing finding: that about 13 per cent of the world's population said they would move to another country if they had the opportunity. If this were to occur, the number of global migrants would not be its current 230 million but almost one billion making their future elsewhere. Despite rising levels of economic growth in Africa, in the Caribbean and in the Indian sub-continent, as well as in the Middle East, the pull of the richer countries is obvious. About one quarter of those surveyed (23 per cent – which translates to 150 million adults) stated that they would choose to migrate to the United States, with Canada, France, Saudi Arabia, Australia, Germany and Spain – also like the UK – leading attractions. As many as 7 per cent stated a preference to migrate to the United Kingdom.[14]

These high survey figures contrast with an annual global flow which has, until recently, been around 15 million migrants (the post-Syrian conflict figures are not yet available). A closer analysis of that 15 million tells us that while three million a year, a figure that is now rising fast, were refugees and asylum seekers and two million were spouses and children being reunited with their families, the majority – around ten million – were economic migrants leaving home to work or study. A shortage of manpower and skill in the advanced economies is a pull factor with the economically advanced economies facing slower – and in some cases stalled – population growth and a projected drop in their workforce numbers from today's 800 million to 600 million by 2050.[15]

Pressures to migrate would, of course, lessen considerably if in Africa, the Indian sub-continent or Middle East, economic growth brought higher levels of prosperity. But, according to one major study, Africa's population will more than double to 2.4 billion within the coming 40 years thanks to better healthcare – and thus lower levels of infant mortality and longer individual life spans. Kenya's population will increase from 44 million to 97 million and Nigeria's from 174 million to 440 million by 2050. Somalia is projected to have 27 million people in 2050, up from an estimated 10 million today, and the Democratic Republic of Congo's 71 million population is expected to rise to 182 million.[16] Think of the pressures that could arise: today the EU has a population of 500 million and sub-Saharan Africa around one billion. By 2050, on current projections, the EU population is around the same – 500 million – but Africa will have a population of 2.4 billion. In other words, while today Africa has twice as many people as Europe, by 2050 the figure will be five times as many. This trend has been examined closely by Branko Milanović who puts before us the stark policy choice: either we ensure the poor will become better off in their home countries through higher growth rates or, more likely, when they have the money to do so – and transport costs are far lower than they were – many will leave for the nearest continent, Europe.[17] And they will often come as illegal immigrants. So while there has been a shift over recent years – European Union counted for 18 per cent[18] of all UK immigration in the 1990s but 42 per cent[19] in the year ending September 2015 – this share may represent the high-point of mainland European entry into Britain as, in the next few decades, we return to a more familiar pattern in which the biggest demand is from outside Europe.

Immigration in the UK

Between September 2014 and September 2015 – the latest period for which an annual figure is available – 323,000 more people entered Britain than left it, down four per cent on the record of 336,000 for the year to July 2014. As the BBC has explained half of those migrants,

165,000, are EU citizens who 'came to the UK for work-related reasons' – of whom '96,000, or 58%, had a definite job to go to while 69,000, or 42%, came looking for work.'[20] The Conservative manifesto promise of 2010 that migrant numbers would be reduced dramatically was never honoured.

The number of mainland Europeans working in Britain has increased by 215,000 to two million, according to Labour Force Survey figures for October to December 2015. This compares with the employment of non-EU nationals in the UK which increased by 38,000 to 1.2 million. There were 38,878 asylum applications, including applications for dependants, in 2015 – an increase of 20 per cent compared with the previous year. But there is some discrepancy between the Office of National Statistics figures and those of the National Insurance authorities, with UKIP claiming that more than twice as many European entrants have been given National Insurance numbers than the numbers cited in the immigration statistics.[21] Following a Freedom of Information request from Jonathan Portes – former Chief Economist at the Cabinet Office, who now heads the National Institute of Economic and Social Research (NIESR), and who has shown that it is important in such a controversial area of debate to have accurate statistics – HM Revenue and Customs are to provide the figures on how many National Insurance numbers are actively being used by migrants from mainland Europe.

It has long been argued that there are four key benefits from immigration: 'It is a primary source of innovation and dynamism in our societies,' says one well-known expert, Ian Goldin. He continues 'It responds to labour shortages and serves unmet needs; it meets the demo-graphic and rapidly escalating dependency challenges posed by ageing populations; and it provides an escape from poverty and persecution.'[22]

Not only do most immigrants to our country tend to be in work – 85 per cent of EU citizens in the UK were in employment in 2014 – but more of them work when they come to Britain than they do in any other European country except Portugal and Denmark. Migrants, from both the EU and the rest of the world, are more likely to set up their own businesses – 17 per cent of them do – compared with business creation rates among British adults of just 10 per cent. This is in part because migrants tend not only to be young – their average age in 2011 was 34 whereas the average age of the UK population is over 40 – but also skilled. While one-fifth of the home-grown population have degrees, one-third of migrants do – and, as Hugo Dixon reminds us, British taxpayers did not have to fund these qualifications.[23]

And of course while migrants use our services, there are reciprocal benefits to British citizens living abroad with thousands of our elderly citizens spending their retirement in the south of Europe. A British government report, published this February, reminded us of 'UK citizens living, working and travelling in the other 27 Member States' who 'currently enjoy a range of specific rights to live, work and access pensions, healthcare and public services that are only guaranteed because of EU law. There would be no requirement under EU law for these rights to be maintained if the UK left the EU.'[24]

The pressures on our health, education and community services that British citizens have concerns about arise from the combined impact of population growth and reduced budgets. From its current population of 8.6 million, London is forecast to grow to 11 million by 2050, and possibly as high as 13 million after what the Office for National Statistics says will be one of the biggest ever population increases – a 4.6 million increase – in one decade.[25]

Yet the pressures have to be seen in perspective. One writer, Danny Dorling, says that London is the lowest-density mega-city on the planet: 'The densest part of London is four times less dense than Barcelona, a normal, well-planned European city that Britons all want to visit.' As Andy Beckett writes: 'Liverpool and Glasgow have barely half as many inhabitants now as they had at their peaks in the middle of the 20th century.' He continues, 'while England has roughly

410 people a square kilometre – the second highest in the EU – Wales has only 150, Northern Ireland 135 and Scotland 70'.[26] Improved land use and more effective regional policy within the UK could ease the pressures that arise from congestion in some parts of the country and the waste of resources in others, but it is undoubtedly the case that there is a shortage of affordable homes and that schools, medical facilities, police and other community resources are stretched.

It is the communities affected by rapid and concentrated immigration that need most help to cope. Incomers are often drawn to a small number of localities, sometimes following in the footsteps of compatriots or relatives. Places like Slough (in the 2011 Census, 10 per cent of Slough residents were born in other EU countries)[27] and rural areas of Lincolnshire, such as Ashford – 60 miles from London – have some of the fastest-growing immigrant communities in England. Having grown by 30 per cent in population in 30 years, Ashford now has 78,000 inhabitants; by 2030, planners estimate it will grow by another 30 per cent and exceed 100,000.[28] Kent has been hit particularly hard – with the County Council having to take responsibility for 1,000 unaccompanied children who have arrived in Britain.[29] We have to recognise that while the benefits that can flow from migration are usually spread across the whole of society – for example in higher economic growth – the cost of migration is often borne by a few hard-pressed local communities which prove to be either a magnet for newly arrived people or a stopping-off point and, in recognising that there are clear geographical trade-offs, we need to allocate resources more fairly. This will include asking the EU for a much larger contribution to funding communities under severe stress.

Arrangements for workers, students and family members coming from outside the European Union are all governed by UK domestic law and by our own home-grown immigration rules. As the UK government's own review of non-EU migration states: 'Legal migration is where there was the greatest consensus that retaining national control has worked in the UK's interest by providing the UK with the flexibility to adjust legal migration policy to meet the demands of the UK economy.'[30]

But Europe is at the centre of the controversy over migration for one important reason. The free movement of workers is enshrined in the Treaty on the Functioning of the European Union – and, of course, goes back to Treaty of Rome. This, and the accompanying principle that there will be no discrimination against any worker of any European nationality, is backed up by rules, regulations, secondary legislation and regular judgments by the Court of Justice of the European Union. But free movement is not unrestricted. In theory a migrant cannot live in another member country for more than three months unless they have a job, or some other means of support, if that country does not wish to retain them. But no country has the resources to maintain the register and the identity card system that would be necessary to enforce this, and over time the freedom to move has tended to include family members and those who have yet to find jobs and are looking for work.

The 'Leave' campaign suggests that, because of our welfare system, the UK is more financially attractive than other Member States in Western Europe, although this is unproven. *The Sun* newspaper reports that with an official minimum salary in Romania of just £2,126 a year, migrants will increase their wages six-fold in the UK, with child benefit and tax credits of top of that.[31] Costs of living are of course higher in the UK. The last Labour government came under fire when Romania and Bulgaria joined the European Union, but we acted to apply restrictions up to a maximum of seven years, which meant that immigration was limited up to the start of 2014. In 2007, there were an estimated 34,000 usual residents in the UK with Bulgarian or Romanian nationality. The number of Bulgarians and Romanians rose by 32,000 and 26,000 in 2007–08 and 2008–09 respectively. However, from 2010 to 2014, the number of Romanians and Bulgarians living in Britain increased by over 110,000.[32] The latest available data was published in August 2015, for January to December

2014. This shows the estimated population of Romanian citizens in the UK was 175,000 compared with 128,000 in the previous year. The estimated resident population of Bulgarian citizens was 59,000 compared with 49,000 in the previous year.[33] In fact, since restrictions on Bulgarian and Romanian people working in the UK were lifted at the start of 2014, the number of Romanian and Bulgarians in the UK workforce has risen by 66,000.[34]

The 2010 Conservative manifesto promised to reduce net migration substantially and their 2015 manifesto said 'we will insist that EU migrants who want to claim tax credits and child benefit must live here and contribute to our country for a minimum of four years.'[35] But there is little evidence in academic or other literature to demonstrate that migrants arrive from Europe just to claim benefits and because it is access to work that drives migration, not access to welfare, economists from the government's budget watchdog, the Office for Budget Responsibility, have suggested a four-year ban will have little practical impact on the number of migrants coming to the UK.[36]

As the National Institute of Economic and Social Research have highlighted: 'Most non-EU migrants can't claim benefits until they are permanently settled here, which takes some years, because the conditions under which they're given entry (as workers, students, or family) don't permit them (there are special rules for asylum seekers and refugees) … if they are not in work they can normally not claim Jobseeker's Allowance (JSA) or child benefits in the first three months they are in the country.'[37] There is little evidence that cutting tax credits would have a correspondingly large impact on migration levels. Indeed, a study by Declan Gaffney demonstrates that after assessing the 'net incomes after taxes, benefits and housing costs of low-wage EU migrants shows that, even after factoring in tax credits, EU migrants with two children are no better off in the UK than in other western European countries, while single EU migrants without children are worse off.'[38]

Those who argue that the upside is outweighed by the downside

– or those who suggest there is no upside and only a downside – argue that migration cuts the wages of the country's workers, puts undue pressure on public services and dilutes the common bonds of citizenship, thus lessening national solidarity and support for our welfare state. But work by Jonathan Portes and others has shown that, in general, there is 'no clear empirical evidence that European immigrants have undercut domestic wages in Britain, or "taken jobs" from others.'[39] He suggests that immigration can often increase labour demand and that, as our survey evidence recognised, immigrants often take on jobs that local people do not want to do.

What can be done within the EU?

Because this is a shared European problem, there is a case for sharing the risks and responsibilities across the EU and offering help to communities facing high levels of demand on their services because of migration. The Mayor of London has said that in 'London alone, we will need to find another 165,000 school places in the next five years. We will need to build another 80 secondary schools. That is a big expense for the taxpayer.'[40] The European Union could do more to share costs and risks across Europe under the umbrella of a new European Solidarity Fund built out of Europe's current Asylum, Migration and Integration Fund (from which the UK is to receive €370 million by 2020). This would be a far more comprehensive version of the UK Controlling Migration Fund from which local authorities and services can make claims to help build the new schools, hospitals and housing in areas with disproportionately high level of migration.

UKIP claimed in its European Election campaign of 2014 that 7 per cent of all crime across the 28 EU Member States was caused by 240 Romanian gangs when they in fact account for 7 per cent of the number of criminals, not the amount of crime committed. They also claimed 28,000 Romanians were arrested for crimes in London in the last five years; however the 28,000 figure was for number of arrests not number of people.[41] In fact, annually, for the period of 2010–14, there were between 4,000 and 5,000 European nationals in English and Welsh jails, less than 6 per cent of prison population.[42] But we could do more to remove offenders who may try to use the freedom of movement rules to move from one country into another. Currently, 'EU citizens who are permanent residents cannot be expelled except on "serious grounds" of public policy or security'. Indeed, for EU citizens who have lived in their host country for ten years there needs to be 'imperative grounds' relating to public security. At the moment, Member States can prevent those European citizens who have been expelled from reapplying for entry for three years. A longer period could be agreed and we need, as has been proposed, a 'more targeted use of Interpol green notices to provide warnings and information to other Interpol members about individuals who have committed offences and pose a risk in other countries'.[43]

If we could do more to prevent exploitation in the workplace, then British workers might feel less insecure. The UK Gangmasters Licensing Authority believes that the 'the early stages of exploitation, facilitation and trafficking take place before the victims arrive here', and a European-wide determination to act both through the law and better policing could stamp out exploitative practices which hit the lowest paid and most vulnerable workers hardest.[44] But there is no substitute for the enforcement of existing standards to prevent individual immigrants being exploited and individual local workers being undercut.

The EU and illegal immigration

Yvette Cooper, a former Labour minister who was until recently, Shadow Home Secretary, has proposed tougher checks and controls.

'At a time of extremist and terrorist threats, the countries of the EU also need strong border checks for example to stop their own citizens going to join ISIL,' she argues, 'or to prevent terrorists, extremists or criminals travelling with guns or weapons.'[45] And clearly the European Agency for the Management of Operational Co-operation at the External Borders of the Member States, or Frontex, which up till now has relied on Member States' staff secondments and can only operate in EU Member States at their invitation, has to work as a Border Control Agency and Coast Guard with its own budget and border staff and coast guards capable of being deployed quickly when individual Member States are under pressure.

But what is needed is a comprehensive European-wide strategy for dealing with illegal immigration. 'So far we have a strict separation between interior ministry officials to deal with security problems, diplomats to take care of international issues, and non-governmental organisations for the humanitarian aspect of things. We need professionals who can grasp the three dimensions of the problem,' a former Italian Prime Minister, Enrico Letta, says. 'The Commission and EU governments talk about fingerprints, hotspots, the Calais jungle, but where is the long-term policy?' he has asked.[46]

And while a start has been made towards a new but controversial strategy for protecting the external border (including returning migrants to Turkey in exchange for taking Syrian refugees direct from the region), Europe is increasingly aware that it is dealing with Afghan, Iraqi, Libyan, Eritrean and other refugees and migrants, as well as Syrians. Six states have suspended Schengen – a system designed for a more benign environment – and have reintroduced border checks.[47] Some countries, like Austria, have set upper limits on incomers; some are erecting walls; and a few are implementing a quota system of reallocating refugees from their points of entry to other Member States.[48] Germany is now reducing the number of 'countries of origin' they recognise for asylum claims[49] and are cutting back on the rights of asylum seekers including replacing cash payments with food vouchers.[50] Denmark, one of the first to sign the 1951 Refugee Convention, is restricting the rights of family members to be reunited, intensifying its use of stop and search powers and has passed laws allowing police to seize refugees' assets worth more than 10,000 kroner (£1,000) that have no sentimental value to their owner.[51] And radical proposals have been under discussion, from ending the Dublin Regulations that register asylum seekers at their first port of call in Europe and changing Europe's external border by dispatching joint police forces along Macedonia's border with Greece, to paying Greece – already struggling with 25 per cent unemployment and an over-size national debt – as well as Turkey to house refugees. In the latest proposals it is recognised that to end what is called 'asylum shopping' – whereby refugees search for the best country that suits their needs – a permanent relocation and burden-sharing scheme is needed that would be triggered either immediately or if arrivals in one country reached critical levels.

In response to the EU deal to return refugees to Turkey, the UN Commissioner for Refugees, Filippo Grandi, has warned of breaches to legal safeguards that guarantee the right to a fair hearing for individual asylum seekers and prevent them from being returned to countries where they face persecution. He has urged not just more support for the countries hardest hit but more safe legal ways for people to enter the EU – humanitarian admission programmes, private sponsorships, student scholarships – as well as better provision for unaccompanied children.[52] At a minimum, refugees must have a right to security, to fair process at borders, and to a reason where entry is refused. But there will have to be burden-sharing at a global level: it makes sense to consider help for displaced persons in the same way that we consider help for peace-keeping and, instead of relying on voluntary contributions to fund emergency aid, examine the possibility of a new system whereby countries are assessed for a contribution based on their size and ability to pay, or we share costs through World Bank loans and grants.

So our own government needs to do more to expose and prevent exploitation and the European Union needs to do more to share the risks equally and to tackle the growing problem of illegal migration. And both the UK and the EU need to do more to form a comprehensive strategy to deal with the challenges of the Middle East and Africa.

Opting out of the European Union would come at a cost: while Europe can achieve a great deal acting in concert, we would be less able to deal with illegal immigration and global migration issues if we were acting on our own. What is telling is that, in opinion poll after opinion poll, the British public have shown little confidence in the proposition that withdrawing from Europe will solve the migration problem. Withdrawal will certainly not reduce illegal immigration and may, because there would be less co-operation across Europe, make it worse. There is no easy answer in leaving.

CHAPTER TWELVE

Do we need a European anti-terrorism and security strategy?

The day after I became Prime Minister, on the morning of Friday, 29th June 2007, I was awoken very early to be told of two unexploded car bombs found in Central London – one which was filled with gas canisters and nails found near a night club in Haymarket and the other in a Mercedes-Benz saloon in which a bomb was discovered only after it had been towed away. The 'trick' of exploding one device and shortly afterwards igniting another, in the words of a former Metropolitan Police Commissioner, was 'textbook al-Qaeda'.[1] If either had exploded, large-scale damage would have been done.

A day later, two men attempted to drive a car into the main terminal of Glasgow Airport, with the intention of detonating a bomb when inside. Thankfully, they were prevented from entering the terminal and the bomb failed to explode. One of the men, a doctor, was later charged with conspiracy to commit murder and was sentenced to a minimum of 32 years in prison. The driver of the car died of his injuries in hospital.

These terrorist attempts resulted in the threat-level in the UK being raised to 'critical', the highest of five possible levels. Other incidents followed. On the same day as the Glasgow attack, Liverpool Airport was closed for eight hours and a suspicious vehicle was removed. A few days later, Heathrow Airport's Terminal 4 was closed for a number of hours due to a suspect package being discovered.

The protection of its citizens is the most important responsibility discharged by a national government. Although the global financial crisis consumed an enormous amount of my time as Prime Minister, from day one to the day I left office, the issues raised by terrorism – from daily bombings in Afghanistan and Iraq to day-to-day surveillance in the UK – were an ever-present concern. The measures we took to ensure security in Britain were a constant source of debate and controversy.

In one of my speeches on terrorism, given just before I became Prime Minister, I cited evidence from our security services that up to 2,000 individuals living in the UK were thought to be terrorist risks to the country. And because of the threat posed by these individuals, my colleagues and I spent a great deal of time and effort on improving our strategy for dealing with terrorism – from strengthened border controls and the detention of suspects in the UK to upfront and under-the-radar counter terrorist work around the world. In the process, as Prime Minister, I created a new National Security Council; brought in the former Head of the Royal Navy, Admiral Lord West, as our Minister for Security; ensured that counter-terrorism agencies and police worked with our Home Secretary, Jacqui Smith, to deal with all aspects of terrorism on an interdepartmental basis across government; and doubled the resources devoted to the fight against terrorism.

We were aware that we had a home-grown problem and it was thus wrong to say all terrorist threats came from abroad and to somehow assume that if we shut our borders we would be safe. With large numbers of potential terrorists already in our country, leaving the European Union would not make us safer. For one reality of the modern world always stood out: there could be no effective effort to root out the terrorist threat without co-operation with our allies. In this age, there can be no substitute for a concerted and co-ordinated strategy to deter terrorists, track down suspects and to prevent bombings and shootings.

Europe has seen more terrorist outrages than any other part of the West. Indeed, since 9/11, the four largest attacks in Europe – Madrid (2004), London (2005), Paris (2015) and Brussels (2016) – have claimed more than 400 lives, while in those same 15 years 45 lives have been lost in America from the Fort Hood shooting, the Boston Marathon bombing and the San Bernadino outrage.[2] Europe is home to a disproportionately large number of terrorist suspects and an already substantial home-grown problem is magnified by the flow of extremists from and to the Middle East, Asia and Africa. According to a Soufan Group report from December 2015, 470 Belgian-based extremists have gone to fight in Syria or Iraq together with nearly 800 extremists from Germany, 1,700 from France and 760 from the UK – perhaps 5,000 or so from Europe in total compared with an estimated 250 from America.[3]

The majority of men involved in the Paris terrorist atrocities of November 2015 and the Brussels attacks of March 2016 appear to have been born and raised in either Belgium or France. They reveal a rising number of European-born and educated young people who have been brought up in Europe, radicalised through the Internet or by radical extremist imams and whose hearts are elsewhere.

The response to the Paris attacks showed both the strength and weaknesses of the European Union today. Surprisingly, the French President did not invoke, as America had done in 2001, Article 5 of the North Atlantic Treaty Organisation Treaty to enlist the help of NATO allies but instead he invoked Article 42 (7) of the Lisbon Treaty to summon up a EU response. Article 42 (7) stipulates that 'if a Member State is the victim of armed aggression on its territory, the other Member States shall have towards it an obligation of aid and assistance by all the means in their power, in accordance with Article 51 of the United Nations Charter.' Invoking an obligation for support by 'all means in their power' showed a confidence in the collaborative defence and security efforts of EU Member States.

It quickly became clear however that the invocation of the EU treaty was more symbolic than real and that a co-ordinated response was more about bilateral contacts between Paris and other European capitals than any active mobilisation of the European Union's resources. As Federica Mogherini, the High Representative of the EU for Foreign Affairs and Security Policy, had to clarify: the invocation of the clause did not entail a EU Common Security and Defence Policy (CSDP) mission or operation.[4] The reality was that the weapons available to the EU or Europe-wide institutions were miniscule compared with the resources held by the individual Member States or available to NATO.

In this referendum, the issue of security is in the spotlight. As one commentator, Pierre Briançon, has written: 'All that Europe needed was to appear as if it can't protect its citizens from terrorism … Sixty years ago modern Europe was founded on the assumption that it would be the best way to guarantee peace and security to its citizens. If it looks unable to provide either one, EU politicians are likely to find the populist tide overwhelming.'[5] Or as Rafael Behr has put it in *The Guardian*: 'The lens of British politics has shifted its focus from the economy to security. When that template is applied, EU member-ship is either the necessary mechanism for coordinated anti-terror policy – sharing data, cross-border arrest warrants and intelligence co-operation – or it is an unlocked door through which jihadism sneaks, in refugee garb. This evolution of the argument poses a new, more profound problem for the "in" side.'[6]

Those wishing to 'Leave' tend to ignore the fact that, inside or outside the European Union, we have a home-grown terrorist problem in Britain. They argue that Europe's 'open door' policy is the reason why the terrorist threat is so great. They claim that, although Britain is not signed up to Europe's open-borders system, the free movement of workers puts us at risk. Within minutes of the Brussels bombing, a UKIP press release said the attack showed 'that Schengen-free movement and lax border controls are a threat to our security'.[7] A more sophisticated 'Leave' argument from Sir Richard Dearlove, former head of MI6, is that in any response to a terrorist outrage in Europe the rest of the EU will always need Britain more than we need them. Brussels, he states, is cut out by the Third Party Rule, which means that one nation cannot pass on information to a third party without the originators' agreements and that with the exception of Europol – which is open to non-EU members anyway – the European and Brussels-based bodies in which the UK participates, he suggests, are of little consequence. Outside the European Union, it is contended that, 'the UK-US co-operation over signals intelligence, the Central Intelligence Agency/Secret Intelligence Service/Federal Bureau of Investigation/MI5 liaison and much more would continue as before.'[8] The 'Remain' campaign, on the other hand, argue that there is no better way to deal with the problem of terrorists and terrorism than through cross-border co-operation; that solid and concerted European organisation of the counter-terrorism effort is no longer an option but a necessity; that we in Britain are not subject to the Schengen open borders system – and indeed have our own passport control as people enter the UK – and that we benefit both from our autonomy that allows us to enforce border controls and our ability to co-operate across borders to detect and deter terrorists.

I will suggest that across Europe we will need to develop enhanced systems for gathering and sharing intelligence. The Member States should also be willing to learn from each other the best practices for preventing radicalisation. No multilateral institution other than the European Union – not NATO, not any individual Member State on its own, nor the USA without Europe – can effectively mobilise all the diplomatic and economic resources we need to address the root causes of terrorism in the Middle East. Of course we need our European neighbours to be more organised and efficient. Indeed, it is reported that at the time of the Belgium bombings, Belgium had 150 of its 700 security officer places unfilled and spent only €50 million a year on counter-terrorism. But we in Britain will benefit if the strength that Europe has as a bloc – including our ability to pool and share resources and to achieve more through economies of scale – is better mobilised.[9]

The European wide problem that we face cannot be ignored. In total 149 people died in terrorist attacks in Europe in 2015; in 2014 there were four deaths. A report by Europol in July 2015 highlighted the increase in the number of terrorist attacks. In 2014, a total of 201 attacks – the vast majority of which were foiled or failed – were reported by seven EU Member States. A total of 774 individuals were arrested for terrorism-related offences and cases were completed against 444 individuals. And Britain did not escape. In fact, in 2014, Britain was targeted more than any other country: half the reported terrorist incidents were in the UK.[10]

We currently do not know how many European residents are attached to terrorist cells. While in 2006 we thought that 2,000 individuals were potential terrorist threats, the number today is around 3,000 in need of surveillance.[11] And if constant and comprehensive surveillance is necessary some experts argue that 15–20 agents are needed per person.[12] The group we need to worry about most are the 350 of the estimated 700 people from the UK who travelled to support or fight for jihadist organisations in Syria and Iraq and have since returned.[13] But the criss-crossing of borders shows a need for – and reveals gaps in – a European intelligence system attempting to follow thousands of potential terrorists in and out of – and across – Europe.

While once we thought of ISIL operating in Europe through 'lone wolves,' it is now clear that they operate a sophisticated network with, in the words of a *Der Spiegel* investigation, their 'own infrastructure in Europe, under the radar of most intelligence services, cells consisting of first, second and third-tier militants' – who are in contact with Syria; have logistics on the ground; are supported, including by a number of 'sleeper' cells; and have an advantage over security services in that they are 'perfectly in command of cooperation across European national borders.'[14] The Paris attack leader, Abdelhamid Abaaoud, was well-known to European police as 'intelligence agencies had identified him as a link between ISIS leadership in Syria and European terror cells', but 'he is believed to have moved between several European countries without being apprehended'.[15] Indeed, in 2015, he is reported as boasting in an ISIL publication of how he had travelled between Europe and Syria, stating: 'All of this shows that a Muslim has nothing to fear from the intelligence services of the Crusaders.'[16]

And the attacks in Paris also highlight the difficulties intelligence services have in tracking terrorists' movements when they can use advanced technology to hide their plans. Michael Rogers, Director of the American National Security Administration, said in February 2016 that the terror attacks in Paris 'would not have happened' if it wasn't for encrypted communications apps. He said the spread of smartphone apps that encrypt the content of messages are making it 'much more difficult' to stop terror attacks.[17] This, of course, is likely to lead to serious pressure from the West's counterterror agencies on technology companies such as Apple, Google and others to decrypt where there is a proven need to do so. Indeed, the Director of Europol, Rob Wainwright, has demanded 'a more constrictive legislative solution' for the 'problem of encryption' that provides a better balance between privacy and security and goes beyond police powers to intercept private phone calls as the right to intercept does not exist when it comes to encrypted communications.[18]

But the attacks in Paris and Brussels have led to considerable frustration over the lack of a co-ordinated approach. 'We need to invest in a unitary structure for security and defence,' argued Italy's Prime Minister, Matteo Renzi, as he called for 'constant, punctual and continuous co-operation' among EU security services in the aftermath of the attack in Brussels. He continued that the European Union has been 'discussing and fighting' over common defence since 1954 and that 'We need a European pact, a pact for liberty and security.'[19]

But inflammatory as the language may be, Renzi's comments reflect a basic fact: that national security agencies do not link up as they should to ensure terrorist incidents in one country are properly investigated in another.

In December 2015, after the second Paris attack, European Justice Ministers, including the British Home Secretary, Theresa May, agreed greater co-operation by interconnecting national DNA, fingerprinting and vehicle registration databases, as well as swapping information on terrorist financing. The bigger idea is that anyone entering or leaving the Schengen Area should have their details checked against a Europe-wide database that stores information on wanted terror suspects and people linked to organised crime – a database that gives the UK access to the details of suspected terrorists and wanted criminals to ensure they are unable to enter our country. Participation remains voluntary and happens outside EU institutions. Eighteen months ago there were only 1,000 names on the Schengen Information System database; even now there are just 8,000 as there is no obligation for countries to deposit information and many intelligence agencies fear their sources could be exposed.[20] But there is no centralised database that would register all third-country travellers coming in and out of the Schengen Area – something the German government is pushing for – that would link the Schengen Information System, the European fingerprint database for asylum seekers and the Schengen Visa Information System.[21]

Creating the proposed European Passenger Name Record – which would compel airlines to give passenger data over to EU authorities[22] – and a Europe-wide set of crime records and a pan-European taskforce to combat identity document fraud, as being pushed for by the French government, could lead to more effective prevention and investigation.[23] Other measures include an automated fingerprint recognition system , extending the European Criminal Records Information System (ECRIS) to third country nationals and better control of firearms.

After 9/11 America created a well-resourced Counterterrorism Centre, to encourage government agencies to share information, and a new Director of National Intelligence. Europe's own Counter Terrorism Centre, being created by Europol and run by a former British intelligence officer, now needs resources as there is a push for greater integration of European and international security databases. Rob Wainwright of Europol has recently emphasised that reinforcements are needed to 'help get through all the different information needs that we're processing' after only six countries seconded staff. Indeed, the European Counter Terrorism Centre has only 35 experts currently assigned to it from national security authorities, a staff complement of only 75 in total. Yet as Wainwright has noted: 'We do not have operational powers like the FBI. That is not the purpose of Europol.'[24]

And Europe is unlikely to endorse proposals for enhanced security co-operation as radical as creating a European FBI or CIA (as the Belgium PM has advocated), which would need a treaty change, or even accept the proposal of the President of the Commission, Jean Claude Juncker, for a 'security union' and 'common security standards'. Some talk of the Five Eyes intelligence alliance – comprising Australia, Canada, New Zealand, the United Kingdom and the United States – as a model, and when *Politico* conducted a survey to gauge European leaders' priorities in response to the terror threat, it found that the biggest demand of all was for better intelligence sharing.[25] Europe should be able to agree wider co-operation on a 'need to share' not just a 'need to know basis'. And there is support for a professional network of intelligence co-operation on a similar basis to the European Civil Protection Mechanism that co-ordinates responses to conflicts and natural disasters and involves not just the sharing of information but the co-ordination of responses – a benefit to all countries that would not be realised if nation states retreated into their own shells.

The European response

Of course the primary responsibility in the fight against terrorism lies with the Member States. But as Theresa May has said, it is the need to co-operate – and thus the supporting, convening and co-ordinating role which the EU can play to respond to the cross-border nature of what are common threats – that led her to support the 'Remain' campaign. 'On the security front there are good reasons for us to be members of the European Union,' she wrote. 'What's important is that we work with others to ensure that we can respond,' she concluded.[26] And when it came to a choice as to whether to opt-out of the European Union's justice and home affairs powers, she decided to opt back in on important measures on the recommendations of the Crown Prosecution Service and police.

At present, Britain benefits from having both the power to conduct its own border checks and from the checks carried out by other EU Member States when individuals enter the continent. Our additional border checks help to prevent illegal weapons entering the UK, including the Kalashnikov assault rifles which have been used in terrorist attacks in Europe. And as a result of a deal with France, the UK enjoys a 'security barrier' that ensures migrants are checked on French soil – at the French coast – before they even reach Britain. These 'juxtaposed border controls', with British border guards based at the French port of Calais instead of Dover, have become significant because of the claims made by both the French and British governments that Calais would cease to operate its border controls for Britain if we left the EU.[27]

A tightening up of checks on Europe's external borders – vital for the detection of terrorists – is long overdue. As Hugo Dixon argues: 'A terrorist who comes into Greece via a dinghy from Turkey posing as a refugee couldn't just pop up in London. He would first have to navigate our border checks. These controls, admittedly, aren't perfect. But quitting the EU wouldn't make them any better. Quite the opposite. We'd find it even harder to catch jihadis if we weren't swapping intelligence as effectively with our erstwhile partners across the Channel.' He continues: 'We now have the best of both worlds. We are not exposed to Schengen's leaky borders, but we play a big role in designing European counter-terrorism policies. The Paris attacks are a reason to stay in the EU, not quit.'[28]

And we benefit from the European Union's ability to use its strength to deal with the cross-border nature of threats. In 2000 the European Union authorised the Director of Europol to enter into negotiations with non-EU states. Today, Europol has agreements with 14 non-EU countries: Colombia, Albania, Liechtenstein, Canada, Macedonia, Iceland, Moldova, Montenegro, Norway, Serbia, Switzerland, Monaco, Australia and the United States. And it now has strategic agreements in place with Bosnia and Herzegovina, Russia, Turkey and Ukraine. The nature of these agreements can vary, ranging from operational co-operation to technical or strategic discussions. Some have suggested that with many non-EU countries signed up, such arrangements will be as strong outside the European Union but this is to forget that European Member States benefit from enhanced co-operation, including permanent communication links and the regular exchanges of criminal data and more co-ordinated investigative techniques.[29]

A former Secretary General of Interpol, Ronald Noble, has argued the Schengen Agreement 'is like hanging a sign welcoming terrorists to Europe'.[30] However, the current Director of Europol, Rob Wainwright, has said that Britain would be 'much less effective' at fighting terrorism in the future if we left the EU.[31] Leaving, the current head of the Metropolitan Police has said, would be a 'bureaucratic nightmare' and he has argued that an increased security risk during a two-year renegotiation period 'is one of the things that people would have to address'.[32] And in an article for *The Daily Telegraph*, former CIA chief, David Petraeus, has argued that leaving would 'deal a significant blow to the EU's strength and resilience at exactly the moment when the West is under attack from multiple directions … the best way to defend ourselves is precisely by deepening military, intelligence, and diplomatic cooperation across the Western world, by working together with our partners on the continent and elsewhere to strike at the terrorists in their sanctuaries and tackle the underlying drivers of radicalization. The EU, for all its imperfections, is a vital player in this effort.'[33]

And although we are not in the Schengen Area, in February 2015 – after the Charlie Hebdo attacks – we saw the benefit in deciding to join the Schengen Information System, which gives the UK access to the details of suspected terrorists and wanted criminals to ensure they are unable to enter the country.[34] The EU-wide Prüm Convention for sharing fingerprints and DNA, which Britain will access next year, reduces the time taken to match DNA from 143 days through Interpol to fifteen minutes and is thus an important tool to help in the exchange information to catch criminals.[35]

In the past six years, 785 European Arrest Warrants have been issued by British police forces to repatriate UK nationals accused of crime and terrorism from other European nations and 6,165 suspected offenders have been removed from Britain to stand trial in their home countries at the request of European courts.[36] While Sir Richard Dearlove argues that the warrants' 'importance has been exclusively criminal and few would notice its passing'.[37] Sir Hugh Orde, former President of the Association of Chief Police Officers has said: 'These new figures demonstrate why being in Europe is so vital to the safety of Britain's streets. For our police forces, the ability to quickly deport foreign criminals and bring villains back to face British justice is invaluable.'[38] This view has been reinforced by Lord Hannay who has contradicted Sir Richard by demonstrating that arrest warrants cover terrorist offences. And as Theresa May has said: 'You don't need bilateral agreements with everybody. It's also the case that there are a number of countries who outside of the EAW don't extradite their nationals so if you are not part of that EAW there might be some people who you wouldn't be able to see being extradited.'[39] Indeed, after the 1995 Paris Métro bombing, one suspect was held in British custody for more than seven years before he could be extradited to Paris and convicted. Now there is no such wait as shown when a man linked to the Charlie Hebdo shootings was immediately returned to Paris from Bulgaria.[40]

Ensuring that there is no hiding place for terrorist finances, much of which comes from oil smuggling or extortion, is another area of co-operative activity worldwide and within the European Union. After 2001 the G8 countries took steps to increase their joint efforts to root out terrorist finance and ensure that there was no safe haven for those who financed terrorist activity. In December, a military-style operation codenamed 'Tidal Wave II' brought countries together, including the USA, the UK and France. This operation has included British and French planes bombing ISIL oilfields in Eastern Syria which Defence Secretary, Michael Fallon, has described as 'key infrastructure targets' from which ISIL derives over 10 per cent of its oil revenue. The Americans have also targeted oil lorries to help cut of the flow of ISIL controlled oil.[41]

Can we also learn from each other in formulating our national programmes to prevent radicalisation? Few will disagree that we are now in a generational battle for hearts and minds of young people which cannot be won by military means alone. We are in a war of propaganda against terrorist organisations whose main thesis is the impossibility of co-existence of Muslims and non-Muslims and this is happening in a Middle East and North Africa where terrorists can exploit the deeply engrained inequalities within the region and try to popularise a storyline that blames the West for just about everything that's wrong with the world. France has, in the words of one respected commentator, Gilles Kepel, allowed '"virtual and mental enclaves," growing rejection of common values, and heightened social, political and economic marginalization' of the young. This is partly due to the neglect of the employment needs of immigrants.

Indeed, as Kepel puts it, 'their war of enclaves could not exist if there were no enclaves'. France needs to be more inclusive, he argues, but is having to counteract the 'calculated and alarming surge in radical Islamic separatism exemplified by Salafism'. While the resentment in the poor suburbs has social roots – essentially the residents' are excluded from a tight jobs market – rioters have expressed frustration in a vocabulary borrowed from a violent interpretation of Islam.[42] But counter-radicalisation programmes are not succeeding because the residents do not see themselves as French and the French state has long been uncomfortable with entrusting sensitive de-radicalisation work to religious or civil authorities. Germany, Sweden, Denmark and Britain boast well-respected 'disengagement' programmes to detect and dissuade would-be terrorists. Some countries, including our own, emphasise building community resilience against violent extremism; others stress a family approach, working with suspects' families to bring them back from jihadism; and others have tried modern forms of group therapy. As the European Agenda on Security for the period 2015–20 acknowledges, Europe would benefit from a wider exchange of experiences of how we best prevent terrorist recruitment and de-radicalise converts to violence. This includes a Centre of Excellence to collect and disseminate expertise on anti-radicalisation, a more coherent legal framework to deal with foreign fighters, as well as action with the IT industry to counter terrorist propaganda on the Internet and in social media.

Again Britain cannot deliver a comprehensive response in all these areas alone, but is influential enough to help shape collective European efforts. If we were outside the EU, Britain could certainly continue to co-operate with other countries on a bilateral basis – we could still work through Europol – but we would be far less effective in our approach to identifying, tracking and arresting would-be terrorists and to counteracting their propaganda. By sharing intelligence, pooling resources and by co-ordinating our approach to counter terrorism, European countries can add value to and enhance each others' security.

The question is how, outside of the EU, we would be able to deliver the comprehensive approach that is needed to deal with deep-seated problems in the Middle East and Africa and to limit the damage to Europe from the spill-over effects from conflicts in countries from Syria and Iraq to Libya and sub-Saharan Africa. Some may argue that NATO, which has recently undertaken out-of-area operations, could perform this task but NATO is not in business to offer the combination of diplomatic presence, development aid and support for economic reconstruction that is needed. Sooner or later European nations will have no choice but to come together to forge such a policy. And if we want to deal with the causes of terrorism and address the root problems which are leading millions to seek sanctuary and a future life in Europe, we must work together within the EU.

Defence of the realm

Terrorism was seen as the biggest threat to our security according to a recent survey by Chatham House – and policies that focused on counter-terrorism and border-control were seen as the top priorities for the defence of the realm. But these are not the only threats that the British public are concerned about and from which they demand protection. Our future in Europe is being decided at a time when, as the survey shows, British people are of the view that we are in a far less safe and more unstable and uncertain world. While sceptical about the value of entering further wars, another top priority is security against possible aggression and conflict. In the wake of aggression by Russia in Ukraine, 'two-thirds of the public think that President Putin is a threat to the security of the EU, and one in five regard Russia as a "very big" threat.' And the public are clear that we need to co-operate in our national interest to secure our defence. As Thomas Raines of Chatham House shows: 'NATO is considered "vital" to the UK's security by 36% of the public, with a further 25% saying it is "important". Only 14% think that NATO is no longer relevant. Older respondents are more likely to say that NATO is vital (half of those aged over 60), compared with just one-quarter of those aged 18–24.'[43]

When I heard President Hollande invoking not NATO but European-wide co-operation after the attacks on Paris last year, it brought me back to deep conversations I had in 2007 and 2008 with President Sarkozy. Then he proposed intensified British-French co-operation. What he had in mind was not just the usual proposals for joint expeditionary forces and for joint research, but for co-operative work more generally on the British and French nuclear deterrents and a common approach to their modernisation. There was no inherent contradiction between Anglo-French co-operation and our membership of NATO; it was at this time that he was bringing back France into the inner core of NATO.

That co-operation with President Sarkozy was taken on by the new Coalition government and led to the signing of two defence treaties at Lancaster House: on defence and security, and on nuclear co-operation. This is referred to as the Lancaster House Agreement. These treaties enhanced defence and security co-operation between our countries' armed forces and entailed the pooling and sharing of materials and equipment, the building of joint facilities, and indus-trial and technological co-operation. They amounted to what the official statement said was 'a historic commitment to build a long-term partnership in defence and security, reflecting our common history, interests, values and responsibilities, and understanding of the threats we face, and an unprecedented token of our mutual confidence.'[44] And most recently, France and the UK have worked more closely together, including with the joint air campaign against Libya in 2012 and the campaign against ISIL following the Paris attacks.

Plans promoting defence co-operation are not new. But recent co-operation reverses the post-1945 stand off when European defence co-operation foundered not just on British reticence to join a European defence policy but on French suspicion of Germany which had led to the collapse in 1954 of the project for a European Defence Community. For years, Franco-German military co-operation was hindered by major differences over relations with the US, over nuclear weapons – which France possessed but Germany did not – and because of Europe's opposition to German re-armament which was matched by an understandable German reluctance to support the use of military force as an instrument of foreign policy.

West European security, however, was assured by NATO even after France withdrew from its military command in 1966. With both hostile to Russian aggression, France and Germany's defence interests started to converge in the early 1980s after French President Mitterrand supported Chancellor Kohl's decision to approve the stationing of medium-range US nuclear weapons in Germany. Interest in greater co-operation grew as Germany feared America might draw down its forces in Western Europe and reduce its strong commitment to Western European security. But Kohl did not propose EU joint action – there were then 12 members – nor even an advance guard of the founding six but a bilateral initiative – what became in 1987, with Mitterrand's agreement, a joint Franco-German brigade as the 'core of a future European army'.[45] Later Kohl and Mitterrand 'resolved to upgrade and transform the small Franco-German brigade (4,200 soldiers) into a 45,000-strong "Eurocorps", open to other Member States, to engage in peace-making, peacekeeping and humanitarian missions and to contribute to the defence of Western Europe under the terms of the NATO and WEU treaties.' Other Member States were invited to contribute to the Eurocorps. Only three, however, did so: Belgium (1993), Spain (1994) and Luxembourg (1996).[46] And while the Eurocorps has since been deployed in various UN, NATO and EU missions, there was no groundswell for a European army. All that has happened is that several other EU Member States, including Greece, Italy, Poland, Austria and Romania, are now represented among the headquarters staff of the Eurocorps, along with Turkey and the US.

France, under de Gaulle, wanted a European nuclear capability distinct from NATO. In an ideal world the US would have liked a more or less united Western Europe under British leadership taking far more responsibility for its own security, with European armies enlarged and with all European nuclear weapons pooled and subject to some kind of American veto on their use. But France saw NATO as 'an appendage' of American policy and de Gaulle became convinced France should be part of a European and not a NATO force, favouring the creation of a European nuclear command within NATO and a new Council of Ministers within NATO. Once again Britain feared that a distinct pan-European initiative would give America an excuse for cutting back on its commitment to Europe. But while de Gaulle proposed an executive committee of NATO – comprising the US, UK, France, Germany and Italy – his successor quietly dropped the proposal. And while Europe formally agreed to have its own Common Defence and Security Policy, attempts at cohesion were undermined by disagreements over the US-led invasion of Iraq in 2003.

A far more significant development has been the growth over the last 20 years – without great fanfare in Britain – of French and British co-operation on defence. Together France and Britain, with only 25 per cent of the EU's population, are responsible for 42 per cent of Europe's total defence spending and 80 per cent of defence research and development spending in defence.[47] Given that Germany's armed forces are smaller than those of the EU's other two 'big powers' and less capable of being deployed overseas, a European military inter-vention capacity built around an Anglo-French nucleus has until recently been a far more credible European presence than a Franco-German-based force.

In 1997, in the wake and midst of the wars in Yugoslavia, 'which had dramatically revealed the EU Member States' incapacity to wield military power independently of the US',[48] Tony Blair promoted a defence treaty with the French. And as Stephen Wall, Tony's former EU adviser, recalls he managed to go further than any previous Prime Minister in securing co-operation. He writes: 'European defence is the principal area of European policy where the Labour government moved British policy' including integrating European forces with a rapid reaction capability and co-ordinated military planning at a European level.[49] At Saint-Malo it was agreed that the common defence policy must have the capacity for collective action backed up by credible military forces, the means to decide to use them and a readiness to do so in order to respond to international crises.

Of course in the past there have been some crucial differences between France and the UK that have led to tensions – including the use of the French veto on military targets during the air campaign in Kosovo in 1999 and the opposition by Paris to the invasion of Iraq in 2003 – but last year saw co-operation intensified with the launch of 'Exercise Griffin', a joint exercise showing the close partnership that exists between France and the UK, involving 1,000 British and French personnel. This complemented the joint operations against the Taliban in Afghanistan and off the Horn of Africa, alongside the UK and French engagement side-by-side against ISIL, in the Mediterranean and in the EU training and advisory mission in Mali. As the UK government highlights: 'Together, we are engaged in air-policing duties within NATO. The UK has provided strategic air transport and surveillance support to French operations in Mali and the Central African Republic. France has supported the UK's Tornado deployment to help the Nigerian Government in its fight against Boko Haram. And French Atlantique Maritime Patrol Aircraft have operated from RAF Lossiemouth in Scotland.'[50] And in December 2015, the Royal Navy warship HMS *Defender* joined the French aircraft carrier *Charles de Gaulle* in the Indian Ocean to support the

French in operations against ISIL including airstrikes on the terrorist organisation in Syria and Iraq.

Future co-operation will deepen the joint actions of the two armed forces. A French Brigadier-General 'is to become second-in-command of one of the UK army's two frontline divisions from August, as part of the permanent exchange of senior personnel that reinforces deepening Anglo-French military co-operation.' As the *Financial Times* reported: 'The move is a permanent posting, raising the prospect that a French general could take British troops into combat should the commanding officer be unavailable.'[51]

By the early 2020s, with Britain's new aircraft carriers, the UK and France will aim to have the ability to deploy a UK-French integrated carrier strike group incorporating assets owned by both countries. The two countries are developing a joint technological and industrial roadmap for drones including a joint Technology and Operational Demonstration programme. And there is 'unprecedented co-operation' over the nuclear weapons programme, with a new joint facility at Valduc in France evaluating materials and overall performance of both countries' weapons supported by a joint Technology Development Centre at Aldermaston in the UK.[52]

The greater intensity of Franco-British co-operation comes at a time when collective action, as a joint statement affirms, has to be stepped up to deal with 'the proliferation of weapons of mass destruction and ballistic missiles, terrorism, cyberattacks, maritime and space security.'[53] For the first time since the Second World War, the recent British Defence Review 'elevated Germany to a top tier ally, alongside France and the United States' and in the words of Michael Fallon, Germany and Britain 'are already working closely together within NATO and in the fight against Daesh. Now I want to see more collaboration on operations, missions and training and deeper industrial co-operation.'[54] This includes an initiative on Transatlantic Capability Enhancement and Training with the general aim that both countries 'work together to ensure NATO remains strong and united; tackle

terrorist threats; build capacity outside of Europe; and enhance the
interoperability between their Armed Forces.'[55] In 2015 Germany
committed itself to increase defence spending by 6.2 per cent over the
next five years and to what they called 'widened NATO engagement'.[56]
And while previously Germany abstained, seeing 'significant dangers
and risks' in military intervention in Libya, Germany's parliament in
December 2015 approved a military campaign against ISIL in Syria
short of direct German airstrikes that includes six Tornado reconnais-
sance jets, a frigate in support of the French aircraft carrier *Charles de
Gaulle*, refuelling aircraft and up to 1,200 military personnel.[57]

But how does this increase in defence co-operation fit in with
membership of the European Union and how does it relate to NATO?
For 60 years Britain has publicly praised the idea of enhanced
Europe-wide co-operation on defence but stopped short of exclusive
European action. Although her speech was seen to be Eurosceptic,
Mrs Thatcher's intervention recognised that Europe 'cannot rely
forever on others for our defence ... each member of the Alliance
must shoulder a fair share of the burden ... We should develop the
EU, not as an alternative to NATO, but as a means of strengthening
Europe's contribution to the common defence of the West ... let us
never forget that our way of life, our vision and all we hope to achieve,
is secured not by the rightness of our cause but by the strength of
our defence.'[58]

Closer co-ordination and co-operation between the EU and other
institutions, principally NATO, in ways which support our national
priorities and build Euro-Atlantic security is a key theme of the
current National Security Strategy and Strategic Defence review,
which also favours joint European action on cyber threats and a
shared effort to help other states develop their security capacity.[59]
'Leave' campaigners argue that NATO is happy to include non-EU
members and can operate out-of-area, and they question the value of
a common European Defence and Security Policy. But it should be
recognised that there are three distinctive threats on Europe's borders

– aggression from Russia, and instability flowing from both the Middle East and Africa – that require the continent to co-operate more closely. These threats require not only military co-operation through NATO, but also other responses including aid, diplomacy, economic support and 'soft power' – measures that NATO cannot take but the European Union can. And while many in America now talk of a 30-year-war in the Middle East and urge their country to avoid precipitate action, European nations have no choice but to deal with the immediate threats on their doorstep. The reality is that Europe cannot avoid addressing the flows of refugees and needs a comprehensive strategy for tackling the terrorist threats that come from the region.

Russia

Russian assertiveness is a direct threat to the security of Europe. Russian action in Georgia, the takeover of Crimea and the threat it poses to Ukraine has led the NATO Secretary General, Jens Stoltenberg, to pronounce that, 'what Russia has done in Ukraine is not defensive; to annex [Crimea] … that is an act of aggression'.[60] The agreement that each notify the other of forthcoming military exercises was, of course, breached – Russia claiming a get-out clause when 'snap' decisions have to be made. From April 2014 all military co-operation under the NATO-Russia Council ended. Suspicions also run so high that Eastern European states want tougher 'red lines', not just preventing NATO-Russia Council meetings discussing military issues but restricting apolitical dialogue – something that may suit Russia which seems to have no interest in updating inspection regimes or in offering greater transparency about military drills.

The crisis in Ukraine also represented a break from 70 years of Cold War and post-Cold War history in that negotiations with Russia have been led not by America but by Germany and France (Britain could have been involved as one of the 1995 guarantors of Ukraine's independence but stood aside). Under the Minsk deal, negotiated by Chancellor Merkel and President Hollande with US and British support, 'Moscow must withdraw forces from eastern Ukraine and end its support for separatists; Kyiv must allow elections and greater autonomy for the country's relatively pro-Russian east; and the US and Europe will lift sanctions on Moscow.'[61] Not all has worked out: the original timetable – for the end of 2015 – has already been missed and the Ukrainian government is arguing that their promises of greater autonomy for the East will only follow after the withdrawal of Russian forces.

Ukraine is home to the Russian naval base at Sevastopol on the Black Sea which houses Russia's Black Sea Fleet and Mediterranean Task Force. Russia wants Ukraine to be part of its sphere of influence and wants a Eurasian customs union to counter the European Union. But Russian assertiveness and aggression are a real threat which, it is agreed, demands a united European response. One defence expert, Elizabeth Pond, sums it up, 'Menacingly, Putin boasted that his troops could be in Kyiv within two days if he so ordered; and could reach the capitals of Estonia, Latvia, Lithuania, Poland and Romania, all NATO member states, just as fast.' And there is little doubt that Russia has been 'testing Nato defences of the Baltic and Atlantic states daily on the seas and in the air – and endangering passenger flights by sending bombers with their transponders turned off into airspace that civilian liners use. On 18 February, RAF jets were scrambled after two Russian military aircraft were spotted off the coast of Cornwall.'[62]

This has been accompanied by a build-up of Russian military spending, despite the fall in oil revenues. In October 2015, *The Moscow Times* reported that 'Russian military expenditure has been rising since 2011, when the government launched a massive 20 trillion rubles ($700 billion at the time) rearmament drive aimed at modernizing some 70 per cent of the Russian armed forces by 2020 … this will put Russian military spending ahead of the United States' as a percentage of national income.[63] And there is a crossover to the Middle East. Retired General Leonid Ivashov, once a high-ranking Russian Defence Ministry official and now the President of the Academy of Geopolitical Problems in Moscow, is quoted as declaring that 2016 is to be a decisive year 'in which Russia takes a leading role in the Middle East, thereby challenging the West and re-establishing its civilising determination. Russia is becoming an independent geo-political actor.' He says that 'Russia has redefined its goals and will distance itself from the West, thereby breaking America's dominant role' and he believes that the Middle East will be the focus of conflict.[64]

'To our east we see in Russia an actor who is eager to return to the power politics of yesteryear,' stated Ursula von der Leyen, the German Defence Minister: 'Without unity and resolve among Europeans, we have no chance against this.'[65] It is in response to this that Germany has not only committed to raise its defence spending but to strengthen tank forces in response to the Ukraine crisis. Scandinavian nations are 'investing in military capability in response to the Russian threat,' notes another defence expert, Elizabeth Quintana of Royal United Services Institute (RUSI).[66] An EU advisory mission was established in Ukraine in 2014 to assist with policing and the rule of law to tackle the crisis as it occurred. In June 2015 Michael Fallon announced that the UK would 'contribute 3,000 personnel to the NATO Very High Readiness Joint Task Force (VJTF) from 2016 … The VJTF is part of the NATO Readiness Action Plan (RAP), which provides a comprehensive package of measures to respond to changes in the security environment on NATO's borders and further afield that are of concern to Allies.'[67] As a result, the UK has deployed several thousand personnel from all three armed services on a range of NATO reassurance exercises in Eastern Europe and in October 2015 Fallon announced UK troop deployments to the Baltic states and increased training for the Ukraine Armed Forces. The UK took the lead in the NATO 'land training exercise' in the Baltic states, underlining our continued support to the region. Exercise 'Arrcade Fusion' took place in Estonia, Latvia and Lithuania and was led by the British Army, accompanied by a number of supporting personnel from the Royal Navy and Royal Air Force. As the UK government explained: 'Around 1,400 troops from 18 NATO nations' took part in the exercise, which began and ran through November. The UK committed '800 troops and around 350 Army logistics vehicles.'[68]

But perhaps the most insidious development is Russia's renewed efforts to influence the West and Europe in particular through funding political parties across Europe, using social media, disseminating propaganda, and sponsoring corrupt leaders and organisations particularly in Eastern European states. In the past Russia took such measures to pursue a global goal. Now it does so to influence the development of Europe. This attempt at influence cannot easily be addressed with hard power or by military means. Instead, the European Union has to use its soft power – its diplomacy, its aid budget, its neighbourhood agreements – to address this new phenomenon. If a common European approach did not exist, it would have to be created to deal with a problem such as this.

Instability in neighbouring regions

The threats to peace and stability on Europe's Eastern borders are not just from Russian intervention in Ukraine. Ongoing EU missions, involving UK troops and a civilian rule-of-law mission in Kosovo and operations in Bosnia and Herzegovina, are now helping to maintain peace in the Balkans.

If a distinctively European response to threats to the East has become necessary, a comprehensive European response to the instability of the Middle East and North and sub-Saharan Africa becomes more essential by the day. Europe is now leading in African missions – establishing border assistance missions in Libya; civilian missions to support internal security forces in the Sahel region of Africa, including in Niger, where they face threats from terrorist organisation Boko Haram; and in tackling piracy against international shipping off Africa's coast. UK troops have been in Nigeria, and European countries are helping the internal security forces in Mali and Niger. The European 'official view' is: 'The current instability in the Sahel and the cross-border nature of the security threats confirm the relevance of the regional approach taken in the European Union strategy for security and development in the Sahel region, adopted in March 2011.'[69] The 'Annual Report from the High Representative of the European Union for Foreign Affairs and Security Policy to the European Parliament' highlights the promotion of democracy including election observation in Guinea Bissau, Malawi, Egypt, Mozambique and Tunisia.

Europe's role in the Middle East is now well known. It is an essential part of a broader-based coalition – France, Germany, Italy, the UK and the Netherlands linking with America and Australia – which plays a key regional role and that came together in Paris in 2016 to discuss the 'Coalition effort to tackle Daesh, how best to exploit further opportunities as the campaign moves into a new phase and options for intensifying the military operation in against Iraq and Syria' to support stability.[70] As the UK government has set out, Europe has come together with others to address the challenges of 'regional instability, large-scale humanitarian need, mass migration and human trafficking, and exploitation of weak governments or ungoverned space by terrorist groups and criminals'.[71]

America

What is very clear is that American leaders, quite rightly, want Europe to do more for itself. In 2011, in his valedictory visit to Europe before retiring, the then US Defence Secretary, Robert Gates, spoke of America's '"dwindling appetite" to serve as the heavyweight partner in the military order that has underpinned the US relationship with Europe since the end of World War II.'[72]

In fact, as I have shown earlier we have seen a continuous drawdown of US military forces from Europe from the high of 440,000 in 1957 to an all-time low of around 67,000 in 2015.[73] But Gates warned of further changes, complaining that the United States was tired of engaging in combat for those who 'don't want to share the risks and the costs … The blunt reality is that there will be dwindling appetite and patience in the US Congress – and in the American body politic at large, to expend increasingly precious funds on behalf of nations that are apparently unwilling to devote the necessary resources or make the necessary changes to be serious and capable partners in their own defense.'[74] And he gave his advice that 'if current trends in the decline of European defence capabilities are not halted and reversed, future US political leaders – those for whom the Cold War was not the formative experience that it was for me – may not consider the return on America's investment in NATO worth the cost.'[75]

Gates referred to the Libya mission – an initiative announced by France and Britain but, as he claimed, one that had to be managed by the US. Up against what might be considered an insubstantial foe, the Anglo-French campaign had been running short of munitions after just a few missions and had to turn to the US for assistance.

In recent polls, it has been shown that more than 50 per cent of Americans say that the 'United States "should mind its own business internationally and let other countries get along the best they can on their own" – the highest number ever recorded since the Pew research series started asking the question 50 years ago.' And recent polls have also found a majority agreeing 'that it was "more important" that the United States "not get too involved in the situation in Ukraine" than that it "take a firm stand".'[76] It is of course Donald Trump's view that Europe should look after itself.

But the real tension in US foreign policy, as I have found, is not between isolationism and internationalism but, as Robert Kagan highlights, between America acting out of a narrow self-interest – which has led them to be cautious of external commitments – and acting because they saw American intervention as a global responsibility and thus making America a regional power in every region, maintaining the balance of power in Europe and the Middle East as well as in Asia and the Americas. It is Kagan's argument that no other nation in history, including Britain in its days of Empire, has ever played such a role on a global scale and that for most of the post-war years there would not have been a stable balance of power in Europe or the Middle East without the United States. But as Niall Ferguson has written it has had to play that role while always stretched militarily and financially and sometimes without great public support.[77]

While in the face of the Russian threat, US Defence Secretary Ash Carter announced in February 2016 that the US 'will quadruple annual spending ... including sending more forward-located combat equipment to the European front lines', it has been presented in a narrow and limited way – as an effort in 'reassurance' for Europe.[78] As he said, 'The US-European Command has called for the posting of up to three brigades "as part of the United States" commitment to increased assurance and deterrence.'[79]

Similarly, America has stepped up its efforts in tackling the terrorist threat in the Middle East, with drones often hitting more than a dozen ISIL targets in a day. As David Ignatius has recently written, America is and remains 'the indispensable stabilizing power' in the Middle East, as shown with its leadership in negotiating the nuclear treaty with Iran, and the recent ceasefire in Syria as well as its evolving relationships with Middle East states.[80] But in his State of the Union address of 2016 President Obama made clear that while ISIL may 'pose a direct threat to our people' its actions 'do not threaten our national existence'. He is taking a long-view: that 'even without ISIL, ... instability will continue for decades in many parts of the world – in the Middle East, in Afghanistan, parts of Pakistan, in parts of Central America, in Africa, and Asia.' He recognises: 'Some of these places may become safe havens for new terrorist networks; others will fall victim to ethnic conflict, or famine, feeding the next wave of refugees.' 'The dangers facing Americans,' he said, are 'not because of diminished American strength. In today's world, we're threatened less by evil empires and more by failing states.' These Middle East threats are rooted at least partially in 'a transformation that will play out for a generation'.[81]

But while America is far enough away from the Middle East for it to feel its borders are less under threat, every day Europe's borders are directly and immediately under threat – leaving European nations with no choice but to act both to address 'the next wave of refugees' and stop places becoming 'safe havens for new terrorist networks'. We have to act now to avoid decades of instability.

So while America and Europe share the same distaste for instability in the Middle East and share the same desire to do something about it, it is Europe that is, at least today, more directly affected and at risk. We know that for the long term, the US wants a partnership in which Europe itself assumes more responsibility. And we know that there are continuing problems in Ukraine, Syria, Iraq and Libya, as well as a general instability across the Middle East and North Africa. And we know that NATO cannot on its own address questions that run far beyond the military – nor can any one European country. It is difficult to see any alternative to co-ordinating European resources, intelligence, aid and diplomacy. And it is clearly in Britain's interests to have a say in the direction of such a strategy.

Better use of resources

Collectively, as the European Political Strategy Centre points out, 'Europe is the world's second largest military spender. But it is far from being the second largest military power – a clear consequence of inefficiency in spending and a lack of interoperability.'[82] According to the European Defence Agency, enhanced co-operation by European Union Member States is 'the solution to acquire and maintain critical capabilities'.[83] And with 84 per cent of all equipment procurement transacted at a national level, there are clear benefits from greater co-operation.[84] The European Union estimated '€600 million could be saved from sharing of infantry vehicles and €500 million from having a collective system of certification of ammunition.'[85]

Britain could be one of the largest beneficiaries of a more co-ordinated approach. In 2015 Britain contributed $60 billion out of a total NATO spend of $900 billion – 7 per cent of all NATO defence spending, which makes us by far the biggest contributor after the US. Our spending is much more than Germany's $40 billion, France's $44 billion, Spain's $11 billion and Netherlands $9 billion.[86] So Britain should benefit from the September 2014 NATO pledge to 'halt any decline in defence' and to 'aim to increase defence expenditure in real terms as GDP grows', and 'aim to move towards the 2% guideline within a decade.'[87]

The evidence suggests that the promise that NATO countries made to reverse their decline in spending has been honoured. 'A curious thing is happening in continental Europe: defence spending is rising,' Elizabeth Quintana wrote in May 2015. 'France joined a growing number of European nations including Germany, Sweden, the Netherlands and Poland to increase defence spending,' something acknowledged by NATO chief Jens Stoltenberg in January.[88]

Co-operation could reduce the threat to the UK – and to every other advanced country – from cyber-attacks, to risks at airports, power stations and key institutions. Here we have agreed on the first EU-wide cyber legislation requiring technology firms and those running critical services to report cyber-breaches and setting minimum standards of cybersecurity for banks, energy and water firms.[89] Only a concerted effort against what has been called the Dark

Web – hidden parts of the Internet in which ISIL operates – will undermine what has been called a 'constellation' of computer servers that underpins their hidden online operations.[90]

So there is a powerful case for a more co-ordinated and more effective deployment of defence resources across Europe; a need for both burden-sharing and the integration of defence resources to meet agreed objectives. This is to reinforce the American presence, not to dilute it nor to prepare for an American withdrawal. And indeed many smaller European countries share the sentiment expressed by the then Danish Prime Minister during the Iraq War controversy that Europe's security is 'better guaranteed by "the American superpower" than by the fragile balance of power amongst Germany, France and England.'[91] But through European Union co-operation we can pool and utilise a broad range of resources and skills from across Europe – including diplomatic, civilian and financial expertise to tackle conflict and promote peace, the resource NATO cannot bring to bear. The role of the European Union, as UK Europe Minister David Lidington put it, is to help 'ensure that the significant progress made in recent years does not slip back towards political instability and ethnic violence, right on our doorstep'.[92] This is at no cost to NATO which in an official statement makes clear: 'Sharing strategic interests, NATO and the European Union co-operate on issues of common interest and are working side by side in crisis management, capability development and political consultations. The European Union is a unique and essential partner for NATO.'[93]

There is another reason why European co-operation is possible where it was difficult in the past. The search for an equilibrium in Europe, to prevent one power becoming too dominant, has been a centuries-long preoccupation. It arose from the days when an over-powerful European country could dictate militarily what happened not just in Europe but in the rest of the world. With Europe now a smaller part of the world's population – and a smaller part of the world's economy – the old balance-of-power considerations of the past matter less than collective security in dealing with Russia, the Middle East and North Africa.

Limits to co-operation

But there are limits to co-operation. In March 2015 the European Commission President, Jean-Claude Juncker, expressed support for the creation of a European Union army. 'With its own army, Europe could react more credibly to the threat to peace in a Member State or in a neighbouring state,' Mr Junker declared, adding that 'a common European army would convey a clear message to Russia that we are serious about defending our European values.' He added that an EU army would 'bring significant saving' in terms of purchasing military equipment. But the European Union is unlikely to have a single army to match its single currency. Other countries hold to the same positon as the UK government who responded that 'defence is a national, not an EU responsibility and that there is no prospect of that position changing and no prospect of a European army.'[94] In fact, Britain has recently blocked EU proposals, backed by France, Spain, Italy, Poland and Germany, that 'would have paved the way for developing a new fleet of unmanned surveillance drones and a European Air Force comprised of heavy transport and air-to-air refuelling planes.'[95]

Here again the issue for Britain's future is how to get the balance right between the autonomy countries desire and the co-operation that is in our interests. Getting that balance right starts from an understanding that individual nation states, including the UK, are unlikely to sacrifice, at least in the near future, long-held views about where they stand on the most vital of defence issues – including on the role of nuclear weapons.

A review of the difficulties of agreeing a common European position on nuclear disarmament makes the point. For the last 25 years the European Union has tried to co-ordinate the positions of Member States and to agree a common European position on disarmament, non-proliferation and peaceful use of nuclear energy. Indeed, it is argued that 'since the 1990s the EU Member States have always agreed on a common position to be presented at each NPT (Nuclear Non-Proliferation Treaty) Review Conference, delivered by a single representative on behalf of the EU as a whole.'[96] But, if it looked as if there was a common position on disarmament in 2010, in the preparations for the 2015 Review Conference, it proved impossible to reconcile differences on disarmament.

Countries once willing to compromise were determined to protect their own autonomous positions. Europe's two nuclear weapon states (France and the UK) are joined by four NATO members (Belgium, Germany, Italy and the Netherlands) who host US tactical nuclear weapons on their territory under the nuclear sharing arrangements, and there are 16 more NATO members who are protected by the NATO umbrella. The European Union, however, also contains six states who are not members of NATO, two of whom (Finland and Sweden) use nuclear plants for energy production and four (Austria, Cyprus, Ireland and Malta) who have repudiated even the civilian use of nuclear energy. In addition, as recorded by a seasoned observer of these talks, some European Union states like Denmark, Finland, Sweden, Norway and Iceland are in a Nordic disarmament coalition and others including Austria, Cyprus, Finland, Ireland, Malta and Sweden are part of a Humanitarian Initiative pushing for more immediate disarmament.[97]

'The EU Member States are able to agree only on the very general thesis that nuclear disarmament should be pursued as one of the NPT goals,' Michal Smetana concludes, 'Viewpoints on the timing and nature of the steps to be taken towards a nuclear weapon-free world vary dramatically ... In general, the individual Member States seemed to focus predominantly on their own agenda and activities within specific regional, political or issue-based coalitions and

groupings, and took significantly more divergent positions on particular issues than in the past.'[98]

The balance is unlikely to change soon in favour of a common
uniform European position. No Eurosceptic need fear that Britain
will be dragged against its will into an agreement to disarm or to take
action against its will. We will continue to be able to act in our own
self-defence with safeguards written in. But here again getting the
balance right between autonomy and co-operation emerges as the
central issue. 'If it leaves the EU,' concludes Robin Niblett, 'Britain
will find itself truly the junior and dependent partner in an unbal-
anced, bilateral security relationship with the US.'[99] And if we act
alone or restrict co-operation to a military alliance then our foreign
and defence policy ambitions cannot be afforded or achieved. The
way forward will be to work more closely with our neighbours, and
through this co-operation, increase our ability to act effectively
without losing our freedom to act. In an unstable and uncertain
world – and up against instability in the Middle East and Africa and
aggression from Russia, the conclusion is quite straightforward: if the
European Union is weaker, the United Kingdom will be less secure.
And this is what the British people appear to think. By two to one in
the recent Hope not Hate poll I cited earlier, our fellow British citizens
think we are safer because of European co-operation on security and
counter-terrorism. In response to the statement, '*In an unstable world,
European countries will be more secure by sticking together and
promoting shared values,*' 46 per cent agreed and only 19 per cent
disagreed. And in response to the statement, '*Leaving the EU would
be a risk because we would lose the ability to co-operate on security and
counter-terrorism issues*', 44 per cent agreed and 27 per cent disagreed.

Conclusion:
Leading, Not Leaving

In the first half of 2014 I was completing a book that put my case for Scotland staying part of Britain.

In advance of the Scottish independence referendum of September 2014, I wanted to present my own patriotic view of what Scotland's future could be.

I wanted to show that the needs and aspirations of the Scottish people could best be advanced as part of a reformed United Kingdom and that there was no contradiction between being a patriotic Scot and a supporter of the Union.

To show my patriotic credentials, it made sense to start from my own Scottish background. I could trace my family's roots back three hundred and more years within Scotland and indeed within one county of Scotland, the Kingdom of Fife – and trace how, from a farming background rooted in the land of Fife, our family fared from the time of the Union in 1707.

My bloodline could be tracked back through both my father and mother. I was Scottish born-and-bred and from a Scottish family that could be traced back as far as records of birth, marriages and deaths were available – to the early 1700s, three centuries and nearly fifteen generations ago.

Just after I sent off my book on Scotland to my publishers, I found myself talking to my friend, the author Alistair Moffat, who also ran a company that analysed DNA through a very simple saliva test that he had perfected – not dissimilar to the one used by the current Arch-bishop of Canterbury to check his parentage. And so to complete my work into the family tree I decided to take a saliva test and waited for the results.

To my astonishment everything that I assumed was now questioned by the findings: through the DNA test they could trace back my roots far beyond Scotland – and they did not, indeed, start in Scotland at all.

I was neither part of the Pictish race, nor the original Scots, nor the Angles, nor the Gaels.

My family's roots, the research suggested, lay in Scandinavia – not in Norway, from where many of today's Scottish families' bloodlines can be traced but in Sweden.

Almost certainly, as he found, my ancestors had travelled by sea from Sweden to England in search of prosperity and the evidence suggests they left Sweden around the 9th or 10th centuries.

And from there we were able to piece together, through family stories handed down over the years and by a process of deduction, a picture of immigrants who, having arrived on the North Sea coast of England, moved northwards within England to the Border country between Scotland and England.

Like many in their time they had probably been Border reivers – and lived a difficult and violent life on that fraught border in the 15th, 16th and possibly right up to the early 17th centuries before moving north.

And so the early story of my family's roots started to come together.

My older brother remembered that my father had told him of our Border roots and that our ancestors had indeed spent time working in the hills and valleys between Scotland and England.

Indeed, he had told him a family story passed down through the generations that our ancestors were forced to flee the Borders – and that Brown was not our original name. To escape from our pursuers, we had to change our name.

I then studied the history of the Borders around this time and read about the families who were rounded up and accused of being Border reivers; as the Union that brought Scotland and England together was in the process of being created – first with the Union of the Crowns in 1603, when James VI of Scotland became King James I of England too – there was a desire to ease tensions on the borders and see law and order restored. Orders went out to arrest anyone suspected of being part of raiding parties to steal livestock from England, and from each other. Proclamations calling for families to be outlawed and hunted down were issued. Many families were identified as likely culprits, and members were arrested and then executed, often without trial. Some managed to escape from capture by fleeing the Borders. And some had to change their name to avoid being hanged or – the cheaper way of executing convicts at that time – being drowned.

What started off as a search for an identity that appeared to be purely Scottish in origin ended up as a discovery of my migrant roots – indeed an understanding that almost all of our families, at some stage, have been migrants – and my European roots: Scandinavian ancestry, an English journey and time on the borderlands between two countries before becoming the Fife family we have been for 300 years.

And so it is with most families in Britain. As Norman Davies recalls in *The Isles*, the DNA of the oldest British skeleton was analysed and found to have continental roots, leading him to suggest we were all Europeans then and we are all – to a large extent – Europeans now.[1]

So those who write off our European heritage are, at least in part, writing off their own heritage. But I have not founded my case for remaining part of the European Union on genealogy: my case is based on what Europe can yield for us in the future. And in this book I have tried to make a positive, principled and patriotic case for Britain's membership of the European Union.

At the outset I placed the referendum debate in its historical context, showing that, in the aftermath of the Second World War, Britain still saw its economic future in Commonwealth trade and its political future in its strong association with America. Reluctant to engage in plans for European co-operation, we missed out on our chance to lead the continent. Even as we came to recognise that the new Commonwealth could never be as effective a platform for British economic progress and influence as the old Empire, we still found it difficult to envisage a relationship with Europe with which we were comfortable – one that could both accord with our view of the importance of the transatlantic partnership and not appear to put our autonomy at risk.

Even when we joined the European Economic Community in the 1970s, entry was little celebrated either as a triumph of enhanced co-operation or as a step towards a more a cosmopolitan world – or even as the embrace of a more European identity – but viewed more as a transaction, an exercise in practical co-operation that would protect the post-war peace and, most of all, help an economically weakened Britain catch up with our more prosperous neighbours in the West of Europe.

But if the debates in Britain from the 1940s to the 1970s started from a conventional position – what was best for us as a sovereign nation in a world of Great Powers – the 1980s brought the opening up of the global economy and from then on waves of global change – seismic shifts in industries, occupations and lifestyles – that have made our world very different from the imperial age.

It has taken a long time for us to realise that globalisation – and the increasing interdependence of peoples and nations – changes not just which national industries thrive and what jobs we have but also the very nature of our engagement with the world, particularly with the rest of Europe. Ironically, the very governments who championed the opening up of markets were slow to recognise that we had moved from a world defined by Great Powers – and indeed for a time defined by American pre-eminence alone – to a world defined by our international interdependence.

The 1997–2010 Labour government tried to rise to the challenge of a new world. In the age of interdependence, a country like ours, we believed, would deliver for the British people less through the direct exercise of military power important as that is and more through the influence we built – through our transatlantic partnership, our leadership of the Commonwealth, our participation in the European Union, and our engagement with – and inside – international institutions and with emerging powers like China. For too long, we believed, Britain had neglected our European links. A Britain that was stronger in Europe would be stronger in the world and co-operation between Europe and America could be a bigger force for global progress. So we set out after 1997 to do better where we had done worst before 1997: in building a stronger relationship with our neigbours in Europe.

The 1980s and 1990s proved to be a turning point not just because of the scale, scope and speed of globalisation but because of the popular reaction against globalisation as the downsides of global change started to become apparent. Faced with rapid de-industrialisation in the West – as Asia became the world's manufacturing centre – working families became aware of the greater insecurities that characterised their everyday lives. Their jobs were less secure, their living standards under greater pressure and the prospects for their children more uncertain. And while the upside of globalisation has been a widening of opportunities for millions, the downside has brought discontent and anger among working families who feel they have lost out. Many feel they are not globalisation's children but globalisation's orphans. Many more have come to the view that Britain has changed out of all recognition and is not the country they were born into. And they blame multinational organisations and supranational institutions – from international companies and global banks to the European Union itself – for the insecurities they face and demand that someone, somewhere shelter, protect, insulate and make them more secure. This has, as have I suggested, led to demands to 'bring control back home' and 'put control back in our own hands.'

The theme of this book is that in a new era of international interdependence it makes no sense to retreat from the cross-border cooperation, that is necessary to address climate change, financial instability, illegal migration and terrorism, just as it makes no sense for proud nations to submerge their strong sense of national identities into some superstate. I conclude that to meet and master the challenges we confront – to balance the legitimate desire for as much autonomy as possible with the need to co-operate to secure our interests – we should team up with our neighbours to manage globalisation in the interests of working people. Indeed, it might be the only way to bring that 'runaway train' back to doing what we want it to do.

I have suggested that we have moved on from the early years of the century – and the high watermark of federalist ambition – and that the EU operates less according to the structures Eurosceptics identify as federalist than according to a form of intergovernmentalism – decisions made through negotiation between individual states. This should not come as a surprise: in the enlarged European Union of 28 members, every single country, as proud of their own distinctive traditions and culture as we are, is unwilling to suppress their national identity in favour of a blanket uniformity and each country is, like Britain, searching for the right balance between the autonomy it desires and the co-operation it needs. Our independent position on the Euro and on Schenghen shows that we do not give automatic support to every proposal for integration, but we do not either automatically oppose any proposal. The test is what is of benefit to Britain. The Europe of the future is unlikely to be a United States of Europe but, instead, a United Europe of States: independent-minded nation states who share similar values, travelling to the same destinations at different speeds or, as often is now the case, travelling on separate tracks and sometimes too with different destinations in view.

I try to demonstrate how across a range of decisions that concern every family in our country – the economy and jobs, social justice, migration, energy and climate change, defence and security – Britain can argue for, and achieve, the best balance between national autonomy and international co-operation for the 21st century. I also suggest that Europe should think of itself as Global Europe, and by that I mean a Europe that looks outwards to the rest of the world, builds stronger relationships with Asia, the Middle East and Africa, and works in partnership with the United States and others to shape the international institutions of the future.

At the heart of this book is the contention that our ties – economic, cultural, political and diplomatic – to mainland Europe are far more extensive, intricate, complex and of more benefit to us than we are often prepared to acknowledge. From the research of Professor Iain Begg at the London School of Economics, who has estimated the scale of employment linked to membership of the EU, we can show that more than three million jobs depend on demand from our European neighbours.[2] By guaranteeing the free, unimpeded movement of goods and services across frontiers the Single Market offers us more than a free trade area can ever give us. And when we ask the right question – what exactly is the best balance between autonomy and co-operation if we are to deliver the most job opportunities and the best economic prospects for British people in the future? – we find that our best interests are served by rapid reform of the Single Market through the opening up of European finance and the digital and services sectors to British firms. I suggest that if we are to maintain the proper balance between autonomy and co-operation then the more the European Single Market works by 'mutual recognition' of Member States' domestic standards – which starts from the presumption that decisions made in one country can be recognised in another – the better.

Balancing autonomy and co-operation in the interests of Britain means we continue to retain the freedom to pursue our own national policies on tax, public expenditure and employment, and thrive or falter on decisions we make in our own Parliament. Even Euro-enthusiasts have come a long way from believing that harmonisation and homogeneity are necessarily the best ways forward.

In this book, I have devoted a chapter to the Euro and to the complex issues that our government had to resolve in choosing whether to adopt or reject it. There were clear advantages – lower transaction costs and trading costs across countries, as we eliminated the need for currency exchange within Europe – and the possibility of lower interest rates for Britain in the long-term, and, over time, lower inflation. But there were disadvantages – our economic cycle was different, our housing market in particular was unique, and by joining we would lose our power to make interest-rate decisions in line with our own economic cycle, would be forced to fall back on fiscal fine-tuning and we would probably have suffered a Euro-induced recession around 2005, ending up with even lower growth rates than we have now.

But it makes no sense to ignore the benefits companies and industries gain from co-operation on economic policy including the benefit from joint action to secure the stability of the financial system. And so we opposed – and I continue to reject – the idea of an economic Berlin Wall separating Euro and non-Euro areas. Of course it is right to have safeguards that decisions made by the Eurozone will not undermine the European Single Market but, from protecting the integrity of the banking system to G20 initiatives on growth, from framing global trade policies to dealing with the economics of climate change, closer co-operation in framing macroeconomic policies in a multi-currency Europe is in our interests. So I am of the view we need not consign ourselves to a back-seat role when it comes to discussions of Europe's economic future, we should instead push our way to the centre.

The way ahead

What then of the future? Is the case for being part of Europe strengthened or diminished by the challenges lying ahead of us? One fact is clear: as a recent Chatham House-YouGov survey states, 63 per cent of the public (including 58 per cent of Labour voters) believe that the UK should 'seek to remain a great power,' and only one in five say the 'UK should accept it is no longer a great power'.[3] While most (60 per cent of the public) agree with the statement, 'the UK is expected to do too much internationally [and] the UK should do less and others should do more', there are still large majorities of the view that the UK has a 'responsibility to maintain international security' – 69 per cent believe this. Meanwhile, 58 per cent believe that the 'UK should provide troops for peacekeeping missions' and 56 per cent believe Britain 'should help lead the global response to climate change'.[4]

Understandably, the top public priority for international action in Britain's national interest is to protect ourselves against terrorism. Respondents emphasise the security of our borders and a counter-terrorist strategy, something that cannot be achieved without co-operation with our neighbours. The second priority chosen by the public is what is called 'resource security' – work on delivering a sustainable environment in the light of climate change that again requires international agreements. A third priority is security against possible aggression and conflict, and while NATO is considered vital and European membership evokes little enthusiasm, there has, however, been a shift in public attitudes in one respect: 30 per cent of the public now thinks 'that the UK's closest ties should be to the EU', compared to 25 per cent who prefer America. And while Conservatives and UKIP supporters tend to prefer the US over the European Union, Labour and Liberal Democrats opt for European co-operation.[5]

Of course, as we have shown, Winston Churchill thought of a world of interlocking circles with Britain exercising influence at the

intersection. His interlocking circles were Empire and the Commonwealth, the transatlantic relationships and Europe. In each of these
relationships, Churchill thought of Britain as a leader, particularly as
the leader of Empire and an equal with the USA. But the world, as
we have seen, changed fast around him.

The old distinctions between 'over here' and 'over there' have
become blurred. We cannot say that pollution, financial contagion,
terrorism or the movement of peoples are 'over there' and we have
found that we cannot quarantine extremism in one country, cauterise
pollution in one region or separate any one continent off from the
pressures of migration. Indeed, building walls has not been
successful: the 40 countries that have built barriers on their borders
– and done so with 65 other countries – have been discovering that
it is more effective to build bridges than erect walls.[6] And if even the
smallest country can affect us directly, then their loss may not be our
gain and Britain's international relations should not be seen as a
Zero-sum game; while we must never compromise on our strong
support for human rights and democracy it makes no sense to act in
an exclusive way and fail to seek the widest circle of working relationships. And it makes no sense at all to distance ourselves from our
nearest neighbours with whom we trade most and whose co-
operation we need for our security as well as our prosperity.

While military might gave states the most direct and tangible
capacity to direct events – Stalin famously asked how many divisions
the Pope had[7] – we now have to take into account both our greater
dependence upon each other and, by acknowledging limits to the use
of hard power, must think of how we persuade allies – rather than
coerce, threaten or intimidate them. This includes other potential
partners that are not to be found on a map – national and international non-governmental organisations, charities, foundations and
companies who may share our objectives and be persuaded to work
with us to shape agreed outcomes.

While Britain remains one of a number of countries of a size and capacity to influence the rest of the world, we will do best when we act in concert with others rather than on our own. I suggested earlier that since 2010, as a result of its reluctance to identify positively with the EU, the Conservative Government presented Britain, in the words of Robin Niblett, as 'a hub or a bridge or a connecting node in a networked world', reaching out to China, India, Brazil, South Africa and the emerging economies with whom trade has been rising fastest. They saw this not as complementary to but as an alternative to working closely within the European Union.[8] However, presenting ourselves to the world as akin to convener of events and conferences – even ones at the centre of global attention – can take us only so far and will not give us the level of influence that matches our ambitions. Niblett has argued against the view that Britain can maximise its influence without choosing between the many possible channels of influence and without taking engagement in Europe more seriously. His view is that a nation like ours, with limited resources, has no choice but to concentrate our energies where we can achieve greatest results. And while, as he puts it, 'Britain's multiple vectors of inter-national influence are … useful foreign policy assets', we also need a 'strong geo-political base' – namely Europe – from which to meet large geo-political challenges and ensure our prosperity and security.[9]

A calm and objective consideration of our interests – particularly of the threats to our security from instability near to home – may lead us to a similar conclusion. 'If one ticks off a list of our likely preoccupations over the next few decades – poverty, disease migration, terrorism, energy, climate change and economic compet-itiveness,' writes Stephen Wall pointedly, 'all of them require Britain to work with our European partners and many of them will require not the lengthy lowest common denominator approach of intergov-ernmental negotiation but the effective decision-making and subse-quent enforcement which can only be achieved by the so-called Community method … Britain as never before needs Europe.'[10]

Europe is where our greatest economic interests lie, are likely to continue to lie, and – because mainland Europe is but a few miles away – this will be true 'in' or 'out' of the European Union. That being the case, it is better to be in a position to shape Europe rather than be shaped by it. And, despite our past reluctance to see our engagement in Europe in this light, there is no reason why it should be at the expense of our American relationship or resisted by our American partners. A Britain that is stronger in Europe is likely to be strengthened in its relationship with America and others.

In the immediate future, as I have tried to show in the previous chapter, Britain faces three profound challenges on our and Europe's doorstep that impact upon us and our security priorities in a way that is different from America: first, Middle East instability – including both the threat from terrorists and the flow of migrants out of the region; second, the looming problem also on Europe's borders that emanates from Africa where instability is breeding terrorist groups and causing large movements of people into Europe; and, third, Russian aggression on the European Union's eastern borders. As I suggested, American and European interests do not diverge but current American and European priorities are not entirely the same – with America more focused on Asia and China, in particular – while Europe has no alternative but to address urgent problems that arise from mass migration and terrorist threats.

But what of the future? Richard Hass, the President of the US Council of Foreign Relations, has warned that 'an America that is distracted and divided is less likely to be willing or able to take the lead in promoting security in the Middle East, Europe, or Asia, or in meeting global challenges'.[11] Yet the Europe of the future cannot afford to stand back not just because the threat to our security continues to be immediate and ever present, but because there can be no long-term solution to the problems of both the Middle East and Africa that will slow migration, diminish the terrorist threat or bring stability without a comprehensive approach to these regions. And that approach will require physical support, diplomatic engagement, aid to deal with crises and, more importantly for the long term, help with economic reconstruction to provide an alternative vision of a Middle East future through which the rising generation of 200 million young people can have hope that there is a middle way between tyranny and terrorism. We have to address therefore not just the spillover effects from instability in these regions but, if we are to feel more secure, the root causes of that instability. And because we need to work with countries in the Middle East on social, economic and political reform, such a strategy could not be delivered by NATO alone even if it has a continuous out-of-area presence, nor by one country alone. Britain is, quite simply, now too small to implement a Middle East strategy on its own but is big enough to be a leading partner in a European-led initiative.

Some would say that we should be prepared to act but only on an *ad hoc* basis and only for the time there is an emergency. However, as none of these basic social, economic and political challenges is going to disappear in the next decade, we need more than a case-by-case response to each crisis and more than a short-term and inter-mittent engagement with troubled countries: we will not only need a comprehensive approach that uses all the levers available to us but we will require a continuing and long-term commitment to work with troubled countries to ensure stability.

It will soon become obvious that a similar approach will be needed in forging a better European relationship with Africa. Just as the Middle East needs a 21st-century Marshall-style Plan to deliver educational, employment and economic opportunities, political reform and inter-regional co-operation, so too we need to build a more comprehensive and longer-term relationship that helps Africa move from poverty to prosperity. Today Africa comprises 16 per cent of the world's population; by 2030 it will rise to 19 per cent. In 2015 60 per cent of Africa's population were aged under 25 – and yet Africa is home to 1.5 per cent of the world's manufacturing, 0.45 per cent of the world's inward investment and over 33 million children who are not in primary school.[12] Unless we work with the continent, Africa cannot catch-up economically and will remain on the fringes of the world economy – its people increasingly angry at their marginalisation. Indeed, Africa's problems are so deep-seated that there is a case for Europe leading a coalition with America – and, I would add, China – to work with African governments to build the Africa of the future. A few years from now it may be more difficult for us to carry such influence but today a strong American-European partnership remains the best starting point for managing globalisation better and the best building block for working towards a fairer and more equitable global order.

Europe's importance to world peace and stability was at the heart of President Kennedy's words in 1962 when he called for a Declaration of Independence. In that speech he proposed 'forming a concrete Atlantic partnership, a mutually beneficial partnership between the new union now emerging in Europe and the old American Union founded here 175 years ago'. And he explained why in arguments that are still relevant today:

Acting on our own, by ourselves, we cannot establish justice throughout the world; we cannot insure its domestic tranquillity, or provide for its common defence, or promote its general welfare, or secure the blessings of liberty to ourselves and our posterity. But joined with other free nations, we can do all this and more. We can assist the developing nations to throw off the yoke of poverty. We can balance our worldwide trade and payments at the highest possible level of growth. We can mount a deterrent powerful enough to deter any aggression. And ultimately we can help to achieve a world of law and free choice, banishing the world of war and coercion ... for the Atlantic partnership of which I speak would not look inward only, preoccupied with its own welfare and advancement. It must look outward to co-operate with all nations in meeting their common concern. It would serve as a nucleus for the eventual union of all free men – those who are now free and those who are vowing that someday they will be free.[13]

Europe is not only the main focus for our economic interests but vital to our security. And, if the greatest threats to the UK are now close to our borders, Britain should not, in the words of Dr Robin Niblett, ever move from 'the first team' to the 'reserve bench.'[14] Instead, we should see the advantages of co-operation: at a minimum, participating on equal terms with our nearest neighbours, and at our best, where we can and if we make the effort, as a leader that would make Europe, as Niblett says, 'the principal source of international leverage'.[15] Not only does membership of the European Union offer us the chance to design, propose and push new EU initiatives that are in Britain's and Europe's interests but by combining our resources, often in partnership with America, we have the capacity to deliver far better outcomes than ever we could achieve on our own. Freed by virtue of globalisation from the old balance of power constraints that made European nations gang up against each other to avoid one power becoming over-dominant, Europe not only wants a collective approach to its security but also there is less opposition than ever before from Germany and France to Britain playing a leading role. And we have further advantages: while certain responsibilities of membership of the European Union are requirements in the form of obligations, many are not. We have successfully opted out of the Euro, Schengen and, where it was in our interests to do so, foreign policy decisions.

It is important to recognise that we have – and will continue to have – our own armed forces who take action only on the instruction of the British Government and the UK Parliament. Just as our tax, spending and currency arrangements are decided in Britain, so too is the future of our army, navy and air force. But security co-operation is in our interests when dealing with common threats and contributes to best use of scarce resources in doing so. With this freedom to act independently or to act in collaboration, and the right to choose how we respond, we can balance the autonomy we desire with the co-operation we need, recognising the benefits from Britain joining in co-operative actions which cannot be achieved if we act in isolation – and, as a result, we will be stronger in facing Russia, able to moderate the power of the strongest and provide a champion for small countries who support reform and want a Europe that looks outwards.

Defence co-operation will be strengthened principally within NATO. But through our willingness to work together as a European Union comes an additional benefit: our very co-operation as allies is in itself a deterrent to potential aggressors. We do not, however, surrender our autonomy in doing so: not only have we maintained our position on nuclear deterrence, despite numerous unsuccessful attempts within Europe to bind us to a common position, but in foreign, defence and security policy we retain our independent decision-making power, co-operating when it is in our interests to do so.

I have suggested that European leverage is of benefit not only to address the challenges that threaten our security but to enhance prospects of trade with America (where a treaty is being negotiated) and with China. And I have argued it is in Britain's national interest to set minimum social standards across Europe in order to stop the good European employer, whether it be a business or a country, from being undercut by the bad and the bad by the worst. I have shown how European co-operation can assist us using to best effect our unique natural resources not only in oil and gas but in wind and wave power. Environmental policy cannot work to reduce pollution significantly if only Britain cuts its emissions and the rest of Europe does not, but co-operation offers more than that: by integrating our wind and wave power into the widest possible pool – mixing it in with more guaranteed sources – we stop the waste of renewable resources; ensure the security of our supplies of energy; keep energy costs down for consumers; and, of course, cut carbon emissions.

Migration poses the most difficult question because an unfair accusation has become an accepted wisdom amongst many who believe that we have sacrificed our autonomy – by agreeing to freedom of movement of European workers across Europe – for nothing in return. In truth, however, we benefit directly from co-operation with our nearest neighbours as we confront illegal migration. Going forward, we need to co-ordinate our actions to secure tougher controls on Europe's external borders, to develop a system for a fair distribution of refugees across the continent, to negotiate arrangements with third-party countries from where most migrants come and to help the Middle East and North and sub-Saharan African countries to retain their populations by ensuring that millions who are considering migration have the chance of prosperity at home. So, without close co-operation, we cannot track the flow of illegal immigrants or get to the root of the problem that leads them to land on our shores. With close co-operation – arrest warrants, surveillance and negotiated agreements with countries of origin to return illegal immigrants – we can achieve much more.

Five ways to lead Europe

Of course the risks from leaving the European Union cannot be left unstated, including the fall-out from unintended consequences. One possible outcome of a 'Leave' vote is a second Scottish referendum on independence. And, if England was to be permanently outside the European Union the pressure would be on Scotland to adopt the Euro rather than the pound. We should counterpose this with a vision of a European Union ready to champion more direct partici-pation by the regions and the nations.

The Northern Ireland DUP leadership is calling for a 'Leave' vote

– which, if successful, would reintroduce border controls and custom points and destabilise the 'Good Friday' agreement. Sinn Féin have retaliated with a call for a border poll to end partition. To this, we should counterpose a positive vision in which Europe mobilises its economic resources to strengthen cross-border co-operation and narrow long-standing inequalities within Ireland.

We have a duty also to inspire people about the opportunities arising from Europe by focusing on the positives where the EU can help improve standards of living and quality of life in the future.

Before 23 June 2016, voters should hear more not just about the positive benefits that European membership brings to Britain today but what it can bring to Britain in the future. And a forward-looking agenda might highlight five ways Europe can do better by the British people.

First: Focus on the half a million new British jobs that can be created in the next ten years from reforms to the Single Market – opening up the digital economy (which can contribute 25 per cent of increased output), the energy market (15 per cent), and the service and other sectors, including financial services and capital markets (just under 60 per cent), through offering economies of scale, lower production, transaction and distribution costs and easier access to finance.

Second: European help for hard-pressed industrial communities hit by closures and restructuring. At the same time as we seek a future for steel manufacturing in Britain, additional new jobs can come from the European infrastructure initiative by insisting Britain benefits now from a 15–16 per cent share of the €315 billion European Investment Plan – and this should be in addition to substantial Social Fund and other support for our steel communities.

Third: Act together to create a fairer society. We have shown that European co-operation can lead global efforts to reduce tax avoidance and tax evasion by forcing the exchange of information between national tax authorities. Faced with the loss of €1 trillion in tax receipts to fund public services, a European initative – pushed through the G20 and the Organisation of Economic Co-operation and Development – can lead the way. There should be no hiding place for tax evaders and no safe haven for tax avoiders.

Fourth: Reduce the pressures from migration in the areas which worry fellow citizens most – the NHS, schools, and social housing. Our most affected communities should be benefiting from a new European Solidarity Fund built out of Europe's current Asylum Migration and Integration Fund, (from which the UK is to receive by 2020 €370m), a far more comprehensive version of the UK Controlling Migration Fund which can provide extra support for local areas that face unexpected pressures. And we should extend co-operation among security, intelligence and policing authorities across Europe to tackle the criminal mafias, the people smugglers and the gangmasters that exploit migrants and increase unlawful immigration from the Middle East and Africa. While helping refugees who need our support, we need to back up our own system of border controls with a better European co-ordination of security forces.

Fifth: Build a European strategy for addressing the root causes of Middle Eastern and African instability. While most of our terrorist threats come from home-grown terrorists – and reforms in security co-operation among security services will help reduce this – the roots of terrorism lie outside Europe. And if we are to thwart terrorism, slow the flow of migrants from the Middle East and Africa and do something to answer the more basic problem – grievances of millions of young people in the Middle East and Africa who are being taught the only alternatives are tyranny and terrorism – we will need a comprehensive Middle East and Africa strategy as bold as the 1940s Marshall Plan. This cannot be delivered by NATO which is a defence and military alliance unable to undertake the comprehensive 'out-of-area' effort that requires the use of aid, economic muscle and soft power. And while America shares our interests in these regions, it is looking at the Middle East from a long-term perspective. For Europe, moreover, migration and terrorism are immediate and urgent problems on our own doorstep that have to be addressed. The European-led Marshall-style Plan, which is needed urgently, would use all our weapons – military, diplomatic, financial and economic – to help build stability and prosperity in these regions.

All these immediate challenges – from terrorism to job creation and other longer term challenges from pollution to dealing with Russian aggression – show how, at every turn, it is important, in our national interest, to get the balance right between the autonomy we desire and the co-operation we need.

And we can only succeed in meeting and mastering these challenges by *leading in* Europe. Not being 'half-out', as we currently appear to many; not being 'fully out', where the Eurosceptics would want us to be, but by pushing our way to Europe's centre where and when it matters. That's how we can be in the vanguard, advancing British interests by shaping Europe and through our influence in Europe shaping the world. And this is how, on reflection, the British people appear to see it. By two to one – 41 per cent to 21 per cent among those who expressed an opinion – citizens agreed with the Hate not Hope opinion poll statement that '*Britain does best when it is a leading country within the European Union.*'

In the spirit of a country that defeated fascism on the continent of Europe it is simply not British to be on Europe's side-lines especially when we are in an insecure and unstable world which faces the same challenges as us. It is certainly not the Britain I know best to relegate ourselves to the periphery when big security decisions that affect our safety as citizens have to be made not only in NATO but in the European Union.

Only 70 years ago Britain's power lay in directing an Empire we imagined would last forever. So we downplayed our role in Europe even when we were in a position to be its leader. We took time to understand that there was a new world in the making. Now as the world's economy has now gone global, our era is marked out by the interdependence and interconnectedness of the world's peoples. And Britain, the most outward-looking, internationalist and globally connected power in Europe, is in a position to help lead Europe into this new world. We should seize the opportunity.

Being that leader will allow us to once again to display the qualities that made Britain's worldwide reputation for championing democracy and fair play. These are the values we showed when we led the fight against fascism, and then helped rebuild Europe from the ruins of war. The same values we showed when we stood up to dictators in Eastern Europe, helped restore peace on the edge of Europe in the Balkans and fought anti-Semitism.

These are the same values that we showed when we worked to establish the European Convention of Human Rights, defended democracy, resettled refugees and stood in solidarity with those fleeing persecution.

They are the values upon which Britain helped build European co-operation in what had been a war-torn and divided continent. These were the values we showed when we invited the countries of Eastern Europe in as the Cold War came to an end and when we offer the hand of friendship – irrespective of race or religion – to all those who embrace democracy, liberty and equality of opportunity. This is the Britain I know and love – the Britain that should be leading Europe not leaving it. For 'Brex-it' read 'Lead-it'.

Notes

INTRODUCTION

1 Centre for Economics and Business Research, UK Jobs Supported by Exports to the EU: CEBR Analysis of UK Jobs Associated with Demand from the European Union', (London, CEBR, 2014), p. 12.
2 In total, 770,000 people are employed across the UK automotive sector, including retail and servicing. Of this number, 161,000 are employed directly in manufacturing and 78,000 in the supply chain.
3 Confederation for British Industry, 'Our Global Future' (CBI, London, 2013).
4 Office for National Statistics, 'Top 50 UK International Export Destinations, 2015', (London, ONS, 2015).
5 Bank of England, *EU Membership and the Bank of England* (Bank of England, London, 2015), p. 9.
6 Figure complied by Britain Stronger in Europe using data from Her Majesty's Revenue and Customs. Available online at: http://www.strongerin.co.uk/the_economy
7 In 1973, the value of UK imports and exports were together worth around 40 per cent of UK GDP, but by 2014 they were worth close to 60 per cent of GDP. Since 1973, trade volumes have grown at twice the rate of GDP. See Bank of England, 'EU Membership and the Bank of England', p. 18.
8 Mark Carney, Letter to Rt Hon Andrew Tyrie MP, (7 March 2016). Available online at: http://www.bankofengland.co.uk/publications/Documents/other/treasurycommittee/other/governorletter070316.pdf
9 John Curtice, 'Revealed: Two thirds of British voters are Europsceptics – but they aren't convinced we should leave', *The Daily Telegraph*, (24 February 2016). Available online at: http://www.telegraph.co.uk/news/newstopics/eureferendum/12171049/Revealed-Two-thirds-of-British-voters-are-Eurosceptics-but-they-arent-convinced-we-should-leave.html
10 John Curtice, 'The Two Poles of the Referendum Debate: Immigration and the Economy', *What UK Thinks: EU*, (28 January 2016). Available online at: http://whatukthinks.org/eu/immigration-and-the-economy-the-two-key-issues-in-the-referendum/

11 Robert Ford and Nick Lowles, 'Fear & Hope 2016: Race, Faith and Belonging
    in Today's England', (2016), p.55. Available online at: http://www.barrow
    cadbury.org.uk/wp-content/uploads/2016/03/Fear-and-Hope-report-1.pdf

12 'In the end, it looks as though it will principally voters' hard-headed judge-
    ments about the economy that will prove decisive', writes Curtice, who has
    been among the most prescient of polling experts in recent years. 'Put it this
    way,' another prominent analyst Matthew Godwin writes, 'among those who
    felt both under threat from the EU and that Brexit would be economically
    beneficial, support for Brexit surpassed 80 per cent. But among those who had
    only been won over by the identity case but not the economic, then Brexit
    remained a minority view, supported by around 40 per cent.' Taking his cue
    from *The Daily Telegraph* poll of mid-March 2016 the question voters are
    asking, says Sir Lynton Crosby in even blunter terms is: 'are the economic risks
    of remaining in the EU bigger or smaller than the impact of uncontrolled
    immigration that voters believe could result?' 'The outcome,' concludes
    Curtice, 'is likely to turn on whether voters go with their doubts about the
    cultural consequences of EU membership.' John Curtice, 'EU referendum:
    Economy will be decisive in making voters' minds up', *The Independent*, (23
    February 2016). Available online at: http://www.independent.co.uk/voices/
    eu-referendum-economy-will-be-decisive-in-making-voters-minds-
    upa6892096.html. Matthew Goodwin, 'If Boris Johnson wants to win, he
    needs to lake less about sovereignty and more about the economy',
    BrexitVote, (13 March 2016). Available online at: http://blogs.lse.ac.uk/
    brexitvote/2016/03/13/if-boris-johnson-wants-to-win-he-needs-to-talk-less-
    about-sovereignty-andmore-about-the-economy/. Sir Lynton Crosby,
    'Remain or leave? It all rests on the risk factor', *The Daily Telegraph*, (14 March
    2016). Online at: http://www.telegraph.co.uk/news/politics/12194138/Remain-
    or-leave-It-allrests-on-the-risk-factor.html

13 Global flows of goods, services, and finance rose 15-fold from $2 trillion in
    1980 to $29 trillion in 2007. It then subsequently declined as a result of the
    global financial crisis and recession, before rising again and reaching $28
    trillion in 2014. It has been projected by the McKinsey Global Institute that
    this figure could triple – to $84 trillion – by 2025. McKinsey Global Institute,
    'Global Flows in a Digital Age'. (New York, McKinsey, 2014).

14 John F. Kennedy, 'Address at Independence Hall, Philadelphia', July 4, 1962.
    Online by Gerhard Peters and John T. Woolley, *The American Presidency
    Project*. http://www.presidency.ucsb.edu/ws/?pid=8756.

15 Adrian Hyde-Price, 'European Security in the Twenty-First Century:
    The Challenge of Multipolarity' (Abingdon: Routledge, 2006), p.102

CHAPTER 1

1 Janan Ganesh, *From a Reluctant European: memo to the Prime Minister* (Open
   Europe, London, January 2015); 'Special Report', *The Economist*, (17 October
   2015). Available online at: http://www.economist.com/sites/default/files/
   20151017_ukeu.pdf

2   Speech by Lord Lamont, Guildhall Conference, (19 October 2015). Available
     online at: http://businessforbritain.org/2015/10/19/speech-by-lord-lamont-to-
     guildhall-conference/

3   Charles Moore, 'By choosing not to lead, Obama has left the West dangerously
     exposed', *The Daily Telegraph*, (11 March 2016). Available online at:
     http://www.telegraph.co.uk/news/worldnews/northamerica/12191637/
     By-choosing-not-to-lead-Obama-has-left-the-West-dangerously-
     exposed.html

4   Denis MacShane, *Brexit: How Britain Will Leave Europe* (London, I.B. Tauris,
     2015), p. 204.

5   Stephen Wall, *A Stranger in Europe: Britain and the EU from Thatcher to Blair*
     (Oxford, Oxford University Press, 2008), p.200.

6   Vernon Bogdanor, 'Footfalls echoing in the memory. Britain and Europe: the
     historical perspective', *International Affairs*, vol. 81, no. 4 (2005), pp. 689–701.

7   Jeremy Paxman, *The English: A Portrait of a People* (London, Penguin, 2001),
     p. 200.

8   Norman Moss, *Nineteen Weeks: America, Britain, and the Fateful Summer of
     1940* (Boston and New York, Houghton Mifflin-Harcourt, 2003), p. 203.

9   Vernon Bogdanor, 'Britain and the Continent', Gresham College Lecture,
     (17 September 2013). Available online at: http://www.gresham.ac.uk/
     lectures-and-events/britain-and-the-continent

10 David Cannadine, *The Undivided Past: History Beyond Our Differences*
     (London, Allen Lane, 2013), p. 259–160.

11 David Abulafia, 'Britain: apart from or a part of Europe?', *History Today*,
     (11 May 2015). Available online at: http://www.historytoday.com/
     david-abulafia/britain-apart-or-part-europe

12 Norman Davies, *The Isles: A History* (Papermac, London, 2000), p. 7.

13 *Ibid*, p. 8.

14 *Ibid*.

15 *Ibid*, pp. 8-9.

16 *Ibid*, p. 38.

17 Robert Tombs, *The English and their History: The First Thirteen Centuries*
     (London, Penguin, 2015), p. 7.

18 Davies, *The Isles*, p. 9.

19 *Ibid*.

20 Response to David Abulafia composed by David Andress, Richard Blakemore,
     Thomas Charlton, Neil Gregor, Rachel Moss, Natalia Nowakowska, Charlotte
     Riley and Mark Williams, 'Fog in Channel, Historians Isolated', *History Today*,
     (18 May 2005). Available online at: http://www.historytoday.com/various-
     authors/fog-channel-historians-isolated

21 'The Open Sea', *The Economist*, (17 October 2015).

22 Chris Rhodes, *Tourism: Statistics and Policy* (London, House of Commons
     Library, 2015), p. 9.

23 European Commission, 'Children in Europe start learning foreign languages
     at increasingly early age', press release, (20 September 2012). Available online
     at: http://europa.eu/rapid/press-release_IP-12-990_en.htm

24 Sam Wilson, 'Britain and the EU: A long and rocky relationship', *BBC News*, (1 April 2014). Available at: http://www.bbc.co.uk/news/uk-politics-26515129

25 Bogdanor, 'Britain and the Continent'.

26 James Ellison, 'Is Britain more European than it thinks?', *History Today*, (February 2012). Available online at: http://www.historytoday.com/james-ellison/britain-more-european-it-thinks

27 Robert Kagan, 'Superpowers Don't Get to Retire', *New Republic*, (May 2014). Available online at: https://newrepublic.com/article/117859/allure-normalcy-what-america-still-owes-world

28 Hugo Young, *This Blessed Plot: Britain and Europe from Churchill to Blair* (London, Macmillan, 1998), p. 96.

29 David Cannadine, 'Apocalypse When?' in Peter Clarke and Clive Trebilcock (eds.), *Understanding Decline: Perceptions and Realities of British Economic Performance* (Cambridge, Cambridge University Press), p. 274.

30 David Cannadine, *In Churchill's Shadow: Confronting the Past in Modern Britain* (London, Penguin, 2002), p. 34.

31 *Ibid*.

32 *Ibid*.

33 Michael Charlton, *The Price of Victory* (London, BBC, 1983), p. 20.

34 Charles de Gaulle, *War Memoirs*, vol. 2 (New York, Viking, 1959), p. 227.

35 Sabine Lee, *Victory in Europe? Britain and Germany Since 1945* (London, Routledge, 2001), p. 48.

36 Donald Maitland quoted in Young, *This Blessed Plot*, p. 101.

37 David Gowland and Arthur Turner, *Reluctant Europeans: Britain and European Integration 1945–1998* (London, Routledge, 2000), p. 16; Peter Hennessy, *Having it So Good: Britain in the Fifties* (London, Allen Lane, 2007), pp. 36–37.

38 Benn Steill, *The Battle of Bretton Woods: John Maynard Keynes, Harry Dexter White, and the Making of a New World Order* (New Haven, Princeton University Press, 2013), p. 191.

39 For Churchill's 'three circles' speech see Winston Churchill, *Europe Unite! Speeches, 1947 & 1948* (London, Cassell, 1950), pp. 417–418.

40 Vernon Bogdanor and Robert Skidelsky, *The Age of Affluence, 1951–1964* (London, Macmillan, 1970), p. 198.

41 Gowland and Turner, *Reluctant Europeans: Britain and European Integration 1945–1998*, p. 10.

42 *Ibid*, p. 86.

43 *Ibid*, p. 84.

44 David Gowland, Arthur Turner and Alex Wright, *Britain and European Integration Since 1945: On the Sidelines* (London, Routledge, 2010), p. 24.

45 Manifesto by the National Executive Committee of the British Labour Party on European unity (May 1950). Available online at cvce.eu.

46 Oliver Franks, *Britain and the Tide of World Affairs* (Oxford, Oxford University Press, 1955), p. 23.

47   John Gallagher, *The Decline, Revival and Fall of the British Empire: The Ford Lectures and Other Essays* (Cambridge, Cambridge University Press, 1982), p. 146.

48   Kevin Jefferys, *Labour Forces: From Ernest Bevin to Gordon Brown* (London, I.B. Tauris, 2002) p.19.

49   Oliver Franks, *Britain and the Tide of World Affairs*, p. 12.

50   Victor Sebestyen, *1946: The Making of the Modern World* (London, Palgrave Macmillan, 2014), p. 78.

51   *Ibid*, p. 12

52   John Darwin, 'A Third British Empire? The Dominion Idea in Imperial Politics' in Judith Brown and Wm. Rodger Lewis (eds.), *The Oxford History of the British Empire: Volume IV: The Twentieth Century* (Oxford, Oxford University Press, 1999), p.85.

53   Michael Jago, *Clement Attlee: The Inevitable Prime Minister* (London, Biteback Publishing, 2014), p. 188.

54   Congressman Emmanuel Cellar quoted in Richard N. Gardner, *Sterling-Dollar Diplomacy* (Oxford, Clarendon Press, 1956), p. 237.

55   Robert Self, *British Foreign and Defence Policy Since 1945: Challenges and Dilemmas in a Changing World* (London, Palgrave Macmillan, 2010), p. 77

56   Kenneth O. Morgan, *Callaghan: A Life* (Oxford University Press, 1997), p. 60.

57   Gowland and Turner, *Reluctant Europeans*, p. 31.

58   *Ibid.*

59   Sebestyen, *1946: The Making of the Modern World*, p. 75.

60   *Ibid*, p. 74.

61   Mark Phythian, *The Labour Party, War and International Relations, 1945–2006* (London, Routledge 2007), p. 29.

62   Peter Jones, *America and the British Labour Party: The Special Relationship at Work* (London, I.B. Tauris, 1997) p. 79.

63   Nicklaus Thomas-Symonds, *Attlee: A Life in Politics* (London, I.B. Taurus, 2010), p. 197.

64   Sebestyen, *1946: The Making of the Modern World*, p. 74.

65   See Edmund Dell, *The Schuman Plan and the British Abdication of Leadership in Europe* (Oxford, Clarendon, 1995).

66   Sean Greenwood, *Britain and European Integration Since the Second World War* (Manchester, Manchester University Press, 1996), p. 19.

67   *Ibid*, p. 20.

68   *Ibid*, p. 21.

69   *Ibid*, p.23.

70   *Ibid*, p.24.

71   *Ibid.*

72   John Saville, *The Politics of Continuity: British Foreign Policy and the Labour Government, 1945-46* (London, Verso, 1993), p. 20.

73   Gowland and Turner, *Reluctant Europeans*, p.31.

74   *Ibid*, p.141.

75   Franks, *Britain and the Tide of World Affairs*, p. 38.

76 Roland Quinault, *British Prime Ministers and Democracy: From Disraeli to Blair* (London, Bloomsbury, 2011), p.170.

77 Peter Hennessy, *The Prime Minister: The Office and Its Holders Since* 1945 (London, Palgrave Macmillan, 2001), p.173.

78 Vernon Bogdanor, 'Britain and the Continent'.

79 Walter Lippmann in correspondence with Senator J. William Fulbright. See Randall Bennett Woods, *Fulbright: A Biography* (Cambridge, Cambridge University Press, 1995), p. 143.

80 Hugh Corbet and David Robertson (eds.), *Europe's Free Trade Area Experiment: EFTA and Economic Integration* (Oxford, Permagon, 1970), p. 48.

81 Gowland and Turner, *Reluctant Europeans*, p. 39.

82 Dr Joseph Retinger, Secretary of the European Movement, in conversation with Ernest Bevin. See MacShane, *Brexit: How Britain Will Leave Europe*, p. 41.

83 Young, *This Blessed Plot*, p. 42.

84 Memorandum by Sir Ivone Kirkpatrick on the political implications of the Schuman Plan (11 May 1950). Available online at cvce.eu.

85 Young, *This Blessed Plot*, p. 64.

86 *Ibid*, p. 55.

87 Dell, *The Schuman Plan*, p. 151.

88 P. M. H Bell, *France and Britain, 1940-1994: The Long Separation* (London, Routledge, 1997), p. 117.

89 Ernest Bevin quoted in Gowland and Turner, *Reluctant Europeans*, p.78.

90 Dell, *The Schuman Plan*, p. 176.

91 Vernon Bogdanor, *From New Jerusalem to New Labour: British Prime Ministers from Attlee to Blair* (London, Palgrave Macmillan, 2010), p. 34.

92 Alan S. Milward (ed.), *The Rise and Fall of a National Strategy: The UK and The European Community, 1945-1963* (London, Frank Cass, 2002), p. 100.

93 Cannadine, *In Churchill's Shadow*, p.35.

94 John Darwin, *The Empire Project: The Rise and Fall of the British World-System, 1830–1970* (Cambridge, Cambridge University Press, 2009), p. 569.

95 Alistair Horne, *Harold Macmillan: Politician, 1894–1956* (London, Macmillan, 1989), p. 351.

96 Young, *This Blessed Plot*, p. 76.

97 Geoffrey Best, *Churchill: A Study in Greatness* (London, Hambleton, 2001), p. 293

98 Martin Gilbert (ed.), *Churchill: The Power of Words* (London, Bantam, 2012), p. 403.

99 Dean Acheson, *Present at Creation: My Years at the State Department* (New York, Norton, 1969), p. 600.

100 W. Scott Lucas, *Divided We Stand: The Suez Crisis of 1956 and the 'Anglo-American Alliance'* (London, LSE, 1991), p. 26.

101 Vernon Bogdanor, 'From the European Coal and Steel Community to the Common Market', Lecture to Gresham College, (12 November 2013). Available online at: http://www.gresham.ac.uk/lectures-and-events/from-the-european-coal-and-steel-community-to-the-common-market

102 David Reynolds, *Britannia Overruled: British Policy and World Power in the Twentieth Century* (London, Longman, 1991), p. 183.

103 Jean Monnet, *Memoirs* (London, Collins, 1978), p. 306.
104 Oliver J. Daddow, *Britain and Europe Since 1945: Historiographical Perspectives on Integration* (Manchester, Manchester University Press, 2004), p. 81; Bogdanor, 'From the European Coal and Steel Community to the Common Market'.
105 Greenwood, *Britain and European Integration*, p. 51.
106 *Ibid.*
107 Trevor C. Salmon, *Building European Union: A Documentary History and Analysis* (Manchester, Manchester University Press, 1997), p. 51.
108 Paul Addison, *Churchill: The Unexpected Hero* (Oxford, Oxford University Press, 2005), p. 234.
109 Dell, *The Schuman Plan*, p. 231.
110 Greenwood, *Britain and European Integration*, p. 53.
111 *Ibid*, pp. 56-57.
112 *Ibid*, p. 60.
113 *Ibid*, p. 61.
114 *Ibid*, p. 66.
115 Young, *This Blessed Plot*, p. 83.
116 *Ibid.*
117 D.R. Thorpe, *Supermac: The Life of Harold Macmillan* (London, Random House, 2011), p. 311.
118 Richard Aldous and Sabine Lee (eds.), *Harold Macmillan and Britain's World Role* (Basingstoke, Macmillan, 1996), p. 135.
119 Greenwood, *Britain and European Integration*, pp. 76–77.
120 Charlton, *Price of Victory*, p. 306.
121 *Ibid*, p. 34.
122 David A. Nichols, *Eisenhower 1956: The President's Year of Crisis – Suez and the Brink of War* (New York, Simon and Schuster, 2012), p. 138.
123 US State Department (Office of the Historian), *Foreign Relations of the United States, 1955-57*, vol. xvi, Document 46, Memorandum of a Conversation, 11 Downing Street, London, August 1, 1956. Available online at: https://history.state.gov/historicaldocuments/frus1955-57v16/d46
124 Thorpe, *Supermac*, p. 338.
125 Robin Renwick, *Fighting with Allies* (New York, Times Books, 1996), p 205.
126 See James M. Boughton, 'North-West of Suez: The 1956 Crisis and the IMF', *IMF Staff Papers*, vol. 48, issue 3 (Washington D.C., IMF, December 2001), pp. 425–446.
127 US State Department (Office of the Historian), *Foreign Relations of the United States, 1955-57*, vol. xvi, Document 502, Message from President Eisenhower to Prime Minister Eden, 5 November 1956. Available online at: https://history.state.gov/historicaldocuments/frus1955-57v16/d502
128 George Humphrey, US Secretary of the Treasury, to Macmillan, who replied: 'That's a frosty message you have for me, George.' See Archie Brown, *The Myth of the Strong Leader in the Modern Age* (London, Vintage, 2014), pp. 324–25.
129 Tony Judt, *Postwar: A History of Europe Since 1945* (London, Random House, 2011), p. 292.

130 Ronald Hyam, *Understanding the British Empire* (Cambridge, Cambridge University Press, 2010), p. 36
131 Young, *This Blessed Plot*, p. 111.
132 Greenwood, *Britain and European Integration*, p. 88.
133 Hennessy, *Having it So Good*, p. 365

CHAPTER 2

1   Michael Charlton, *The Price of Victory* (London, BBC, 1983), p. 307.
2   D.R. Thorpe, *Supermac: The Life of Harold Macmillan* (London, Random House, 2011), p. 317.
3   For further information see Peter Hennessy, *Having it So Good: Britain in the Fifties* (London, Allen Lane, 2007), pp. 481–87
4   *Ibid*, p. 483.
5   *Ibid*, p. 483.
6   *Ibid*, p. 482.
7   *Ibid*.
8   Charles de Gaulle, *Memoirs of Hope: Renewal and Endeavour* (New York, Simon and Schuster, 1971), p. 188.
9   Richard Aldous and Sabine Lee (eds.), *Harold Macmillan and Britain's World Role* (Basingstoke, Macmillan, 1996), p. 132.
10 Hugo Young, *This Blessed Plot: Britain and Europe from Churchill to Blair* (London, Macmillan, 1998), p. 113.
11 Roger Liddle, *The Europe Dilemma: Britain and the Drama of EU Integration* (London I.B. Taurus, 2014), p. 5
12 Harold Macmillan, *Pointing the Way, 1959–61* (London, Macmillan, 1972), p. 316.
13 Ronald Hyam and William Roger Louis (eds.), *The Conservatives and the End of Empire, 1957–1964 Part II: Economics, International Relations and the Commonwealth* (London, The Stationery Office for the Institute for Commonwealth Studies, 2000), p. 93.
14 Frank Heinlein, *British Government Policy and Decolonisation, 1945–63: Scrutinising the Official Mind* (London, Routledge, 2002), p. 172.
15 Hennessy, *Having it So Good,* p. 574.
16 *Ibid*, p. 594.
17 *Ibid*.
18 *Ibid*, p. 593.
19 *Ibid*.
20 *Ibid*.
21 Joseph Frankel, *British Foreign Policy: 1945–1973* (Oxford, Oxford University Press for the Royal Institute of International Affairs, 1975), p. 162.
22 Harold Macmillan, *Pointing the Way, 1959–61* (London, Macmillan, 1972), p. 324
23 *Ibid*.
24 Miles Jebb (ed.), *The Diaries of Cynthia Gladwyn* (London, Constable, 1995), p. 195.

25 Lionel Bell, *The Throw that Failed: Britain's Original Application to Join the Common Market* (London, New European Publications, 1995), p. 156.

26 Hennessy, *Having it So Good*, p. 594.

27 Alistair Horne, *Macmillan: 1957–1986*, vol. 2, (London, Macmillan, 1988), p. 285.

28 *Ibid.*

29 Greenwood, *Britain and European Integration*, p. 126.

30 Hyam and Louis, *The Conservative Government and the End of Empire, 1957–1964*, pp. 213–14

31 N. Piers Ludlow, *Dealing with Britain: The Six and the First UK Application to the EEC* (Cambridge, Cambridge University Press, 1997), p. 254.

32 Derek Scott, *Off Whitehall: A View from Downing Street by Tony Blair's Advisor* (London, IB Taurus, 2004), p. 191.

33 Ivor Richard, *Europe or the Open Sea? The Political and Strategic Implications for Britain in the Common Market* (London, C. Knight, 1971), p. 86.

34 Horne, *Macmillan*, vol. 2, p. 319.

35 *Ibid.*

36 *Ibid.*

37 *Ibid.*

38 Isabelle Tombs and Robert Tombs, *That Sweet Enemy: The British and the French from the Sun King to the Present* (London, Random House, 2010), pp. 624–65.

39 *Ibid*, p. 603.

40 Niall Ferguson, *Kissinger: 1923–1968: The Idealist* (London, Penguin, 2015), p. 566.

41 Charlton, *Price of Victory*, p. 297.

42 Stephen Wall, *The Official History of Britain and the European Community, Vol. II: From Rejection to Referendum, 1963–1975* (London, Routledge, 2012), p. 7

43 Tony Judt, *Postwar: A History of Europe Since 1945* (London, Random House, 2011), p. 308.

44 George Ball, *The Discipline of Power: Essentials of a Modern World Structure* (London, The Bodley Head, 1968), p. 69.

45 *Ibid.*

46 Harold Macmillan, *At the End of the Day, 1961–63* (London, Macmillan, 1973), p. 339.

47 Wall, *Official History of Britain and the European Community*, p. 42.

48 Young, *This Blessed Plot*, p. 182.

49 Giles Radice *Offshore: Britain and the European Idea* (London, I.B. Taurus, 1992), p. 20.

50 Robert Self, *British Foreign and Defence Policy Since 1945: Challenges and Dilemmas in a Changing World* (London, Palgrave Macmillan, 2010), p. 77.

51 David Gowland and Arthur Turner, *Reluctant Europeans: Britain and European Integration 1945-1998* (London, Routledge, 2000), p. 115.

52 Ben Pimlott, *Harold Wilson* (London, Harper Collins, 1992), pp. 350–51.

53 Kevin Jeffreys, *Leading Labour: From Keir Hardie to Tony Blair* (London, IB Taurus, 1999), p. 112.

54   Roy Jenkins, *A Life at the Centre* (London, Macmillan, 1991), p. 145.

55   John Campbell, *Roy Jenkins: A Well-Rounded Life* (London, Vintage, 2015) p. 215.

56   Jim Tomlinson, *The Labour Governments: 1964–70: Economic Policy*, vol. 3, (Manchester, Manchester University Press, 2004), p. 23.

57   Young, *This Blessed Plot*, p. 187.

58   R.H.S. Crossman, *The Diaries of a Cabinet Minister, Minister of Housing, 1964–66*, vol. I (London, Hamish Hamilton and Jonathan Cape, 1975), p. 570.

59   Scott Newton, 'The Sterling Devaluation of 1967, the International Economy and Post-War Social Democracy', *The English Historical Review*, vol. 125, no. 515 (August 2010), pp. 912–945.

60   Kenneth O. Morgan, *Callaghan: A Life* (Oxford University Press, 1997), p. 274.

61   Glen O'Hara, 'The Limits of US Power: Transatlantic Financial Diplomacy under the Johnson and Wilson Administrations, October 1964 – November 1968', *Contemporary European History*, vol. 12, no. 3, (2003), pp. 257–278.

62   Jonathan Colman, *A 'Special Relationship'? Harold Wilson, Lyndon B. Johnson and Anglo-American Relations 'at the Summit', 1964–8* (Manchester, Manchester University Press, 2004), pp 155–56.

63   William Roger Louis, *Ends of British Imperialism: The Scramble for Empire, Suez and Decolonization, Collected Essays* (London, Tauris, 2006), p. 558.

64   S.R. Ashton, *East of Suez and the Commonwealth 1964–1971: East of Suez* (London, The Stationery Office, 2004), p. 127.

65   David Gowland *et. al*, *Britain and European Integration Since 1945*, p. 68.

66   Barbara Castle, *The Castle Diaries, 1964–1976* (London, Papermac, 1990). p. 75.

67   George Brown, *In My Way* (Harmondsworth, Penguin, 1972), p. 205.

68   Young, *This Blessed Plot*, p. 190.

69   *Ibid*, p. 191.

70   *Ibid*.

71   *Ibid*, p. 195.

72   Sean Greenwood, *Britain and European Integration Since the Second World War* (Manchester, Manchester University Press, 1996), p. 148.

73   Statement by Harold Wilson on the United Kingdom's application for membership to the EC (London, 2 May 1967), available online at cvce.eu.

74   Young, *This Blessed Plot*, pp. 193–94.

75   *Ibid*, p. 192.

76   Peter Paterson, *Tired and Emotional: The Life of Lord George-Brown* (Chatto & Windus, London, 1993), p. 286.

77   Young, *This Blessed Plot*, p. 196.

78   Press conference held by General de Gaulle at the Elysée (27 November 1967). Available online at cvce.eu.

79   Wall, *The Official History of Britain and the European Community*, p. 181.

80   Stephen Wall interviewed by Thomas Raineau (Université de Paris-Sorbonne). Transcript available from Churchill College, Cambridge. Available online at: https://www.chu.cam.ac.uk/media/uploads/files/Wall.pdf

CHAPTER 3

1   Edward Heath quoted in N. Piers Ludlow, *Dealing with Britain: The Six and the First UK Application to the EEC* (Cambridge, Cambridge University Press, 1997), p. 226.

2   Henry Kissinger, *Years of Upheaval* (Boston, Brown & Company, 1982), p. 141.

3   Michael Charlton, 'How (and Why) Britain Lost the Leadership of Europe (3): The Channel Crossing', *Encounter*, vol. 57, No. 3 (October 1981), p. 25.

4   Desmond Dinan, *Origins and Evolution of the European Union* (Oxford, Oxford University Press, 2006). p. 170.

5   Vernon Bogdanor, *The People and the Party System: The Referendum and Electoral Reform in British Politics* (Cambridge, Cambridge University Press, 1981), p. 38.

6   For more information on international leaders' views on Heath see Philip Ziegler, *Edward Heath: The Authorised Biography*, (London, Harper, 2010).

7   *Ibid*, p. 281.

8   John Campbell, *Edward Heath: A Biography* (London, Random House, 2013), p. 359.

9   Stephen Wall, *The Official History of Britain and the European Community, Vol. II: From Rejection to Referendum, 1963–1975* (London, Routledge, 2012), p. 401.

10 Vernon Bogdanor, 'Entry into the European Community, 1971–73', Lecture to Gresham College, (11 March 2014). Available online at: http://www.gresham. ac.uk/lectures-and-events/entry-into-the-european-community-1971-73

11 Edward Heath, *The Course of My Life: My Autobiography* (London, Hodder & Stoughton, 1998), p. 381.

12 Sean Greenwood, *Britain and European Integration Since the Second World War* (Manchester, Manchester University Press, 1996), pp. 151–152.

13 Edward Heath, speech in Brussels, (22 January 1972). Available online at: cvce.eu

14 Helen Parr, *Britain's Policy Towards the European Community* (London, Routledge, 1996), p. 17.

15 Hugo Young, *This Blessed Plot: Britain and Europe from Churchill to Blair* (London, Macmillan, 1998), p. 255.

16 Harold Wilson, speech on Britain's membership to the EEC, (17 July 1971). Available online at cvce.eu.

17 Kenneth O. Morgan, *Callaghan: A Life* (Oxford, Oxford University Press, 1997), p. 395.

18 Adrian Williamson, 'The case for Brexit: lessons from the 1960s and 1970s', History and Policy website (5 May 2015). Available online at: http://www.historyandpolicy.org/policy-papers/papers/the-case-for-brexit-lessons-from-1960s-and-1970s

19 Alex May, *Britain and Europe Since 1945* (London, Routledge, 1999), p. 58.

20 Andrew Glencross, 'Looking Back to Look Forward: 40 Years of Referendum Debate in Britain', *Political Insight*, vol. 6, issue 1 pp. 25–27, (April 2015).

21 Sir Stephen Wall, GCMG, interviewed by Thomas Raineau (Université de Paris-Sorbonne), Churchill, College Cambridge.

22 Derek W. Unwin, *The Community of Europe: A History of European Integration Since 1945* (London, Routledge, 2000), p. 199.

23 Tony Benn, *Against the Tide: Diaries 1973–1976* (London, Hutchinson, 1980), p. 343.

24 *Ibid.*

25 *Ibid.*

26 *Ibid*, p. 344.

27 Kenneth O. Morgan, *Michael Foot: A Life*, (London, Harper, 2007), p. 274.

28 *Ibid.*

29 *Ibid*, p. 327.

30 *Ibid.*

31 Campbell, *Roy Jenkins*, p. 215.

32 *Ibid*, p. 448.

33 *Ibid*, p. 446.

34 David Gowland and Arthur Turner, *Reluctant Europeans: Britain and European Integration 1945–1998* (London, Routledge, 2000), p. 146.

35 Justin Gibbs, *Britain, Europe and National Identity: Self and Other in International Relations* (London, Palgrave Macmillan, 2014), p. 183.

36 Ziegler, *Edward Heath* (London, Harper, 2010).

37 David Butler and Uwe Kitzinger, *The 1975 Referendum* (London and Basingstoke, Macmillan, 1976), pp. 279–280.

38 See HM Government, *Britain's New Deal in Europe* (London, HM Stationery Office, 1975).

39 Young, *This Blessed Plot*, pp. 288–89.

40 See HM Government, *British membership of the European Community* (HM Stationery Office, 1973).

41 Margaret Thatcher, Speech to the College of Europe, 'The Bruges Speech', (20 September 1988). Available online at cvce.eu.

42 *Ibid.*

43 *Ibid.*

44 Laurence Peter, 'Thatcher's Bruges speech 'not anti-EU' – former aide', BBC, (27 September 2013). Available online at: http://www.bbc.co.uk/news/world-europe-24301837

45 John Campbell, *The Iron Lady: Margaret Thatcher: From Grocer's Daughter to Iron Lady* (London, Vintage, 2012), p. 258.

46 Peter Riddell, *Hug Them Close: Blair, Clinton, Bush and the 'Special Relationship'* (London, Politico's Publishing Ltd, 2003), p. 47.

47 Matthew Smith, *Policy-Making in the Treasury: Explaining Britain's Chosen Path on European Economic and Monetary Union* (London, Palgrave Macmillan, 2014), p. 77.

48 House of Commons Statement on Rome European Council, (30 October 1990). Available online at Thatcher Foundation website: http://www.margaretthatcher.org/document/108234.

49 *Ibid*, p. 314.

50 See Iain Begg, 'Margaret Thatcher maintained a difficult relationship with Europe, but she was far from a figurehead for Euroscepticism', in LSE Public Policy Group, *The Legacy of Margaret Thatcher*, (London, LSE Public Policy Group), pp. 28–31.

51 See Stephen Wall, *A Stranger in Europe: Britain and the EU from Thatcher to Blair* (Oxford, Oxford University Press, 2008).

52 See John Major, *The Power to Choose: The Right to Own*, (London, Conservative Political Centre, 1991), p. 42.

53 Young, *This Blessed Plot*, p. 424.

54 Young, *This Blessed Plot*, p. 465.

55 *Ibid*, p. 466.

56 John Major, *John Major: The Autobiography* (London, HarperCollins, 1999), p. 343.

57 *Ibid*.

58 *Ibid*, p. 344.

59 *Ibid*, p. 345.

60 Speech by Norman Lamont to the Conservative Party Conference (9 October 1991).

CHAPTER 4

1   See Gordon Brown, *The Change We Choose: Speeches, 2007–2009* (Edinburgh, Mainstream, 2010), pp. 17–29.

2   John F. Kennedy: 'Address at Independence Hall, Philadelphia,' July 4, 1962. Available online by Gerhard Peters and John T. Woolley, The American Presidency Project. http://www.presidency.ucsb.edu/ws/?pid=8756

3   See Danny Quah, 'The Global Economy's Shifting Centre of Gravity', *Global Policy*, vol. 2, no. 1., (2011). pp. 3–9.

4   House of Lords Select Committee on Soft Power and the UK's Influence, *Persuasion and Power in the Modern World* (London, The Stationery Office, 2014), p. 25.

5   Moises Naim, *The End of Power: From Boardrooms to Battlefields and Churches to States, Why Being in Charge Isn't What It Used to Be* (New York, Basic Books, 2013), p. 16.

6   Peter Hennessy, *Having it So Good: Britain in the Fifties* (London, Allen Lane, 2007), p. 483.

7   *Ibid*.

8   Joseph S. Nye, *The Future of Power* (New York, PublicAffairs, 2011), p. 19.

9   *Ibid*, p. xv.

10 *Ibid*, p. xvi; Joseph S. Nye, 'Public Diplomacy and Soft Power', *The Annals of the American Academy of Political and Social Sciences*, vol. 16, no. 1, pp. 94–109.

11 Tony Blair, 'Making the case for Britain in Europe' speech, (27 July 1999). Available online at: http://www.theguardian.com/business/1999/jul/27/emu.theeuro2

12 *Ibid*.

13 *Ibid.*
14 Jon Lunn, Vaughne Miller and Ben Smith, *British Foreign Policy since 1997*, House of Commons Research Paper, 08/56, (London, House of Commons Library, June 2008), p. 31.
15 Tony Blair, Speech at Lord Mayor's banquet, (10 November 1997). Available online at: http://collections.europarchive.org/tna/20060403085217/ http://pm.gov.uk/output/Page1070.asp
16 Tony Blair, *A Journey* (London, Hutchinson, 2010) p. 438.
17 Clare Short, *An Honourable Deception? New Labour, Iraq and the Misuse of Power* (London, Free, 2004), p. 273; Robin Cook, *The Point of Departure* (London, Simon and Schuster, 2003), p. 133.
18 Christopher Meyer, *D.C. Confidential*, (London, Phoenix, 2006), p. 261.
19 Robert Self, *British Foreign and Defence Policy Since 1945: Challenges and Dilemmas in a Changing World* (London, Palgrave Macmillan, 2010), p. 146.
20 See The Labour Party manifesto 2005, *Britain Forward, Not Back*, (London, Labour Party, 2005), p. 84.
21 Statement by Jack Straw to the House of Commons (6 June 2005). Giuliano Amato, *The European Constitution: Cases and Materials in EU and Member States' Law* (Cheltenham, Edward Elgar, 2007), p. 63.
22 Stephen Wall, *A Stranger in Europe: Britain and the EU from Thatcher to Blair* (Oxford, Oxford University Press, 2008).
23 Oliver J. Daddow, New Labour and the European Union: Blair and Brown's Logic of History (Manchester, Manchester University Press, 2011), p. 23.
24 *Ibid.*
25 Tony Blair, Speech on the Future of Europe, (2 February 2006). Available online at: http://webarchive.nationalarchives.gov.uk/+/number10.gov.uk/ page9003
26 Daddow, *New Labour and the European Union*, p. 21.
27 Wall, *A Stranger in Europe*, p. 215.
28 *Ibid.*
29 Daddow, *New Labour and the European Union*, p. 30.
30 See *Official Publication of the Commonwealth Heads of Government Meeting 2009*, (London, FIRST on behalf of the National Secretariat for CHOGM, 2009) pp. 96–97.
31 Interview with Katie Couric of CBS Television, (14 April 2008).
32 Brown, *The Change We Choose*, p. 28.
33 Gordon Brown speech at Lord Mayor's Banquet Speech (12 November 2007).
34 Robert Kagan, 'The United States must resist a return to spheres of interest in the international system'. Available online at: http://www.brookings.edu/ blogs/order-from-chaos/posts/2015/02/19-united-states-must-resist-return-to-spheres-of-interest-international-system-kagan
35 Gordon Brown speech, 'Speech on Business Priorities for a "Global Europe"' (14 January 2008).
36 *Ibid.*
37 Daddow, *New Labour and the European Union*, p. 27.
38 House of Lords Select Committee, *Persuasion and Power*, p. 86.

39 *Ibid.*

40 *Ibid*, p. 87.

41 Timothy Garton Ash, '9½ vital questions for our would-be leaders on Britain's role in the world', *The Guardian*, (21 April 2010).

42 See Robin Niblett. 'Britain's Place in the World', Lord Garden Memorial Lecture, (25 June 2015).

43 Robin Niblett, *Britain, Europe and the World Rethinking the UK's Circles of Influence* (London, Chatham House, 2015), p. 19.

CHAPTER 5

1   McKinsey, *Global Flows in a Digital Age* (New York, McKinsey, 2014).

2   Gary B. Magee, 'Manufacturing and technological change' from Roderick Floud and Paul Johnson (ed.), The Cambridge Economic History of Modern Britain, Volume II: Economic Maturity, 1860–1939 (Cambridge: Cambridge University Press, 2004), p.81

3   Chris Rhodes, *Manufacturing: international comparisons* (London, House of Commons Library, June 2015), Briefing Paper No. 05909, p.4. Correct figure is 3 per cent.

4   Figures compiled using data from the following: Maddison Project, Historical Statistics of the World Economy 1–2008 AD: www.ggdc.net/maddison/maddison-project/home.htm; Jutta Bolt, Marcel Timmer, Jan Luiten van Zanden, GDP per Capita since 1820-2014, (Paris, OECD, 2014); and United Nations, Industrial Development Organisation, Growth and Distribution Pattern of the World Manufacturing Output: A Statistical Profile, (Vienna, United Nations, 2014)

5   *Ibid.*

6   Lucy Siegle, 'Britain's rag trade revival', *The Guardian*, 15 February 2014. Online at: http://www.theguardian.com/fashion/2014/feb/15/britains-rag-trade-revival-marks-and-spencer.

7   'Made in China?', *The Economist*, 14 March 2015

8   Dyson press release, 'Dyson digital motor technology gets a $100 million boost', (22 February 2013)

9   Richard Dobbs et al, 'The world at work: Jobs, pay, and skills for 3.5 billion people', McKinsey Global Institute, June 2012. Online at: http://www.mckinsey.com/global-themes/employment-and-growth/the-world-at-work

10 International Labour Organisation statistics.

11 See Stephen Broadberry and Tim Leunig, *The Impact of Government Policies on UK Manufacturing since 1945* (London, Foresight, Government Office for Science, 2013) and Chris Rhodes, Manufacturing: Statistics and Policy (London, House of Commons Library, 2015)

12 Deloitte, *From Brawns to Brain: The Impact of Technology on Jobs in the UK* (London, Deloitte, 2015), p. 7.

13 'The real cost of cheap clothes', NBC News, 13 March 2013. Online at: http://www.nbcnews.com/video/nightly-news/51871485#51871485

14 Department for Business, Innovation and Skills, *Hollowing out and the Future of the Labour Market* (London, BIS, 2013), pp. 26–28.

15 Carl Frey and Michael A. Osborne, *Agiletown: The Relentless March of Technology and London's Response* (London, Deloitte, 2014), p. 5.

16 Larry Elliott, 'Coalition has presided over plunge in living standards, says TUC', *The Guardian*, (28 April 2015). Available online at: http://www.theguardian.com/politics/2015/apr/28/coalition-presided-over-plunge-living-standards-tuc-frances-ogrady

17 James Browne and William Elming, *The Effect of the Coalition's Tax and Benefit Changes on Household Incomes and Work Incentives* (London, Institute for Fiscal Studies, 2015), p. 1.

18 Branko Milanović, 'We're Experiencing the Greatest Reshuffling of Income Since the Industrial Revolution', *The World Post*, 22 July 2015. Available online at: http://www.huffingtonpost.com/branko-Milanovic/economic-power-west-asia_b_7849724.html

19 Branko Milanovic, *Global Inequality: A New Approach for the Age of Globalization* (Cambridge, Harvard University Press, 2016)

20 Larry Elliot, 'Trade policy is no longer just for political nerds: it matters in the UK and US', *The Guardian*, 27 March 2016. Available online at: http://www.theguardian.com/business/2016/mar/27/trade-policy-uk-eu-referendum-us-bernie-sanders-donald-trump-ttip-globalisation

21 Branko Milanović, 'Introducing Kuznets waves: How income inequality waxes and wanes over the very long run', *Vox*, (24 February 2016). Available online at: http://www.voxeu.org/article/introducing-kuznets-waves-income-inequality

22 Milanović *Global Inequality*. (2016)

23 *Ibid.*

24 Felipe Ossa, 'The Economist Who Brought You Thomas Piketty Sees "Perfect Storm" of Inequality Ahead', *New York*, (24 March 2016). Online at: http://nymag.com/daily/intelligencer/2016/03/Milanovic-millennial-on-millennial-war-is-next.html

25 Chris Belfield et al, 'Living Standards, Poverty and Inequality in the UK: 2015', Institute for Fiscal Studies, 2015, p.4. Online at: http://www.ifs.org.uk/uploads/publications/comms/R107.pdf

26 Robert Peston, 'Quelle Catastrophe! France with Robert Peston'. BBC 2, last broadcast on 19 March 2015.

27 'Cost of Living', The University of Manchester. Available online at: http://www.manchester.ac.uk/study/experience/student-life/living-costs/

28 Anthony Giddens, *Runaway World* (London, Profile, 2002)

29 Robert Tombs and Isabelle Tombs, *That Sweet Enemy: The French and the British from the Sun King to the Present* (New York: Random House, 2007), p. 645

30 Matthew Goodwin and Caitlin Milazzo, *Britain, the European Union and the Referendum: What Drives Euroscepticism?* (London, Chatham House, 2015), p.5

31 Nathan Gardels, 'Why the World Is Falling Apart', *The World Post*, (28 March 2016). Available online at: http://www.huffingtonpost.com/nathan-gardels/world-falling-apart_b_9553982.html

32 Goodwin and Milazzo, *Britain, the European Union and the Referendum*, p.5

33 Matthew Goodwin, 'What is the likely effect of different arguments on Britain's EU referendum?', (27 November 2015). Available online at: http://whatukthinks.org/eu/what-is-the-likely-effect-of-different-arguments-on-britains-eu-referendum/

34 Catherine de Vries and Isabell Hoffmann, *Border Protection and Freedom of Movement What people expect of European asylum and migration policies* (Berlin, Bertelsmann Stiftung, 2016), p. 11.

35 'Turning right', *The Economist*, 4 January 2014.

36 Nicholas Vincour, 'Marine Le Pen takes sharp left turn', *Politico*, 11 December 2015. Online at: http://www.politico.eu/article/marine-le-pen-goes-left-socialist-sarkozy-communist/

37 Blathnaid Healy, 'Far-right parties gain popularity in Europe after Paris attacks', *MashableUK*, 14 January 2015. Online at: http://mashable.com/2015/01/14/far-right-europe-paris-attacks/#d54yJ7vFV8qa

38 Paul Ames, 'Forget left and right, Europe's new politics are all over the place', *GlobalPost*, (27 March 2015). Available online at: http://www.globalpost.com/article/6502630/2015/03/27/europes-left-and-right-are-out-radical-center

39 Goodwin and Milazzo, 'Britain, the European Union and the Referendum', p. 8

40 http://www.epc.eu/pub_details.php?cat_id=17&pub_id=6377

41 Paul Mason, 'Podemos: how Europe's political centre is being eaten by the radical left and nationalist right', *The Guardian*, 21 December 2015. Available online at: http://www.theguardian.com/commentisfree/2015/dec/21/podemos-europe-political-centre-radical-left-nationalist-right-spain-anti-austerity-party

CHAPTER 6

1 Denis MacShane, *Brexit: How Britain Will Leave Europe* (London, I.B. Tauris, 2015), p. 70.

2 Norman Davies, *Europe: A History* (London, Pimlico, 1997), p. 1119

3 Desmond Dinan, *Origins and Evolution of the European Union* (Oxford, Oxford University Press, 2006). p. 21.

4 Jim Yardley, 'Has Europe Reached the Breaking Point?', *New York Times*, (December 15, 2015). Available online at: http://www.nytimes.com/2015/12/20/magazine/has-europe-reached-the-breaking-point.html?_r=0

5 Jean-Claude Juncker, 'State of the Union 2015: Time for Honesty, Unity and Solidarity', (9 September 2015). Available online at: http://europa.eu/rapid/press-release_SPEECH-15-5614_en.htm

6 Helmut Schmidt, Speech to the SPD part conference in Berlin, (4 December 2011). Available online at: https://www3.spd.de/scalableImageBlob/23344/data/20111204_speech_schmidt-data.pdf

7 Dirk Leuffen, Berthold Rittberger and Frank Schimmelfennig, 'The European Union as a System of Differentiated Integration', *Political Science Series*, Working paper no. 137, (2014).

8   BBC, 'EU reform deal: What Cameron wanted and what he got',
    (20 February 2016). Available online at: http://www.bbc.co.uk/news/
    uk-politics-eu-referendum-35622105

9   *Ibid.*

10 Gavin Thompson and Daniel Harari, *The economic impact of EU membership
    on the UK* (London, House of Commons Library, 2013), p. 25.

11 Lawyers in for Britain, *The UK and the EU: Benefits, Misconceptions and
    Alternatives* (2016), p. 34.

12 Jonathan Lindsell, *The Norwegian Way: A case study for Britain's future
    relationship with the EU* (London, Civitas, 2015), p. 9.

13 John Cridland, 'Leaving Europe would be bad for British business',
    The Guardian, (17 May 2013). Available online at:
    http://www.theguardian.com/commentisfree/2013/may/17/business-better-
    off-staying-in-europe

14 See Open Europe, *Top 100 EU Rules Cost Britain £33.3bn* (London, Open
    Europe, 2015).

15 Claude-Alain Margelisch, 'Market access: an important pillar of the growth
    strategy', (2 September 2013). Available online at:
    http://www.swissbanking.org/en/20130813-5010-rede_cma_final-rga.pdf

16 Open Europe, 'Britain's EU immigration debate: Norway and Switzerland are
    not the answer', (November 2014). Available online at:
    http://openeurope.org.uk/intelligence/immigration-and-justice/norway-
    and-switzerland/

17 Confederation for British Industry, *Our Global Future* (CBI, London, 2013),
    p. 153.

18 Michael Gove, 'EU referendum: Michael Gove explains why Britain should
    leave the EU', *The Daily Telegraph*, (20 February 2016). Available online at:
    http://www.telegraph.co.uk/news/newstopics/eureferendum/12166345/
    European-referendum-Michael-Gove-explains-why-Britain-should-leave-
    the-EU.html

19 Philip Stephens, 'Boris Johnson is wrong. Parliament has the ultimate
    authority', *The Financial Times*, (25 February 2016). Available online at:
    https://next.ft.com/content/26b6a12c-daf2-11e5-a72f-1e7744c66818

20 Nicholas Watt and Rowena Mason, 'Cameron appeals to Boris Johnson not to
    join Brexit camp', *The Guardian*, (21 February 2016). Available online at:
    http://www.theguardian.com/politics/2016/feb/21/cameron-boris-johnson-
    brexit-nigel-farage-george-galloway-uk

21 Tony Blair, 'Britain's role in Europe', (23 November 2001). Available online at:
    http://www.theguardian.com/world/2001/nov/23/euro.eu1

22 Bagehot, 'Boris Johnson is wrong: in the 21st century, sovereignty is always
    relative', *The Economist*, (21 February 2016). Available online at:
    http://www.economist.com/blogs/bagehot/2016/02/bojo-breaks-ranks

CHAPTER 7

1 Nissan Motor Manufacturing UK statistics. In 2000, Nissan exceeded the barrier of 300,000 cars for the first time and, in 2010, exceeded 400,000 cars produced a year. In 2012 the total exceeded 500,000 for the first time.

2 Nissan's supply chain supports 21,000 jobs in Sunderland and 40,000 jobs across the UK.

3 KPMG, *The UK Automotive Industry and the EU: An Economic Assessment of the Interaction of the UK's Automotive Industry with the European Union* (London, KPMG, 2014), p. 5.

4 Trevor Mann, 'Britain is our bridgehead to Europe because of its world-class talent', *The Daily Telegraph*, (29 November 2015). Available online at: http://www.telegraph.co.uk/finance/comment/12023939/Britain-is-our-bridgehead-to-Europe-because-of-its-world-class-talent.html

5 See *The Society of Motor Manufacturers and Traders, Motor Industry Facts, 2015* (London, SMMT, 2015), p 8; Chris Rhodes and Dominic Sear, *The Motor Industry: Statistics and Policy* (London, House of Commons Library, 2015), p. 6.

6 *Ibid*, p. 3.

7 KPMG, *The UK Automotive Industry and the EU*, p. 1.

8 *Ibid*, p. 3.

9 *Ibid*, p. 1.

10 *Ibid*.

11 *Ibid*.

12 Rhodes and Sear, *The Motor Industry: Statistics and Policy*, p. 9.

13 KPMG, *The UK Automotive Industry and the EU*, p. 3.

14 *Ibid*.

15 *Ibid*.

16 *Ibid*.

17 Centre for Economics and Business Research, *UK Jobs Supported by Exports to the EU: CEBR Analysis of UK Jobs Associated with Demand from the European Union* (London, CEBR, 2014), p. 12.

18 KPMG, *The UK Automotive Industry and the EU*, p. 1.

19 *Ibid*, p. 17.

20 World Bank statistics, Exports of Goods and Services (per cent of GDP) data.

21 Bank of England, *EU Membership and the Bank of England* (Bank of England, London, 2015), p. 3.

22 *Ibid*.

23 Mark Carney, 'The European Union, Monetary and Financial stability, and the Bank of England', (21 October 2015). Available online at: http://www.bankofengland.co.uk/publications/Pages/speeches/2015/852.aspx

24 BBC, 'Scotch whisky "worth £5bn to UK economy"' (28 January 2015). Available online at: http://www.bbc.co.uk/news/uk-scotland-scotland-business-31003387

25 Scottish Whisky Association, *The Economic Impact of Scotch Whisky Production in the UK* (SWA, Edinburgh, 2015), p. 9.

26 See Centre for Economics and Business Research, *The Impact of the UK being in the Single Market* (CEBR, London, 2015).

27 Brian Ardy, Iain Begg and Dermot Hodson, *UK Jobs Dependent on the EU* (South Bank University European Institute, London, 2000).

28 CEBR, *UK Jobs Supported by Exports to the EU*, p. 3.

29 Confederation for British Industry, *Our Global Future* (CBI, London, 2013), p. 86.

30 Association of the British Pharmaceutical Industry statistics.

31 David Crow, Andrew Ward and Kate Allen, 'Brexit would be a 'mistake'', say global pharma leaders', *The Financial Times*, (25 January 2016). Available online at: https://next.ft.com/content/9216298e-bf67-11e5-846f-79b0e3d20eaf

32 *Ibid.*

33 CBI, *Our Global Future*, p. 69.

34 Kate McCann, 'Lord Darzi: Leaving the EU would be "disastrous" for UK science and health', *The Daily Telegraph*, (2 April 2016). Available online at: http://www.telegraph.co.uk/news/2016/04/02/lord-darzi-leaving-the-eu-would-be-disastrous-for-uk-science-and/

35 The European Medicines Agency has 600 members of staff and has been based in London since it started in 1995. Both Sweden and Denmark are reported to be seeking to be the new home of the EMA in the event of Britain leaving the EU.

36 McCann, 'Lord Darzi: Leaving the EU would be "disastrous" for UK science and health', *The Daily Telegraph*, (2 April 2016).

37 John Chave, 'UK industry would be weakened by exit from EU', *The Pharmaceutical Journal*, vol. 293, no 7819 (July 2014).

38 Richard Bergström, 'EU-UK: What Brexit would mean for our industry', European Federation of Pharmaceutical Industries and Associations website, (March 2013). Available online at: http://pharmaviews.eu/eu-uk-what-brexit-would-mean-for-our-industry/

39 TheCityUK, *A practitioner's guide to Brexit* (TheCityUK, London, 2015), p. 8.

40 UK Trade & Investment, *UK Financial Centres of Excellence* (UKTI, London, 2015), p. 2.

41 Capital Economics, *The Economic Impact of 'Brexit'* (Capital Economics, London, 2016), p. 22.

42 Karel Lannoo, 'Britain's Finance Industry Needs the EU', *Wall Street Journal*, (26 January 2016). Available online at: http://www.wsj.com/articles/britains-finance-industry-needs-the-eu-1453840160

43 Bank of England, *EU Membership and the Bank of England*, p. 26. These firms range from commercial and investment banks to insurers, asset managers and hedge funds.

44 *Ibid*, p. 9.

45 HM Government, *Review of the Balance of Competences between the United Kingdom and the European Union The Single Market: Financial Services and the Free Movement of Capital* (HM Government, London, 2014), p. 39.

46 John Springford and Philip Whyte, *The Consequences of Brexit for the City of London* (Centre for European Reform, London, 2014), p. 2.

47 Jill Treanor, 'HSBC could switch 1,000 banking jobs to France after a Brexit
    vote', *The Guardian*, (15 February 2016). Available online at:
    http://www.theguardian.com/business/2016/feb/15/uk-better-in-reformed-
    europe-says-hsbc-chair

48 Alex Brummer, 'We can thrive outside Europe', *Daily Mail*, (20 February
    2016). Available online at: http://www.dailymail.co.uk/debate/article-
    3455466/We-thrive-outside-Europe-Mail-s-City-Editor-ALEX-BRUMMER-
    pro-EU-explains-changed-mind.html

49 *Ibid.*

50 CEBR, UK Jobs Supported by Exports to the EU, p. 15.

51 See Centre for Economic and Business Research, *British Jobs and the Single
    Market* (London, CEBR, 2014).

52 Centre for Economic and Business Research, *The Impact of the UK being in
    the Single Market* (London, CEBR, 2015), p. 5.

53 Tim Congdon, *How much does the European Union cost Britain?* (London,
    UKIP, 2014), p. 9.

54 See Paolo Cecchini *et al.*, *Europe 1992: The Overall Challenge* (Brussels,
    Commission of the European Communities, 1988); Paolo Cecchini with
    Michel Catinat and Alexis Jacquemin, *The European Challenge 1992. The
    Benefits of a Single Market* (Aldershot, Wildwood House, 1988).

55 CEBR, *The Impact of the UK being in the Single Market* (London, CEBR, 2015),
    p. 16.

56 Organisation for Economic Co-operation and Development, *OECD Economic
    Surveys: European Union 2014* (Paris, OECD, 2014), p. 33.

57 See Stephen Booth, Christopher Howarth, Mats Persson and Raoul Ruparel,
    Kick-Starting Growth: How to Reignite the EU's Services Sector (London, Open
    Europe, 2013).

58 See George Osborne speech, Germany's BDI industry body in Berlin,
    (3 November 2015). Available online at: https://www.gov.uk/government/
    speeches/ let-britain-and-germany-work-together-as-partners-for-a-
    european-union-that-works-better-for-all-of-us-says-chancellor

59 John Springford, *Offline? How Europe can catch-up with US technology*
    (CER, London, 2015), pp. 4–5.

60 *Ibid*, p. 8.

61 See John Thornhill, 'Europe needs its own breed of unicorn', *Financial Times*,
    (26 October 2015). Available online at: https://next.ft.com/content/
    7dae9ace-7996-11e5-933d-efcdc3c11c89

62 CEBR, The Impact of the UK being in the Single Market (London, CEBR,
    2015), p. 20.

63 See Open Europe, *Top 100 EU Rules Cost Britain £33.3bn* (London, Open
    Europe, 2015).

64 Jacques Pelkmans, 'Mutual Recognition: Economic and Regulatory Logic in
    Goods and Services' in Thomas Eger and Hans-Bernd Schafer (eds.), *Research
    Handbook on the Economics of European Union Law* (Edward Elgar,
    Cheltenham, 2012) p. 117.

CHAPTER 8

1   In 2008, 15 countries were part of the Eurozone: Austria, Belgium, Cyrus,
    Finland, France, Germany, Greece, Ireland, Italy, Luxembourg, Malta, Nether-
    lands, Portugal, Slovenia and Spain. Estonia, Latvia, Lithuania and Slovakia
    have subsequently joined the Euro.
2   US banks were leveraged by a factor of 12, according to the conventional
    metric of banks' assets to capital. European banks, in contrast, were leveraged
    by a factor of 20. See Barry Eichengreen, *Hall of Mirrors: The Great Depression,
    The Great Recession, and the Uses-and Misuses-of History* (Oxford, Oxford
    University Press, 2015), p. 97.
3   Helmut Schmidt, 'Germany in and with and for Europe', (11 December 2011).
    Available online at: http://www.pro-europa.eu/index.php/en/library/
    understanding-europe/480-germany-in,-with-and-for-europe
4   Riccardo Fiorentini and Guido Montani (eds.), The European Union and
    Supranational Political Economy (London, Routledge, 2015), p. 251.
5   Eurostat, General Government Gross Debt – annual data.
6   In 2014, general government gross as a percentage of GDP for these countries
    was as follows: Greece, 178.6 per cent; Spain, 99.9 per cent; Portugal, 130.2 per
    cent; Ireland, 107.5 per cent.
7   2014Q4 compared to 2008Q1.
8   See Karl Lamers and Wolfgang Schäuble, *Reflections on European Policy*
    (CDU/CSU Parliamentary Faction, Bonn, September 1994). Reprinted
    in English in Karl Lamers, *A German Agenda for the European Union*
    (The Federal Trust for Education/Konrad Adenauer Foundation, London,
    1994).
9   Karl Lamers and Wolfgang Schäuble, 'More integration is still the right goal
    for Europe', *The Financial Times*, (31 August 2014). Available online at:
    https://next.ft.com/content/5565f134-2d48-11e4-8105-00144feabdc0
10 See François Villeroy de Galhau and Jens Weidmann, 'Europa braucht mehr
    Investitionen', *Süddeutsche Zeitung*, (8 February 2016). Available (with
    translation) online at: http://www.sueddeutsche.de/wirtschaft/euro-
    raum-europa-braucht-ein-gemeinsames-finanzministerium-1.2852586
11 Francesco Guerrero, 'Eurozone needs a Finance Minister', Politico website,
    (23 February 2016). Available online at: http://www.politico.eu/article/
    eurozone-needs-finance-minister-padoan-economic-banking/
12 See Jean-Claude Juncker, Donald Tusk, Jeroen Dijsselbloem, Mario Draghi
    and Martin Schulz, *Completing Europe's Economic and Monetary Union*
    (European Commission, Brussels, 2015).
13 Boris Johnson, 'There is only one way to get the change we want – vote to
    leave the EU', *The Daily Telegraph*, (22 February 2016). Available online at:
    http://www.telegraph.co.uk/opinion/2016/03/16/boris-johnson-exclusive-
    there-is-only-one-way-to-get-the-change/
14 House of Lords, EU Economic and Financial Affairs Sub-Committee:
    Evidence, (2 October 2013), p. 197. Available online at: https://www.politic-
    shome.com/event/house-lords/44116/house-lords-business-27-january-2016

15 Alex Barker, 'Britain's EU deal: the results and the verdict', *Financial Times*, (20 February 2016). Available online at: https://next.ft.com/content/7c90bfec-d76e-11e5-829b-8564e7528e54

16 Charles Grant, 'Cameron's deal is more than it seems', *Centre for European Reform Bulletin*, no. 117, (April/May 2016), p. 3.

17 Peter Müller and Christoph Scheuermann, 'Brexit Danger: The EU Strategy to Keep Britain from Leaving', *Der Spiegel*, (5 January 2016). Available online at: http://www.spiegel.de/international/europe/eu-seeks-to-avoid-brexit-at-all-costs-a-1070389.html

18 *Ibid.*

19 Richard Baldwin, Francesco Giavazzi, 'The Eurozone Crisis: A Consensus View of the Causes and a Few Possible Solutions', (7 September 2015). Available online at: http://www.voxeu.org/content/eurozone-crisis-consensus-view-causes-and-few-possible-solutions

20 Jean Pisani-Ferry, 'The Social Roots of Political Realignment in the West', CaixinOnline, (22 December 2015). Available online at: http://english.caixin.com/2015-12-22/100891333.html

21 See Martin Sandbu, *Europe's Orphan: The Future of the Euro and the Politics of Debt* (Princeton, Princeton University Press, 2015).

22 Ben Bernanke, 'Greece and Europe: Is Europe holding up its end of the bargain?', Brookings Institute website, (17 July 2015). Available online at: http://www.brookings.edu/blogs/ben-bernanke/posts/2015/07/17-greece-and-europe

23 Maria João Rodrigues, 'A New Future for the Eurozone', Politico website, (2 February 2016). Available online at: http://www.politico.eu/article/why-the-eurozone-needs-new-economic-policy-breakaway-schengen-recession/

24 See Shekhar Aiyar, Bergljot Barkbu, Nicoletta Batini, *et.al.*, *The Refugee Surge in Europe: Economic Challenges* (New York, IMF, 2016).

CHAPTER 9

1 HM Government, *Review of the Balance of Competences between the United Kingdom and the European Union: Social and Employment Policy* (London, HM Government, 2014), p. 5.

2 Martin Rhodes, 'The Social Dimension of the Single European Market: National versus Transnational Interests', *European Journal of Political Research*, vol. 19, p.261.

3 John Turner, *The Tories and Europe* (Manchester, Manchester University Press, 2000), p. 121; Margaret Thatcher, *The Downing Street Years* (London, Harper Collins, 1993), p. 750.

4 Sarah Hogg and Jonathan Hill, *Too Close to Call: Power and Politics – John Major in No.10* (London, Little, Brown and Company, 1995), p. 155.

5 Stephen Wall, *A Stranger in Europe. Britain and the EU from Thatcher to Blair* (Oxford, Oxford University Press, 2008) p. 124.

6   Stephen Wall interviewed by Thomas Raineau (Université de Paris-
    Sorbonne). Transcript available from Churchill College, Cambridge.
    Available online at: https://www.chu.cam.ac.uk/media/uploads/files/Wall.pdf
7   Douglas Hurd, *Memoirs* (London, Little, Brown, 2003), p. 461.
8   Hogg and Hill, *Too Close To Call*, p. 151.
9   John Major, *John Major: The Autobiography* (London, HarperCollins, 1999), p. 285.
10 *Ibid*, p, 281.
11 *Ibid*.
12 *Ibid*, p. 282.
13 *Ibid*, pp. 281-82.
14 Hogg and Hill, *Too Close To Call*, p. 151.
15 *Ibid*, p. 154.
16 *Ibid*.
17 Hugo Young, *This Blessed Plot: Britain and Europe from Churchill to Blair*
    (London, Macmillan, 1998), p. 431.
18 Major, *The Autobiography*, p 286.
19 *Ibid*.
20 Douglas Hurd, *Memoirs*, p. 462.
21 *Ibid*.
22 Young, *This Blessed Plot*, p. 432.
23 Major, *The Autobiography*, p. 375.
24 Richard Howitt, 'Brexit could undermine the rights of disabled people',
    The Guardian, (11 March 2016). Available online at:
    http://www.theguardian.com/social-care-network/2016/mar/11/brexit-
    could-undermine-the-rights-of-disabled-people
25 The European Accessibility Act will set common accessibility requirements
    for certain key products and services that will help people with disabilities at
    EU level to participate fully in society. For further information see:
    http://europa.eu/rapid/press-release_IP-15-6147_en.htm
26 Joe Dromey, *Common Rights in a Single Market? The EU and Rights at Work
    in the UK* (London, IPA and Friedrich-Ebert-Stiftung, 2015), p. 12.
27 HM Government, *Review of the Balance of Competences: Social and
    Employment Policy*, p. 48.
28 *Ibid*, p. 67.
29 Leonardo Morlino and Gianluigi Palombella (eds.), *Rule of Law and Democracy:
    Inquiries into Internal and External Issues* (Leiden, Brill, 2010), p. 179.
30 *Ibid*.
31 See Thorsten Schulten, 'Towards a European minimum wage policy? Fair
    wages and social Europe', *European Journal of Industrial Relations*,
    vol. 14, no. 2, (2008), pp. 421–439.
32 For further information see Thorsten Schulten, *Contours of a European
    Minimum Wage Policy* (Friedrich-Ebert-Stiftung, London, 2014).
33 There is no clear, universally accepted definition of social dumping. The
    European Commission describes the practice as a situation 'where foreign
    service providers can undercut local service providers because their labour
    standards are lower'.

34 Iain Begg, Fabian Mushövel and Robin Niblett, *The Welfare State in Europe: Visions for Reform* (London, Chatham House, 2015), p. 11. Data taken from Eurostat.

35 *Ibid.*

36 Begg, Mushövel and Niblett, *The Welfare State in Europe*, pp. 12–13. These models are built on concepts developed by Gøsta Esping-Andersen and Maurizio Ferrera. For further information see Gøsta Esping-Andersen, *The Three Worlds of Welfare Capitalism* (Princeton, New Jersey: Princeton University Press, 1990) and Maurizio Ferrera, 'The "Southern Model" of Welfare in Social Europe', *Journal of European Social Policy*, 6:1, 1996, pp. 17–37.

37 Anthony Giddens, Patrick Diamond and Roger Liddle (eds.), *Global Europe, Social Europe* (London, Polity, 2006), p. 3.

38 Tony Blair, Speech to the European Parliament, (23 June 2005). Available online at: http://www.theguardian.com/politics/2005/jun/23/speeches.eu

39 Giddens, Diamond and Liddle, *Global Europe, Social Europe*, p. 11; Roger Liddle, 'Equipping Europe for Globalisation: what can be done at the EU level?', *A Social Model for Europe* (Policy Network, London, 2006), pp. 21–26.

40 Angela Merkel has frequently used in the past. For example, *The Financial Times* quotes her as saying the following during an interview with the paper in December 2012: 'If Europe today accounts for just over 7 percent of the world's population, produces around 25 percent of global GDP and has to finance 50 percent of global social spending, then it's obvious that it will have to work very hard to maintain its prosperity and way of life […] All of us have to stop spending more than we earn every year.' See Quentin Peel, 'Merkel Warns on Cost of Welfare', *Financial Times*, (16 December 2012). Also see George Osborne speech, Open Europe Conference, (15 July 2015).

41 HM Government, *Review of the Balance of Competences between the United Kingdom and the European Union: Cohesion Policy* (HM Government, London, 2014).

42 Eurostat data.

43 Dawid Sawicki, 'Rising inequality in the Eurozone underlines the need for a fiscal union', LSE Brexitvote website, (3 August 2015). Available online at: http://blogs.lse.ac.uk/europpblog/2015/08/03/rising-inequality-in-the-eurozone-underlines-the-need-for-a-fiscal-union/

44 17.2 per cent of the population in the EU-28 in 2014 were at risk of poverty after social transfers, meaning that their disposable income was below their national at-risk-of-poverty threshold.

45 Dawid Sawicki, 'Rising inequality in the Eurozone underlines the need for a fiscal union', (3 August 2015).

46 HM Government, *Review of the Balance of Competences: Cohesion Policy*, p. 44.

47 *Ibid*, p. 46.

48 Wolfgang Münchau, 'Britain's pro-Europe campaigners are losing the argument', *The Financial Times*, (3 April 2016). Available online at: https://next.ft.com/content/66283476-f74c-11e5-96db-fc683b5e52db

49   Kate McCann, 'Lord Darzi: Leaving the EU would be "disastrous" for UK
     science and health', *The Daily Telegraph*, (2 April 2016). Available online at:
     http://www.telegraph.co.uk/news/2016/04/02/lord-darzi-leaving-the-eu-
     would-be-disastrous-for-uk-science-and/
50   Hogg and Hill, *Too Close To Call*, p. 156.
51   The Royal Society, *UK Research and the European Union: The Role of the EU in
     Funding UK Research* (Royal Society, London, 2015), p. 12.
52   *Ibid*, p. 14.
53   *Ibid*, p. 16.
54   John Morgan, 'Brexit: the perks and pitfalls for higher education', *Times
     Higher Education Supplement*, (16 July 2015).
55   Pallab Ghosh, 'EU exit "risks British science"', BBC website, (26 February
     2016). Available online at: http://www.bbc.co.uk/news/science-environment-
     35668682
56   McCann, 'Lord Darzi: Leaving the EU would be "disastrous" for UK science
     and health', *The Daily Telegraph*, (2 April 2016).
57   Oliver Wright, 'EU referendum: Leading UK scientists warn against conse-
     quences of Brexit', *The Independent*, (23 December 2015). Available online at:
     http://www.independent.co.uk/news/uk/politics/eu-referendum-leading-uk-
     scientists-warn-against-consequences-of-brexit-a6784886.html
58   *Ibid*.

CHAPTER 10

1   John Kemp, 'Super grid: China masters long-distance power transmission',
    Reuters, (19 June 2014). Available online at: http://www.reuters.com/article/
    us-china-electricity-grid-kemp-idUSKBN0EU19B20140619
2   Ministry of Foreign Affairs of the People's Republic of China, 'Xi Jinping
    Delivers Important Speech at UN Sustainable Development Summit, Stressing
    to Realize Common Development of All Countries from New Starting Point
    of Post-2015 Development Agenda', (27 September 2015). Available online at:
    http://www.fmprc.gov.cn/mfa_eng/zxxx_662805/ t1302359.shtml
3   Jeremy Plester, 'Wind from Britain, solar from the Sahara, geothermal from
    Iceland', *The Guardian*, (22 November 2015). Available online at:
    http://www.theguardian.com/news/2015/nov/22/european-supergrid-
    renewable-energy
4   Speech by Chancellor Angela Merkel, 'Opening Ceremony of the 61st
    Academic Year of the College of Europe in Bruges', (2 November 2010).
5   Dieter Helm, 'The EU Energy Union. More than the sum of its parts?',
    Centre for European Reform, (November 2015). Available online at:
    http://www.cer.org.uk/publications/archive/policy-brief/2015/eu-energy-
    union-more-sum-its-parts
6   *Ibid*.
7   European Commission, 'Energy'. Available online at: http://ec.europa.eu/
    clima/policies/international/paris_protocol/energy/index_en.htm

8   BBC, 'EU referendum: Row over claim Brexit would push up bills', *BBC*, (24 March 2016). Available online at: http://www.bbc.co.uk/news/uk-politics-eu-referendum-35887477

9   PBL Netherlands Environmental Assessment Agency, 'Trends in global CO_2 emissions: 2015 Report', (The Hague, 2015), p. 5

10 Bruegel Policy Brief, 'Making Low Carbon Technology support smarter', (August 2015). Available online at: http://bruegel.org/2015/08/making-low-carbon-technology-support-smarter/

11 *Ibid.*

12 Jill Rutter and William Knighton, 'Legislated Policy Targets', *Institute for Government*, (August 2012). Available online at: http://www.instituteforgovernment.org.uk/sites/default/files/publications/Legislated%20policy%20targets%20final.pdf

13 Sara Stefanini, Kalina Oroschakoff and Andrew Restuccia, '5 takeaways on the Paris climate deal', *Politico*, (14 December 2015). Available online at: http://www.politico.eu/article/5-takeaways-paris-climate-deal-cop21-global-warming/

14 European Commission, '2013 Energy Strategy'. Available online at: http://ec.europa.eu/energy/en/topics/energy-strategy/2030-energy-strategy

15 Environmentalists for Europe, 'Europe is saving your beach', *Environmentalists for Europe*, (24 March 2016). Available online at: http://environmentalistsforeurope.org/articles/

16 RSPB, 'State of Nature Report', (2013). Available online at: https://www.rspb.org.uk/Images/stateofnature_tcm9-345839.pdf

17 Environmentalists for Europe, 'Europe is saving your beach', *Environmentalists for Europe*, (24 March 2016).

18 Green Alliance letter to Liz Truss MP. Available online at: http://www.green-alliance.org.uk/EU_letter_to_Liz_Truss_MP.php

CHAPTER 11

1   Populus, 'Hope not Hate, Poll of adults in England', Research Objectives and Methodology, (February 2016), p. 54.

2   Populus, 'Hope not Hate, Poll of adults in England', Spreadsheet, (February 2016) (Table 194).

3   *Ibid.* (Table 112).

4   *Ibid.* (Table 113).

5   *Ibid.* (Table 194).

6   John Curtice, 'How deeply does Britain's Euroscepticism run?' (London, NatCen, 2016), p. 8.

7   Populus, 'Hope not Hate, Poll of adults in England', (February 2016) (Table 264).

8   Oliver Hawkins, 'Migration Statistics', (London, House of Commons Library, 25 February 2016). Available online at: www.parliament.uk/briefing-papers/sn06077.pdf

9   United Nations Press Release, '232 million international migrants living abroad
     worldwide – new UN global migration statistics reveal', (11 September 2013).

10   The UN Refugee Agency, 'Facts and Figures about Refugees'. Available online
     at: http://www.unhcr.org.uk/about-us/key-facts-and-figures.html

11   Ian Goldin, 'How immigration has changed the world – for the better', *Oxford
     Martin School, University of Oxford*, (21 January 2016). Available online at:
     http://www.oxfordmartin.ox.ac.uk/opinion/view/320

12   Migration Policy Centre, European University Institute, 'Migration profile:
     Syria', (2016). Available online at: http://cadmus.eui.eu//handle/1814/39225

13   Ian Goldin, Geoffrey Cameron and Meera Balarajan, 'Exceptional People:
     How Migration Shaped Our World and Will Define Our Future' (Princeton,
     Princeton University Press, 2012), p. 222–223.

14   Jon Clifton, '150 Million Adults Worldwide Would Migrate to the U.S.', *Gallup*,
     (20 April 2012). Available online at: http://www.gallup.com/poll/153992/150-
     million-adults-worldwide-migrate.aspx

15   Ian Goldin, 'How immigration has changed the world – for the better', *World
     Economic Forum*, (17 January 2016). Available online at:
     http://www. weforum.org/agenda/2016/01/how-immigration-has-changed-
     the-world-for-the-better

16   Mike Pflanz, 'Africa's population to double to 2.4 billion by 2050', *The Daily
     Telegraph*, (12 September 2013). Available online at:
     http://www.telegraph.co.uk/news/worldnews/africaandindianocean/
     10305000/Africas-population-to-double-to-2.4-billion-by-2050.html

17   Demos, 'On Income Inequality: An Interview with Branko Milanovic', (14
     November 2014). Available online at: http://www.demos.org/blog/11/14/14/
     income-inequality-interview-branko-milanovic

18   The Migration Observatory, 'Long-Term International Migration Flows to
     and from the UK', Table 1. Available online at:
     http://www.migrationobservatory.ox.ac.uk/briefings/long-term-
     international-migration-flows-and-uk

19   See Oliver Hawkins, *Migration Statistics*, (25 February 2016).

20   BBC, 'Net migration at 323,000 prompts EU referendum row', *BBC*, (25 February
     2016). Available online at: http://www.bbc.co.uk/news/uk-politics-35658731

21   *Ibid.*

22   Ian Goldin, 'Encouraging more, better managed, migration should be part of
     our economic strategy for growth', *LSE blog*, (6 July 2012). Available online at:
     http://eprints.lse.ac.uk/48408/1/blogs.lse.ac.uk-Encouraging_more_better_
     managed_migration_should_be_part_of_our_economic_strategy_for_
     growth.pdf

23   Hugo Dixon, 'The In/Out Question; Why Britain should stay in the EU and
     fight to make it better', Excerpt in 'The inflow: European migration into
     Britain', *In Facts*. Available online at: http://infacts.org/briefings/the-inflow-
     european-migration-into-britain/

24   Tobias Buck, 'British expats worry about Brexit in Costa Blanca', *The Financial
     Times*, (22 March 2016). Available online at: http://www.ft.com/cms/s/0/
     86f26cda-ef90-11e5-aff5-19b4e253664a.html# axzz430498XLW

25 Andy Beckett, 'Is Britain full? Home truths about the population panic', *The Guardian*, (9 February 2016). Available online at: http://www.theguardian.com/world/2016/feb/09/is-britain-full-home-truths-about-population-panic

26 *Ibid.*

27 Slough Borough Council, 'Migration: Facts, figures and trends'. Available online at: http://www.slough.gov.uk/council/joint-strategic-needs-assessment/migration.aspx

28 Andy Beckett, 'Is Britain full? Home truths about the population panic', *The Guardian*, (9 February 2016)

29 Patrick Wintour, 'Ministers urged to spell out details of UK plan to take in Syrian children', *The Guardian*, (28 January 2016). Available online at: http://www.theguardian.com/world/2016/jan/28/ministers-urged-to-spell-out-details-of-plan-for-uk-to-take-in-syrian-children

30 HM Government, 'Review of the Balance of Competences between the United Kingdom and the European Union, Asylum and non-EU Migration,' (HM Government, London, February 2014), p. 7.

31 Nick Parker and Sian Hewitt, 'Inside the Roma Beverly Hills as it's revealed they send home £541m', *The Scottish Sun*, (7 February 2016). Available online at: http://www.thescottishsun.co.uk/scotsol/homepage/6914825/Camerons-EU-brake-will-not-stop-migrants-cashing-in.html

32 Office for National Statistics, 'Population by Country of Birth and Nationality Report', August 2015 (ONS, London, 2015)

33 Office of National Statistics, 'Bulgarian and Romanian migration to the UK', August 2015 (ONS, London, 2015).

34 Matt Dathan, 'EU migrations working in Britain soars by more than 200,000 in ONE YEAR as one in six jobs are taken by foreigners', *The Daily Mail*, (17 February 2016). Available online at: http://www.dailymail.co.uk/news/article-3450762/Unemployment-UK-stays-ten-year-low-earnings-edge-1-9.html

35 BBC, 'EU reform deal: What Cameron wanted and what he got', *BBC*, (20 February 2016). Available online at: http://www.bbc.co.uk/news/uk-politics-eu-referendum-35622105

36 Patrick Wintour and Ian Traynor, 'EU renegotiation: Cameron faces Brussels deadlock over migrants' benefits', *The Guardian*, (18 December 2015). Available online at: http://www.theguardian.com/politics/2015/dec/17/david-cameron-compromise-eu-migrants-benefits-summit

37 Jonathan Portes, 'Migrants, benefits and the UK's renegotiation: questions and answers', *National Institute of Economic and Social Research*, (9 November 2015). Available online at:http://www.niesr.ac.uk/blog/ migrants-benefits-and-uks-renegotiation-questions-and-answers-updated#.Vt_t8jbcvug

38 Marley Morris, 'IPPR Briefing, Unlocking the EU free movement debate', (London, IPPR, December 2015), p. 5.

39 Jonathan Portes quoted by Ian Goldin, 'Out of the kitchen, into the economic reality: Why Europe needs migration', *Oxford Martin School, University of Oxford*, (4 July 2012). Available online at: http://www.oxfordmartin.ox.ac.uk/opinion/view/167

40 Boris Johnson, 'If Denmark can treat foreigners differently, then so can Britain', *The Daily Telegraph*, (13 December 2015). Available online at: http://www.telegraph.co.uk/news/newstopics/eureferendum/12048621/If-Denmark-can-treat-foreigners-differently-then-so-can-Britain.html

41 Channel Four, 'FactCheck: is there a Romanian crimewave?', *Channel 4, Fact Check*, (19 May 2014). Available online at: http://blogs.channel4.com/factcheck/factcheck-romanian-crimewave/18207

42 HM Government, 'Prison population 2014', Table A1.10 Prison population by nationality, 2002 to 2014, England and Wales

43 See Morris, 'Unlocking the EU free movement debate', (December 2015), p. 14.

44 *Ibid*, p. 13.

45 Yvette Cooper, 'Yvette's response to comments about the future of borders', (1 February 2016). Available online at: http://www.yvettecooper.com/yvette_s_response_to

46 Pierre Briançon, 'Enrico Letter: So what are European governments doing?', *Politico*, (12 February 2016). Available online at: http://www.politico.eu/article/enrico-letta-so-what-are-european-governments-doing-migration-crisis/

47 Leo Cendrowicz, 'The end of Schengen? Restrictions by Denmark and Sweden are 'threatening Europe's passport-free zone', *The Independent*, (4 January 2016). Available online at: http://www.independent.co.uk/news/world/europe/the-end-of-schengen-restrictions-by-denmark-and-sweden-are-threatening-europes-passport-free-zone-a6796696.html

48 Andrea Thomas and Valentina Pop, 'Austria to Set Limit on Migrants Entering the Country', *The Wall Street Journal*, (20 January 2016). Available online at: http://www.wsj.com/articles/dutch-leader-warns-europe-needs-urgent-fix-to-migrant-influx-1453285192

49 Keersten Knipp, 'Safe countries of origin?', *Deutsche Welle*, (29 January 2016). Available online at: http://www.dw.com/en/safe-countries-of-origin/a-19012766

50 Stefan Wagstyl, 'Berlin agrees steps to curb migrants as Merkel faces backlash', *The Financial Times*, (29 September 2015). Available online at: http://www.ft.com/cms/s/0/dd6620bc-66b4-11e5-97d0-1456a776a4f5.html#axzz45FlSs8PL

51 David Crouch and Patrick Kingsley, 'Danish parliament approves plan to sieve assets from refugees', *The Guardian*, (26 January 2016). Available online at: http://www.theguardian.com/world/2016/jan/26/danish-parliament-approves-plan-to-seize-assets-from-refugees

52 Statement by High Commissioner, 'Women refugees and asylum seekers in the European Union, Ceremony to mark International Women's Day Filippo Grandi, United Nations High Commissioner for Refugees to the Chamber of the European Parliament Strasbourg', (8 March 2016). Available online at: http://www.unhcr.org/56dec2e99.html

CHAPTER 12

1   BBC, 'PM defiant over al-Qaeda threat', *BBC*, (1 July 2007). Available online at:
    http://news.bbc.co.uk/1/hi/uk/6258062.stm

2   Daniel Benjamin, 'Why Europe can't fix its terrorism problem, and why the
    US probably won't be next', *Politico*, (23 March 2016). Available online at:
    http://www.politico.eu/article/why-europe-cant-fix-its-terrorism-problem/

3   The Soufan Group, 'Foreign Fighters, An Updated Assessment of the Flow of
    Foreign Fighters in Syria and Iraq', (December 2015), p. 7-10.

4   European Parliament Briefing, 'The EU's mutual assistance clause, first ever
    activation of Article 42 (7) TEU', (November 2015).

5   Pierre Briançon, 'An attack on European legitimacy', *Politico*, (23 March 2016).
    Available online at: http://www.politico.eu/article/an-attack-on-european-
    legitimacy-terrorism-war-eu-skepticism/

6   Rafael Behr, 'As Le Pen rises in Europe's liberal dream is disappearing in front
    of our eyes', *The Guardian*, (9 December 2015). Available online at:
    http://www.theguardian.com/commentisfree/2015/dec/09/le-pen-europe-
    liberal-dream-disappearing-britain-eu

7   Christopher Hope, Steven Swinford, Peter Foster and Laura Hughes 'Brussels
    attacks: Europe is acting as a 'welcome sign' to terrorists, warns former Tory
    leader', *The Daily Telegraph*, (22 March 2016). Available online at:
    http://www.telegraph.co.uk/news/worldnews/europe/belgium/12201677/Bruss
    els-attacks-Europe-is-acting-as-a-welcome-sign-to-terrorists-warns-former-
    Tory-leader.html

8   Richard Dearlove, 'Brexit would not damage UK security', *Prospect*,
    (April 2016). Available online at: http://www.prospectmagazine.co.uk/
    opinions/brexit-would-not-damage-uk-security

9   Sputniknews, 'Broken Belgium and Fragmented Government Blamed for
    Terror Attack', *Sputniknews*, (29 March 2016). Online at:
    http://sputniknews.com/europe/20160329/1037134893/belgium-terror-
    government-faillures.html

10 Europol Report, 'European Union Terrorism Situation and Trend Report
    2015', (6 July 2015). Available online at: https://www.europol.europa.eu/
    content/european-union-terrorism-situation-and-trend-report-2015

11 Sam Jones, 'UK puts 3,000 extremists on "Jihadi John" watchlist', *The Financial
    Times*, (27 February 2015). Available online at: http://www.ft.com/cms/
    s/0/35a081fa-bea9-11e4-8d9e-00144feab7de.html#axzz415ppcEy4

12 Sam Jones, James Politi and Anne-Sylvaine Chassany, 'Clamour grows for EU
    'security union' to combat terror', *The Financial Times*, (23 March 2016).
    Available online at: http://www.ft.com/cms/s/0/a0c06508-f11c-11e5-aff5-
    19b4e253664a. html#axzz430498XLWaxzz430498XLW

13 Sky News, 'Warning of up to 5,000 jihadists in Europe', *Sky News*,
    (19 February 2016). Available online at: http://news.sky.com/story/1645171/
    warning-of-up-to-5000-jihadists-in-europe

14   Der Spiegel Online, 'Postcard from a Failed State? Attacks Cast Light on Belgium's State Crisis', *Der Spiegel Online*, (25 March 2016). Available online at: http://www.spiegel.de/international/europe/terror-attacks-cast-light-onbelgian-identity-crisis-a-1084151.html

15   Mariano Castillo and Paul Cruickshank, 'Who was Abdelhamid Abaaoud, suspected ringleader of Paris attack?', *CNN*, (19 November 2015). Available online at: http://edition.cnn.com/2015/11/16/europe/paris-terror-attack-mastermind-abdelhamid-abaaoud/

16   See Der Spiegel Online, 'Postcard from a Failed State? Attacks Cast Light on Belgium's State Crisis', *Der Spiegel Online*, (25 March 2016).

17   Michael Isikoff, 'NSA chief: "Paris would not have happened" without encrypted apps', *Yahoo*, (17 February 2016). Available online at: https://www.yahoo.com/politics/nsa-chief-paris-would-not-have-happened-without-184040933.html

18   Zoya Sheftalovich, 'Encryption a problem in terrorism investigations: Europol', *Politico*, (24 March 2016). Available online at: http://www.politico.eu/article/encryption-probe-in-terror-investigations-probe-say-europol/

19   Sam Jones, James Politi and Anne-Sylvaine Chassany, 'Clamour grows for EU "security union" to combat terror', *The Financial Times*, (23 March 2016). Available online at: http://www.ft.com/cms/s/0/a0c06508-f11c-11e5-aff5-19b4e253664a.html#axzz430498XLW

20   Michael Birnbaum, 'A terror attack exposed Belgium's security failings. Europe's problem is far bigger', *The Washington Post*, (28 March 2016). Available online at: https://www.washingtonpost.com/world/europe/a-terror-attack-exposed-belgiums-security-failings-europes-problem-is-far-bigger/2016/03/28/47be66ac-f39d-11e5-a2a3-d4e9697917d1_story.html

21   Janosch Delcker, 'Germany to press for entry-exit registry in Schengen area', *Politico*, (24 March 2016). Available online at: http://www.politico.eu/article/germany-to-press-for-entry-exit-registry-in-schengen-area-thomas-de-maiziere/

22   Hugo Dixon, 'After the Paris attacks, staying in Europe is more important than ever', *The Guardian*, (3 December 2015). Available online at: http://www.theguardian.com/commentisfree/2015/dec/03/paris-attacks-europe-ukip-britain-eu-jihadis

23   See Sam Jones, James Politi and Anne-Sylvaine Chassany, 'Clamour grows for EU "security union" to combat terror', *The Financial Times*, (23 March 2016).

24   Zoya Sheftalovich, 'Europol needs more staff from EU nations to respond to terrorist attacks', *Politico*, (24 March 2016). Available online at: http://www.politico.eu/article/europol-needs-more-staff-from-eu-nations-to-respond-to-terrorist-attacks/

25   Vince Chadwick, 'Policymakers: Share intel but don't betray liberty', *Politico*, (7 April 2016). Available online at: http://www.politico.eu/article/politico-caucus-policymakers-share-intel-but-dont-betray-liberty-brussels-terror-attacks-counter-terrorism-isil-security/

26 Alice Thomson and Rachel Sylvester, 'Leaving EU would put our security at risk, claims May', *The Times*, (23 March 2016). Available online at: http://www.thetimes.co.uk/tto/news/politics/article4719456.ece?acs_cjd=true

27 Peter Dominiczak and Michael Wilkinson, 'Britain "faces influx of 50,000 asylum seekers" if it leaves the European Union', *The Daily Telegraph*, (8 Feb 2016). Available online at: http://www.telegraph.co.uk/news/newstopics/eureferendum/12145781/David-Cameron-warns-of-migrant-camps-in-southern-England-if-Brexit-vote.html

28 Hugo Dixon, 'After the Paris attacks, staying in Europe is more important than ever', *The Guardian*, (3 December 2015). Available online at: http://www.theguardian.com/commentisfree/2015/dec/03/paris-attacks-europe-ukip-britain-eu-jihadis

29 Europol, 'Member States'. Available online at: https://www.europol.europa.eu/ content/page/member-states-131

30 Christopher Hope, Steven Swinford, Peter Foster, Europe Editor and Laura Hughes, 'Brussels attacks: Europe is acting as a 'welcome sign' to terrorists, warns former Tory leader', *The Daily Telegraph*, (22 March 2016). Available online at: http://www.telegraph.co.uk/news/worldnews/europe/belgium/ 12201677/ Brussels-attacks-Europe-is-acting-as-a-welcome-sign-to-terrorists-warns- former-Tory-leader.html

31 BBC, 'Brexit will make it "harder" for UK to fight terrorism', *BBC HARDtalk*, (8 February 2016). Available online at: http://www.bbc.co.uk/news/ world-europe-35524017

32 See Alice Thomson and Rachel Sylvester, 'Leaving EU would put our security at risk, claims May', *The Times*, (23 March 2016). Available online at: http://www.thetimes.co.uk/tto/news/politics/article4719456.ece?acs_cjd=true

33 David Petraeus, 'David Petraeus: Brexit would weaken the West's war on terror', *The Daily Telegraph*, (26 March 2016). Available online at: http://www.telegraph.co.uk/news/newstopics/eureferendum/12205094/ David-Petraeus-Brexit-would-weaken-the-Wests-war-on-terror.html

34 UK Government, 'UK joins international security alert system', (10 February 2016). Available online at: https://www.gov.uk/government/news/uk-joins-international-security-alert-system

35 UK Government, 'Government sets out case for joining Prüm', (26 November 2015). Available online at: https://www.gov.uk/government/news/ government-sets-out-case-for-joining-prum

36 Nigel Morris, 'EU referendum: Brexit campaigners accused of risking return to days of "Costa del Crime"', *The Independent*, (11 March 2016). Available online at: http://www.independent.co.uk/news/uk/politics/eu-referendum-brexitcampaign-accused-of-risking-return-to-costa-del-crime-days-a6926461.html

37 See Richard Dearlove, 'Brexit would not damage UK security', *Prospect*, (April 2016).

38 See Nigel Morris, 'EU referendum: Brexit campaigners accused of risking return to days of "Costa del Crime"', *The Independent*, (11 March 2016).

39 See Alice Thomson and Rachel Sylvester, 'Leaving EU would put our security at risk, claims May', *The Times*, (23 March 2016).

40 Stronger In, 'EU essential to UK security, say former Home Secretaries', Stronger In, (1 December 2015). Available online at: http://www.strongerin.co.uk/eu_essential_to_uk_security_say_former_home_secretaries#dXeF07bTrvZUlMm0.97

41 Sky News, 'RAF bombs IS oil wells in Tidal Wave II mission', *Sky News*, (5 December 2015). Available online at: http://news.sky.com/story/1598804/raf-bombs-is-oil-wells-in-tidal-wave-ii-mission

42 Gilles Kepel quoted in Emma-Kate Symons, 'A new book says Islamists and the far right work hand-in-hand to promote jihad in France', *Quartz*, (16 December 2015). Available online at: http://qz.com/574889/islamists-and-the-far-right-work-hand-in-hand-to-promote-jihad-in-france/

43 Thomas Raines, 'Internationalism or Isolationism? The Chatham House – YouGov Survey' (London, Chatham House, January 2015), p. 21.

44 UK Government, 'UK-French defence cooperation reaffirmed on fifth anniversary of Lancaster House Agreement', (3 November 2015). Available online at: https://www.gov.uk/government/news/uk-french-defence-cooperation-reaffirmed-on-fifth-anniversary-of-lancaster-house-agreement

45 Douglas Webber, 'The Politics of Differentiated Integration in the European Union: Origins, Decision Making and Outcomes' (Monash University, European and EU Centre, October 2012) p. 17.

46 *Ibid.*

47 European Defence Agency, 'Defence Data Portal'. Available online at: http://www.eda.europa.eu/info-hub/defence-data-portal/EDA/year/2013#3

48 Douglas Webber, 'The Politics of Differentiated Integration in the European Union: Origins, Decision Making and Outcomes' (Monash University, European and EU Centre, October 2012) p. 18

49 Stephen Wall, 'A Stranger in Europe: Britain and the EU from Thatcher to Blair', (Oxford: Oxford University Press, 2008).

50 UK Government, 'UK-French defence cooperation reaffirmed on fifth anniversary of Lancaster House Agreement', (3 November 2015). Available online at: https://www.gov.uk/government/news/uk-french-defence-cooperation-reaffirmed-on-fifth-anniversary-of-lancaster-house-agreement

51 Mark Odell, 'French general given top UK army job', *The Financial Times*, (8 February 2016). Available online at: http://www.ft.com/cms/s/0/dd0313ec-ce78-11e5-831d-09f7778e7377.html#axzz41I9w6ZNG

52 UK Government, 'UK–France Summit 2010 Declaration on Defence and Security Co-operation', (2 November 2010). Available online at: https://www.gov.uk/government/news/uk-france-summit-2010-declaration-on-defence-and-security-co-operation

53 *Ibid.*

54 UK Government, 'Defence Secretary welcomes deeper security relationship with Germany', (25 January 2016'. Available online at: https://www.gov.uk/government/news/defence-secretary-welcomes-deeper-security-relationship-with-germany

55 *Ibid.*

56 Deanna Corbett, 'Germany to Boost Defense 6.2% Over 5 Years', *Defense News*, (20 March 2015). Available online at: http://www.defensenews.com/ story/defense/policy-budget/budget/ 2015/03/20/germany-budget-defense-spending-increase-nato-terrorist-merkel/25073443/

57 The Daily Telegraph, 'Germany joins fight against Isil after parliament approves military action in Syria', *The Daily Telegraph*, (4 December 2015). Available online at: http://www.telegraph.co.uk/news/worldnews/europe/ germany/12032948/ Germany-joins-fight-against-Isil-after-parliament-approves-military-action-in-Syria.html

58 Margaret Thatcher Foundation, 'Speech to the College of Europe (The Bruges Speech)'. Available online at: http://www.margaretthatcher.org/ document/107332

59 UK Government, 'National Security Strategy and Strategic Defence and Security Review 2015', (23 November 2015). Available online at: https://www.gov.uk/government/publications/national-security-strategy-and-strategic-defence-and-security-review-2015

60 Deutsche Welle, 'NATO not interested in arms race with Russia', *Deutsche Welle*, (24 June 2015). Available online at: http://www.dw.com/en/nato-not-interested-in-arms-race-with-russia/a-18539611

61 Michael Crowley, 'Obama's Ukraine policy in shambles', *Politico*, (29 February 2016). Available online at: http://www.politico.com/story/2016/02/obama-ukraine-russia-putin-219783

62 Elizabeth Pond, 'Russia vs the west: the consequences of Putin's invasion of Ukraine', *New Statesman*, (5 March 2015). Available online at: http://www.newstatesman.com/politics/2015/03/russia-vs-west-consequences-putin-s-invasion-ukraine

63 Matthew Bodner, 'Russian Military Spending to Increase by Less Than 1% Next Year', *The Moscow Times*, (26 October 2015). Available online at: http://www.themoscowtimes.com/news/article/russian-military-spending-to-increase-by-less-than-1-next-year/540362.html

64 Der Spiegel Online 'The War of Western Failures: Hopes for Syria Fall with Aleppo', *Der Spiegel Online*, (17 February 2016). Available online at: http://www.spiegel.de/international/world/the-siege-of-aleppo-is-an-emblem-of-western-failure-in-syria-a-1077140.html

65 Jeevan Vasagar, 'Germany pledges to raise defence spending', *The Financial Times*, (1 March 2015). Available online at: http://www.ft.com/cms/s/0/ 4b2737f6-c00e-11e4-a71e-00144feab7de.html#axzz42D008tkh

66 Elizabeth Quintana, 'Rising European Defence Budgets?', RUSI, (1 May 2015). Available online at: https://rusi.org/commentary/rising-european-defence-budgets

67 UK Government, 'UK to increase contribution to NATO task force', (8 June 2015). Available online at: https://www.gov.uk/government/news/ uk-to-increase-contribution-to-nato-task-force

68   UK Government, 'UK Armed Forces lead NATO exercise in the Baltics',
      (10 November 2015). Available online at: https://www.gov.uk/government/
      news/uk-armed-forces-lead-nato-exercise-in-the-baltics

69   European Union External Action, '*Common Security and Defence Policy
      Briefing*', (September 2014).

70   UK Government, 'Defence Secretary meets counterparts to discuss defeating
      Daesh', (20 January 2016). Available online at: https://www.gov.uk/
      government/news/defence-secretary-meets-counterparts-to-discuss-
      defeating-daesh

71   UK Government, 'National Security Strategy and Strategic Defence and
      Security Review 2015', (23 November 2015). Available online at:
      https://www.gov.uk/government/publications/national-security-strategy-
      and-strategic-defence-and-security-review-2015

72   Michael Birnbaum, 'Gates rebukes European allies in farewell speech',
      The Washington Post, (10 June 2011). Available online at:
      https://www.washingtonpost.com/world/gates-rebukes-european-allies-in-
      farewell-speech/2011/06/10/AG9tKeOH_story.html

73   Stefen Soesanto, 'Europe needs less soldiers – but more European ones',
      NATO Review. Available online at: http://www.nato.int/docu/review/2015/
      Also-in-2015/europe-defense-budget-military-soldiers/EN/

74   Thome Shanker, 'Defense Secretary Warns NATO of 'Dim' Future', *The New
      York Times*, (10 June 2011). Available online at: http://www.nytimes.com/
      2011/06/11/world/europe/11gates.html?_r=0

75   Ian Traynor, 'US defence chief blasts Europe over Nato', *The Guardian*,
      (10 June 2011). Available online at: http://www.theguardian.com/world/
      2011/jun/10/nato-dismal-future-pentagon-chief

76   Robert Kagan, 'Superpowers Don't Get to Retire: What Our Tired Country
      Still Owes the World', Brookings, (26 May 2014). Available online at:
      http://www.brookings.edu/research/opinions/2014/05/26-superpowers-
      dont-retire-kagan

77   Niall Ferguson, 'Colossus: The Rise and Fall of the American Empire',
      (London: Penguin Group, 2009).

78   Ivo Daalder, 'Ghost of European re-nationalism', *Politico*, (10 February 2016).
      Available online at: http://www.politico.eu/article/ghost-of-european-
      re-nationalism/

79   Paul Dallison, 'US to increase troop numbers in Europe', *Politico*, (30 March
      2015). Available online at: http://www.politico.eu/article/us-to-increase-
      troop-numbers-in-europe/

80   David Ignatius, 'The U.S. remains essential in a shifting Middle East',
      The Washington Post, (1 March 2016). Available online at: https://www.
      washingtonpost.com/opinions/the-us-remains-essential-in-a-changing-
      middle-east/2016/03/01/47f352e6-dfe7-11e5-9c36-e1902f6b6571_ story.html

81   President Barack Obama, 'State of the Union Address, as delivered', (January
      2016). Available online at: https://www.whitehouse.gov/the-press-
      office/2016/01/12/remarks-president-barack-obama-%E2%80%93-
      prepared-delivery-state-union-address

82 European Commission, European Political Strategy Centre, 'In Defence of Europe', (15 June 2015). Available online at: http://ec.europa.eu/epsc/ publications/notes/sn4_en.htm

83 European Defence Agency, 'Pooling and Sharing'. Available online at: http://www.eda.europa.eu/what-we-do/eda-priorities/pooling-and-sharing

84 European Commission, European Political Strategy Centre, 'In Defence of Europe', (15 June 2015). Available online at: http://ec.europa.eu/epsc/ publications/notes/sn4_en.htm

85 *Ibid.*

86 NATO, 'The Secretary General's Annual Report 2015', (28 January 2016). Available online at: http://www.nato.int/cps/en/natohq/opinions_127331.htm

87 BBC, 'Nato defence spending falls despite promises to reverse cuts', *BBC*, (26 February 2015). Available online at: http://www.bbc.co.uk/news/ world-31619553

88 Elizabeth Quintana, 'Rising European Defence Budgets?', RUSI, (1 May 2015). Available online at: https://rusi.org/commentary/rising-european-defence-budgets

89 BBC, 'Europe agrees response to cyber-attacks', *BBC*, (8 December 2015). Available online at: http://www.bbc.co.uk/news/technology-35038424

90 Malcolm Nance, 'Five ways to devastate ISIL', *Politico*, (24 March 2016). Available online at: http://www.politico.eu/article/five-ways-to-devastate-isil/

91 Douglas Webber, 'The Politics of Differentiated Integration in the European Union: Origins, Decision Making and Outcomes' (Monash University, European and EU Centre, October 2012) p. 18.

92 UK Government, 'EU Common Security and Defence Policy: The UK Perspective', (27 June 2012). Available online at: https://www.gov.uk/ government/speeches/eu-common-security-and-defence-policy-the-uk-perspective

93 NATO, 'NATO-EU: a strategic partnership', (28 September 2015). Available online at: http://www.nato.int/cps/en/natohq/topics_49217.htm

94 BBC, 'We need a European army, says Jean-Claude Juncker', *BBC*, (9 March 2015). Available online at: http://www.bbc.co.uk/news/world-europe-31796337

95 Bruno Waterfield, 'David Cameron fights off EU army plan', *The Daily Telegraph*, (19 December 2013). Available online at: http://www.telegraph.co.uk/news/worldnews/europe/eu/10528852/ David-Cameron-flies-to-Brussels-determined-to-fight-EU-drones-programme.html

96 Michal Smetana, 'Stuck in disarmament: The European Union and the 2015 NPT Review Conference' (2016) p. 142.

97 *Ibid.*

98 *Ibid.*

99 Dr Robin Niblett, 'Britain, Europe and the World: Rethinking the UK's Circles of Influence', (London, Chatham House, 9 October 2015). Available online at: https://www.chathamhouse.org/publication/britain-europe-and-world-rethinking-uk-circles-influence

CONCLUSION

1   Norman Davies, *The Isles: A History* (Oxford: Oxford University Press, 2000), p. 4–5.

2   http://www.europarl.org.uk/resource/static/files/ukjobs.pdf

3   Thomas Raines, *Internationalism or Isolationism? The Chatham House-YouGov Survey* (London, Chatham House, 2015), p. 7.

4   *Ibid*, p. 7–8.

5   *Ibid*, p. 32.

6   Tara John, 'This is Why Border Fences Don't Work', *Time*, 22 October 2015. Available online at: http://time.com/4080637/this-is-why-border-fences-dont-work/

7   Michael Moran, 'The Pope's Divisions', Council on Foreign Relations, 3 February 2006. Online at: http://www.cfr.org/religion/popes-divisions/p9765

8   Robin Niblett, *Britain's Place in the World* (London, Chatham House, 2015), p.7–8. Available online at: https://www.chathamhouse.org/sites/files/ chathamhouse/field/field_document/20150623Britain per cent20in per cent20the per cent20World.pdf

9   Robin Niblett, *Britain, Europe and the World: Rethinking the UK's Circles of Influence* (London, Chatham House, 2015), p. 3.

10 Stephen Wall, *A Stranger in Europe: Britain and the EU from Thatcher to Blair* (Oxford, Oxford University Press, 2008) p. 219

11 Richard N. Hass, 'The State of the United States', *Project Syndicate*, 30 March 2016. Available online at: https://www.project-syndicate.org/commentary/ america-turning-inward-by-richard-n—haass-2016-03

12 United Nations, 'Population Prospects: The 2015 Revision, Key Findings and Advance Tables', Working Paper No. ESA/P/WP.241 (2015), p.1 and 7–9; Alexis Akwagyiram, 'Made in Africa: Is manufacturing taking off on the continent?', BBC News, 29 May 2014. Online at: http://www.bbc.co.uk/news/world-africa-27329594; UNCATD, 'World Investment Report 2015: Reforming International Investment Governance' (2015), p.iii; and UNESCO Institute for Statistic's database, UIS.Stat. 33,192,738 children of primary school age were out-of-school in Africa in 2013.

13 John F. Kennedy: 'Address at Independence Hall, Philadelphia.', July 4, 1962. Online by Gerhard Peters and John T. Woolley, *The American Presidency Project*. http://www.presidency.ucsb.edu/ws/?pid=8756.

14 Niblett, *Britain, Europe and the World*, p. 10.

15 *Ibid*, p. 3.